Freedom in Entangled Worlds

Eben Kirksey

FREEDOM IN ENTANGLED WORLDS

West Papua and the Architecture of Global Power

DUKE UNIVERSITY PRESS   DURHAM AND LONDON   2012

Duke University Press gratefully

acknowledges the support of The

Graduate Center Foundation at the

City University of New York, which

provided funds toward the publication

of this book.

FRONTISPIECE: *The flamboyant and controversial West Papuan independence advocate Theys Eluay stands in his own home before a display bearing an English caption: "The Greatest Leaders." The display, a black-and-white photograph of John F. Kennedy and Indonesian president Sukarno, recalls freedom dreams from an earlier historical moment and unexpected entanglements with global power. Photograph by Kiki van Bilsen.*

To Jane and Will Kirksey,
for their unconditional support and love,
and to the spirit of Elsham Papua.

Contents

Flying Fish, Flying Tourists

Fishermen from Biak, a small island off the coast of New Guinea, lure flying fish into traps with magic songs. "Facing to Java in the west, then Fiji in the east, then Australia in the south, and Japan in the north, the fishermen call out to their scaly relatives," reports Danilyn Rutherford, a cultural anthropologist. Rutherford's book about national belonging on Biak, *Raiding the Land of the Foreigners*, reveals surprising tricks used to catch the fish. Borrowing foreign phrases and inventing new words, the fishermen startle and amuse their airborne prey. A coy American catcall remembered from the Allied occupation of the island in 1944—*Hey woman! Come on!*—captivates the fish with strange language. The fishermen extend invitations to a wild party. Buzzing along the surface of the water like miniature bomber planes, the shiny fish veer off their flight paths and into the fishermen's canoes. Ashore the fishermen reveal their bait and switch: the flying fish, honored guests at a lively feast, are roasted whole and eaten.

Flying tourists, like flying fish, are also courted by Biak performers. In the mid-1990s, Indonesia's national airline, Garuda, flew a regular route from Los Angeles to Jakarta via Honolulu, Biak, and Bali. At midnight local time, the jet made an hour-long fueling stop on Biak's runway. By predictable routine, groups of bewildered transnational travelers were deposited in a tiny airport transit lounge. The tourists functioned as bait, drawing crowds of Biak villagers to the glass airport windows. "Briefly detained on their weekly migration," writes Rutherford, the tourists "were also the fish."[1]

In June 1994 I unexpectedly found myself in this waiting room as I was en route to be a high-school exchange student in Indonesia. Biak was dark beyond the glow of the airport lights. Sweet fumes from clove cigarettes hung in the air. Posters depicting indigenous people wearing penis gourds and

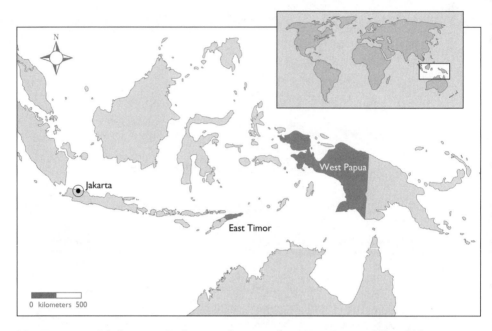

West Papua in a global context. In the eyes of cartographers, New Guinea is shaped like a cassowary, a large flightless bird endemic to the island. The tail end of the cassowary is the independent country of Papua New Guinea (PNG). A straight line along 141° east longitude separates PNG from West Papua, the half of the island under Indonesian control. The bird's head is in West Papua. Biak is the small northernmost island in the bay above the bird's neck. *Map by Damond Kyllo.*

vibrant bird of paradise feathers adorned the walls. Dancing in grass skirts and performing songs for the international travelers, a local string band replicated idyllic images of the Pacific islands. After the music concluded, I was ushered back into the plane and whisked away to Java, the center of power in Indonesia—an archipelago of some 17,500 islands that stretches east from Biak for over three thousand miles. Over the next six months, I attended high school in one of Java's sprawling cities and picked up the ability to speak the Indonesian language. Still, this unexpected airport encounter lingered in my memory.

Biak is part of West Papua, the half of New Guinea under Indonesian control. European and American adventurers have long traveled to West Papua hoping to discover people living outside of history, tribes supposedly living in the Stone Age.[2] The Biak string band that greeted me at the airport was clearly playing to this timeless ideal. Rutherford's work later led

A man from the Mee tribe in the traditional dress of highland West Papua. *Photograph by Eben Kirksey.*

me to understand that the performers were trying some bait-and-switch magic of their own during the nightly refueling stops—secretly laying the groundwork for a surprising trap.³ Tourists expecting a tranquil paradise, or perhaps an encounter with Stone Age peoples, are routinely shocked to discover a military occupation beyond the airport gates.

The people of West Papua first raised their independence banner, the Morning Star flag, on December 1, 1961. At the time they were Dutch colonial subjects, lured by the dreams of national freedom then sweeping the planet. Two weeks later the Indonesian military invaded and began what was arguably genocide.⁴ During the coming decades of Indonesian occupation, thousands of indigenous West Papuans were killed in bombing raids, displaced by military operations, subjected to arbitrary detention, executed, or "disappeared."⁵ Forced sterilization campaigns and neglect of basic public health programs resulted in slower, perhaps more insidious, declines in West Papuan populations.⁶

Few outsiders can distinguish Papua New Guinea, the neighboring country that is familiar to anyone who has taken an introductory anthropology course, from West Papua. Officially known as Irian Jaya, until the name was changed in 2000, this seemingly remote place easily slips out of geographic memory.[7] With similar conflicts raging in other parts of the globe—Tibet, Palestine, and Darfur—West Papuans have had difficulty in getting the international community to take notice. The reaction of many people upon hearing about yet another underreported and asymmetrical war is to simply turn away.[8] As a result, West Papuan activists have become savvy at capturing the attention of tourists and other visiting foreigners. The dancers at the airport were the first of a long line of West Papuans who grabbed hold of my imagination with surprising images, actions, and dreams. Years later, when I set out to study West Papua's independence movement, I was drawn into a struggle for freedom that I was just coming to understand. I found myself starting to expect the unexpected.

Only a handful of West Papua's 263 distinct language groups have been studied by cultural anthropologists in long-term ethnographic research projects.[9] This book does not claim either the depth of these localized studies or the thoroughness of a historical account based on the study of a definitive archive. Rather, it traces ideas about freedom, ideas contained in the Indonesian word *merdeka* (free, independent, liberated), as they moved through time and among West Papuan cultural groups.[10] This book charts the contours of West Papua's independence movement as it gained ground over a ten-year period, from 1998 to 2008, and beyond. What follows is not a monograph with pretensions to completeness. Instead I offer partial perspectives, a story of compromises, situated within multiple entangled worlds.

Like the Biak fishermen who appropriated the catcalls of the Allied troops, I have borrowed words and ideas from others. This book is intertextual, a fusion of multiple different stories. Conversations with the scholarly literature—meditations on timely debates in anthropology, cultural studies, and political theory—appear as a subtext throughout the book in expansive footnotes.[11] My own observations—as a transit passenger, as a bystander at Indonesian military massacres, and as an advocate who accompanied West Papuan activists in political meetings—serve as a route into published materials, obscure historical documents, and spoken testimony.[12] I deploy multiple genres and narrative forms: figurative indigenous parables alongside literalist accounts of history, personal memoir alongside ethnographic description. The result is an unconventional anthropological study, a multisited ethnography, about people and political formations in motion.[13]

Indigenous leaders, visionaries, and ordinary people let me record their tales. Over the course of my research, I conducted more than four hundred interviews, mostly in the Indonesian language and a creole slang called Logat Papua.[14] Some stories I heard will be familiar to anyone who follows daily news reports from other conflict zones—stories about torture, about U.S. government support for a military occupation, and about aspirations for independence. Other stories surprised me. I learned about a government campaign of terror initiated by "Mrs. Dracula" and about how my ancestors, the whites, stole the magic of modernity.[15] Indigenous activists used images of inequality and terror as well as figures of hope—of multiple messiahs and promised lands—to probe the bounds of realism and realistic possibility.[16]

Amid campaigns of state violence, West Papuans embraced the sort of hope that arises only in times of complete hopelessness.[17] People from all walks of life searched future horizons for signs of coming transformations.[18] At the same time, indigenous activists began to find small cracks in the architecture of power. They began to secure financing from multinational corporations, political support from foreign governments, and concessions from the Indonesian occupiers. Studying the strategic engagements of West Papuans and listening to their remarkable dreams, I developed an argument about freedom in entangled worlds. In short, wedding the strategy of collaboration with an expansive imagination opens up surprising opportunities in the field of historical possibility.

List of Key Characters

OCTOVIANUS MOTE, a journalist and public
intellectual from the Mee tribe, was the bureau
chief of *Kompas*, a daily newspaper in West Papua's
capital, Jayapura. In 1999 he played a key role in
setting up the meeting between the Team of 100
leaders and President B. J. Habibie (see chapter 2).
Narrowly escaping a botched assassination
attempt, on the heels of this historic event, Mote
was granted political asylum in the United States. As a visiting fellow at
Cornell University and Yale University, he recruited me to help explore the
halls of the U.S. Congress as he searched for possibilities of freedom for
his people in a seemingly impossible geopolitical situation (see chapter 6).
Photograph courtesy of Elsham Papua.

DENNY YOMAKI served as the secretary of Elsham
Papua, the Institute of Human Rights Study and
Advocacy. Personal entanglements with Wasior, a
seemingly remote town that was suddenly rocked
by violence as a BP natural gas project started up
nearby, led Yomaki to launch an investigation into
Indonesian military covert operations (see
chapter 3). Serving as a guide to epistemologically murky realms, where
supernatural specters masked surprising collaborations, Yomaki helped me
translate ephemeral rumors into forms of knowledge that then traveled
to the halls of global power (see chapter 4). *Photograph courtesy of Elsham
Papua.*

ANTONIUS WAMANG, a farmer from the
Amungme tribe, was indicted by a U.S. grand jury
in 2004 for involvement in the murder of two
American schoolteachers. After the Indonesian
authorities failed to apprehend Wamang, FBI
special agents convinced him to surrender on
Indonesian soil in January 2006. Using bait-and-
switch tactics, the FBI promised Wamang a trial in
America and then promptly delivered him to

the Indonesian police. Wamang had contacts with Indonesian security
forces before the attack that killed the teachers. Ambivalent and contingent collaborations between Wamang and Indonesian agents coproduced
an act of terror (see chapter 5). *Photograph by Eben Kirksey.*

JOHN RUMBIAK was the charismatic founder
of Elsham Papua (the Institute for Human Rights
Study and Advocacy) who began to travel the
globe on a quest to bring rights and justice within
reach of his people. Critical of organized religion,
Rumbiak espoused secular freedom dreams. Faith
in the power of international law and the ethical principles of human rights led Rumbiak to collaborate with powerful institutions in distant

lands (see chapter 4). Ultimately this trust was exploited and betrayed
by U.S. government agents (see chapter 5). *Photograph courtesy of Elsham
Papua.*

PAULA MAKABORY, a human rights researcher
with Elsham Papua, worked to expose the role of
undercover Indonesian military agents in murdering two American teachers near a gold mine
operated by Freeport McMoRan. Following death
threats, Makabory obtained political asylum in
Australia. *Photography courtesy of Mary Wareham.*

GENERAL MELKIANUS AWOM participated in
the first guerrilla actions by the Organisasi Papua
Merdeka (OPM) in 1965. Evading detection from
the authorities for decades, Awom helped keep
a fighting spirit alive. At the First Voice Honey
Center, his jungle hideout, General Awom worked
to create a realm of spiritual and symbolic autonomy. Still, he found that he could not escape ma-
terial entanglements with enemy forces. General
Awom harbored freedom dreams from distant lands, hopes that were not
entirely his own. *Photograph by Eben Kirksey.*

BENNY GIAY is a Protestant pastor and a cultural
anthropologist from the Mee tribe. A prolific
writer, Dr. Giay has published a number of books
about charismatic West Papuan leaders. Drawing
from the liberation theology of Latin America,
the writings of U.S. intellectuals in the civil rights
movement, and the philosophy of the Frankfurt
school, he has explored the promise of the messi-
anic idea (see introduction). In 1998 and 1999,
Dr. Giay helped initiate dialogue with the Indonesian government (see
chapter 2). He later became an outspoken critic of West Papuan nationalist
leaders, whose visions of freedom showed little promise of getting beyond
a new regime of postcolonial suffering (see chapter 6). *Photograph courtesy
of Elsham Papua.*

FILEP KARMA, a civil servant in the governor's
office, rallied crowds in July 1998 under the Morning Star flag, West Papua's banner of independence
(see chapter 1). For a moment, Karma embodied
the messianic multiple—a spirit dancing about
like liquid mercury, moving in different directions,
and coalescing around multiple future events, fig-
ures of hope. On December 1, 2004, Filep Karma
was arrested for again raising the Morning Star and sentenced to fifteen
years in prison for "rebellion." Amnesty International is spearheading a
campaign for Karma's release. *Photograph by Eben Kirksey.*

Freedom in Entangled Worlds

Introduction

When I started research for this book, I planned to study West Papuan resistance to Indonesian rule and the forces of globalization. Unexpected discoveries forced me to rethink the terms of my research. Collaboration, rather than resistance, turned out to be the primary strategy of this political movement. West Papuan revolutionaries demonstrated an uncanny knack for getting inside institutions of power. Building coalitions with unlikely allies — making strategic engagements with foreign governments, multinational corporations, and even elite Indonesian politicians — they brought specific political goals within reach. Yet as West Papuans achieved near-term objectives, they found that the politics of collaboration restricted the scope and scale of their interventions. In the face of impossibility, people began to harbor seemingly unrealistic dreams.

This book explores a series of interrelated questions: What are the prospects of finding limited rights and justice while trapped within unwanted entanglements? When worlds are at war, bent on mutual annihilation, why do people collaborate across lines separating enemies from allies? How does one find freedom in an era of global interdependence, when national sovereignty and independence are inherently compromised? In short, I argue that freedom emerges when people collaborate with existing institutions of power while imagining sweeping transformations on future horizons. Imaginative dreams bring surprising prospects into view when translated into collaborative action.[1]

Strategies of collaboration or purely imaginary dreams often fail when they operate alone. Collaboration, by itself, can quickly lead to co-optation. Hope can produce paralysis. Passively waiting for dreams to be fulfilled without taking steps to actualize them resigns the future to fate.[2] This book chronicles the history of indigenous activists who wed collaboration with imagination. As West Papuans linked expansive dreams to established institutions, historical possibilities multiplied beyond control.

In opening, I offer two stories that illustrate my argument about freedom in entangled worlds, about the interplay of collaboration and imagination. The first story, about a woman who was kept by Indonesian soldiers as a sexual slave, grapples with the ethical and existential dilemmas faced by people who try to exceed the conditions of their exploitation. This is an account about the limited possibilities that emerge with strategies of collaboration in situations of extreme power asymmetry. A second story—a fantastic tale involving magic, soccer, and gold—depicts the elusive nature of freedom in the current moment of global history. Presented side by side, these two tales set the stage for the remainder of the book, where I chronicle revolutionary possibilities and political actualities that emerged in West Papua.

Collaboration

Ester Nawipa, then a girl of fifteen, awoke with a start one night. A blinding light shone through the windows of the one-room house she shared with her extended family. At the time she was living in a highland village two hours' walk from Enarotali, the nearest town. "Night was usually pitch black, nobody had electricity," Ester told me years later in the living room of a trusted mutual friend. "We were all wondering who was outside with a big flashlight. Then men suddenly started banging on the door. They were soldiers. Nobody answered the door, so they kicked it in. 'You are going to be our new girlfriend,' they told me. 'You must come with us to our barracks, Post 753.'"

The day before, Ester had unintentionally caught the eye of a soldier when she sold him vegetables at the market. She had been wearing a grass skirt and a net bag made of bark string modestly covering her back—the traditional dress of highland West Papua—which left her breasts exposed. Like other members of the Mee tribe, some one hundred thousand people living around a series of large highland lakes, her family subsisted by farming sweet potatoes and raising pigs. Selling vegetables allowed Ester's family to buy a few choice factory goods. Her cousin, who had joined the military a few years earlier, was one of the only extended family members with a wage-paying job. It was Ester's cousin who led the soldiers to her house that night.[3]

Carrying sweet potatoes to the market in Enarotali, a city in the highlands that is in the territory of the Mee tribe. *Photograph by Eben Kirksey.*

"The soldiers shot their guns into the air when we protested about them taking me away," Ester continued. "One of my uncles said: We could all end up dead here—it's better if you just go with them." This cynical declaration by Ester's uncle reflects widespread sentiments in the highlands of New Guinea that place sociopolitical and economic considerations ahead of the welfare of individual women.[4] Before missionaries outlawed polygamy in the late twentieth century, rich men in the Mee tribe accumulated many wives who toiled in sweet potato gardens and took care of pigs.[5] In the early twenty-first century, men continued to regard their young female kin as economic assets who were redeemable for a bride price at marriage.[6] Ester's uncle calculated that keeping the peace with the Indonesian soldiers was more important than future prospects of bride wealth.[7]

The next day, Ester reluctantly went with the solders to their barracks in Enarotali. She had no choice. Six different soldiers in the Indonesian military raped her over the course of a year. The men never used condoms. Later Ester became the exclusive "girlfriend" of the commander of the

Lake Paniai as seen from Enarotali. *Photograph by Eben Kirksey.*

post. "Things with the commander weren't that bad. His subordinates were rougher," she told me. With her newfound status as the commander's girl-friend, the other soldiers began to be deferential to Ester. She used her special status to become a peacemaker. "No villagers were ever shot while I was there. When soldiers' tempers would rise, I would steal their guns and hold on to their magazines of bullets. I had to intervene a lot. There were nearly thirty close calls while I was the commander's girlfriend—I might have saved thirty people from getting shot."

When I interviewed Ester, she was twenty-five, one year younger than I was at the time. She insisted that I publish this story with her real name.[8] In committing her story to the public record, Ester was coming to terms with the difficult choices she was forced to make as a girl. She was overcoming feelings of shame and embracing a sense of indignation. During our conversation, she made it clear to me that she did not choose to sleep with the soldiers. She made it equally clear that she did not just passively resign herself to fate. Despite being trapped in an extreme situation of exploitation, she managed to assert herself in a subtle way. Ester exceeded the conditions of her exploitation. She became a voice of peace, of human rights, of freedom.[9]

Ester asked me to tell the international community about what it was like to grow up amid a military occupation in the 1980s and 1990s. Young

Post 753, the army barracks in Enarotali where Ester was forced to live.
Photograph by Eben Kirksey.

Indonesian soldiers were not supplied with a living wage. They raped, killed, and extorted money from West Papuans with impunity. Sexual slavery and sexualized torture were commonplace. Indonesian troops also routinely beat, electrocuted, and shot civilians. At the time Ester told me her story, in August 2002, human bodies were turning up along roadsides and beaches. Some of these bodies had the marks of torture.[10] In talking to me, Ester was risking a similar fate. Braving soldiers' flaring tempers in her youth— when she seized their bullets and guns to protect people—made Ester want to take a defiant public stand as an adult. She offered me her words with the modest hope that they would someday help West Papuans enjoy basic human rights.

When Ester told me about using her unwanted relationship with the commander to save peoples' lives, I began to think about other people who maneuver within entanglements. Ester's story challenged me to rethink the politics of collaboration. I began to find parallels between her lived experiences and the experiences of West Papuan independence activists who were trapped in an Indonesian military occupation and extreme power asymmetries on the wider global stage. I came to understand that people who are stuck in subordinate positions often have few options other than engaging with dominant institutions and building coalitions with agents of power.

Compromises can open up the field of possibility in situations of seeming impossibility.

Why do collaborations work? Anna Tsing, a cultural anthropologist who also studies out-of-the-way places in Indonesia suggests that "collaborations are the hopeful edge of a political project."[11] Clever engagements can bring specific goals within reach, even when collaborators do not share the same interests. Risking an alliance with "the enemy" has the prospect of moving beyond eternal standoffs between opposing interest groups. "Collaborations create *new* interests and identities," continues Tsing, "but not to everyone's benefit."[12] Seemingly beneficial alliances can quickly collapse into relations of raw exploitation.

While making clever engagements, West Papuans found their imaginations and political coalitions stuck in entanglements that were difficult to escape. "Entanglement suggests knots, gnarls, and adhesions rather than smooth surfaces," in the words of Donald Moore, an anthropologist who studies struggles over land in Zimbabwe. Entanglements form "an inextricable interweave that ensnares; a compromising relationship that challenges while making withdrawal difficult if not impossible. Attempts to pull apart such formations may unwittingly tighten them."[13] The notion of entanglement points to the constraints of past connections as well as emergent possibilities.[14] Rather than pulling apart knotty and gnarled formations, I found many political agents struggling for change from within. Strategic compromises transformed dominant systems of power and changed situations where withdrawal was difficult or impossible.

West Papuans came to draw me, a young anthropologist, into their collaborative projects. Recruited as a believer and a partisan, I became involved in the social movement that I had set out to study as a doctoral student. My counterparts encouraged me to meet with people whom I had not previously imagined as potential allies. Donning a suit and tie, I joined indigenous activists, sometimes against my better judgment, in meetings with corporate executives and government officials. Often our specific "asks," or requests for action, were ignored. In the face of indifference, I learned the importance of securing incremental and partial victories. Sometimes our encounters with officials resulted in bringing a new ally into a fragile, contingent coalition that backed a particular initiative.[15]

Following West Papuans to the chambers of the British Parliament in London and the halls of Capitol Hill in Washington, I came to study institutions of power as a participant observer. My research became entangled in a hotly contested murder investigation, activism against U.S. military aid to Indonesia, and a host of ethical dilemmas. Working alongside West Papuans who were seeking alliances with seemingly hostile groups, drawing on foreign ideological elements, and building connections with powerful institutions, I learned about the ethics and politics of navigating entangled worlds.[16]

While negotiating complex compromises, West Papuan activists told me that they were still anticipating elusive horizons of transformation in the future. West Papuan leaders who were adept at collaborating with power told me about their hopes for a time when the rules would change. They were imagining miracles that would let them escape their present entanglements. I discovered plans for reconfiguring the system of global hegemony. Visionaries imagined a future where they would give away their natural resources in grand humanitarian gestures, rather than passively watch their homeland be drained of timber, gold, copper, and natural gas. I found my friends praying for me, for the United States, and for the "higher rulers of humanity" at the United Nations so that we would learn to genuinely embrace the principles of human rights—to see things to which we had been blind in the past.

Ester, too, prayed that God would forgive her sins and deliver her from evil. She pragmatically engaged with power while waiting for a dramatic transformation of her life circumstances. Trapped in a system of sexual slavery, she believed that divine intervention might be her only route to a complete escape. One day a wonderful surprise liberated her from the Indonesian soldiers: she became pregnant. "None of the other girls being held at the barracks had become pregnant before," Ester told me. Rampant sexual infections and rough treatment likely prevented them from having children. "My baby was a miracle," she said.

When Ester's belly began to grow, none of the soldiers wanted to have sex with her anymore. She was free to leave the army barracks. Ester traveled to the lowland city of Nabire, where she had her baby in peace. Freedom for Ester was thus embodied in the flesh and blood of her firstborn. She has since married a West Papuan church worker and now has five children. Someday Ester hopes to follow her husband's path and pursue advanced theological training herself. Ester spent an agonizing two years in an Indonesian military barracks and nonetheless developed a remarkable ability to actualize limited freedoms. She taught me that it is possible to maneuver for rights and justice in compromised situations while still holding on to hope for a future to come.[17]

Figures of Imagination

Days after interviewing Ester Nawipa, I chartered a missionary plane to the eastern highlands to investigate reports of Indonesian military operations among the Yali, a group of some thirty thousand people. The day before my flight, I paid a mandatory visit to the airport hangar, where I was weighed along with my baggage. Shortly after dawn the next morning, I was airborne. The only other passenger, a Yali church worker, had canceled at the last minute. I rode shotgun. In my lap a backup control wheel swiveled, tracing the pilot's maneuvers. We left the hot and humid lowlands, flew over expansive stands of forest and swamp, climbed past rolling foothills, and wove through jagged mountain peaks. The plane banked sharply to the left and dove to the main Yali landing strip—some two hundred yards of grass that dropped off over a steep precipice at one end.

On the landing strip, as the pilot prepared for his departure, a Yali man startled me with a provocative question: "Are you here to help the West Papuan people?"[18] I paused, weighing the implications of my possible responses. "*Yes*," I said, turning over letters of introduction that I had obtained from well-known church leaders and human rights workers. Six men quickly escorted me into a nearby building. Light filtered through cracks in the wood-plank walls, and a shortwave radio crackled from a small booth in the corner. They shut the door.

Behind the closed door, I explained to the assembled Yali leaders that I was a student working on a dissertation about nationalism and violence. I was surprised by the savvy of these culture brokers. Having been the subjects of two doctoral projects—Siegfried Zöllner's theological study of religion and Klaus-Friedrich Koch's ethnography of warfare—these Yali men quickly understood the nature of my mission. They offered me a list of research topics. Was I interested in hearing about the activities of local guerrillas? Would I like to learn about the local branch of the Panel, a peaceful nationalist group? State violence and human rights? The coming of the gospel? In the coming days, I stayed in an abandoned room at the local health clinic. I returned regularly to the radio shed to meet with these men, and we had conversations that wandered over each of these topics. We also strayed into unforeseen territory, off the map of this list of potential research projects.

The day after my arrival, Silas Kiwak, a tall, wiry man who was an elder in the Protestant Church, summoned me back to the radio shed. There he told me about the history of the world. "In the beginning the ancestors of the first whites and the first blacks played soccer together. They played soccer here on a landing strip. Even today you can see the remains of that old landing strip," Kiwak said as his eyebrows danced behind a pair of wire-rimmed glasses. "Back then," he continued, "all sorts of machines were freely available. We had airplanes, radios, and electric generators. Everybody had shoes, soccer balls, outhouses, and rice."[19]

This story threw me off balance. Instead of talking about the recent series of violent assaults by Indonesian security forces that I had come to investigate, the latest incidents in a long history of suffering, Kiwak told me a tale that flew in the face of everything I knew about history.[20] He told me about a modern age that had come and gone—an era of abundance and peace, a past that might suddenly come again. The time of the first human ancestors, Kiwak said, had a short period of abundance with enough material goods for everyone. These good years came after a chaotic period of perpetual earthquakes, monstrous shape-shifting pigs, and powerful tree-kangaroo shamans.[21] Listening carefully to this uncanny tale, I came to realize that it was about present inequalities and future possibilities as much as it was about the past.

Life under Dutch colonialism was hardly utopic for most West Papuans. Racism and material inequality were ever present in tales of early colonial adventures.[22] Local accounts of history are now dominated by memories of major development campaigns launched by the Dutch shortly after they first set up permanent colonial outposts in West Papua's highlands. In the 1950s many new machines and types of clothes suddenly arrived. With the departure of the Dutch in the 1960s and the arrival of Indonesians, foreign wares became relatively scarce. During my visit in 2002, few Yali had factory-made clothing, shoes, or other choice goods. Discovery Channel images of the Yali—of men wearing long penis gourds and of bare-breasted women wearing grass skirts—were the most valuable commodities that had been brought out of their land recently.[23] Rice, grown in distant Javanese and Balinese paddies, was an imported luxury food. Access to airplanes, radios, and electric generators was only available to a select few.

Kiwak's story hinged on an act of deceit: "The whites told the blacks to gather together on the soccer field. Our ancestors, the blacks, were told to shut their eyes and pray. They complied. As the prayer was finishing one of the black men opened his eyes. He saw the last white person disappearing into a hole in the earth. This black man shouted out. All the goods had van-

We are not in Kansas.
Photograph by Terry McClain.

ished. Everyone assembled on the field opened their eyes and witnessed the promise of the last departing white man. The last white said he would return one day with the goods. Then he entered the hole, and it closed shut behind him."

With this tale, I was forced to face myself as others see me, as a "white."[24] White men are viewed with ambivalence throughout the highlands of New Guinea—as people who act greedily in self-interest and as a people who ushered in a time of relative peace and prosperity.[25] In this particular tale, the departing promise of the last white man suggested that a major transformation of the global order, a past to come again, might be just around the corner. Silas Kiwak's story illustrated the elaborate deceptions, industrial secrets, and legal constructions that sustain white magic: the magic of modernity.[26] Upon concluding his tale, he regarded me with a twinkle in his eye, inviting me to respond. But I was at a loss for words.

Silas Kiwak's prowess for telling stories was widely revered among the Yali. He drew on multiple sources for inspiration. Like many other intellectuals in Melanesia, the chain of Pacific islands that stretches east from New

Guinea toward Fiji, he had gained renown for making connections between seemingly different tales and resolving contradictory elements among them.[27] Fusing Christian parables and local myths with accounts of history, he told me about the origin of social and economic injustice. His account of the ancestors represented more than just a catalog of desirable commodities; it contained visions of the past and the future collapsing together in revolutionary time.

Some aspects of reality are best represented with figural stories rather than accounts that claim to be strictly literal.[28] This parable about a figural hole can only be understood in relation to a literal hole in the highlands of West Papua that contains vast subterranean wealth. Freeport McMoRan, a company based in the United States, has taken home approximately $1.9 billion each year from a huge open-pit mine in West Papua.[29] Every day the mine produces some 1,800 metric tons of copper and 9,000 troy ounces of gold.[30] This project is extracting the largest known deposit of gold on the planet. It is the world's third-largest open-cut copper mine. A photographic image that was recently released by NASA gives a vivid picture of the hole from outer space.

Freeport began building their mine in West Papua on an auspicious day: exactly 1,971 years after the memorialized birth of Christ. "On Christmas Day 1971, the first convoy of trucks, carrying 500 tons of cargo, drove into the town site at milepost 68," writes Forbes Wilson, former president of Freeport Indonesia Inc. "We were now able to begin construction of the town."[31] Freeport's arrival heralded not a new era of abundance and peace but rather the sharp disappointment that comes with unfulfilled promises. Access to Freeport's "cargo" was restricted to the whites and their local collaborators.[32]

The sudden and unexpected delivery of wealth in 1971 set the stage for the hybrid historical parable that Silas Kiwak told me some thirty years later. The Yali story of the hole, an ancestral tale that was reinvented to make sense of new historical circumstances, used the promise of the departing whites to refer to the possibilities contained in Freeport's open-pit mine and other, yet unopened holes. Kiwak's figural hole referenced literal possibilities. Promises from powerful outsiders might someday be fulfilled.

Kiwak's tale contained elements of messianic consciousness, a mode of thought that was introduced and reinforced in West Papua by European and American missionaries.[33] True followers will enjoy a blissful rapture with the Second Coming of the Messiah, according to missionaries who spread

A hole. This picture of the open-pit Freeport mine was taken by an astronaut in June 2005, at an elevation of 191 nautical miles, with a Kodak electronic still camera. The hole is about 2.5 miles wide. There are also extensive mining tunnels at the site. Access roads for trucks hauling ore and waste rock are visible along the sides of the pit. *Image ISS011-E-9620, NASA Earth Observatory.*

the Good News in West Papua.[34] Church workers promised that the return of Christ would usher in the millennium, one thousand years of peace, righteousness, and utopia.[35]

Hopes connected to the arrival of a messiah contain "the attraction, invincible élan or affirmation of an unpredictable future-to-come (or even of a past-to-come-again)," in the words of Jacques Derrida, the French philosopher who is one of the founders of deconstruction.[36] "Not only must one not renounce the emancipatory desire," writes Derrida, but "it is necessary to insist on it more than ever."[37] Silas Kiwak's story certainly contained the emancipatory desire described by Derrida. It was not tied to the figure of Christ; nor was he fixated on a period of one thousand years. Instead Kiwak held on to promises contained in the magical hole of the white ancestors, a figure that embodies hopes for ending global economic inequalities.

Figures are graphic representations, like drawings. "To figure" also means to have a role in a story.[38] Following Nathan Bailey's *Dictionarium Britannicum* of 1730, figures might be regarded as "a fashioning, a resemblance, a shape; also a chimerical vision."[39] They bring desires together into stable objects of hope and serve as anchoring points for dreams.[40] Some figures, like Ester Nawipa's miraculous baby, are the material embodiment of personal hopes. Mythic elements help animate historical figures like Jesus Christ or President Obama, who gather up the hopes of the masses and produce the conditions for collective action. Figures can be material objects or structures, like Freeport's giant hole filled with gold and copper. They can contain injustices as well as expansive desires.[41]

The hole of the Yali is a figure of hope that, when taken by itself, produced paralyzing inaction. The magic of modernity may one day be revealed by the whites, but passively waiting for this dream to be fulfilled does not require making concrete interventions.[42] Despite evidence of the perils of blind faith, and at the risk of repeating the naive gullibility of the black ancestors who shut their eyes to pray, Silas Kiwak was nonetheless waiting for the Second Coming of modernity. He regarded whites and other outsiders with hopeful ambivalence. Kiwak hoped that the figural stolen goods would one day be returned.

Benny Giay, a cultural anthropologist and theologian from the Mee tribe, is critical of the church, the Indonesian government, and foreign companies for promoting the idea that the Messiah, or other figures animated by a messianic spirit, will usher in a better future for West Papua. "West Papuans have been left in the waiting room," says Giay, "to wait for outsiders to bring peace, happiness and justice."[43] The institutions of power operating in West Papua have ultimately failed to channel the messianic spirit, Giay argues. Following the programs of action dictated by hierarchical institutions for many years—passively praying, or hoping for development funds, with few noticeable results—produced a sense of collective frustration.

The Indonesian government gets a windfall of taxes every year from mining precious metals and petroleum in West Papua. In 2009, Freeport paid $1.4 billion in taxes to the central government.[44] In the same year, West Papua still ranked last out of Indonesia's thirty-three provinces on the Human Development Index, a measure of life expectancy, literacy, and standard of living.[45] "Modern institutions have promoted the messianic idea," concludes Giay, "but these same institutions have failed to offer systematic instruction and direction to make West Papuans aware of their potentials, their strengths."

After decades of failed promises, West Papuans have held on to the messianic spirit and have channeled it in surprising directions. Under shrewd leadership, imaginative dreams began to ignite a mass movement and reconfigure relations of power. At the dawn of the twenty-first century—as disappointments in church bureaucracies, multinational companies, and Indonesian institutions continued to mount—indigenous intellectuals began to pin collective hopes on multiple figures and objects of desire. When expansive dreams became concrete as specific events appeared on future horizons and particular leaders embodied the messianic spirit, a wildly popular social movement exploded with revolutionary activity.

Entangled Worlds: Collaboration Meets Imagination

When social movements bring imagination and collaboration together, they generate moments of political electricity. If institutions of power are impenetrable, then gathering together and demanding the impossible—the resignation of the president, say, or an independence referendum—can have surprising results. Cracks in the architecture of power signal that the possibilities are multiplying. When the masses harbor expansive hopes and savvy leaders penetrate powerful institutions, coordinated action can bring particular objects of collective desire within reach.[46]

Taking to the street en masse is just one visible way of making worlds, of collaborating and doing things together.[47] Social worlds, according to a classic definition from sociology, are arenas established by the limits of communication.[48] They are communities of practice and discourse engaged in collective action.[49] Diffracting these classic definitions through my own keywords, I suggest that social worlds are forged when imagination comes together with collaboration.[50] Sharing dreams about a messianic figure or a future event produces the conditions for united worldly action.

Social worlds are often at war. Battles over supporters, land, money, and scarce natural resources are constantly taking place.[51] Perhaps a state of open war is preferable to a false sense of peace. In a book titled *War of the Worlds* Bruno Latour argues: "It might after all be better to be at war, and thus to be forced to think about the diplomatic work to be done, than to imagine that there is no war at all and keep talking endlessly about progress, modernity, development—without realizing the price that must be paid in reaching such lofty goals."[52] Diplomatic work, transforming former enemies into temporary allies, is often necessary to bring specific objectives within reach. Freedom in entangled worlds can thus be found by maneuvering for rights and justice within a nested matrix of global power, rather than establishing an illusion of complete sovereignty.

My understanding of "entangled worlds" is also informed by theories of the modern world system, first developed by Immanuel Wallerstein a sociologist and historian. World systems theory suggests that global capitalistic production was based on inequality from the start: strong "core" states exploited labor and resources from weak "peripheral" territories.[53] Wallerstein regards the world capitalist system as a unified whole that remained stable over the *longue durée* of history, even as different European nations and later the United States assumed the role of global hegemon.[54] I accept Wallerstein's basic premise about how inequality is built into the global system of capitalistic production. But as I maneuvered among competing social worlds in West Papua, I found that this global system is not unified. The modern system is structured by oblique powers, multiple worlds jockeying with each other, rather than a single, all-encompassing world hegemon.[55]

Amid conditions of coercion, maintaining perceptible boundaries among worlds is often difficult, especially since some people always inhabit the borderlands, living in between powerful countervailing forces.[56] Competing visions from multiple worlds—dreams of prosperity, political autonomy, or security—tug at the imaginations of leaders, their die-hard supporters, and people on the margins.[57] Sometimes people switch sides. As representatives of social worlds engage in strategic compromises, seeking concessions from other groups, they risk finding their dreams captured, of developing a commitment to more than one community.[58]

Freedom in entangled worlds means negotiating complex interdependencies, rather than promoting fictions about absolute independence.[59] Contingent alliances, sometimes even with the enemy, can open up possibilities in seemingly impossible situations. Amid warfare among worlds, coalition building and serious diplomacy generate limited freedoms for people who are stuck in conditions not of their own choosing. Still, strategies of engagement can fail. When institutions of power are impenetrable, speculative fictions and figures generate new critical insights and plans for action. When leaders wed strategies of collaboration with figures that captured the imagination of the masses, when leaders bring these two elements of freedom together, the future contains open-ended possibilities.

The word "freedom" has entered the lexicon of global war; it has become one of many words that bulldoze over our dreams.[60] When the Bush administration launched Operation Iraqi Freedom, it generated powerful new associations with this word, links that jeopardized liberty, sovereignty, choice, and free will. President Bush linked war and a coup d'état to freedom to rally popular support for his invasion and occupation of Iraq. This book aims to reclaim the hopeful possibilities contained in *freedom*, displacing prevailing notions with visions from the periphery of the modern world system.

Collective aspirations in West Papua were wrapped around an abstract ideal, *merdeka*, a charged slogan containing imaginative dreams and programs of collaborative action. *Merdeka*, a loose equivalent of "freedom," contains multiple layers of meaning, figures of hope, and objects of desire.[61] *An Indonesian-English Dictionary*, in the custom of such indexes, establishes a simple equivalence between the word *merdeka* and three English words: free, independent, and liberated.[62] When West Papuans began linking their aspirations to merdeka in the mid-twentieth century, they inherited a rich history of previous translations and appropriations from much earlier periods.[63] The word's etymology can be traced to two Sanskrit words: *maha* (great, mighty, strong, lustrous, brilliant, powerful) and *ṛddhi* (growth, prosperity, success, good fortune, wealth, abundance; also accomplishment, perfection, supernatural power).[64] Ideas about merdeka developed in insular Southeast Asia under some 350 years of Dutch economic adventures and colonial exploits.[65]

Merdeka became the rallying cry of Indonesian freedom fighters in the twentieth century during their struggle for independence from Dutch colonialism. At this moment, local dreams in Indonesia linked up with large-scale collective actions. The spark of anticolonial nationalism caught and became a conflagration, sweeping the globe like wildfire.[66] Nationalism had become "modular," according to Benedict Anderson who is perhaps the single most influential theorist on nationalism in recent years. The module of the independent nation-state was "transplanted, with varying degrees of self-consciousness, to a great variety of social terrains, to merge and be merged with a correspondingly wide variety of political and ideological constellations."[67] Newspapers and literary novels were vehicles of nationalism, helping to popularize standard national languages.[68] Emergent groups of literate citizens came to form what Anderson called imagined communities, groups of people who would never know each other face-to-face but nonetheless shared an image of their communion.[69]

After gaining independence, postcolonial nations found themselves grappling with Cold War imperialisms and predatory multinational corporations. Members of newly sovereign imagined communities were mired in a fresh era of postcolonial suffering.[70] After the modular nation was imported to Indonesia, after the country achieved independence from the Dutch, dreams of merdeka from earlier periods resurfaced—ideas about prosperity and local autonomy. "Long after Indonesian sovereignty was recognized by the world," writes Anderson, who is also an Indonesian specialist, "the search for 100 per cent *merdeka* [liberty] was to continue and was to remain sentenced to disappointment. But hopes are still with us."[71] At the periphery of the country—in provinces where military excesses bred widespread discontent—people lost hope in Indonesian nationalism. Merdeka came to inspire breakaway nationalist movements in the Indonesian provinces of Aceh, West Papua, Maluku, and East Timor.[72] Merdeka formed Indonesia. The same rallying cry began to pull the nation apart.

The political dimensions of imagination have been theorized by Robin Kelley, whose book *Freedom Dreams* argues that the visions of social movements should be evaluated according to their inherent merits, not by whether they have succeeded. "Alternative visions and dreams inspire new generations to continue to struggle for change," writes Kelley, though "virtually every radical movement failed because the basic power relations they sought to change remain pretty much intact."[73]

As the dawn of the twenty-first century approached and West Papuans rallied in the streets, the possibility of success seemed imminent—the near-term goal of achieving national independence seemed close at hand. Activists were not only hoping to instate the "modular nationalism" that they would inherit from abroad. People began dreaming that another world was possible. After liberating themselves from Indonesian occupation, indigenous visionaries planned to roll back injustices on a global scale. The merdeka movement came to be allied in spirit and principle with the anti-globalization movement that emerged with the protests in November 1999 against the World Trade Organization in Seattle. In Europe West Papuans found common cause with an allied political project, the alter-globalization movement. Alter-globalization (*autre-mondialisation*, "other worlding" in French) is a vision of another world order where global humanistic values are given primacy over the market economy.[74]

The more than 263 indigenous groups in West Papua seemed to be "vanishing worlds" in the mid-twentieth century, soon to disappear amid the forces of Dutch colonialism, Indonesian nationalism, and global capitalism. In the early twenty-first century, these indigenous people began to reassert themselves in surprising ways.[75] As American and European power showed signs of decline, reemerging indigenous worlds began to gain ascendancy, shifting and realigning prevailing hegemonies.[76] The future was up for grabs as West Papuan indigenous groups united around the idea of merdeka—each diffracting national and international hopes, freedom dreams, and figures through their local idioms.[77]

Among the hundreds of indigenous worlds I brushed up against in West Papua, one group in particular stands out. The Mee people, the tribe of Ester Nawipa and Benny Giay, feature prominently in this book. When the Dutch colonial authorities built an administrative headquarters at Enarotali in 1938, their first highland outpost, they gave the Mee educational opportunities offered by the modern world. When I was an undergraduate, I spent three months with the Mee of the Siriwo River Valley, a group of hunter-gatherers living in the foothills. This experience gave me a point of entry to senior Mee leaders, some of the most influential intellectuals in West Papua, when I later began studying the merdeka movement in graduate school.

Following merdeka through heterogeneous cultural worlds, I found that it was not fixed on any one thing but instead contained expansive freedom dreams about many different future events, potential messiahs, and imaginative figures.[78] Tacking back and forth between fantastic tales and historical realism, this book chronicles West Papua's independence movement for more than a decade, from 1998 to 2008 and beyond, charting the interplay between political engagement and withdrawal, between effective action and expansive dreaming.

In 1998 a series of events took place that surprised everyone, even those who were involved. Thousands of West Papuans took to the streets to demand freedom from Indonesia. At this moment, amid an economic crisis and regime change, the field of historical possibility appeared completely open. Imagination linked up with the politics of collaboration, and it seemed that anything could happen at any moment. Long-standing promises from the modern world—promises contained in international treaties, human rights law, and development discourse—suddenly seemed as if they would be fulfilled.[79]

When Indonesian authorities tried to destroy West Papua's movement for merdeka with raw force, killing students and other civilians in a series of massacres in 1998, freedom fighters reappeared in unexpected places. They popped up within the architecture of power. Strategic collaborations and compromises, rather than strategies of pure resistance, produced surprising victories. In 2000, independence began to seem plausible when elite

My ties to the Mee tribe led Dr. Benny Giay, a theologian and cultural anthropologist, to adopt me as a graduate student. He became a formal member of my Ph.D. committee at UC Santa Cruz, commenting on my dissertation drafts remotely from West Papua. Here we are pictured together in Washington on the sidelines of the 2007 American Anthropological Association meetings, moments after he graced the title page of my dissertation with his signature. *Photograph by Octovianus Mote.*

West Papuan leaders staged a massive congress with financial support from multinational corporations.

Fresh violence—an Indonesian military campaign targeting West Papuan independence leaders with assassination and intimidation—suddenly undercut the momentum of the movement in 2001 and 2002. At this moment, imagination became unhinged from strategies of political collaboration. Amid the renewed campaign of violence, West Papuans embraced a sort of hope that arises only in times of complete hopelessness.[80] People from all walks of life searched for signs of coming transformations. Their freedom dreams pushed the bounds of realism, and of realistic possibility.

With the election of U.S. president Barack Obama in 2008, the people of West Papua took his slogan of hope and filled it with their own collective desires. "The thrill of imagining that things could be otherwise," in the words of Danilyn Rutherford, led West Papuans to find "pleasure and potency by inhabiting the slippery 'we' of 'yes we can.'"[81] Even as Obama failed to fulfill expectations that had been placed on him, the collective imagination of West Papua animated multiple other figures of hope. Activists pinned their imaginings on literal pipelines channeling gold and natural gas out of West Papua, as well as figural tubes embodying unjust economic interdependencies. Following dreams that depart along multiple lines of flight, I offer a history of multiple futures.[82]

I. BREAKOUT

1998–2000

The King Has Left the Palace

JAVA, MAY 1998

Multiple environmental, political, and social crises began to rock Indonesia in 1997. An El Niño drought hit Southeast Asia in August, coinciding with the start of the Asian financial crisis that left millions of people holding devalued currency. The drought led to massive forest fires, smog clouds, and widespread crop failures. A "poison fog blanket" covered the region, in the lurid words of one journalist. The island of New Guinea was hit by an erratic snowfall, as well as by outbreaks of diseases such as malaria, tuberculosis, diarrhea, and cholera. Over seven hundred people reportedly died from illness and famine in West Papua alone. In the first three weeks of 1998 there were more than thirty outbreaks of violence in Indonesia, which is more than the whole previous year. In Java, Indonesia's center of political power, social unrest spread like wildfire.[1]

For many Indonesians, these crises were oddly signs of hope—they fueled speculation about revolutionary transitions on the horizon.[2] The corrupt regime of Major-General Suharto, who had been president for over thirty years, was beginning to fail. Disharmony in natural and social realms has long been read as a sign of deteriorating political power by the Javanese, one of the dominant ethnic groups in Indonesia. "The signs of a lessening in the tautness of a ruler's power and of a diffusion of his strength are seen equally in manifestations of disorder in the natural world—floods, eruptions and plagues—and in inappropriate modes of social behavior—theft, greed, and murder," writes Benedict Anderson in *Language and Power*, a book about political cultures in Indonesia. "A ruler who has once permitted natural and social disorders to appear," Anderson continues, "finds it particularly difficult to reconstitute his authority. Javanese would tend to believe that, if he still had the power, the disorders would never have arisen."[3]

As the crisis deepened, Javanese mystics worked to determine the cause of the problems. Sujono Humardhani, a member of Suharto's inner circle, consulted an experienced diviner about the disturbances. Reportedly a magic nail fixing Java to the cosmos had come unglued. The island was adrift. Sujono tried to mend the cosmological problems as events got worse and worse. Engineers felled a tree from a sacred forest, cut all the branches off, and drove it into the ground in central Jakarta, Indonesia's capital city. When Sujono reported back to the diviner about the completed ritual, he learned that his mission had failed. The spiritual center of Java was not in Jakarta, according to the diviner. The tree had been driven into the ground at the wrong spot. Sujono died shortly thereafter—before he had the opportunity to conduct a nailing ceremony in the proper place—leaving Indonesia floating loose in a cosmological sea.[4]

Reports about the unpinning of Java, and the failure to nail it back down, initially circulated only among Suharto's inner circle—spreading feelings of uncertainty in the Presidential Palace.[5] The story then leaked to foreign diplomats and spread further afield.[6] Tales laced with exotic and mystical elements can easily feed stereotypes about irrational "Orientals" whose thought patterns and political processes are in essence different from Western rationality.[7] Stories about the island coming unglued are not evidence of peculiar idiosyncrasies in Javanese thought. Rather, as this unfolding chronicle will demonstrate, these reports fueled collective consciousness about revolutionary possibilities—a force that has been at work in many different cultural locations and historical moments.

President Suharto had assumed power in 1965 as massacres of alleged communists left from five hundred thousand to one million dead. By the end of his administration, the extended Suharto family had amassed a fortune worth an estimated $15 billion. A sense of policed calm was in force for most of his rule. Under Suharto's New Order regime, "events" and "incidents" were hidden from public view. The Indonesian state tried to tightly manage political and military affairs so that an all-encompassing order would prevail where nothing seemed to happen. In the decade leading up to the protests of May 1998, Suharto's practice of promoting only favored army officers and bureaucrats had bred widespread resentment within the rank and file.[8] As exciting rumors about internal trouble in the Presidential Palace spread, the disgruntled middle management contemplated insubordination, subversion, and revolt. The year 1998 was full of events and incidents. Time was clearly not proceeding in an ordinary, orderly, fashion.

Triggering a specific event, the resignation of Suharto, became the central focus of grassroots political mobilization in late-twentieth-century Indonesia.

The homogeneous, empty time of the Suharto regime was quickly giving way to a new era when the Indonesian people began to focus their collective energy on particular figures and anticipate coming horizons of transformation. The collective excitement of the Indonesian people, an expectation of sweeping changes that could come at any moment, was driven by a messianic spirit.[9] Messiahs, like many other figures, embody hope in their flesh and blood. Seeing "every second of time [as] the strait gate through which the Messiah might march" produces a revolutionary consciousness, in the words of Walter Benjamin, the celebrated German philosopher from the Frankfurt School.[10] Benjamin sought to establish a new concept of the present with his ideas about messianic time. He referred to the "time of the now" where every moment contains the open-ended possibility of sudden transformation.[11]

In 1998 collective Indonesian desires for sudden transformations were not pinned on a specific messiah. Instead of anticipating a messiah marching through the gate, this movement imagined the moment when Suharto would be forced to march out through the gates of the Presidential Palace, never again to return. Suharto became a figure who embodied all the ills facing the nation—a doppelganger of the messiah, representing evil rather than hope. As the people of Indonesia collectively anticipated Suharto's departure, a prefigured horizon of change, they dreamed about sweeping transformations that would come to every sector of society.

Messianic desires can operate beyond the confines of any particular figure. Jacques Derrida has described a universal structure of feeling that works independent of any specific historical moment or cultural location: "The universal, quasi-transcendental structure that I call *messianicity without messianism* is not bound up with any particular moment of (political or general) history or culture."[12] Derrida's sense of expectation is thus not oriented toward a specific program, event, project, or messiah.[13] His messianicity is "without content," in contrast to messianism, which contains specific objects of desire. The promise of messianicity, for Derrida, opened up a new way of thinking about historicity—not a new history or still less a "new historicism" but a hopeful sort of awareness about what might be possible. In short, Derrida was fishing for language to represent the background of possibility that exists at any given historical moment.[14]

Rather than embracing Derrida's messianicity without messianism, the people of Indonesia pinned their freedom dreams on specific figures, events, and political projects.[15] Diverse social worlds united around the cry of *Reform!* Human rights activists, members of Islamic organizations, environmental campaigners, and even some of Suharto's longtime political supporters found common cause across ideological boundaries. Former enemies became temporary allies. Aspirations for freedom from arbitrary military violence, poverty, and exploitation by transnational capitalism fused to form a reinvigorated postcolonial nationalism. The reform movement embodied messianism rather than Derrida's contentless messianicity. Activists hoped for a specific prefigured event, Suharto's resignation, against a wider background of historical possibility.[16]

News spread in grassroots networks that the wave of demonstrations was expanding, reportedly reaching cities in remote provinces like Jayapura in West Papua and Kupang in Timor.[17] Many Indonesians thought that the resignation of Suharto would resolve the problems of places that had borne the brunt of decades of military abuse. West Papuans came to have a silent and symbolic existence in the movement for national reform, present in the Indonesian collective imagination.[18] But the visions of Indonesian leaders ultimately failed to inspire many West Papuans. "We didn't care who was president, we weren't interested in reform," said Octovianus Mote, a journalist from the Mee tribe, in a telephone interview. "We did not feel like we were part of Indonesia's imagined community," he continued, code-switching from the West Papuan dialect of Indonesian into the English language of social theory. "There was a small demonstration against Suharto in Jayapura, but not many people came."[19]

Around the world, activists associated with the growing alterglobalization and antiglobalization (*autre-mondialisation*) movement began to stage protests in solidarity with the Indonesian students. Unexpected allies also emerged from the seats of global power. Then Speaker of the U.S. House of Representatives, Newt Gingrich, a Republican Christian with messianic visions of his own, suddenly came to endorse the goal of ousting Suharto.[20] The long arm of U.S. foreign policy began fanning the flames of economic and social crises in Indonesia with the explicit intent of producing regime change. An International Monetary Fund (IMF) bailout plan lifted government subsidies on rice and fuel. This triggered further price hikes and widespread protests.[21]

On the heels of the IMF bailout, *Time* magazine depicted anarchic, anticapitalist chaos: "Shopping malls were looted and torched, car dealerships were destroyed, the new toll road from the airport was commandeered by lawless mobs who threatened to set fire to cars that did not hand over cash on demand."[22] The Indonesian army hired thugs to spread violence.[23] Chinese shop owners, long resented for their perceived domination of the economy, began to install fortifications against looters that came to be ironically called "gates of reform" (*pintu reformasi*).[24] Countless people of Chinese descent were robbed, beaten, or raped. Some 1,188 people, many of them looters trapped in burning shopping malls, lost their lives. The U.S. Embassy in Jakarta began airlifting expatriates out of Indonesia, and all nonessential government representatives were ordered to leave the country. Indonesian government employees, even members of armed forces, began to support the reform movement. Riding the waves of popular outcry, powerful segments of Indonesia's elite began to imagine the dawn of a new era of personal freedom out from under Suharto's towering shadow.[25]

When military troops shot four student protesters dead at Trisakti University, the people of Indonesia were shocked. Outraged students, reinvigorated with moral authority, flooded the streets.[26] Students began occupying Indonesia's parliament on May 18, 1998, and showed no signs of leaving until the long-awaited event came to pass. The country held its breath, waiting. In this moment, nobody knew what to expect. Would the Indonesian military crack down and bring the reform movement to a definitive, bloody, end? Or would the prefigured event take place? Would Suharto be forced to walk through the gates of the Presidential Palace, never again to return?

Secular messianic hopes, expansive desires attached to a single imagined event, were the driving force behind these revolutionary student actions. Amid the fray, nobody knew if the student activists would be routed or if they would emerge triumphant. Defeat is an integral part of messianic moments, according to Fredric Jameson, a literary critic. "The very idea of the messianic brings the whole feeling of dashed hopes and impossibility along with it," writes Jameson. "You would not evoke the messianic in a genuinely revolutionary period, a period in which changes can be sensed at work all around you."[27] During the student occupation of parliament, nobody knew if the protesters were dreaming about the impossible or totally reconfiguring the field of historical possibility. Departing from Jameson, I suggest that the messianic is indeed involved in revolutionary moments, whether or not the revolution is successful. Uniting behind secular messianic hopes, the people of Indonesia collectively imagined a seemingly impossible future event.[28]

Suharto stepped down quietly on May 21, 1998, and euphoria swept Indonesia. In this moment, the power of imagination touched the field of historical possibility.[29] But in the months after Suharto's fall, it gradually became clear to the Indonesian people that human-rights abuses, corruption, nepotism, poor labor conditions, and a host of other injustices would continue unabated. The reform movement began to fragment. After their common enemy was gone, the temporary coalition of groups with conflicting viewpoints collapsed. As Suharto's longtime cronies struggled to redefine themselves in a new political landscape, segments of Indonesia's elite who had helped fan the flames of popular protest began to rearticulate unpopular policies from the Suharto era.[30] As leaders representing multiple social worlds jockeyed for power, the common goal of reform was lost.

Perhaps these failures would come as no surprise to Derrida, who cultivated an idea of messianicity that is literally empty, oriented away from specific events, political projects, or messiahs.[31] If messianicity is a sentiment of expectant hope, without an object, then, he reasons, it cannot be taken apart, and it cannot fail.[32] Despite these failures, perhaps Derrida would share my commitment to thinking critically about what one might do in postrevolutionary moments, after an event like the fall of Suharto. Does one give up on the messianic after a particular moment fails to actualize every element of expansive dreams? Or does one appreciate what has changed and maintain an openness to the possibility of future changes?[33]

When Indonesia's prefigured messianic event took place in May 1998, when Suharto left the Presidential Palace, the moment was a concrete victory for the people, even if collective hopes quickly gave way to disappointment.[34] The power vacuum that emerged opened up opportunities for multiple political projects that had lain dormant during decades of homogeneous, empty time. While Java was floating loose in the cosmos, indigenous activists at the periphery of the nation began to pin their hopes on other figures and seemingly impossible desires. Building on the momentum of the reform movement, the people in these far-flung provinces began to take this political energy in new directions. Rallying behind merdeka—dreams of freedom that contained heterogeneous desires and multiple figures—people in East Timor, Aceh, and West Papua imagined futures outside Indonesia's national fold. Reimagining distinct social worlds, emergent formations that were at odds with dominant elements of the reform movement, indigenous activists took the messianic spirit in surprising directions.

CHAPTER ONE

The Messianic Multiple

Collecting nectar from the flowers at the top of coconut trees was one of the Itchy Old Man's favorite pastimes. This old timer, who had flaky skin and oozing sores all over his body, liked to make the nectar into palm wine. Shunned by villagers, he lived poor and alone in a shack on the edge of an isolated beach.[1] The Itchy Old Man is the unlikely messiah of parables from Biak, the island off of West Papua's north coast where I met indigenous tricksters in an airport transit lounge when I was a high school exchange student. Under the repulsive skin of this mythical hero are secrets of wealth and power, according to Danilyn Rutherford, who has described how this strange figure was trapped in a cycle of excessive scratching, an unbearable conjoining of pleasure and pain. Rutherford's book, *Raiding the Land of the Foreigners*, chronicles how the Itchy Old Man miraculously shed his skin and embarked on an epic journey around the world.[2] On this mythical journey he brought material wealth and a new world religion to the faithful. Drawing on Rutherford's work, and my own sources of inspiration, I offer an account of his story to illuminate a messianic logic that produced revolutionary possibilities in West Papua.[3]

One morning the Itchy Old Man found that his palm wine containers had been drained by a thief: the bamboo tubes that he placed in a tall palm tree each night to catch flower nectar were empty. Determined to catch the thief, he spent the next night perched in the treetop. Just before dawn, The Itchy Old Man caught the Morning Star in the act of stealing wine. Struggling in the Itchy Old Man's grasp, the star bargained for freedom.

"The sun is rising, look. You have to release me so that I can go home. Come on, what do you want? Wealth?" asked the Morning Star.

"Wealth? I already have it all," replied the Old Man.

"Come on, let me go. I've got to get back. What are you asking for? Brains and beauty?"

"Brains and beauty?" he cried, sounding offended. "I already have all of that."

In rejecting these offers, the old codger indicated that something might be hiding underneath his crusty skin. The increasingly desperate Morning Star was eventually able to give the Itchy Old Man something that he desired: a woman. Offering up a magic piece of fruit, the star passed along instructions about how to use it to impregnate the lady of his choice.

The Itchy Old Man waited until Princess Insoraki, a gorgeous maiden who was the daughter of an important chief, was bathing in the sea. He threw the small magical fruit toward the princess. The fruit floated up and hit her right breast. "Yesus!" she cried. ("Yesus," in the Biak language, means "my breast!") At this moment, as she clutched her bosom, Princess Insoraki miraculously conceived. After Princess Insoraki returned home, her nipples turned black and began to itch. In the coming weeks, a rash spread all over her body. Her belly began to swell.

After a full term of pregnancy, the princess gave birth. Everyone—especially the princess herself—was puzzled about the identity of the infant's father. The baby boy proved to have uncanny abilities; it could walk and talk just days after birth. So the family of the princess hoped that this miraculous boy would be able to identify his father. They invited all the men on the island to a huge dancing feast. The young dandies first danced in front of the boy, but they failed to attract his attention. Middle-aged dancers were also met with indifference. Finally the elderly men hobbled out into the arena. Shuffling behind all the other men, whirling his bony limbs about in an ungainly jig, was the Itchy Old Man.

When the baby boy called out and identified the Itchy Old Man as his father, the party broke into chaos. In utter disgust, everyone deserted this island, bringing all the goods they could carry and destroying the rest. The Itchy Old Man, Princess Insoraki, and their son were left behind.

This unfamiliar story about an Immaculate Conception set the stage for the emergence of the Messiah himself. Once the commotion had died down, the baby boy grew hungry. He asked Princess Insoraki for food, but she told him to go to his father. The Itchy Old Man flaked off a piece of his scaly skin and offered it up for his son to eat. It tasted like the most delicious food imaginable. As his son ate, the Itchy Old Man heaped ironwood logs into a huge pile.

After setting the pile alight, the elderly man leapt into the raging blaze. Antique porcelain, shell armlets, food, beads, and other valuables fell out of the fire as his crusty skin burned away.

When the flames died down, a handsome youth with shining brown skin emerged from the remnants of the bonfire. The Itchy Old Man had become the Lord Himself—"Manseren Mangundi." Revealing more of his powers, Lord Manseren drew a picture of a ship on the beach. When he stamped his feet, an actual ship—a small steamboat—materialized on the water.

Lord Manseren began a trip that would change the course of world history, offering a new life of material plenty and salvation for true believers. In a word, he offered merdeka to people who gave him a proper reception.[4] First Lord Manseren visited the dispersed relatives of Princess Insoraki who had fled after the dance party. Transforming his body back into the guise of the Itchy Old Man, he tested the sincerity and faith of her kin. Promising eternal life and material wealth, he asked his mother-in-law to lay her body down on the beach to serve as a slide for his boat. The request was rejected as outlandish; Insoraki's mother knew that her body would be broken by the weight of the heavy vessel. Other Biak notables spat on the Itchy Old Man when he tried to come ashore.

Disgusted, the hero traveled west along with Princess Insoraki and their son. Lord Manseren left West Papua and began an epic voyage. His son, who had been named at the miraculous moment of conception ("Jesus! My breast!"), disembarked from the steamship in Palestine and began sowing the seeds of a new world religion.

When Lord Manseren arrived in Europe, he catalyzed the Industrial Revolution. In a small Dutch village, he found people living just like West Papuans—they were fishing, hunting, and growing sweet potatoes. Receiving a warm welcome, the traveler from a far-off land bestowed factory-made shirts and trousers on the Dutch villagers. Lord Manseren also divulged the secret knowledge necessary to reproduce the material wealth of industrialization.

Standing dominant history on its head and revoicing biblical scripture, this fable combines cosmological ideas from West Papuan worlds and global culture.[5] The promises of the Itchy Old Man, about eternal life and material wealth, are like the promises wrapped up in the magic of modernity—about economic development and health. This parable illustrates how the faithful obtained merdeka. This tale "does not simply figure the fictive origin of social differences," writes Rutherford, "but also promises transformations" that are still to come.[6] Rutherford's work about the long-standing engagements of the Biak people with the outside world uses the Itchy Old Man myth to explore the limits of the nation on this seemingly remote Indonesian island, looking inward and backward in time. Departing from the course Rutherford has already charted in *Raiding the Land of the Foreigners* (2003), I use this same story to frame the historical trajectory of the West Papuan nationalist movement over a decade, looking outward and forward.

The Itchy Old Man embodies a revolutionary form of consciousness, a sense of expectation that keeps the identity of the Messiah up for grabs. Those who follow the logic of this allegory are cautiously searching for a savior who might suddenly appear at any moment in an unexpected guise.[7] While waiting for an appearance of Manseren Mangundi, the Lord Himself, no one knows exactly what to expect. Another old man with scabies? A visiting foreign dignitary? Perhaps a phantom steamship on the horizon? If the ancestors of the Biak people lost the chance to learn the secrets of merdeka when they rejected the Itchy Old Man, perhaps there is a way to give this figure a proper welcome in contemporary times.

The Itchy Old Man does not live "in a fictive site beyond the horizon," writes Rutherford, but instead animates an "in-between" space where imagination bridges the gap between old and new worlds.[8] This shapeshifting figure inhabits an elusive place where expansive fantasies touch the field of historical possibility. If Derrida calls on us to wait for mysterious possibilities that are utterly unfigurable, that are beyond our imaginative horizons, the revolutionary logic of the Itchy Old Man offers a model for *pre*figuring coming changes while maintaining a radical openness to *re*figuring hopes when a desired object fails to materialize.[9]

This tale informs my idea of the messianic multiple—a sense of expectation that is oriented to future horizons populated by many different saviors and imagined events. Rather than fixing on the arrival of any single messiah, this logic is like liquid mercury: it dances about, moving in different directions, coalescing around multiple figures of hope.[10] Operating in the imagination of a single person, the messianic multiple animates a cautious form of hope, flitting from object to object, probing the field of historical possibility. When it catches hold of a crowd, a multitude of creative agents, the impossible comes within reach.[11] Anything can happen at any time when this sort of collective imagination meets up with collaborative action.

The spirit of the messianic multiple was on the loose in 1998. After one particular prefigured event in Indonesia, the resignation of Suharto, dreams were refigured around multiple objects emerging on imagined horizons. Stumbling onto the scene amid powerful countervailing forces, I found that West Papuan activists were bringing a seemingly impossible collective dream, plans for establishing an independent nation, into contact with the field of historical possibility. In startling encounters with indigenous activists, I learned about improbable conspiracies among world leaders. Wrangling with intractable bureaucracies and meeting people who refracted global history through a strange lens, I found that messianic dreams were capturing my imagination.

The United Nations, He Has Sins

Poring over regional journals, I became determined to conduct research in West Papua for my senior thesis as an undergraduate major in anthropology and biology at New College of Florida. I found an article written in 1958 by Dr. J. V. de Bruijn, reviewing the ethnographic literature and reporting that West Papua is "an earthly paradise for anthropological research" with "numerous opportunities for anthropological studies of cultures barely influenced or even untouched by Western culture."[12] When I read this article some forty years later, in the mid-1990s, few new studies had been conducted. Compared to Papua New Guinea—the site of classic anthropological studies like Malinowski's *Coral Gardens and Their Magic*, Margaret Mead's *Growing Up in New Guinea*, and a multitude of more recent works—West Papua remained terra incognita. Hoping to fill some of the gaps in the anthropological literature, I crafted grant proposals to investigate how the El Niño drought of 1997 impacted indigenous groups in West Papua's highlands.[13]

In early 1997, I applied to study abroad at Bird of Paradise University (Universitas Cenderawasih), the largest state institution in West Papua, through the Indonesian embassy in Washington. Months passed with no word from Jakarta, Indonesia's capital. I clung to increasingly unrealistic hopes for a visa. Having completed all my paperwork, without anything left to do, I waited for a decision from an inscrutable center of power. While I harbored improbable dreams for a personal miracle in the realms of Indonesian bureaucracy, signs of major changes in the world order captivated my imagination.

Admittedly, I was fascinated by, deeply fearful of, and inextricably implicated in, the messianic promises of the third millennium, the fabled era that began to unfold as my fieldwork was taking place.[14] Like many people my age in the United States—members of what some commentators have dubbed the "millennial generation"—I felt a growing sense of anticipation as the Y2K approached on the horizon.[15] I had lost faith in the predictable march of progress and the bureaucratic institutions governing the modern world. Personally I was never a believer in organized religion. Still, I found secular elements of the messianic idea beginning to move within me.

At the moment when I was about to give up hope of ever visiting West Papua, surprising developments in Jakarta were all over the news. Suharto had just resigned. Paying another visit to the Indonesian embassy, I found a consular officer who was willing to help. Perhaps inspired by the infectious spirit of the reform movement, or finding my special permission from Jakarta locked away in a dusty embassy filing cabinet, this official approved my visa on June 4, 1998, fifteen days after Suharto's fall.

A week later I arrived in Abepura, a suburb of Jayapura, the capital city of West Papua. I rented a small room in a maze of cinderblock walls, tin roofs, and gravel alleyways. Nine West Papuan and Indonesian students became my flat mates in a ramshackle boardinghouse that had been cobbled together out of plywood and tin roofing. Our shared cooking facilities consisted of a counter, a garden hose, and a portable kerosene stove.

There was a marked lack of enthusiasm for talking about the 1997 El Niño drought. The rains had come months before. As I tried to go about a narrowly defined program of anthropological research, as I attempted to study the drought, West Papuans began to make and commemorate history in the streets. Enrolling in anthropology classes at the university, trying to steer clear of political activity, my own life quickly fell into a mundane routine. I became a regular patron at the university library, where I read through a treasure trove of theses written by West Papuan students and a haphazard collection of books in Indonesian and English.

Agus, a short, older man with a deeply creased face who wore a soul patch—a small beard on the lower lip that was once equally popular in rural parts of West Papua and metropolitan centers of style in the global North—waylaid me near the library one afternoon. He asked me to return the next day, around the same time, with a tape recorder. When I showed up, as promised, he launched into a monologue in thickly accented Logat Papua: "On this little tape I want to record a statement. If you go to the Global World Body's place of gathering, please pass on this language," he said. We were standing outside the library, with passersby looking at us askance. "This language is named the rough language, villager language, that I am talking. You can translate it into refined English if you want, to pass it along."

Agus was the first of many West Papuan activists who tried to gain my ear. I was perhaps expecting to encounter a representative of an indigenous culture who would teach me about the opposite of what I already knew: telling me myths in contrast to history, revealing ideas about cyclical time instead of a linear model, describing immanent gods instead of a transcendent God.[16] Instead of these predictable differences, I discovered startling and disquieting tales when I tried to listen carefully to indigenous voices.[17] Seemingly familiar stories were related to me in unfamiliar ways. As Agus told me about his freedom dreams—trying to use the language of history, law, and human rights—I found myself struggling to keep up.

Agus talked about the U.S. officials who betrayed his nation, but at the time I was unable to understand. "Kennedy, and his secretaries, have sins," Agus told me. "He already saw, but he pretended not to know. He already saw, but he plays dumb. It doesn't matter, just kill them." I tried hard to follow his wandering narrative, without dates, where the identities of different historical actors and institutions bled together. Agus knew that his people had been betrayed by global power brokers. But he was only able to partially translate his knowledge into a recognizable historical narrative. "My message is that the United Nations, he has sins," Agus said. "Above the UN is God, below him are governments. Is that the Global World Body? Is that the UN? Does the UN rule the kingdom of heaven? No, he is just a regular human."

I left this encounter feeling uneasy and confused. Already socialized into the political culture of Indonesia, I knew that Agus was telling me about things that the government deemed sensitive. We would both get in serious trouble, even in the new era of reform, if the authorities caught us talking politics. Was there truth to this story about the Kennedy family and the United Nations? Or was Agus just rambling, perhaps delusional? Only years later, after long hours spent reading archival documents and piecing together different events in other interviews, did I begin to appreciate the complexity of the historical events that Agus was trying to tell me about that afternoon outside the library.

In 1962, after a protracted military conflict between the Dutch and the Indonesians over the future of West Papua, the Kennedy administration intervened. One cynical U.S. official, Robert Komer, a balding and bespectacled former CIA analyst who was a key architect of Kennedy's policy on Southeast Asia, argued in an internal memo: "A pro-Bloc (if not Communist) Indonesia is [an] infinitely greater threat . . . than Indo possession of a few thousand square miles of cannibal land."[18] The words of Agus echoed in my head when I later came across these historical sources. "Kennedy may be dead, and his secretaries may be on pensions, but their sins must not be covered up. It must be transparent, it must be open, to save those of us who remain, the dregs of a race that is being killed."

West Papuans, who have long been viewed as peoples without history, are well aware of the historical agreements, events, and actors that enabled Indonesia to take over their land. Translating West Papuan historical consciousness into no-nonsense historical narrative is no easy task. Robert F. Kennedy, the president's brother and then attorney general, traveled to Indonesia and Holland in February 1962 to begin talks about this disputed territory. U.S. officials helped broker the New York Agreement, a cease-fire between the Dutch and the Republic of Indonesia that was signed on August 15, 1962. This accord effectively transferred West Papua from Dutch to Indonesian control via a temporary UN protectorate. The treaty guaranteed West Papuans the right to participate in an "act of self-determination" that would give them the opportunity to decide "(a) whether they wish to remain with Indonesia; or (b) whether they wish to sever their ties with Indonesia."[19] A referendum that clearly presented this choice never took place.[20] In 1969 Indonesia staged the so-called Act of Free Choice where 1,022 handpicked Papuan delegates, representing a population of around one million, unanimously declared their desire to join Indonesia.

"In the opinion of the Western observers and the Papuans who have spoken out about this, the Act of Free Choice ended up as a sham," concludes Pieter Drooglever, who wrote an 854-page historical monograph on the subject. After extensive research in Dutch government archives, as well as a careful study of UN, U.S., and Australian records, Drooglever wrote: "A press-ganged electorate acting under a great deal of pressure appeared to have unanimously declared itself in favor of Indonesia."[21] Cold War politics and the interests of "big power," concludes the historian John Saltford, meant that independence for West Papua was never considered to be a serious option once the New York Agreement of 1962 was signed.[22]

The promise of an act of self-determination contained in the New York

Agreement took on heightened significance amid broader political crises that were sweeping Indonesia in 1998. In June of that year, at the moment when Agus spoke to me outside the library, people throughout West Papua saw new horizons of possibility opening up. Unbeknownst to me at the time, a letter from U.S. congressional representatives was circulating in West Papua, spreading like wildfire as activists made hundreds of photocopies and handed them out to trusted kin and friends. The letter was addressed to Indonesia's new president, B. J. Habibie, and called for dialogue on the political status of East Timor and West Papua. The leading signatories were representative Christopher Smith, a Republican from New Jersey, and representative Patrick Kennedy, the son of senator Ted Kennedy and a Democrat from Rhode Island. With the Kennedy family name on this letter, many West Papuans believed that global power brokers were ready to right historical wrongs.[23]

Amid an audible political buzz on the streets, I struggled to find certainty about my immigration status. The stamp in my passport from the Indonesian embassy in Washington was only good for two months, and I needed to extend it another six months to complete my course work at the university. Again, I found myself waiting for minor bureaucratic miracles. On July 1, 1998, I began the day by waiting in line at the immigration office. Years later, when I started researching the merdeka movement in earnest, I learned that this day was the twenty-seventh anniversary of the transmission of an independence manifesto over a single-sideband (SSB) radio. My journal entries over the next few days chronicled my struggle to navigate Indonesian officialdom and my initial attempts to understand the political developments taking place all around me:

Wednesday, July 1, 1998
Early this morning I went to the Immigration Office in downtown Jayapura. After I quietly waited for over two hours, the officials told me that I needed an additional letter of support from Bird of Paradise University before they could process my visa extension. I passed by a small demonstration outside the Regional People's Provincial Assembly (DPRD) after I left Immigration. Beyond a core group—a tight knot of people who were passionately chanting and dancing—people were casual and friendly. An hour later the group of protesters had swelled to about 100 people. Police in riot gear surrounded the protesters, while several thousand quiet onlookers stood by. Later in the day I heard that the Morning Star flag, the banner of West Papua's independence movement,

had been waved at this event. In the afternoon I traveled an hour and a half by a series of public buses to meet with a high-level university official. I asked for a letter required by the Immigration Office. He promised to produce it by tomorrow morning.[24]

Thursday, July 2, 1998

This morning there was a massive show of force by the police and army in downtown Jayapura. Hundreds of troops lined the streets. As I walked to the post office to check my e-mail at the cybercafé, the streets were strangely silent. No demonstrators were in sight. From there I went directly to campus, picked up the letter, and then delivered it to Immigration. After I waited for several hours, the immigration officials changed what they told me the day before. They asked me to return in late August, so that I could extend my visa just as the new semester is about to begin at the university.

Friday, July 3, 1998

Today I introduced myself to the head of the anthropology department at the university. I presented him with all my documents, and then we walked together to the other side of campus. Along the road we bumped into Michael Howard, a visiting professor from Simon Fraser University. A small group of protesters gathered nearby, in front of the main university buildings at the side of the road. A truck full of Indonesian troops, Mobile Brigade (Brimob) police in riot gear, drove by on the road. I could see many of the troops turn their heads in apparent surprise to look at the demonstration. But the truck did not stop. Professor Howard left, and then some other staff from the anthropology department joined our conversation. One of the staff members had just returned from a Discovery Channel filming expedition to the remote Mamberamo River. He laughed with us about the field methods of the British film crew and the American anthropologist who accompanied them. When a question was asked during filmed interviews, the people would ask for money before answering.

Our conversation was suddenly interrupted by people running from the direction of the demo. Immediately everyone around me began to run. Most kept an amused air. I managed to get into a nearby canteen, along with most of the people who had been talking with me. The proprietor quickly locked the door and pulled the curtains over the windows.

We continued our conversation as people flashed by the windows. Several minutes later intense bursts of popping explosions began. Firecrackers? Soon we all realized that this was gunfire. It must be rubber bullets and blanks, we agreed. The shooting continued in drawn-out clouds for several minutes. Then a pause. Suddenly the explosions began again—this time much closer. We all scrambled to find limited protection under tables and against the wall. After several minutes of silence we all returned to our seats and sheepishly ordered sugary lime drinks. We chatted nervously. When we could see other students and professors calmly walking outside, we left the canteen by the back door. After slipping out a back gate of the campus, which was being guarded by students, we heard the first news of students being shot. One law student was shot in the head—the bullet entered near his eye and exited out the back of his head along with most of his brains. A young middle-school girl, an uninvolved bystander, had also just been shot in the leg.[25]

One of the anthropology lecturers who had been in the canteen with me was so scared that he could hardly talk. He was Indonesian, a recent arrival from Java. He feared retribution from the West Papuan students. "Does reform always have to be like this?" he asked.

Walking along one of the side streets near campus, we ran into some professors from the English language department. "Why did the shooting start?" we asked. There were rumors that the students had been throwing stones. Someone else said that the students had roughed up an Indonesian intelligence agent who was spying on the demonstration. "We are seeing the beginning of a revolution," they joked.

Over the course of a few days, I made abrupt transitions from the dead halls of Indonesian bureaucracy into lively spaces where the pulse of revolutionary momentum was accelerating. For a brief moment, when I ran with my newfound friends from the anthropology department into the canteen ahead of the Indonesian police, we were swept up in the crowd "all happy and excited over this bit of fun."[26] Then, in the space of a few minutes, we collectively experienced a rapid succession of affective responses from nervous anxiety to raw fear to humor. With this sudden rush of emotions, we did not know what to expect. It seemed like anything could happen at any time.

Wild rumors started to circulate about my presence on the margins of the demonstration at Bird of Paradise University. The students were telling each other that Amnesty International had sent me to campus on a fact-finding mission. When some of my new West Papuan friends intimated that they knew about my human rights work, I protested; I tried to convince them that I really was just an exchange student in the anthropology program. Some seemed to believe me. Others, with a wink and a nod, promised not to blow my cover. "Be careful," one West Papuan student cautioned as we relaxed together on the front porch of my boardinghouse on the night after the demonstration. "Indonesian spies are starting to follow you."

Shaken by the violence at Bird of Paradise University and worried about getting in trouble with the cops, I spontaneously decided to leave Jayapura the following day. I had befriended a Belgian entomologist who promised to introduce me to a Mee community, a group of hunter-gatherers living in the Siriwo River Valley. Hoping to leave the trouble behind in Jayapura, I set out to conduct what I then saw as real anthropological research in the hinterlands.

Skirting a police blockade in downtown Jayapura the next afternoon— Saturday, July 4, 1998—I jostled along with other sweaty bodies toward the harbor. Along with several thousand West Papuan and Indonesian passengers, I boarded an ocean liner, a passenger ferry in the Indonesian government Pelni fleet that plies fixed routes with predictable regularity. Undoubtedly many of my fellow travelers were, like me, fleeing recent unrest. The ship was destined for Biak, the original home of the Itchy Old Man. In Biak I planned to get on another boat, a ferry to Nabire, a coastal city with logging roads leading to Mee lands in the Siriwo River Valley. Instead of a predictable journey, however, the passenger ship delivered me straight into another protest.

Sunday, July 5, 1998, 7:00 a.m.
Our ship has just docked in the Biak harbor, and outside a crowd is chanting, "*Papua merdeka!*" The Morning Star flag is flying on a nearby water tower. As soon as the ship docked, several young men boarded and ran around the ship waving banners and shouting. Other passengers are saying that these men are now asking for money. My newfound friend and traveling companion, the Belgian entomologist, appears to be the only other foreigner on the passenger ship. The harbor is devoid of any Indonesian government authorities. These youths have reportedly been occupying the harbor for the last several days. My connecting ferry to Nabire is nowhere in sight.

Unbeknownst to me at the time, the people of Biak had endowed this passenger ferry with special significance. Rumors spread ahead of the ship that powerful foreigners were aboard.[27] In the words of Rutherford, who has already published a nuanced analysis of the dynamics that unfolded in the Biak harbor, "evidence of foreign attention brought to mind not only the gaze of outsiders, but also their impending presence." Several weeks later,

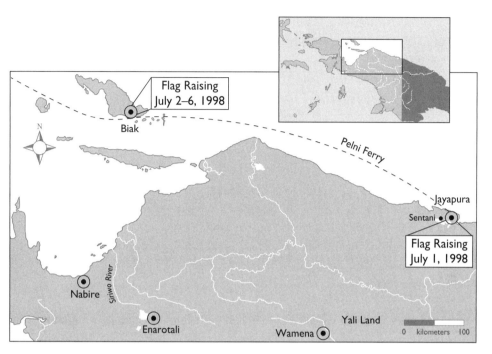

West Papua's north coast. *Map by Damond Kyllo.*

Rutherford arrived in Biak to interview her trusted long-term friends about recent events. One of her friends talked about going to meet the ship that I happened to be on. As he was leaving home, his neighbor asked him with great excitement, "Has the foreigners' ship arrived?"[28]

Years later I interviewed an elder Biak cultural leader who helped me understand the excitement that had been building in the crowd: "There was something that was awaited with much anticipation by the West Papuans. In three days the UN was to arrive. This anticipation gathered the masses, pulled in the masses from the villages."[29] On July 4, 1998, the day before the ship's scheduled arrival, when the Morning Star flag was already aloft in the Biak harbor, it was announced that Jamsheed Marker, special envoy of UN secretary general Kofi Annan, would be passing through Jakarta. Marker had been sent by Annan after pressure from Portugal, the former colonial power in East Timor. At the same time as the flag raising in Biak, there were four days of clashes between pro- and anti-Indonesian groups in East Timor that left at least two people dead. The mandate of this UN envoy was limited to reviving the stalled dialogue between Indonesia and Portugal about East Timor's future.[30] Members of the crowd in the Biak harbor were nonetheless waiting to see if a UN envoy was on board the passenger ferry as it docked. More rumors began to circulate. CNN journalists were reportedly on board.

The tale of the Itchy Old Man did not feature publicly in speeches that rallied the crowd as they greeted the passenger ferry arriving in Biak's harbor on July 5, 1998. Still, Rutherford suggests that members of this crowd were reading into the speeches, finding evidence that an imagined state of pleasure and perfection was about to arrive.[31] The figural steamboat driven by the Lord Himself, who traveled the high seas spreading the seeds of world religions and the magic of modernity, helps explain the collective excitement about the arrival of the literal boat that I happened to be on. As passengers tried to disembark, people thronged aboard, caught up in the excitement of the moment. Members of the waiting crowd were carefully scrutinizing the passengers, searching for messianic figures who might be traveling in disguise.

Months earlier a small prayer group had formed in Biak. The prayer group was named after two biblical figures, the prophet Deborah and the warrior Barak, who together led an army of ten thousand.[32] Members of this prayer group began to think of themselves as biblical Israelites. Instead of living in Egypt under oppression of the Pharaoh, they were living in Indonesia, the largest Islamic nation in the world. Hoping to follow in the footsteps of mid-twentieth-century Israelites, the members of the Deborah and Barak prayer group quietly began laying the spiritual groundwork for creating their own nation. The prophesied coming of a particular messiah, the Second Coming of Christ, was inspiring messianic visions as the year 2000 approached on the horizon. In Christian communities around the world, including parishes in Biak, possibility of the imminent return of Jesus to earth became very real.[33]

Shortly after the fall of Suharto, exhilarating news began arriving in Biak. Members of the Deborah and Barak prayer group heard about the demonstration outside the provincial assembly—the peaceful protest I had glimpsed after one of my visits to the immigration department. They heard that the Morning Star flag had been raised in Jayapura. Rumors began to spread that a powerful outsider was about to arrive in Biak.

On the evening of July 1, 1998, the same day as the Jayapura protest, Tanjung Karma, a member of a prominent Biak family, conferred with the leaders of the Deborah and Barak prayer group. They decided to mobilize immediately for a flag raising. There was a person from the outside, said Tanjung, who would speak to the Biak crowd during the event. Filep Karma, Tanjung's brother, who happened to be passing through Biak, was this "person from the outside." Filep was a civil servant in the governor's office in Jayapura, who had become savvy about foreign worlds during earlier studies in the Philippines. In the Biak tongue, Filep Karma was regarded as an *amber beba*, "a big foreigner."[34]

Separately, Filep Karma had already been caught by the revolutionary spirit. Reading the letter from U.S. congressmen Patrick Kennedy and Christopher Smith that was circulating through underground activist networks had spurred him to action. Years later, Karma, a civil servant in the provincial administration of the Indonesian government, told me: "When I read that letter from the members of the U.S. Congress, it lit my passion for the struggle on fire." Karma became determined to lead local Biak groups in raising the Morning Star flag. "It happened spontaneously," Karma recalled. "We didn't have a planning meeting. I didn't really know the people in Biak, and they didn't really know me."

After getting inspired to do something, Filep Karma was at loose ends. He did not have a Morning Star flag. "I had seen the flag before, but I didn't remember what it looked like. We looked all over Biak but couldn't find one." Teaming up with an elderly Biak matron who has since passed away, Karma set out to make a flag. "Sewing would have taken too long; the police would have caught us by the time we were done. So we bought some white cloth along with blue and red spray paint."

Before dawn the next day, July 2, the freshly painted Morning Star flag was raised atop the water tower in Biak's harbor. With the flag overhead, Filep Karma gave a public speech that linked Christian rhetoric to desires for merdeka: "The struggle in West Papua, and my own struggle, is based on the primary law of the Bible. This law was lovingly given to us by the Lord, your God."[35] Karma urged the people gathered—at that point just several dozen, members of the Deborah and Barak prayer group and a few others—to use peaceful tactics of resistance.

Revolutions are unexpected for everyone, even their organizers.[36] At first just a few people gathered in the streets of Biak. The flag began to draw larger and larger crowds. By noon more than a thousand people had joined them. Filep Karma urged the crowd to "defend the flag only using the Bible and hymns as weapons." He told the assembled masses: "Indonesian law states that security personnel or police can let bullets fly if their life is at

A truck that was destroyed by protesters on July 2, 1998.
Photograph by Eben Kirksey.

risk. If we are only armed with the Bible and hymns, then the police will not shoot us."[37] At 2:30 that afternoon, a joint police and military operation attempted to disperse the crowd at the base of the water tower. They launched canisters of tear gas into the crowd with no apparent effect. When a low-ranking police officer, a second-class sergeant, beat an elderly demonstrator named Thonci Wabiser, the crowd spontaneously retaliated, demolishing a truck belonging to Indonesian security forces. During this confrontation, thirteen members of the security forces sustained injuries. Two of these men, reportedly in critical condition, were evacuated to Java for medical treatment. The security forces eventually retreated and, for the time being, left the demonstrators at the base of the water tower in peace.[38]

Looking to the future rather than to violent ends, Derrida draws a helpful distinction between the apocalyptic and the messianic.[39] Departing from the work of Marx, who perhaps imprudently writes about the end of history (in the name of the beginning of a different one), Derrida describes a "desert-like messianism." His *messianicity without messianism* is like an "abyssal and chaotic desert, if chaos describes first of all the immensity, excessiveness, disproportion in the gaping hole of the open mouth."[40] Perhaps a few West Papuans were quietly holding on to the spirit of contentless messianicity, waiting for the unexpected to appear out of an empty abyss, while they were gathered under the water tower. But the public speeches and accounts from survivors suggest otherwise—that the crowd harbored visions of merdeka that teemed with heterogeneous content.

There was not a clear consensus about a single object of desire as the crowd rallied under the flag. In other words, the people who took part in this event were not fixated on any one thing.[41] Instead the crowd anticipated many different things, a messianic multiple. The growing excitement was animated by both secular and religious hopes. Will UN special envoy Jamsheed Marker come to witness the demonstration? Perhaps Kofi Annan himself? Will CNN journalists arrive? The Itchy Old Man? Jesus? Or maybe the messianic spirit was already working in Filep Karma, prompting his bold actions. Imagination met collaborative action in this moment. As the crowd defiantly gathered under the water tower, a single future event came into view against the broader background of historical possibility. The protesters imagined the moment when West Papua would be granted independence. In a speech under the Morning Star flag, Filep Karma declared:

> We, the people of West Papua, pledge to struggle to uphold the ideal of the independence of West Papua.
>
> We, the people of West Papua, declare that the Republic of Indonesia cannot interfere in the affairs of West Papua.
>
> We, the people of West Papua, ask that our security be guaranteed by the United Nations and by no one else.[42]

With this statement, Karma was trying to welcome "distant audiences, earthly and divine."[43] But Karma's speech ultimately failed to find a proper reception among heavenly hosts or abroad. In contrast to the Indonesian student reformers—whose freedom dreams were heard by elite national politicians, international activists, and key world leaders—Filep Karma's words were heard only by his local followers and the security forces stationed nearby. Still, for the assembled crowd, his speech helped bring a seemingly impossible desire, national freedom, within reach.

Some revolutionary movements anticipate changes that will occur solely as a result of outside intervention, while others see that concrete action in the world is necessary.[44] The Biak protesters took bold steps when they took to the streets. By staging the demonstration in the harbor and raising the Morning Star flag, they amped up the momentum of the revolution. Yet after this initial action, the group lacked direction. They waited in vain for outside help. At the time, no one knew if the demonstration would end in bloody defeat or in recognition of the demands for independence articulated by Karma. Like the Indonesian students who occupied parliament, everyone held their breath to see if their collective hopes would be actualized.[45] Everyone was waiting, searching future horizons for signs of what might come next.

Sunday, July 5, 1998, 3:00 p.m.

We waited for the excitement to die down before getting off the ship. Many offices in the harbor had been ransacked and covered with graffiti proclaiming freedom for West Papua. Papers were strewn all over the lawn. No police or military troops were to be seen, and all the shops in the nearby market were boarded up. The entomologist and I stopped to chat with protesters who were guarding the gate to the harbor. They told us that a crowd had turned over a police truck and injured a number of officers a few days ago. Surprisingly no West Papuans have yet been killed in retaliation. A Hercules troop carrier flew in yesterday, they said, carrying about five hundred soldiers. The men whom I talked with at the gate were afraid that there could be a major retaliation any time. They were afraid to leave the dock area. If they leave the safe space of the harbor, the men said, the military would single them out and kill them.

The men standing watch at the gate to the harbor were visibly disappointed when they realized that they were talking to the only two foreigners who had arrived on the ship. We were disoriented from our overnight journey and sweaty from the midmorning sun. Everyone quickly surmised that we were not emissaries from the United Nations. Looks of dread began to spread over the faces of the young men. They were anticipating violent retribution by Indonesian troops at any moment.

Christian messianic hopes are often accompanied by ambivalent fears. Pessimism about the course of current history is often wedded to desires for ultimate salvation.[46] The Great Tribulation, which has perhaps already begun, will end horrifically for unbelievers and gloriously for the faithful. Some people gathered under the Morning Star flag in the Biak harbor began to wonder if their own faith was strong enough for them to endure the coming trials. The day after the arrival of the passenger ship, Indonesian security forces launched an all-out assault on protesters who were still camped out under the water tower. In the early morning hours of July 6, 1998, Indonesian soldiers and police officers surrounded the sleeping masses. They opened fire just before dawn.[47]

Monday, July 6, 1998

The entomologist was sure that an Indonesian spy watched us yesterday when we were talking with the West Papuan men guarding the gate to the harbor. He suggested that we stay at a relatively upscale hotel to reduce our chances of being interrogated. After checking in to Hotel Irian, a colonial-era building next to the airport, I ate a lunch of cream of mushroom soup and pasta with marinara sauce. The marinara sauce turned out to be ketchup with seafood.

This morning I heard what sounded like sporadic gunshots from the direction of the harbor. Later people out on the street told me that the harbor had been sealed off by a "leg fence" of Indonesian troops to ensure that none of the protesters would escape. The Morning Star flag had been taken down. Throughout the day I heard reports about how many people had been hunted down and killed. The numbers ranged from two to sixty. One man told me that he saw large groups of people running through the streets that night, fleeing the police and military forces. The people had set up warning systems to let each other know when troops were coming. They would make noise by beating on oil drums. In the early afternoon I heard the loud report of a nearby gun. I peered around my door, and all the people whom I could see were staring across the road in the direction of the airport runway. A man had apparently just been shot at point-blank range. I ate dinner, rice and fried egg, at a small canteen in the airport. All the other customers in the canteen were soldiers. They wore green camo outfits and carried huge rifles.

Four years later I returned to Biak with the intent of piecing together a clearer picture of what happened at the Biak harbor on July 6, 1998. I approached survivors of the incident through Elsham, a human rights organization that supported my research. Some of the survivors agreed to meet me alone for an interview in the home of a trusted mutual friend. Others wanted to be interviewed together. To avoid attracting undue attention by hosting a meeting in someone's home, I organized a picnic at a remote beach. We quietly chatted in Logat Papua, the creole dialect of Indonesian, with my tape recorder running, while we roasted fresh fish over an open fire.

"Every morning my friends and I took food to the protesters," recounted one of these survivors, a woman from a church near the harbor. She told me about the first moments of the attack: "While we were carrying the food that morning, we saw several army trucks approaching. They told us to wait, but when we saw that they were military, we were afraid and began running with the food and water. They began chasing us with their guns blazing. We screamed, 'The enemy is here!'"[48]

As the attack started, Filep Karma roused his followers, all unarmed civilians, with a hymn. They held hands, sitting in a circle, under the water tower where the flag still flew. They were mowed down as they continued to sing. Another survivor told me: "There were Brimob police in riot gear, army troops (Kopasgad), a company of soldiers from the local Kodim barracks, as well as navy personnel. They formed a letter U around us and then shot at us repeatedly."[49] Another eyewitness reported that the Brimob troops who fired the first shots were ethnic West Papuans. He recognized them as local troops stationed in Biak.[50] During the initial assault, Filep Karma was shot twice—once in each leg—but he survived the incident. Many of his followers were not so fortunate and were killed instantly. Twenty-nine people were killed in this initial assault, according to Karma and a second-hand report from a low-ranking soldier.[51]

Some of Karma's followers, who took his words literally about using the Bible and hymns as weapons, believed that they were miraculously protected. One participant in the flag raising told human rights investigators that he escaped the violence by clutching his Bible and pointing it at his attackers. He told the Indonesian soldiers: "If you all know religion and are the children of God, then continue to shoot." A soldier leveled his gun at this man's chest as he spoke. The soldier fired. By the account of this believer, the bullet miraculously left the gun barrel, swerved under the man's armpit and embedded itself in the concrete at the base of the water tower where the Morning Star flag was still flying.[52] This account of a miracle amid a massacre might also be read as an example of collaboration across enemy lines. Perhaps this soldier was a God-fearing man, who deliberately missed his target after being hailed by the man's biblical language.

Scores of people were loaded onto navy ships that had docked at the harbor. I took pictures of these ships from the hotel where I was staying. One group investigating the incident concluded that "one hundred thirty nine people were loaded on two frigates that headed in two directions to the east and to the west and these people were dropped into the sea."[53] A woman who narrowly escaped this ordeal told me: "I was taken by the troops to a navy ship. The number on the side of the ship was 534 AL. Several of my friends had already been taken aboard. They beat us. Some were already dead. There were women raped right next to me. One soldier, he was from Toraja, saved me. The ship was still close to shore, and he told me to jump. I jumped off the back of the ship, and I swam back to the place where it had been tied up. There I found a hiding place and I waited, from 8:00 in the

This Indonesian navy ship reportedly took scores of Papuan civilians into the middle of the ocean and dumped them overboard to drown. *Photograph by Eben Kirksey.*

morning till 8:20 that night.[54] Fleeting collaborations, alliances among enemies, created moments of hope in the face of disaster.

At least thirty-two decaying bodies later washed ashore on Biak.[55] Indonesian government officials explained that these corpses were transnational travelers: they belonged to victims of a tidal wave that hit the coast over six hundred kilometers away in the neighboring country of Papua New Guinea on July 17, 1998.[56] However, the official explanation does not match the facts. Four bodies washed up on the beaches of Biak on July 10.[57] This was four days after the police opened fire on the demonstrators and one week before the tidal wave struck. Some cadavers were missing their heads, hands, or genitals. One man's body still had a Morning Star flag painted on its chest (red, white, and blue in contrast to the black, red, and yellow flag of Papua New Guinea), and a corpse of a child was found still embracing its mother's body.[58]

The bodies of people who were shot under the water tower were heaped into a small cargo truck. Some of these people were not yet dead. Several eyewitnesses reported that the truck was filled with corpses. It left the harbor and then returned for another load. "I counted fifteen people in the first load," one eyewitness told me. "The truck came a second time, and I counted seventeen people inside. When they opened up the truck bed, I could see lots of blood. In that small truck there was lots of blood."[59] Human rights investigators could not determine what happened to the dead and wounded people who were transported in this truck. Filep Karma, who is now an Amnesty International prisoner of conscience, told me about how to find one mass grave, but forensic archaeologists have not yet visited this site.

West Papuan human rights workers were themselves frightened of possible government reprisals as a result of their investigations into the Biak massacre. Their work proceeded quietly as they gathered up information bit by bit. A pastor who began investigating the July 6 massacre the very next day recounted his emotionally taxing efforts: "I ran into someone from Manero at the market. He asked, 'Father, can you come with me?' 'Where?' 'To Manero, to see the body of a person that washed up on the beach.' Only the body was there. They didn't know where his head had gone. I dug a hole and neatly buried him and I cried."

In contrast to the 1991 Dili massacre in East Timor, which was filmed and photographed by international journalists, little mention of the July 1998 Biak massacre was made in the international media. Few reports emerged. CNN did not cover the event, despite the rumors at the protest. According to the official Indonesian version of this two-day siege, only one person died: "The National Commission of Human Rights and the Armed Forces said one activist died in the incident. He was identified as 27-year-old Ruben Orboy."[60] Elsham, the rights organization, produced a sixty-nine-page report in Indonesian about the massacre titled "Names without Graves, Graves without Names." The report called for an international investigation, but no international human rights organizations have followed up on their call.[61]

Tuesday, July 7, 1998

My connecting ferry to Nabire came into the harbor this morning. On my way out of town, I changed money at Bank Exim and then wandered around the harbor and market. People were just starting to come back to their offices, where they were inspecting the damage done by the demonstrators and the army. Desks had been ransacked, and documents littered the floor in a thick layer. Graffiti covered the walls. I went looking for a pay phone, and someone, not thinking, directed me to the building below the water tower where the Morning Star flag had been flying. I found the phone, but the mouthpiece had been ripped away from the handset. The mouthpiece hung, limp, from a few wires. The buildings under the water tower, which looked like government offices, were reduced to hollow shells spray-painted with flags and slo-gans. It looked like this had been the primary base for the protesters. Bullet holes riddled the walls at chest height. I continued toward the market, where I found a phone. A few market stalls were open. In the street—in between the market and the water tower—stood a disabled truck. All the tires were flat, and the doors had been ripped halfway off their hinges. When I headed back toward the harbor to board the ferry, a host of troops and government officials had arrived to inspect the damage at the water tower. Another group puzzled about what to do with the truck that had been destroyed by protesters in their initial clash with security forces.

Rather than marking an apocalyptic ending, a definitive break with the past, the security forces' use of raw violence to quell the protest became evidence of continuity.[62] The same old tactics of state violence from the Suharto era were being deployed in Indonesia's new era of supposed re-form. At the same time, these old tactics were no longer working. As Indo-nesian security forces deliberated and tried to destroy dreams of merdeka with spectacular violence—launching joint operations involving the navy, army, and police—the movement exploded with activity. In July 1998, West Papuans were evading Indonesian authorities by staging events in multiple places all at once. Even as the protests I witnessed in Jayapura and Biak were disrupted by security force violence, flag raisings were also taking place in Sorong, a city in the Bird's Head region of West Papua, as well as Wamena in the highlands.[63] The struggle for merdeka was spreading under-ground. It was on the move, evading detection by authorities. In a word, the movement was operating according to principles of the rhizome.

Rhizomes, in a botanical sense, are stems that spread laterally in the top-soil and send down roots. In the lexicon of Gilles Deleuze, a French phi-losopher, and Félix Guattari, a psychoanalyst, rhizomes are different from roots. Rhizomes, for Deleuze and Guattari, are figures of political resistance: they ceaselessly establish connections among organizations of power, social struggles, and other heterogeneous forms. These forms are extremely dif-ficult to disrupt or kill. When plants with rhizomes are mowed down, they grow back. When chopped up and left for dead, they resprout. "A rhizome can be cracked and broken at any point," observe Deleuze and Guattari, but "it starts off again following one or another of its lines, or even other lines.[64]

Long before the events of 1998, merdeka had already been moving quietly underground in the form of the rhizome, evading detection and fueling dreams of breakouts into the light of day. "Burrows are rhizomorphic in all their functions," write Deleuze and Guattari, "as habitat, means of provision, movement, evasion, and rupture."[65] During the long decades of the Suharto dictatorship, from 1967 till May 1998, West Papua's guerrilla army, the OPM (Organisasi Papua Merdeka), was imagined as the unified clandestine resistance to Indonesian rule. Initially the OPM had a clearly identified leader: Permenas Ferry Awom, a former sergeant major in the Dutch colonial police, who led a series of armed uprisings in the mountainous region of the Bird's Head Peninsula in 1965. As the OPM emerged, a mind-boggling diversity of other independence groups were also active:

> Napan (*Natural Papua Nasional*), PMPM (*Piagam Masyarakat Papua Merdeka*), Genapa (*Gerakan Nasional Papua*), *Rencana Sepuluh Tahun* (Ten Year Plan), PPPM (*Partai Politik Papua Merdeka*), MU FGS (Melanesian Union From Gak to Sumary), GPM (*Gerakan Papua Merdeka*), IPARI (*Ikut Papua Anti-Republik Indonesia*), Sampari (*Semangat Angkatan Muda Anti-Republik Indonesia*), GKPB (*Gerakan Kemerdekaan Papua Barat*), Panapa (*Partai Nasional Papua*), Petana (*Pecinta Tanah Air*), Okepa (*Organisasi Kemerdekaan Papua*), Sepupu (*Semangat Pemuda Papua*), FKPPB A 69 (*Front Komando Pembebasan Papua Barat Angkatan 69*), FPPB (*Front Pembebasan Papua Barat*), Kaki (*Kampagne Kilat*), Cirap (*Cita-cita Rakyat Papua*), and OMB (*Organisasi Maluku Besar*).[66]

The OPM came to connect these and other independence groups in spirit and principle. After the surrender of Permenas Ferry Awom in November 1970 and his reported murder by Indonesian security forces, the OPM became a rhizome.[67] A multiplicity of competing leaders representing different linguistic and cultural groups became linked together under the umbrella of the OPM — an organized anti-organization. In the 1980s and early 1990s the OPM spread and multiplied underground. During this period occasional demonstrations, flag raisings, and armed confrontations with Indonesian troops signaled that the movement was alive. "You can never get rid of ants because they form an animal rhizome that can rebound time and again after most of it has been destroyed," write Deleuze and Guattari. During the long decades of the Suharto regime, figures of the messianic multiple were largely hidden underground, with activists furtively coming together in hideouts, scattering, like a swarm of ants, at the slightest hint of danger. "The rhizome itself assumes very diverse forms," write Deleuze and Guattari, "from ramified surface extension in all directions to concretion into bulbs and tubers. . . . The rhizome includes the best and the worst: potato and couchgrass, or the weed."[68]

Messianic figures are like the potato or tuber form of the rhizome: they temporarily collect and stabilize revolutionary activity and dreaming. When Filep Karma stepped forward to claim the legacy of the OPM in July 1998 (though he had no ties to the guerrilla soldiers who were lying low in nearby jungles), he momentarily embodied the messianic spirit.[69] After Karma was shot and hauled off to prison, the spirit flitted away to animate new objects, figures, and future events. The logic of the messianic multiple—an expectation of the unexpected that is not fixed on any single thing—gave this social movement flexibility amid shifting historical contingencies. When a specific object of desire failed to materialize or a figure disappeared, new content rushed in to take its place. As a new era of free speech dawned in Indonesia, the messianic spirit of merdeka came to alight on increasingly stable, publicly recognizable figures of hope.

While expecting the unexpected without desiring anything in particular, Derrida worked to keep rhizomorphic potatoes and tubers out of his own messianic desert. Derrida tried to protect the notion of messianicity without messianism from the tools of deconstruction that he helped create with his early work. Deconstruction, in short, means taking apart a symbolic system to show that it contains several irreconcilable and contradictory meanings. If the messianic spirit is emptied of all content, Derrida reasons, then it cannot be taken apart. "The figures of messianism would have to be . . . deconstructed as 'religious,' ideological, or fetishistic formations," writes Derrida, "whereas messianicity without messianism remains, for its part, undeconstructible, like justice."[70] With his work on messianicity, Derrida intended to politicize the masses.[71] But his ideas about waiting for nothing in particular have not inspired mass political movements. Contentless messianicity, an empty promise, goes nowhere.

Trying to keep political and messianic movements beyond the reach of deconstruction is a mistake. Alliances and ideological formations are constructed, and are often deconstructed or reconstructed, as contingencies change.[72] Rather than Derrida's empty messianicity, people who joined the rhizomorphic movement for merdeka were hoping for many different things—a messianic multiple. Even as survivors of the massacre in Biak remembered fleeting glimpses of the messianic spirit—the fiery light in Filep Karma's eyes, the Pelni ocean liner appearing on the horizon—their collective imagination danced away to alight on other events, objects, and figures. When raising a flag on the water tower did not result in the recognition of West Papua as a sovereign nation, the central prefigured event for the crowd, visionaries refigured hopes and desires. Dreams about a messianic multiple, with new figures for probing future horizons, generated hope even in this moment of postrevolutionary disappointment.

Even as survivors were reeling from the terror of the killings in July 1998, even as they were afraid to utter the word merdeka in public, other groups pushed the independence movement forward. West Papuan leaders in distant centers of power, who had previously been staunch supporters of the Indonesian government, were prompted to take up the cause after learning about the bloodbath in Biak and the shootings of students in Jayapura. Burrowing under the noses of Indonesian authorities, the movement entered key nodes in the matrix of power. As merdeka spread out from Biak, it penetrated institutions of domination and linked up with new freedom dreams. Surprising alliances were forged, and the boundaries between enemy and ally began to break down as the infectious spirit of merdeka captured the imagination of West Papuans from all walks of life. The Biak massacre did not mark a violent end to the world of merdeka. Instead it set the stage for a new historical era.

CHAPTER TWO

From the Rhizome to the Banyan

1998–2000

The banyan tree is the symbol of Golkar, the Indonesian political institution that helped sustain President Suharto's regime for thirty-one years. Under Suharto, Golkar was the government party that virtually eliminated all forms of political opposition. Beneath banyan trees, other plant life is shaded out and has difficulty growing. The towering canopy of banyans forms a chaotic network of interlocking branches, covered with thick, dark green leaves. Aerial roots trail off of the branches, fusing with each other, engulfing other plants and objects to form entangled structures. Banyans are polymorphic: some individuals have a single trunk, while other trees grow into a whole grove of interconnected secondary trunks.[1] In tropical regions, banyans assume dominant positions in gardens, crowding out other plants and overgrowing human architecture.

By selecting the banyan tree as their party's symbol, the Golkar leadership invoked an overshadowing structure supported by a multitude of distinct pillars. The idea of Golkar — "functional groups" (*golongan karya*) — emerged under Indonesia's first president, Sukarno, who sought to eliminate the Western system of party politics.[2] Under Suharto's New Order Regime, campaigns of "departyization" and "golkarization" were continued into the early 1970s.[3] During its heyday, the Golkar system "was almost the only organization guaranteeing prestige in official society, [and] the only chance of a political career (albeit under military guidance in an avowedly apolitical atmosphere)."[4] The Indonesian military used the Golkar system to take on a dual function (*dwi-fungsi*) — to have a role in political as well as security affairs. In the policed atmosphere of calm that prevailed in Suharto's Indonesia, the Golkar political party predictably won every major election.

Golkar leaders invoked ties to a much earlier institution of domina-

The logo of Golkar, the banyan party.

tion when they chose the banyan as the symbol of their party. The banyan was *the* emblem of royalty in Javanese precolonial kingdoms.[5] In Javanese palaces, the banyan was seen as a source of potentially dangerous supernatural power.[6] Ghosts lurk among the branches and aerial roots, according to Indonesian folktales.[7] Observers of Indonesian political dynamics in the twentieth century began using the banyan as an allegorical figure, saying that a false sense of calm existed in the shade of this tree.[8] In a popular media article, written when momentum for Indonesia's reform movement was beginning to wane in 2001, Benedict Anderson repeated a famous Indonesian saying: "Under the banyan tree no healthy plants can grow." He continued: "Indonesia's present quarrelsome leaders grew up under its shade, and there is not one who has escaped its corrupting, dwarfing influence."[9]

From the periphery of Indonesia, rather than the central island of Java, where Anderson worked, the Golkar banyan began to look different. Emergent West Papuan independence leaders were not simply corrupted or dwarfed by the banyan. Instead they found surprising possibilities within its totalitarian structure of power. After the demise of Suharto, West Papuan activists began using the banyan for their own revolutionary ends. If Deleuze and Guattari's rhizome is an apt figure for understanding the occasional outbreaks of West Papua's *merdeka* movement in 1970s, 1980s, and early 1990s—sporadic flag raisings, guerrilla actions, political statements over radio waves—perhaps the banyan is a better figure for understanding a new historical period when activists began to undermine, climb, appropriate, and replicate the architecture of domination. The banyan, an arboreal rhizome of sorts, illustrates the maneuvering of indigenous politicians within constrained fields of historical possibility, within multiple entangled worlds. Insights from botany—in dialogue with philosophy, cultural theory,

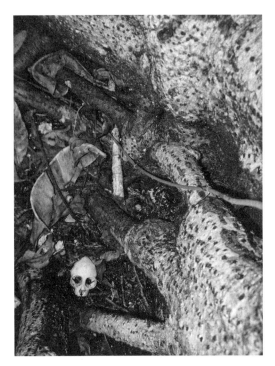

A monkey skull, at the base of a banyan tree, on the Osa Peninsula of Costa Rica. *Photograph by Eben Kirksey.*

and ethnographic observations — offer a way to grapple with human social movements and institutional forms.

The banyan tree is a model of dominant political structures *and* of possible subversions. It shows the possibilities that emerge in entanglements. Whereas the rhizome is "a short-term memory, or antimemory," the banyan contains genealogical roots.[10] While rhizomes are trapped in plateaus — a steady state where climax is avoided — banyans build on inherited structures to generate novel forms. This chapter follows a dense chronology of events, from August 1998 through June 2000, during a period called "the Papuan Spring" by Richard Chauvel, a political scientist who is an expert on Southeast Asia.[11] New collaborations emerged in this era of comparative freedom as indigenous politicians and intellectuals struggled from within the banyan structure. West Papuan activists began to transform radically asymmetrical relations of power from within the very structures that they were trying to change. This chapter traces the contours of the merdeka movement as it morphed from the rhizome into the banyan.

Growing beyond the Rhizome

In the first weeks of July 1998, the Indonesian military tried to destroy the movement for merdeka with raw military force when it emerged in broad daylight. Scattering, embodying the principles of the rhizome, independence activists regrouped underground.[12] Safe in the shadows, the movement reconstituted itself. Groups of trusted friends gathered in the living rooms of private homes, away from the listening ears of Indonesian agents, rehearsing their critiques of the Indonesian government.[13] At these meetings, merdeka was a burrowing rhizome, getting inside people's imaginations. As West Papuan independence activists began to reemerge in new public settings, the movement began to grow beyond the form of the rhizome.

A fact-finding team from the Indonesian National Parliamentary Assembly traveled to West Papua in late July 1998 to investigate the widespread protests and subsequent massacres that had taken place earlier that month. The parliamentarians hosted a dialogue with local leaders of Golkar (the banyan party) and other West Papuan intellectuals. This dialogue took place at an upscale hotel in Jayapura, West Papua's capital. Benny Giay, the Mee anthropologist and theologian, later told me about his own participation in this meeting: "We presented the Indonesian politicians with human rights reports describing killings near the Freeport gold mine, a 1996 military operation in the highlands that left scores of civilians dead, as well as the recent massacre in Biak." After hearing about this litany of abuses from Dr. Giay and other West Papuan leaders, the head of the Golkar party launched into a historical monologue about West Papua's integration into Indonesia. Dr. Giay remembers other West Papuan leaders rolling their eyes when the monologue began.

Then the dynamic in the room changed. "Suddenly, someone stood up," Dr. Giay told me. "It was Theys Eluay." Tall and heavyset, with a white-tinged Afro and frizzy beard, Eluay's formidable presence immediately commanded the attention of all eyes in the room. "Theys shook with anger," Dr. Giay continued. "As he picked up a chair to hurl at the parliamentarians, we restrained him." Theys Eluay interrupted the historical monologue: "We didn't come here to listen to your canned history, but to initiate a dialogue. The problem about the political status of West Papua is not just a national problem but an international problem."[14]

This outburst caught the parliamentarians off guard. Theys Eluay, who had been a Golkar parliamentarian, a trusted member of the banyan party for years, was rejecting Indonesia's historical claims to West Papua. Earlier in the same year, Eluay had lost his position as the Golkar representative to the local parliamentary assembly.[15] He had nothing to lose. "If we can't have a national dialogue," Eluay continued, "we must have an international dialogue."[16] After Eluay stopped fuming from this rapid-fire verbal exchange, he likely experienced a degree of pleasure from this transgression. "Theys Eluay was a flamboyant character. He enjoyed finding himself at the center of attention and controversy."[17]

Days later, Theys Eluay returned all the material artifacts associated with his career as a member of the Golkar team—awards, letterhead, gifts bearing the banyan tree logo—to the local party headquarters. Amid the chaos after Suharto's fall, Theys Eluay was born again. He asked Pastor Bob Ohee to perform a full immersion baptism on him in the Sentani River.[18] In Eluay's own biblical language, he underwent a dramatic conversion: "Before I was Saul, and now I am Paul."[19] Like the Pharisee Saul of Tarsus, who arrested early Christians, the young Theys Eluay had helped Indonesian authorities identify and persecute West Papuan supporters of independence. After seeing a blinding flash of light, Saul changed his name to Paul and changed the direction of his life to become one of the most important early Christian leaders.[20] Following his conversion, Eluay emerged from an entangled position in the Golkar banyan tree as the most prominent independence leader in West Papua.[21]

The people had been dreaming about multiple objects of messianic desire during decades of underground resistance. Hopes for many different prefigured events and saviors had been proliferating. Theys Eluay quickly began to collect and stabilize revolutionary activity and freedom dreams when he emerged as the public face of merdeka. He became the messiah of the movement. Theys Eluay explored new political opportunities within existing structures, exploiting shifting historical contingencies. Like a small parasitic plant beginning to climb up a host tree, like an arboreal rhizome, Eluay's political project grew up and over Golkar networks.

Figural Entanglements

Deleuze and Guattari raided biology for the rhizome without paying attention to the specificity of their figure. The particulars of banyan biology offer a novel perspective on revolutionary political projects, displacing dominant

A strangler fig growing
up and over a host tree.
Photograph by Eben Kirksey.

ways of understanding resistance with a figure that illustrates principles of collaborative engagement. Banyans grow according to some rhizomorphic principles. They are polycentric and have wild connections extending in many different directions. With vast networks of aerial roots that grow into interlocking arboreal structures, banyans exceed the form of Deleuze and Guattari's rhizome. The rhizome "is very different from the tree or root, which plots a point, fixes an order."[22] Polymorphic banyans, in contrast, have a hybrid form: at various points of their life they become rhizomes, roots, and trees.

Banyans are strangler figs. They grow up and around host trees, encircling them with a fused lattice of aerial roots.[23] Like all members of the genus *Ficus*, a diverse grouping that includes about 750 species, banyans produce figs, a fruit that is commonly eaten by birds, bats, and monkeys. Only some *Ficus* species produce figs that are palatable for humans. The strangler is a particularly powerful image for political projects that aim to overtake dominant structures. Strangler figs are famous for cutting off the flow of sap of their hosts and killing them.

The life cycle of stranglers usually begins when a fig-eating creature deposits feces, with seeds, in a suitable spot on a host tree. Small pockets where the branches of trees join the trunk often have enough moist humus for the seed to germinate. As shoots grow upward, roots grow down around the host's trunk.[24] Strangler figs are not true parasites—they do not pump nutrients out of their hosts like mistletoes, for example. Botanists classify stranglers as structural parasites.[25] They use the host tree for architectural support rather than as a source of nutrients.

Banyans are different from rhizomes in that they contain definitive structures. "There are no points or positions in a rhizome, such as those found in a structure, tree, or root," write Deleuze and Guattari. "There are only lines."[26] Emerging banyan trees trace the points and positions of their hosts. Here lies the danger of the banyan as a figure of political emancipation: it can reproduce regimes of domination even as it harbors the promise of liberation.[27]

Even after Theys Eluay publicly rejected Indonesia's claim to West Papua, he secretly began to recultivate relationships with former president Suharto, officials in the Golkar party, and high-level Indonesian military officers.[28] Eluay negotiated complex entanglements among multiple worlds at war. As the independence movement began to morph from an underground rhizome into the latticed structure of the banyan, skeptical observers wondered if he would ultimately be limited or enabled by his connections to the banyan tree party. Would coercive backroom deals reproduce and reinforce exploitative relations, limiting elite freedom fighters to political projects that would not seriously disrupt the status quo?

The Knot Tightens

Entanglements are knotty adhesions rather than smooth surfaces—they form sticky webs that are difficult to escape. When people struggle to free themselves from such attachments, they may unwittingly become even more stuck.[29] Theys Eluay was apparently making a radical departure from the Golkar party line with his declarations about independence for West Papua. Still, his sudden emergence as a freedom fighter can only be understood in terms of radical continuities—links with people whom he knew from his career as an Indonesian politician. As Theys Eluay made public statements challenging the status quo, he secretly strengthened his ties to Indonesia's old guard. He grew closer to former president Suharto, a person historically regarded by most West Papuan nationalists as the number one enemy to their cause.

On August 11, 1998, less than two weeks after his confrontation with the Golkar chairman, Theys Eluay had a secret meeting with Suharto at the recently ousted president's sprawling residential compound in Jakarta.[30] Suharto and his allies were trying to distract the nation's attention from corruption scandals by fanning the flames of freedom in West Papua, according to Dr. Benny Giay. In a book that was later banned by the Indonesian Ministry of Information, Giay wrote: "Certain parties wished to keep the New Order system of President Suharto firmly in place. The power brokers of Jakarta—both civilian and military leaders—did not want their personal interests disturbed by growing demands for reform. In Indonesia's outer regions they promoted local leaders, like Theys Eluay, who had previously been part of the Golkar team. . . . The Indonesian people were demanding a complete elimination of corruption. It was the Suharto family and their cronies who paid for the activities of Theys Eluay in the struggle for freedom in West Papua."[31] When Theys Eluay first emerged as an outspoken advocate for West Papuan rights during his confrontation with the visiting parliamentarians, Giay was one of his close associates. But Giay pulled out of this political group when he learned about the details of Eluay's continued covert ties to Indonesian power brokers. Giay's recent biography of Theys Eluay is a critical analysis of how Suharto and a host of covert operatives manipulated West Papuans who desired freedom. When I later met Giay in person as a first-year graduate student, he encouraged me to investigate Theys Eluay's complex alliances. I took up his suggestion and later invited him to formally become a member of my doctoral dissertation committee (see page 19 for a picture of Dr. Giay and the author).

At the beginning of my undergraduate research in West Papua, I had an outside perspective. In 1998, when I stumbled on the protests in Biak and at Bird of Paradise University, I was a nonpartisan earnestly trying to conduct a narrowly defined anthropological study in the hinterlands. When I set out to study the independence movement as a graduate student, I found myself in a conflict zone where I had to choose sides, allying myself either with the Indonesian government or with West Papuan independence activists. I also quickly discovered that the merdeka movement was split by internal fractures—that intellectuals and human rights activists like Dr. Giay were relentlessly critical of West Papuan "freedom fighters" who were collaborating with the enemy.[32] Through my close relationship with Dr. Giay and other critics of Eluay, I developed a situated perspective of West Papua's independence movement. I also learned about surprising dynamics that were taking place behind the scenes.

The West Papuan "warrior dance" performed by disguised Javanese dancers at the International Tourism Hotel in Jakarta. *Photograph courtesy of Boy Eluay.*

On August 12, 1998, the day after meeting with Suharto, Theys Eluay staged an unusual ceremony at the International Tourism Hotel, a decadent venue frequented by Indonesia's domestic elite.[33] Javanese dancers donned brightly colored loincloths, headdresses, and body paint. Although they were clearly not ethnic West Papuans—with light skin and straight hair, instead of black skin and kinky hair—they performed a "West Papuan warrior dance" while aiming their pink-tasseled bows and arrows at audience members, who watched from behind a railing. Meanwhile musicians worked drums to produce a thudding beat. The performers were evoking images of an exotic primitive, rather than the traditions of a specific West Papuan group.[34] News of this event was not widely reported in West Papua. On the sidelines of the performance, Eluay worked the audience—Indonesian generals, bankers, and high-ranking Golkar politicians—to cultivate support for his new political project.

Theys Eluay thus did not make a clean break from his past when he was born again, though he told the people, "Before I was Saul, and now I am Paul." Eluay was "Sauling around"—flirting with the devil and other figures from his life before he saw the light.[35] Eluay also enjoyed certain pleasures from his transgressions—gifts, cash donations, and even women.[36]

Returning to West Papua on the heels of the strange performance at the International Tourism Hotel, Eluay staged an unprecedented dialogue with a broad cross section of West Papuan leaders about the issue of independence. Three hundred invitations were hand-delivered to prominent intellectuals, journalists, and civil servants. Over seven hundred people arrived, crowding the meeting venue. "Enthusiastic support and fiery oratory from all groups represented at the meeting were focused on one aspiration, the aspiration for freedom," reported one observer. "The words 'Papua Merdeka' (Free Papua) were shouted over and over as tears flowed."[37] This was the first time in nearly forty years that someone had dared to stage such a gathering. Surprisingly, this dialogue about independence was approved in advance by Major General Amir Sembiring, commander of the Indonesian military in West Papua, who had approved the massacre of civilians for raising the Morning Star flag in Biak only weeks before.[38]

Regional newspapers began to splash stories about Theys Eluay's controversial demands for independence across their front pages.[39] Publishing articles about him increased the circulation of *Cenderawasih Pos*, then the only daily newspaper for the whole province of West Papua. There were weeks when Theys Eluay was pictured almost every day on the front page. The headlines read: "Theys Is Weeping," "Theys Is Angry," "Theys Is Sick and Has to Go to Singapore."[40] Regional newspapers did not report about the high-level Indonesian power brokers who began lending institutional and financial support to the cause.

The strange collaborations that enabled Theys Eluay's sudden rise to prominence remained largely unknown to supporters who rallied behind him. The meeting with Suharto, for example, was a closely held secret. Still, supporters who witnessed his flirtations with the devil believed that Eluay was cleverly exploiting Indonesian agents to relentlessly pursue the cause of merdeka. While navigating this situation of extreme power asymmetry, faithful activists who were close to Eluay hoped for a miraculous surprise. As his entanglements with Golkar power brokers grew ever stronger and he fanned the flames of the independence movement, few observers could keep a clear endgame in sight. In relations of mutual exploitation, outcomes are rarely guaranteed.

Roots

Tales about Theys Eluay's historical connections with the Golkar banyan and his past liaisons with powerful leaders of the Indonesian military strangely fueled his popularity when he became the most vociferous leader of the merdeka movement in August 1998. Some were amazed that a close associate of the Indonesian elite, someone who had enjoyed personal benefits from the occupation, had suddenly begun to take the aspirations of the people to heart. Aside from Eluay's close associates, few had specific knowledge about his ongoing collaborations with Suharto and other Indonesian power brokers. The people had faith that his conversion—that his assertion "Before I was Saul, and now I am Paul"—was genuine.

Perhaps Theys Eluay's political project did not fully embrace the promise of the banyan. The logic of his supporters was rhizomorphic: they dismissed history, forgetting about the commitments from his time as a politician in the Indonesian government. Past connections are irrelevant for Deleuze and Guattari's model of uninterruptible connectivity. Marking a sharp break with some of their contemporaries, Deleuze and Guattari distance themselves from genealogy, saying that "it doesn't suggest a popular methodology."[41] They saw genealogical trees as hierarchical, suggesting lines of patrilineal descent. The rhizome is "an anti-genealogy."[42]

Entangled banyans embody elements of genealogy. Their gnarled entanglements illustrate the contingencies of unexpected connections.[43] The method of genealogy, according to Michel Foucault, "opposes itself to the search for 'origins.'"[44] Genealogy involves attention to "the details and accidents that accompany every beginning."[45] If an antigenealogical rhizomorphic logic allowed Eluay to catapult to a prominent position as he rallied the enthusiastic masses behind the cry of *Merdeka!*, some of his opponents within the movement remained focused on his origins.

Theys Eluay had deep roots in the Indonesian nationalist cause. Born on November 3, 1937, he grew up during the tumultuous times of the Second World War—during the Japanese occupation of New Guinea and the Allied bombing campaign. When Indonesia declared independence on August 17, 1945, and began waging a protracted guerrilla struggle against the Dutch, the infectious spirit of anticolonial nationalism captured the young Theys Eluay. As a student at the Dutch-run Hamadi Telegraph School, Eluay started a pro-Indonesia club. Every year on August 17, Indonesia's national Independence Day, he received gifts from Dutch authorities in recognition of his political sympathies. He painted his parents' house white and red, the colors of Indonesia's national flag.[46]

The seeds of West Papuan nationalism, which blossomed at the beginning of the third millennium, were planted by Dutch officials at this moment—during the dying days of their colonial empire. In 1949, at the conclusion of the war for independence, Indonesian leaders secured a key promise from the Dutch. The new nation of Indonesia was to have sovereignty over all Dutch former colonial possessions in Southeast Asia: from Sabang, in the oil-rich region of Aceh, to the easternmost border of West Papua in Merauke. The Dutch later reneged on this agreement and retained West Papua, then called Netherlands New Guinea, as a colony.[47] In the 1950s the Dutch launched an intensive development campaign in West Papua. Later in the same decade, only when it became clear that there was insufficient international support for their New Guinea colony, the Dutch began to prepare the nation that was coming to call itself "West Papua" for self-determination.[48]

Theys Eluay was clearly inspired by Sukarno, the Indonesian president who founded the Golkar party (in office 1945–67). As a leader of the Non-Aligned Movement, Sukarno was an emblematic figure who embodied the hope of postcolonial nationalism. In 1955 Sukarno hosted the Asia-Africa Conference in Bandung, a city in central Java, where delegates from newly formed nations discussed securing human rights, including the right to self-determination, for peoples still under colonial rule.[49] At a time when many members of the West Papuan elite aspired to form their own nation with help from the Dutch, Theys Eluay saw hopeful possibilities in Indonesia's national project.[50]

Sukarno is still remembered for his infamous command in December 1962 to destroy the "puppet state of West Papua" with raw military might. John F. Kennedy and Sukarno worked to seal the 1962 deal that transferred West Papua from Dutch to Indonesian control. West Papuan activists, like Agus, who waylaid me outside of a library to tell me about the sins of world leaders and institutions, remember this deal as an act of betrayal by Kennedy and a land grab by Sukarno. Even after Theys Eluay began to lead West Papua's campaign for independence in 1998, he still displayed a picture of Sukarno and John F. Kennedy in his living room. This photograph of "the greatest leaders" fueled criticism from Eluay's detractors.

In 1969 Theys Eluay was among the 1,022 West Papuan representatives who unanimously "voted" to join Indonesia under close surveillance by the military during the so-called Act of Free Choice. He became a Golkar provincial assemblyman in 1971, during the heyday of Suharto's dictatorship. Haunting memories of Theys Eluay's connections to the Indonesian military stand out from the otherwise unremarkable career of a local banyan party politician. One woman, who wanted to remain anonymous, told me

The flamboyant and controversial West Papuan independence advocate Theys Eluay stands in his own home before a display bearing an English caption: "The Greatest Leaders." The display, a black-and-white photograph of John F. Kennedy and Indonesian president Sukarno, recalls freedom dreams from an earlier historical moment and unexpected entanglements with global power. *Photograph by Kiki van Bilsen.*

that Eluay had helped Indonesian soldiers identify freedom fighters in her local community: "There is a mass grave that contains the bodies of about a dozen Sentani villagers who were killed in the 1980s after being singled out by Theys. The men who ended up in this grave were taken out of their homes in the middle of the night and immediately killed." In a separate incident, Theys Eluay is remembered as the executioner of Julianus Joku, another young man who was openly critical of the Indonesian military.[51] No specific charges were ever filed against Theys Eluay in court. During Suharto's New Order, there were few avenues available to those who had grievances against members of the Golkar establishment.

As a Golkar politician, Theys Eluay had frequent opportunities to publicly air his opinions about West Papuan nationalism. In January 1996, two years before he emerged as the leading spokesperson for the *merdeka* movement, a reporter asked Eluay point blank about the possibility of independence for West Papua. "That talk about *merdeka* is a load of bull," Eluay responded. "We have enjoyed independence since August 17, 1945."[52] This was the date that Indonesia declared independence from the Dutch.

Perhaps Theys Eluay's supporters had to be forgetful, with rhizomorphic short-term memories, as he climbed around in the branches of Golkar's structure of domination. His roots were hazy, lost in the tangle of the rhizosphere. While the rhizomes of Deleuze and Guattari are rooted in antimemories, banyans have clearly visible aerial roots that perform surprising tricks. Entangled strangler figs can make physiological fusions—resulting in a two-way flow of water and nutrients—with members of their own species or with organisms that are sufficiently like themselves. When the roots of two individual fig saplings make contact, they can join with each other to form a mosaic, an organism composed of genetically distinct individuals.[53] The principles of selective fusion of the strangler fig, rather than the rhizome's uninterruptible connectivity, illustrate the processes at work as the movement left Theys Eluay behind.

Binding Articulations

While the vanquished Suharto regime fanned the flames of the independence movement in West Papua, other factions of Indonesia's security forces moved quickly to try to put out the fire. Despite his enduring entanglements with the Golkar banyan tree, Theys Eluay was imprisoned on October 6, 1998, along with four of his close associates. Eluay's public support for independence and subsequent imprisonment turned him into a martyr and increased his popularity among the masses.

Theys Eluay had become a key node in a polycentric, entangled network. When he was temporarily removed, many new leaders stepped forward. Prominent West Papuans in key positions of power—journalists, professors, pastors, corporate executives, and development workers—began to air their aspirations for independence in the vacuum that opened after Eluay was jailed. Suddenly the movement for merdeka came to have multiple potential messiahs, leaders without the complex and checkered past of Eluay. West Papua's independence movement exploded with activity as multiple events and figures of hope began to appear on future horizons.

The movement got inside key structures of power. In understanding the struggle for merdeka as it grew beyond the figure of the rhizome and penetrated multiple institutions, I build on the articulation theory of Stuart Hall, a prominent member of the British cultural studies tradition.[54] Articulation, in a general sense, means making speech sounds and linking things together.[55] As a theory, articulation can be used to break down the common-sense relationships between concepts.[56] Hall worked to understand the conditions that allow different ideological elements or institutions to join together in contingent formations.[57] Rather than keep ideological and political formations beyond the reach of deconstruction, as Derrida tried to do with his ideas about messianicity without messianism, Hall developed tools for thinking about how elements might be taken apart and reconstructed in new configurations.

The entanglements of the banyan might be thought of as binding articulations, connections that are difficult to disrupt. These links are constructed, and they must be well built. With waning institutional support for an ideological element, coalition, or political figure, articulations disappear or are overthrown.[58] Connections have to be actively sustained and constantly renewed. Languishing in jail, Theys Eluay diminished in importance. New coalitions emerged among West Papuan activists who shared long histories of struggle. Whereas Eluay's struggle involved elements of the rhizome, with the forgetfulness of antigenealogy, the emerging multitude more fully actualized the revolutionary promise of a mosaic banyan.

Government institutes, universities, corporations, media outlets, churches, and nongovernmental organizations had all been within Golkar's realm of influence during the Suharto regime. After Suharto's fall, some of these institutions began to assert autonomy from the banyan party. The movement for merdeka replicated the banyan's method of domination. Activists began to rearticulate connections among key institutions of power. Few organizations or government bodies lent public support to the cause. Instead individuals occupying high-ranking positions in different institutions began quietly working together toward the common goal of independence. Like established banyan trees, part of the dominant structure of a tropical forest, these people formed a latticed network of connections—above ground, manifested at public meetings, but through unofficial channels.

If rhizomes "can be connected to anything other, and must be," then connections among West Papuans who were active at this moment in the independence movement were instead tentative and cautious, based on shared histories and mutual trust.[59] Like fig saplings slowly exploring the possibility of physiological fusion, looking for molecular and histological compatibility, West Papuans representing different social formations began to carefully build alliances. Members of private discussion groups, who had vigorously debated the possibility of freedom in safe spaces, began to air their opinions in public. Voicing demands for independence to increasingly wide audiences became a central goal of the movement.

Even as emergent West Papuan leaders linked a diverse array of desires to the idea of freedom in late 1998, they came to orient the hopes of their followers toward a single future event. West Papuan activists took up an idea that Theys Eluay had first proposed in July of that year. During Eluay's heated confrontation with the visiting Golkar politicians, he had demanded a national dialogue. When Indonesian president B. J. Habibie, the hand-picked successor of Suharto, signaled willingness to host such an event, the West Papuan people were ecstatic.[60]

A surprising coalition in support of the national dialogue began to grow beneath the shade of the Golkar banyan. Under the watchful eyes of government officials, the West Papuan people conducted public consultations to select seventy-five delegates representing diverse constituencies: indigenous elders, intellectuals, professionals, religious leaders, historical figures, health workers, women, student activists, and youth leaders. The Indonesian military added twenty-five of their own candidates to the delegation—ethnic West Papuans who were members of the National Parliament or identified themselves as "Indonesian revolutionaries."[61] The delegation that would meet for the national dialogue with President Habibie came to be known as the Team of 100.

Positions in multiple institutions of power gave the Team of 100 collective strength. Still, the delegation was not outside Indonesian regimes of domination but instead struggling for purchase from within. The Indonesian government chartered special planes for all delegates to the national dialogue, who departed from West Papua amid much pomp and circumstance. Theys Eluay could not join the team because he and his inner circle were still under house arrest. The momentum of the independence movement had, for the moment, left Eluay behind.

When the Team of 100 gathered in Jakarta on February 24, 1999, two days before they were to meet with Habibie, their collective sentiments were still undetermined. The freshly selected delegates, some of whom were meeting each other for the first time, stayed at a luxury hotel in Jakarta that had been paid for by the governor. They tentatively tested each other on the issues of the day. Meanwhile Octovianus Mote, who was then the Jayapura bureau chief for *Kompas*, the leading daily newspaper of Indonesia, and others were taking steps behind the scenes to ensure that the Team of 100 would collectively support the call for independence. A mild-mannered intellectual—short, bespectacled, and warm—Mote proved to be a skilled negotiator who was savvy at working behind the scenes. Key players in the Golkar banyan used subtle tactics to influence the agenda of the national dialogue, creating obligations from personal loyalty, hospitality, gifts, gratitude, and respect for elders. Mote and other independence leaders appropriated these same tactics from the banyan party to establish a tight coalition among the diverse groups represented in the delegation.[62]

On the morning of the national dialogue, February 26, 1999, a "political declaration" was presented to the Team of 100. It was a declaration of independence. The facilitators feared that the delegates with government ties would refuse to endorse the statement. Surprisingly all one hundred members, including the controversial "Indonesian revolutionaries," signed. Did these longtime Indonesian collaborators suddenly see new opportunities for themselves in a breakaway nation? "All West Papuans secretly harbor aspirations for independence," Mote later intimated over the phone. "Here even the military agents, who were ethnic West Papuans, revealed their true colors."[63]

Tom Beanal, a charismatic elder statesman from the Amungme tribe, had been selected to read the political declaration. The independence movement had found a new leader in Beanal, a man who did not have the same checkered past as Theys Eluay. After the delegation arrived at the Presidential Palace, anticipation began to build. For decades—during the 1970s, 1980s, and early 1990s—aspirations for freedom had been aired behind the backs of Indonesian officials. When Beanal stood and read the statement, the other delegates anticipated a rare moment of political electricity when they would directly and publicly voice their collective desire for independence in the teeth of power.[64] "We the people of West Papua," Beanal read, "have the intention to leave the Unitary Republic of Indonesia for freedom and for full sovereignty among the other nations on the surface of the earth."[65]

After hearing the political declaration, President Habibie canceled his written speech. He talked with the delegates "heart to heart" and thanked them for making diplomatic efforts: "Your method of presenting your aspirations has been very congenial, in contrast to other regions. Here in Jakarta I have been the object of protest about 3,000 times."[66] Simply airing their demands for freedom at the Presidential Palace was a significant accomplishment. Even so, the Team of 100 sought more than a symbolic victory. Many delegates wanted to extract a promise from the president for an independence referendum.

"The political statement of the people of West Papua is honest and pure," continued Habibie. "It stems from the experiences of the people of Irian Jaya or West Papua."[67] Being hailed as the "people of West Papua" by the president of Indonesia was another major symbolic victory. Until this moment, it had been treasonous to call this place anything but Irian Jaya, the official name bestowed by Suharto in 1972. Habibie took dangerous words and suddenly made them part of acceptable public discourse in Indonesia.

Habibie did not explicitly accept or reject the demand for a special vote on the issue of independence. Ultimately the delegation failed on this point. Still, their symbolic victories were noteworthy: they earned the right to talk about independence in public and the right to call their land West Papua. An underground movement, a purely rhizomorphic formation, could never have staged such diplomatic victories. Arboreal structures that contain stable points and positions, like the banyan, are perhaps better able to interface with existing structures of dominance.

When the Team of 100 flew back home, they were hailed as heroes. The delegates launched a coordinated campaign to spread news of the freedoms earned during the meeting with the president. In villages throughout West Papua, small huts, "communication posts" (*posko*), were established as local clearinghouses of information about independence. Single-sideband radios, a peer-to-peer communication network that linked villages in remote areas, flooded the airwaves with excited freedom dreams.[68] News of the imminent possibility of independence began to spread to all corners of West Papua.

However, even as a new era of political freedom dawned, rogue members of Indonesia's security forces launched a new targeted campaign of violent intimidation. One month after the meeting with the president, Octovianus Mote's next-door neighbor in Jayapura was beaten to death by unknown assailants.[69] "His face was destroyed," Mote told me. "He took what had been intended for me."[70] Immediately after this murder, in late March 1999, Mote sought refuge in the U.S. embassy in Jakarta. Embassy staff ferried him out of the country and helped him begin the tortuous process of obtaining political asylum.

Despite military intimidation tactics and assassination campaigns, excitement among the West Papuan people ran high. Even as I tried to be discreet about my politically sensitive research, I found it impossible to avoid the electricity in the air. People would routinely lean out of public buses and shout *"Papua Merdeka!"* (Free Papua!) as I walked by on the street. But as the months passed, the movement for independence began to flounder. Underground activity had reached a pitched intensity, but no one had emerged as a clear public leader of the moment. The people searched for a new event on the horizon, a messiah, or another figure of hope that might fulfill their collective expectations.

Replication

Theys Eluay suddenly burst into the limelight to reclaim leadership of West Papua's freedom struggle in November 1999. On the heels of the independence referendum in East Timor,[71] he invited thousands to his sixty-second birthday party—honored guests from indigenous organizations, the Indonesian military, the police, and Golkar. After his birthday party, Eluay announced that a series of events would unfold, including flag raisings, further dialogues with Indonesia's president, and internal consultations among West Papuan leaders. These announcements gave the independence movement new legs. In May 2000, Eluay led the emergent nation of West Papua to stage its most spectacular collective event thus far: the Papuan Congress. Some twenty-five thousand people gathered in Jayapura. "There was native finery of all sorts: feather headdresses, shell necklaces, painted bodies," writes Brigham Golden, a doctoral candidate at Columbia University who attended the Congress. "And urbanites of all ages: students, laborers, public servants and professionals. Many carried signs and chanted political slogans."[72]

Forty years earlier, in the 1960s, Indonesia's fledgling Golkar party had been composed of distinct "pillars": workers, peasants, intellectuals, national entrepreneurs, Protestants, Catholics, *alim ulama* (Islamic religious scholars), youths, and former anticolonial guerrilla fighters.[73] Official delegates to the 2000 Papuan Congress replicated similar pillars, representing professionals, historical figures, students, women, and former political prisoners.[74] A multitude of entangled strangler figs fused together in a strong coalition that was publicly working toward revolutionary climax. These indigenous agents inside the banyan architecture were producing visible changes from within the existing structures of domination. Multiple climactic events—the confrontation with the Parliamentary Fact Finding

Team in August 1998, the national dialogue with Habibie in February 1999, the Papuan Congress in June 2000—marked their success. These climaxes generated new horizons of hope and possibility.

Theys Eluay's ability to undermine, climb, appropriate, and replicate the totalitarian Golkar structure of power galvanized his many followers. He was finding surprising political possibilities in a situation of radical inequality. A politics of strategic engagement, collaborating with his "enemies," was opening up startling opportunities even in the face of seemingly insurmountable odds. Eluay skillfully channeled the expansive hopes of the West Papuan people, producing revolutionary friction by bringing freedom dreams into contact with historical reality. Rather than demanding new, utopic, institutional forms, he was deftly exploiting inherited structures for the cause.

Notably absent from the 2000 Papuan Congress were guerrilla fighters, members of the clandestine army that had been waging an underground armed independence struggle for decades. The rhizomorphic strategy of the West Papuan guerrillas had allowed the movement to persist under the steady state of plateau under uncontested rule by the Golkar party. By taking the public stage with a new organizational form, without a place for veteran fighters, Eluay and other urban political leaders alienated many potential supporters in the hinterlands.[75]

At the 2000 Papuan Congress, Theys Eluay was instated as the chairman of the thirty-two-member Papuan Presidium Council. The split between urban activists and rural guerrillas notwithstanding, Eluay tried to organize the independence movement into a hierarchical bureaucracy under his control. The movement was transitioning from the form of many saplings, distinct pillars energetically struggling for purchase on the architecture of power, to a unified structure of domination. At this moment, even as crowds greeted Theys Eluay as the messiah, key West Papuan intellectuals began demanding something other than a breakaway totalitarian state. "Many of us saw the potential of Theys Eluay to become a new dictator," Dr. Benny Giay told me. "Would an independent West Papua under him really be free?"[76]

The symbolic functional pillars that supported the new banyan structure in West Papua—the representatives of professionals, historical figures, students, women, and former political prisoners who reported to the Papuan Presidium Council—were buttressed by material support from the outside. The 2000 Papuan Congress was funded, in part, by Freeport McMoRan, the massive gold and copper mining company with the large hole in West Papua's highlands. Britain's largest company, BP (now officially Beyond Petroleum), also contributed funds to the congress.[77] Having recently acquired shares in a mysterious megaproject in the Bird's Head region of West Papua, BP was supporting revolutionary political dreams even before its own local schemes had substance. With the backing of these multinational corporations, West Papua's independence movement began to seem like a credible threat to the Indonesian government.

Freeport and BP were playing the Indonesians and the West Papuans against each other. These multinational corporations wanted to be in a position of influence regardless of which way the political winds might blow. Their cash gifts articulated and established relations of power.[78] The sudden influx of funds into the coffers of the merdeka movement greased the skids for independence and for further neocolonial interdependencies in a sovereign West Papua. Theys Eluay was on the brink of actualizing one particular vision of merdeka, an independent modular nation organized according to the principles of the Golkar banyan. In August and September 2000, Eluay and his inner circle embarked on an international tour, visiting Australia, the Solomon Islands, the United States, and Holland to leverage support for the cause in the seats of global power.[79]

Eluay's vision of merdeka was clearly not the only one at play in West Papua. Other activists hoped to actualize a broader idea of freedom that would not leave their country beholden to foreign interests. Even as Theys Eluay staged major rallies, drawing excited crowds, regular protests began to form outside his home.[80] Guerrilla fighters and some student activists began to allege that he was "cooperating" (*kerjasama*) with Indonesian agents and foreign corporations. "Theys Eluay was an egg on top of a knife edge," Dr. Giay told me. "Activists came to his house with an arrow. They told him, 'If you sell us out to Indonesia, this arrow will kill you.'"[81] Eluay was precariously balanced in the space where two powerful national projects were colliding. Falling too far to either side would spell his death.

Theys Eluay received gifts from people "who did not want their 'business' in West Papua to be disturbed."[82] Some of these gifts were channeled into the merdeka movement, used to stage events like the 2000 Papuan Congress. Eluay also personally profited from his political maneuvering. One logging company, PT Djajanti, gave Eluay a metallic blue Toyota Kijang sports utility vehicle.[83] Collaborations between elite leaders of postcolonial nationalist movements and imperial agents have caused widespread misery and suffering, according to Partha Chatterjee. Chatterjee would likely view Theys Eluay as having a similar character to many of the nationalist leaders who came before him — as cynically manipulating popular desires for freedom to pursue his own personal interests.[84]

Familiar oppositions between the indigenous urban bourgeoisie and the rural peasantry underlie Partha Chatterjee's critique of elite nationalist leaders. Chatterjee also repeats familiar distinctions between the dynamic character of resisting peoples and the cynical nature of those who had been captured by agents of the state or multinational corporations.[85] Theys Eluay and other West Papuan nationalist leaders were playing high-stakes games. As they successfully captured the power of corporate capital and the state for the cause of merdeka and used it to secure important victories, these leaders became compromised (*con-promises*, with promises).[86] Stuck in a situation not of their own choosing, under a military occupation, these freedom fighters made relatively small-scale interventions within a global world system that was not constructed with their well-being in mind. As leaders like Eluay enjoyed personal freedoms, as their imaginations were captured by the promises of capitalism, they nonetheless secured limited rights and justice for the West Papuan people.

Perhaps Eluay was initially a puppet of the Suharto regime when he first lent support to the issue of independence, creating a distraction from the corruption scandals that were plaguing the former president in Jakarta. But by 2000, Eluay clearly saw a future for himself in a breakaway state. Even as he received death threats from West Papuan activists, "ghosts" (*suangi*), a code word for military intelligence agents, began to haunt the intimate spaces of Eluay's home.[87] Many sensed danger in the air. Amid threats from competing national projects, Eluay became stuck. The focused intensity of revolutionary momentum dissipated as Eluay floundered.

The Plateau

Rhizomes sustain steady states, called plateaus, where climaxes are avoided. As Theys Eluay struggled to navigate complex entanglements, the people of West Papua found themselves stuck in such a plateau: excitement about merdeka ran high, but the movement did not seem to be going anywhere. Plateaus emerge when there is a pitch of intensity that is not automatically dissipated in a climax. Deleuze and Guattari's title *A Thousand Plateaus* celebrates intense activities that veer off in multiple directions, along divergent lines of flight. Strangler figs are famous for killing their host trees. This teleology of climax, however, is in no way guaranteed. A palm tree that has been engulfed, but not choked to death, by a strangler fig illustrates the awkward, yet enduring, relations that persist among entangled "enemies" when a clear endgame is not in sight. As Theys Eluay lost his trajectory toward revolutionary climax, he became stuck in the perpetual state of the plateau. Without clear historical roots in the independence movement, and without a clear vision of the future, Eluay was unable to escape rhizomorphic entanglements — he was not able to fully actualize the revolutionary promise of the banyan.

Examining the roots of the rhizome, making methodological moves that will certainly be unpopular with Deleuzians, reveals that it is a genealogical relative of the Golkar banyan. The plateau, and Golkar's banyan, both can be traced to colonial-era Indonesia. Deleuze and Guattari appropriated the idea of the plateau from Gregory Bateson, an innovative theorist who worked across multiple disciplines, including anthropology, cybernetics, psychology, biology, and semiotics. Quasi-sexual games between mothers and their infant sons in Bali, an Indonesian island, were the central allegory for Bateson's model of the plateau. "The mother will start a small flirtation with the child, pulling its penis or otherwise stimulating it to interpersonal activity," wrote Bateson. "This will excite the child, and for a few moments cumulative interaction will occur. Then just as the child, approaching some small climax, flings its arms around the mother's neck, her attention wanders."[88] Bateson used this approach-and-avoidance game to think about how children might be taught to avoid climax. Playful interactions that result in sustained plateaus are thus quite different from activity that produces orgasms.

Bateson's work in Bali took place in the 1930s, the halcyon days of the Dutch colonial empire in Southeast Asia. Here Bateson thought about social situations that lead to "the substitution of a plateau for a climax." While in Bali, he investigated cultural norms that led people to avoid culminating events. "In general the lack of climax is characteristic for Balinese music, drama, and other art forms," he concluded.[89] He drew formal parallels between these cultural forms and Balinese social organization: "The principal hierarchical structures in the society — the caste system and the hierarchy of full citizens who are the village council — are rigid. . . . An individual may lose his membership in the hierarchy for various acts, but his place in it cannot be altered."[90] Bateson's writing on the steady state of Bali stands as a provocative model of social institutions and cultural forms that do not follow the logic of progressive, step-wise, development.

Peripheral visions of Dutch colonialism are present in Bateson's work on Bali.[91] Still, like many other scholars of Bali, Bateson did not appear to reflect seriously on how histories of colonial domination and anticolonial resistance had an impact on his subjects of study.[92] The steady state of mid-twentieth-century Bali was, in part, a result of a series of massive Dutch military campaigns in the nineteenth century and subsequent policies of indirect rule.[93] By the late 1930s, the time of Bateson's fieldwork, Bali was peaceful and widely regarded as an "earthly paradise." Some Dutch colonists, like the school officials who gave Theys Eluay gifts on Indonesia's national independence day, actively participated in Indonesia's nationalist imaginings. But at this moment most Indonesian revolutionary activity was underground, hidden from foreign anthropologists like Bateson.[94] The Indonesian nationalist movement was burrowing like a subterranean rhizome.

Complex encounters between Balinese culture and Dutch colonialism generated the sociopolitical plateaus that Bateson observed, as well as rhizomes that he did not see. The historical amnesia surrounding Bateson's plateau carried over to Deleuze and Guattari's antigenealogical project. In the steady state of the plateau, the past is forgotten, and future horizons of climactic change seem impossible. Rhizomes often become stuck in plateaus. Only in exceptional moments do they rupture the established order, entering the breakout phase.

The revolutionary promise of the banyan exceeds the form of Deleuze and Guattari's rhizome. Whereas rhizomes are not "roots" or "trees," banyans contain genealogical origins in their knotted entanglements, as well as future possibilities. Banyans trace existing structures. They also contain surprises—the possibility of climax, of choking off institutions of domination or forming novel arboreal structures and establishing new networked architectures of power. Banyans can climb out of the steady state of the plateau: the homogeneous, empty time where nothing ever really happens. Beyond Southeast Asia, the banyan might inspire a subversive politics of engagement. It is a figure of entanglements that are constraining but not determining—impure, corrupted, but not without hopeful aspirations.

The figure of the banyan also contains a warning about the dangers of getting trapped within coercive entanglements.[95] Despite the potential of strangler figs to escape the plateau, to choke off institutions of power in revolutionary climax, Theys Eluay lost sight of imagined goals. The events of 1999 and 2000 certainly involved a series of revolutionary climaxes: the Team of 100 and the Papuan Congress in June 2000 amped up the momentum of the movement. But in the coming months, Eluay and other leaders of the merdeka movement struggled to make progress toward the ultimate climax: achieving the goal of national independence. As the urban elite strained to maneuver within their complex entanglements, visionaries quietly watched from the sidelines, reimagining the scale and scope of necessary transformations. The messianic spirit of merdeka left Theys Eluay, flitting away on multiple lines of flight, reanimating freedom dreams in the hinterlands.

II. PLATEAU

2000–2002

Freeport Sweet Potato Distribution Inc.

Even as independence seemed within reach, the idea of freedom was being pulled in other directions. Powerful forces tried to translate merdeka into money. As the masses rallied for national sovereignty and economic justice, elite West Papuans were given lucrative opportunities by multinational corporations and the Indonesian government. New policies were put in place that promised a greater share of revenue from mining, timber, and petroleum ventures for ordinary people.[1] Individuals began to find possibilities of "freedom," of wealth and prosperity, within the confines of a military occupation and amid resource-extraction projects that were designed to generate profits for foreign investors.

A picture of Yosias Magai, a West Papuan entrepreneur who started a small-scale industrial chicken-and-egg production facility, illustrates the opportunities available to indigenous West Papuans who figure out how to navigate the machinery of corporate benevolence. Magai wears a T-shirt with a single word on the front: freedom. This image was featured in "Underlying Values: Working toward Sustainable Development," a report published in 2006 by Freeport Gold and Copper, the company with the giant hole. The report details Freeport's programs for communities living near the mine—contributions of some $250 million toward basic healthcare, education programs, and grants for small businesses.[2] Descriptions of these programs alongside Magai's image sent a subtle message to Freeport's investors and other stakeholders, suggesting that the company has helped create a stable civil society and domesticated the very idea of freedom.

Philanthropy, an elaborate form of gift giving, is a means of articulating, establishing, or challenging relations of power.[3] Freeport's extensive programs of corporate giving have been roundly criticized by many West Papuans—like the Yali elders who told me the story of the hole—who say that such programs mask underlying relations of exploitation.[4] Charitable

Posing in front of rows of battery cages, a controversial feature
of industrial chicken production, Yosias Magai, a West Papuan
entrepreneur, illustrates the possibilities of freedom for indigenous
people who engage with systems of capitalistic production. This image
also contains ironic juxtapositions—here a new regime of unfreedom,
the confining of nonhumans, promised to liberate a few humans from
poverty.

programs have historically placed indigenous peoples on the receiving end. In the early twenty-first century, as indigenous groups have begun to engage with capitalism in new, surprising ways, some trends in philanthropic giving have started to reverse. For example, the Seminole Tribe of Florida, which surprised observers in 2006 when it used funds from high-stakes bingo games to purchase the international Hard Rock Café chain for $965 million, has begun to donate a share of the profits to local schools, athletic teams, emergency services, and health organizations. In the words of Jessica Cattelino, these philanthropic activities and the Hard Rock Café acquisition "extended the boundaries of Seminole economy and sovereignty across the United States and beyond."[5] Reversing the flow of philanthropic funds, the Seminoles began to reconfigure global relations of power, actualizing freedom dreams that also had currency in West Papua.

A visionary from the Mee tribe, Decky Pigome, began laying elaborate plans for engaging with capitalism and reconfiguring global relations of philanthropic power. In the late 1980s, Pigome founded a new organization that he called Freeport Yawudi Nota. Drawing inspiration from Freeport McMoRan and simultaneously seeking to make a radical break from their greedy practices, Pigome drew up blueprints for an indigenous corporation. In the Mee language, *nota* means sweet potato or, more generally, wealth.[6] The word *yawudi* means to distribute things free of charge. The mission of Freeport Yawudi Nota, or Freeport Sweet Potato Distribution Inc., was to feed people living all across the globe.

The formation of Freeport Sweet Potato Distribution Inc., a new sort of gold and copper company, would be the first step along a path to independence from Indonesia. Like many other West Papuans, Pigome was weary of life under Indonesian military occupation. He dreamed of merdeka. In the late 1980s, when few dared to talk openly about nationalist aspirations, Pigome was planning to use revenue from Freeport Sweet Potato Distribution Inc. to fund the independence movement. Upon obtaining national sovereignty, he planned to launch a grand humanitarian project. With independence, Pigome realized, comes new interdependencies.[7]

Sovereignty for the Seminole Tribe has taken shape through multiple and shifting relations of interdependence—with other governments, corporations, and municipalities.[8] Rather than the nested relations of sovereignty that Native American tribes have negotiated with the U.S. government, Pigome hoped to free his people from Indonesia so that they could directly renegotiate interdependencies with global powers. Fusing principles of international finance with a sort of indigenous socialism, he saw the potential to reroute the flow of natural products so that they would no longer steadily stream from his land into corporate coffers. After ensuring that all West Papuan households had enough wealth to sustain a comfortable existence, Pigome envisioned a foreign aid program to help Indonesia and other poor nations around the globe. In short, Pigome wanted to transform the theft of natural resources into a gift.

Gifts demand gifts in return.[9] In precolonial times, the political influence of *tonowi*, rich men among the Mee highlanders, was established by creating debtors.[10] Younger men borrowed pigs, an essential part of any bride price, from the tonowi. Until the young men established their own teams of pigs and were capable of repaying their debts (with interest), they had to support the tonowi in all matters of politics.[11] Leopold Pospisil, a cultural anthropologist from Yale University who spent eighteen months among the Mee in the 1950s, charted how people strove to become rich men (*tonowi*) by successfully breeding and trading pigs as well as accumulating many wives who toiled in gardens of sweet potatoes—a staple food for humans and pigs alike. A tonowi, according to Pospisil, was able to "expand his herd of pigs indefinitely, thus facilitating an accumulation of great personal wealth."[12]

Pospisil regarded the Mee as "primitive capitalists," as opposed to "primitive communists," a stereotype about indigenous peoples that was popular at the time.[13] Loans structured an indigenous economy that was, in Pospisil's words, "an open, flexible system, in which vertical mobility was one of the major characteristics."[14] Mee bachelors could buy female piglets from established tonowi—with small down payments that were paid in full once the young man realized his first profit from the sale of pork. Yet these "primitives" were doing capitalism differently from agents living in the modern world system. A rich fabric of moral logic demanded that surpluses be redistributed to relatives and exchange partners.[15]

Reimagining West Papua's position in the modern world system, Pigome extended Mee norms about gift giving to the global stage. By giving gifts to foreign worlds, Freeport Sweet Potato Distribution Inc. would gain political allies and economic debtors who could be called on in times of need. Amid the thawing of the Cold War in the 1980s, Pigome dreamed of refashioning aspects of U.S. and Soviet foreign-aid programs. Drawing on mores governing reciprocal exchanges from a seemingly remote corner of New Guinea's highlands, Pigome began to intuitively understand the principles of macroeconomics and soft diplomacy. Dreaming up new ways of maneuvering for rights and justice within a nested matrix of global power rather than harboring hopes for complete sovereignty or autochthony, Pigome was imagining new routes to freedom in entangled worlds.

Decky Pigome inspired dozens of Mee investors—his friends and elder kinsmen—with his dreams. Their modest gifts of one, five, or sometimes twenty dollars enabled him to think and dream without having to work. He hoped to become a modern-day tonowi, using these loans to engage in activities that were calculated to make him and his investors rich. With this backing for his company, he moved to Jayapura, West Papua's capital, where he had enough money to pay rent, eat modest meals of noodles from street vendors, and get around the city by public transport. Pigome spent his days visiting the waiting rooms of Indonesian government offices and banks. There, according to one of his followers, he carefully studied the architecture of the rooms, watching business transactions and drawing copies of posters on the walls in his notebook. Pigome was like an anthropologist conducting an ethnography of the state and global capitalism.[16] He was looking for points of entry, like a strangler fig searching for purchase on a host tree.

Quiet charisma, an understated revolutionary élan, allowed Pigome to capture the imagination of his contemporaries. Playing with the figure and form of the corporation, he pointed toward the prospects of new relationships with foreign worlds—pushing the bounds of realistic possibility. But ultimately Pigome failed to bring his visions into contact with historical reality. He lacked the skills of strategic engagement and practical collaboration with worldly institutions that later generations of West Papuan leaders mastered. After many months of no measurable results, when Pigome's vision failed to materialize, his investors lost confidence. Their loans showed little prospects of being returned. Pigome ultimately failed in his quest to become a modern-day tonowi. He was ostracized. In 1992, Decky Pigome died penniless and alone.

Freedom dreams can have inherent merits whether or not they succeed in the near term.[17] Pigome was ahead of his time, out of joint with history. A decade later, similar visions began to gain traction in other parts of the world. At the 2001 United Nations World Conference on Racism, in Durban, South Africa, a host of sovereign nations mired in postcolonial poverty took up calls for rethinking the logic that structures Third World debt. Conference delegates argued that the poorest regions of the world, especially Africa and the Caribbean, are in fact the creditors of rich nations. This revisionist logic argued that during the colonial period—the first wave of globalization—the theft of indigenous land and the free labor of slavery fueled the development of the North. All major UN conferences seem to coalesce around a theme, and the theme that emerged from Durban was the call for reparations.[18]

At the same moment as Durban, savvy West Papuans were gaining traction within the architecture of the banyan—they seemed to be on the verge of breaking away and plunging Indonesia into a serious economic disaster.

In 1999, Freeport was Indonesia's single largest taxpayer.[19] If West Papua became independent, Indonesia could lose this income. In hopes of forestalling the independence movement, trying to win support from sectors of West Papuan civil society, Indonesian officials began to inject serious funds into the province. Shortly after the 2000 Papuan Congress, 20 billion rupiah ($2.1 million) was given to each of West Papua's fourteen regencies (*kabupaten*).[20] This influx of cash, totaling approximately 280 billion rupiah ($29.5 million), was a special one-time "crash program" grant roughly equal to the Indonesian government's annual operating budget for the entire province.[21] Shortly after these funds were released, a headline of the progressive weekly *Tifa Papua* read: "Crash Program: Will It Dampen the Desire for Independence?"[22]

Indonesian legislators began to draft a "special autonomy" package that contained major economic concessions. Rather than looking to the past, rather than make reparations for historical injustices as proposed at Durban, this plan looked to the future. Initial drafts of the special autonomy package promised West Papua's provincial government 70 to 80 percent of revenue from forestry, fisheries, mining, and natural gas industries. If the legislation passed, the central government would be obligated to increase the annual provincial budget from 280 billion rupiah ($29.5 million) to roughly 3.6 trillion rupiah ($400 million).[23] At the same time that Freeport stepped up their philanthropic programs, the Indonesian government was trying to use gifts to domesticate the very idea of freedom.[24]

Economic justice, a limited form of merdeka, seemed to have arrived with the autonomy package and community development funds from Freeport. Some of the West Papuan activists involved in drafting the special autonomy legislation intimated to me, off the record, that they regarded autonomy as a possible steppingstone to national independence—they hoped to channel funds to the movement. Others came to see autonomy as a thinly veiled Indonesian attempt to buy off West Papua's urban elite. General Mathias Wenda, an influential guerrilla leader, told a blogger: "Our one demand has been clear: full independence for West Papua, politically, socially and above all, economically. There is NOTHING to say about autonomy."[25]

Indigenous visionaries were struggling to keep their freedom dreams alive as speculative fantasies and fictions from foreign lands burrowed into their political imagination.[26] The peaceful struggle for independence was foundering, stuck in a plateau with no climactic events in sight. As Indonesian security forces launched a new campaign of targeted assassinations and once again staged spectacular new displays of violence, West Papua's guerrilla forces began to retaliate. Amid rumors of strange collaborations, where the lines separating enemies from allies blurred, West Papuans found themselves fighting on the front lines of wars that were not entirely their own.

CHAPTER THREE

Entangled Worlds at War

2000–2001

Multiple worlds went to war in West Papua at the dawn of the twenty-first century. Fragmenting imagined communities, divergent millennial prophecies, contending indigenous visions, and rival imperial designs competed with each other for believers and supporters. The promise of national independence competed with diverse other goals—of maintaining security, generating wealth, and reforming the existing government. Veena Das, an anthropologist who writes about violence, asks: "What is it to inhabit a world? How does one make the world one's own? What is it to lose one's world?"[1] Departing from these questions and exploring the interplay between imagination and collaboration, this chapter traces movements of provocateurs and revolutionaries who inhabited borderlands—sites where different worlds came into contact and conflict.

West Papuan freedom fighters were locked in mortal entanglements with three other social worlds: the Indonesian reform movement, government security forces, and global capitalists. Each of these worlds was fragile and vulnerable. Lives were at stake all the time. Even as representatives of opposing visions tried to silence each other, they also found opportunities for collaboration and mutual exploitation. Serious diplomacy, strategic concessions in the interests of other worlds, alternated with duplicitous betrayal and frontal assault. Transgressive interworld liaisons, involving temporary alliances among avowed enemies, enabled agents to advance their own visions even as they were losing support among constituencies at home.

Magic was in the air, masking relations of exploitation, hiding collaborations with the enemy, and generating the conditions for revolutionary surprises. Perhaps the strongest magic of all was contained in the messianic spirit as it played in the imaginations of indigenous activists. Rival worldly prophecies, each with its own events, figures of hope, and objects of desire, animated competing freedom dreams. People became captivated by the alluring promises of multiple worlds, claiming more than one as their own. Even the leaders who were actively creating worlds around them harbored visions with elements from foreign lands and dreamed their enemy's dreams. Without even being aware of it, political agents began to change sides.[2]

World One: Reform

Gus Dur, a nearly blind Islamic visionary who was still recovering from a major stroke, suddenly became president of Indonesia in October 1999 after a surprise electoral upset. After the last-minute resignation of B. J. Habibie, the protégé of Suharto who was up for reelection, Gus Dur won enough votes from parliamentarians in what was the first democratic transfer of presidential power in Indonesian history.[3] Days later Megawati Sukarnoputri, the daughter of Indonesia's first president, Sukarno, was elected by parliament as Gus Dur's vice president. Megawati had been expected to win the presidency, and by all accounts she was disappointed with her position as second in command. Close friends since childhood, and both important voices of political dissent under the thirty-two-year Suharto regime, Megawati and Gus Dur started their administration with a united program of reform.[4] Despite feelings of animosity that developed as they were both vying for the presidency, they had overlapping aspirations for Indonesia's future.

Even as hopes for genuine reform of the Indonesian government had largely been dashed by military violence in West Papua, elsewhere in Indonesia the messianic spirit of the reform movement remained strong. Gus Dur and Megawati, both possible figures of the Messiah, embodied expansive hopes of the nation. A neomodernist vision of liberal Islam and a strong belief in the power of electoral democracy fueled Gus Dur's program of reform. Before becoming president, Gus Dur headed the Nahdlatul Ulama (NU), Indonesia's largest Islamic organization, with an estimated thirty to forty million members.[5] Megawati had cut her teeth as a voice for reform while heading the Indonesian Democratic Party for Struggle (PDI-P). This was one of the few parties outside the Golkar banyan that tried to carve out an autonomous realm for political activity. Nostalgia for the heady days when anticolonial nationalism promised to remake the world—nostalgia for the presidency of her father—fueled Megawati's popularity. Nationalist dreams were reinvigorated with hope. The administration of Gus Dur and Megawati began to turn some of the expansive imaginings of the reform movement into concrete policies.

Syncretic freedom dreams emerging in West Papua found points of correspondence with the hybrid form of Islam practiced by Gus Dur, which fused Hindu and Buddhist elements to an amalgam of indigenous and animist beliefs.[6] Gus Dur "grew up in an enchanted universe in which the spiritual was as real as the material," in the words of his authorized biographer. "The spiritual was not confined to the life to come; it was also part of the here and now."[7] Gus Dur's theology provided a framework for wedding pragmatic strategies of collaboration to the promises contained in messianic visions. Upon taking office in October 1999, he began to capitalize on auspicious moments, generating historic events while still cultivating a sense of mystery about the wider field of possibility.

Dawn of the New Millennium, January 1, 2000

Every day the first rays of the rising sun hit West Papua before any other place in the Indonesian archipelago. Ushering in the dawn of the new millennium during a "working visit," Gus Dur, in one of his first bold moves as president, offered the West Papuan people new hopes.[8] Newspapers reported that the president came "to see the sunrise in the easternmost province at the turning of the year and the turning of the millennium."[9] The year 2000 was anticipated by societies throughout the world as an event that might usher in times of tribulation or an era of utopian bliss.[10] Scriptural promises about the millennium—one thousand years of peace and righteousness—seemed as if they were coming true. Many Christians around the world, including some West Papuans, hoped that Y2K would mark the Second Coming of Christ and the moment of rapture.[11] It seemed as if the time of merdeka was near. When the president arrived, a possible messiah himself, an estimated twenty thousand people greeted him at the Sentani airport, waving the banned Morning Star flag and demanding independence.[12]

On New Year's Eve, Gus Dur ate dinner with West Papuan leaders at the governor's mansion in Jayapura.[13] At midnight, in a lively speech, he announced that he would change the official name of the province from Irian

The Morning Star flag was outlawed until Indonesian President Gus Dur announced, in June 2000, that it could be flown as a cultural symbol. *Photograph by Eben Kirksey.*

Jaya to Papua.[14] The next day, he issued a statement that firmly rejected demands for an independence referendum. Activists, who persisted in calling their unrecognized nation West Papua, had not found in the new president a messiah who would help them usher in a new era of independence. Gus Dur was reclaiming a different sort of messianic promise at the start of the new millennium. He was attempting to reclaim the hope of democracy and postcolonial nationalism at a moment when such projects were failing all around the world.[15]

In the coming months, the president made key symbolic concessions. In June 2000 his administration announced that flying the Morning Star flag would no longer be considered a treasonous act.[16] He also initiated a number of programs to enlist West Papuans in a reinvigorated Indonesian nationalist project. In his state of the nation address in August 2000, he announced that a broad special autonomy package was being drawn up for West Papua.[17]

As Gus Dur instituted a sweeping program of reform throughout Indonesia, many political enemies emerged, including members of the recently ousted regime. From his point of view, two powerful worlds were opposing him. One group, elite businessmen and politicians, wanted to halt trials about Suharto-era corruption cases. The other group, rogue elements in the military, was intent on causing unrest in far-flung provinces to undermine the credibility of his government.[18] Indonesian military agents deployed to outlying parts of the Indonesian archipelago—Maluku, Poso, Kalimantan, West Papua—where they incited violent conflicts. A conservative backlash swept Indonesia during the early months of Gus Dur's presidency as popular support for the military spread among Indonesian citizens who were concerned that their country would start to break apart after the "loss" of East Timor.[19]

In Aceh, another Indonesian province with a strong independence movement, Indonesian security forces intensified a campaign of violence in 1998 and 1999. Human rights abuses in Aceh were widely reported in the media, including stories about sadistic sexual violence and the presence of mass graves.[20] Carefully following these news reports, West Papua's indigenous leaders began to lay plans for preventing the spread of state violence to their own homeland. "We popularized the idea that West Papua should become a Zone of Peace, rather than a Military Operations Zone," said Dr. Benny Giay, who later enlisted me in this initiative.[21] While I was conducting research for my doctoral dissertation, he encouraged me to volunteer my time at Elsham, a human rights organization, and to help document state violence.

Working at Elsham alongside dozens of young West Papuan volunteers, I watched as the Zone of Peace campaign began to unfold in urban areas. As I saw pictures of dismembered corpses and wrote a seemingly endless series of reports about killings, beatings, and torture for Elsham, I began to develop a visceral understanding of some of the key grievances driving West Papua's independence movement. Still, this human rights work was squarely in line with Gus Dur's visions of reform—visions of reining in the security forces and developing an inclusive Indonesian national project.

As part of the Zone of Peace campaign, Elsham was meeting with West Papuan guerrilla fighters, encouraging them to lay down their weapons and continue their struggle through peaceful political channels. My West Papuan friends brought surprising reports back from these meetings—rumors of liaisons between guerrilla fighters and Indonesian intelligence agents, accounts of magical trickery, stories colored with mystery and intrigue.

The headquarters of Elsham Papua (the Institute for Human Rights Study and Advocacy) in the Padang Bulan neighborhood of Abepura. Two of these Elsham activists appear in this book: Denny Yomaki (white shirt, top right) and Daniel Randongkir (third from right). *Photograph courtesy of Elsham.*

Growing weary of writing human rights reports and finding my anthropological imagination captured by these tales from the hinterlands, I set out to meet the guerrillas myself.

World Two: West Papuan Guerrilla Fighters

Possessing only a vague knowledge of the history of West Papua's armed resistance from books, I paid my first visit to a guerrilla leader, Brigadier General Thadius Yogi, a member of the Mee tribe, in April 2001. Securing a seat on one of the irregular flights to Enarotali on a turboprop plane operated by the Catholic Church, I was whisked out of the world of the reform movement. Leaving a realm dominated by the moral certainty of human rights, where things were clearly right or wrong, I found myself struggling to distinguish enemies from allies, historical facts from fictions.

After exchanging a series of notes through a courier, Yogi said that he wanted to meet me in the middle of the night at a house where I was staying as a guest. My host surprised me by agreeing to have Yogi visit. The house

Brigadier General Thadius
Yogi, commander of West
Papuan guerrilla fighters
for the Paniai Region.
Photograph by Eben Kirksey.

was less than two hundred yards away from an Indonesian army barracks.
A platoon of elite mobile brigade police was also stationed nearby. I knew
that Yogi's group was poorly armed, like all other guerrillas in West Papua.
From my friends at Elsham I knew that Yogi only had a pair of bolt-action
Mauser rifles—powerful, but outdated, weapons capable of killing from a
great distance. His men would be no match for professionally trained Indonesian troops armed with high end automatic weaponry. What would happen, I wondered, if Indonesian security forces suddenly caught wind of the
meeting?

It started raining shortly before we heard hushed voices outside. When
Yogi entered the room, he held his right arm horizontally across his chest,
saluted, and then extended his hand straight out toward me. He wore green
fatigues and five gold stars on his shoulders. Golden pins fixed to the breast
of his shirt, his shoulders, and hat were the national emblem of West Papua:
a crowned pigeon clutching arrows and a drum. A colorful patch on his left
shoulder depicted the same emblem. An English motto—One People, One

Downtown Enarotali.
Photograph by Eben Kirksey.

Soul—graced the patch. He also wore a metal tag bearing his full name: Thadius Jhony Kimema Yopari Magai Yogi. An oversized cowry shell necklace was draped over his chest, and his collar was ringed with the teeth of a marsupial called a cuscus. As I beheld his elaborate uniform, I moved to shake Yogi's hand. But he kept his fingers straight and did not engage with my grip.

Nearly twenty men filed in behind Yogi. Two carried the bolt-action Mauser rifles. Others in the entourage were armed with machetes as well as bows and arrows. After sitting down next to where my tape recorder was running, Yogi seized control of the encounter: "So before I proceed, and before we conduct an in-depth analysis, I will lead us in prayer first. There are lots of religions, so you can each follow along with your own prayers."

Yogi opened his prayer in a predictable way: "Lord God, Lord God in Heaven. Lord God, creator of all that fills the sky as well as that which dwells on earth . . . We want to have freedom and complete sovereignty like other nations that are free around the world." Then he painted a remarkable picture of the worldly and otherworldly order: "Lord God, please pass this prayer along to the higher rulers of humanity, to the UN, so that they begin to know about human rights soon. Before we conduct our analysis we ask for blessings in the name of your child, Jesus, Amen."

Elements of Yogi's freedom dreams—visions of national sovereignty, human rights, and divine intervention—originated in distant lands. His petition for divine intervention to the higher echelons (*atasan*) of human governance and to God himself might be seen as a parody of foreign ideals and the institutions that ostensibly promote them. Human rights, one of the freedom dreams appropriated from abroad, should be taught back to the United Nations, according to Yogi. He was reminding God that the UN had failed to guarantee West Papua's right to self-determination as en-shrined in the 1962 treaty brokered by the Kennedy administration.

After the prayer, without waiting for any prodding from me, Yogi launched into a monologue about the guerrilla struggle. His language re-mained formal. A methodical, if not somewhat tedious, account of Yogi's guerrilla activities unfolded as the night wore on. In contrast to Agus, who told me about the sins of Kennedy and the UN, Yogi proved savvy about the prevailing conventions of historical discourse.[22] He started his biographi-cal story in December 1976, when Yogi's group killed four West Papuan men who were campaigning in connection with an upcoming Indonesian na-tional election.[23] After this incident and the deaths of several Indonesian troops near Wamena, the Indonesian military launched Operation Elimi-nate (Operasi Kikis).[24] Hundreds, if not thousands, of West Papuan civil-ians were killed during this operation. Indonesian troops used daisy cut-ter bombs, mortars, and machine guns to fight Yogi and his compatriots.[25] "Initially we did not have any firearms, but later we stole a total of nine weapons from Indonesian soldiers," Yogi said. "We obtained seven rifles and two pistols."[26]

Yogi is one among many regional leaders of West Papua's Tentara Pem-bebasan Nasional (TPN), or National Liberation Army, a polycentric group without a clear hierarchical command structure founded in 1971. The TPN has a relatively restricted membership, in contrast to the OPM (Organi-sasi Papua Merdeka), a widely popular underground organization that, by some estimates, includes all West Papuans and even foreign sympathizers. Today estimates of the number of TPN troops vary wildly; some report that there are fewer than one hundred fighters, while other observers claim that fighters number in the thousands. All sources agree that the weaponry of West Papuan guerrillas is extremely limited and largely outdated.

After concluding my initial interview with Thadius Yogi—after hearing about his epic exploits with the TPN in the 1980s and 1990s—I remained confused about how our encounter had been able to take place less than two hundred yards from an Indonesian military barracks. Yogi talked so much that I was not able to get a question in edgewise. One of his officers, Colonel "Theo Madi," Yogi's bearded and bespectacled intelligence chief, came back to chat with me the next day. Colonel Madi had grown up in the Mee highlands and had earned a master's degree in theology from one of West Papua's leading institutions. When I asked Colonel Madi about Yogi's uncanny ability to avoid detection by the military, he reminded me of the steady rain that began to fall just before Yogi's arrival: "He is nature [alam], he is the clouds, he is the rain. . . . He is here now, but who knows about tomorrow. We look over there and he is gone."[27]

Colonel Madi was offering me glimpses of a magical realm, a universe where carefully planned supernatural maneuvers enabled revolutionary activity right in front of occupying soldiers. As Indonesian troops dominated material reality, Papuans fought for dominance in the world of *alam*, the realm of the supernatural. *Alam* has three distinct meanings in standard Indonesian dictionaries: (1) a world or realm, (2) environment, and (3) knowledge.[28] In the creole slang of Logat Papua, *alam* means nature and supernature. People with knowledge of alam can make startling things happen—from minor weather events to floods, earthquakes, and volcanic eruptions. The rainstorm that began just before General Yogi paid me a visit was evidence, at least in the eyes of Colonel Madi and other followers, of his command over alam.

The idea of alam has broad currency in West Papua.[29] Lively tales about animal tricksters, about shamans and other shape-shifting beings, are staples of religion in New Guinea.[30] In the creole mixtures of West Papuan culture, alam maps onto elements from a diversity of cosmological systems. Beliefs about nature and supernature form part of the ideological fabric that holds the more than 263 West Papuan indigenous groups together in the struggle for merdeka from Indonesia. Faith in superior supernatural powers has arguably inspired underequipped TPN soldiers to fight against seemingly impossible odds. In other words, a collective imagination holds the social world of West Papuan guerrilla fighters together and inspires collaborative action.

The powers of General Thadius Yogi in the domain of alam are rooted in the specifics of Mee mythology. "During times of acute danger, a snake appears and leads Yogi to safety," said Colonel Madi. "The snake's head points to the route of safety while the snake's tail points to the attackers. Yogi simply follows the snake out of dangerous situations."[31] This familiar spirit helped Thadius Yogi because of a long genealogical relationship—members of his clan trace their origins to a monstrous snake.[32] General Yogi's powers were reportedly not just limited to the domain of his clan. "When Indonesian troops come across one of Yogi's freshly vacated campsites," according to Colonel Madi, "it looks like it has been abandoned for months. Grass quickly grows in the fire pit, and tall weeds cover the ground."[33]

General Yogi uses his magic to keep hopes alive for Colonel Madi and many other TPN troops. Farther afield, beyond the guerrilla camps, rumors of the supernatural powers wielded by Yogi and other TPN leaders fueled the quiet proliferation of dreams about merdeka among civilians.[34] As surprising collaborative relationships developed across lines that usually separated enemy from ally, magic came to have a new function in the movement. Supernature, alam, enabled Yogi to overcome some of the contradictions involved in leading a lightly armed revolutionary movement under the noses of a well-equipped occupying force.[35]

Megawati Meets Yogi, May 2000

On May 20, 2000, about a year before my interview with Thadius Yogi, thousands of the Mee people greeted vice president Megawati Sukarnoputri when she visited Enarotali. Megawati was on tour in West Papua to assess the political situation firsthand. Running counterclockwise around her helicopter in a raucous dance, the Mee waved Morning Star flags while shouting a singsong chorus.[36] In front of the crowd stood over fifty barefoot men armed with bows and arrows—Yogi's TPN guerrillas.

Yogi's men wore elaborate uniforms: red or green berets, camouflaged T-shirts with West Papua's national seal stenciled on the front, matching camouflaged shorts, and red shoulder boards indicating their rank. Other members of the crowd were wearing grass skirts and penis sheaths. When Megawati stepped onto the tarmac, the TPN guerrillas presented her with two signs that read "The Papuan peoples ask for freedom" and "Today, May 20, 2000, in the name of all people in the land of West Papua, from the heart of the Morning Star Mountains, we ask for freedom and full sovereignty." Indonesian military troops and several platoons of Brimob (mobile brigade) police lined the airfield as an uncanny performance unfolded.

A view from Enarotali, over Lake Paniai and toward General Yogi's hideout in the hills beyond. *Photograph by Eben Kirksey.*

When I asked Yogi about Megawati's visit, he presented the encounter as a rare opportunity to voice his aspirations: "I simply wanted to present the contents of my own heart, the desire of the people of West Papua." However, he was not afforded the opportunity to directly speak with Megawati. "As I turned to face the vice president," Yogi said, "she saw me and immediately paled. Yeah, she was scared. She pissed herself; she pissed in her pants. And then she ran off. So I didn't get to deliver my message."[37] Megawati was on a stage during this incident, and all the Mee people I interviewed agreed that she lost control of her bodily functions when she saw General Yogi and his TPN troops. Scrambling back up into the helicopter, Megawati canceled her scheduled speech. Her helicopter was reportedly airborne within minutes.

Thadius Yogi scored a clear victory in the eyes of his followers by publicly humiliating a member of the Indonesian elite. Imaginative speculation about how Yogi gained power over Megawati proliferated among his followers. Megawati had real reason to be afraid during her stop in Enarotali, according to Colonel Madi, the Intelligence Chief. "She was visiting the heart of Morning Star Mountains, the heart of the land of merdeka," he told me. Although Indonesian troops with advanced weaponry were keeping a watchful eye over the encounter, Yogi reportedly used his control of alam to gain the upper hand.[38] Despite the imaginative allure of Mee magic, I had a sneaking suspicion that something else was going on.

World Three: Indonesian Security Forces

The encounter between General Yogi and Megawati was staged by Indonesian military agents as part of an elaborate power play. In the months leading up to Megawati's stopover on May 20, 2000, a series of helicopters landed near Yogi's camp. The flight path of these helicopters was clearly seen by many Mee people, who later shared their observations with me. Colonel Armentony, who was then the head of Indonesian Military Intelligence for West Papua, arrived in the first helicopter. A West Papuan guerrilla fighter named Hans Bomai, as well as three other Indonesian intelligence agents, accompanied Armentony. They brought Yogi's troops gifts of rice, coffee, tobacco, sugar, ramen noodles, and condensed milk.[39]

Many of my sources reported that some of the elaborate accouterments enhancing Yogi's performances as a West Papuan "freedom fighter" were entangled objects—gifts from the Indonesian military. The elaborate uniforms of the troops and the colorful signboards displayed to Megawati were reportedly given to Yogi by Colonel Armentony.[40] When I visited Yogi's camp, I found that the seam of his personal uniform was embossed with "TNI-AD," the abbreviation for the Indonesian army.[41] Indonesian military agents were using these artifacts to play up the military threat presented by TPN guerrillas in a staged performance for Megawati.

While the vice president toured the highlands, a group of West Papuan guerrillas was preparing to travel to Jakarta. This trip was facilitated by Major General Albert Inkiriwang, a regional commander of the Indonesian military, who was accompanying Megawati during her encounter with Yogi's men. In a classified letter—intercepted and given to me by human rights activists—Inkiriwang budgeted a total of $73,155 for the trip, as part of Operation Illumination 2000. A line item of this budget requested $750 to enlist Thadius Yogi's participation in the journey.[42] In addition to giving the West Papuan freedom fighters free accommodation, food, and transportation, Inkiriwang proposed that they be provided with safari jumpsuits, batik shirts, shoes, underwear, socks, towels, and miscellaneous souvenirs.[43]

Why would Inkiriwang stage elaborate performances with odd costumes? In short, his motives were money and influence. The presidency of Gus Dur

General Yogi's troops in formation at his hideout. *Photograph by Eben Kirksey.*

threatened to undermine the freedoms enjoyed by the military under Suharto.[44] In previous years, much of the army's budget—as much as 70 to 75
percent, according to credible reports—came from running golf courses,
logging operations, and banks, as well as from contracts to protect foreign
companies, prostitution rings, and nightclubs.[45] These sources of income
were being scrutinized by reform-era politicians who wanted to bring security forces squarely under civilian budgetary control. Furthermore, Gus
Dur was laying plans to eliminate the army's territorial command, a sort of
shadow power structure to the civilian administration.[46] Many army officers, including Major General Inkiriwang and Colonel Armentony, were
seriously invested in preserving the status quo.

Operation Illumination 2000 was contributing to a growing rift between
President Gus Dur and Vice President Megawati over the issue of West
Papua.[47] The president had supported the 2000 Papuan Congress—the historic event led by Theys Eluay that gathered some twenty-five thousand
people together around the rallying cry of *Merdeka!* Megawati saw this as
treasonous. Her father, President Sukarno, had led the charge to "destroy
the puppet state of West Papua" decades earlier. On May 29, 2000, the
opening day of the Papuan Congress, Major General Inkiriwang delivered
a delegation of over forty West Papuan guerrilla fighters to meet with Gus
Dur and Megawati in Jakarta. The delegation, who asked for freedom and

Colonel Armentony (center), of the Indonesian military, meets with General Yogi (second from right). *Photograph courtesy of Elsham.*

peace, brought existing tensions within the Presidential Palace to a head.[48] In the coming months, the vice president became increasingly unsupportive of Gus Dur's attempts at reconciliation with West Papua's leadership.[49] By October 2000, Megawati had joined outspoken critics of the president in calling for a "military solution" to West Papua's problems.[50]

As Indonesian generals and civilian officials jockeyed for position in distant centers of power, rumors spread about foreigners who were foretelling a coming era of prosperity. Sporadic news reports and rumors began circulating about a "megaproject"—a massive natural gas development scheme. Dreams of wealth began to proliferate among the different worlds at war in West Papua. With elusive promises of riches, agents of capitalism worked to capture the imagination of Indonesian government officials, key figures in West Papua's movement for merdeka, and members of the security forces.

World Four: Global Capital

Tales about vast subterranean gas fields under West Papua's western tip had been proliferating since 1996, when the American company ARCO began exploratory drilling in Bintuni Bay. Babies began mysteriously dying in Weriagar, a remote village perched above the gas deposit, during this drilling. All the infants in Weriagar, forty-eight children in all, had died by the time the survey team left.[51] Company reports dismissed claims by villagers, saying that links between infant mortality and exploratory activities were unsubstantiated. Their studies did substantiate claims that the gas field under Weriagar was enormous by any standard, with over twenty trillion cubic feet of proven, probable, and possible reserves.[52]

When BP took over ARCO in 1999, acquiring rights to this gas field and other assets around the world, they named their project to exploit it "Tangguh," meaning strong, hard to defeat, or unstoppable in Indonesian. They claimed that the project would generate more than $198 billion (£100 billion) in revenue.[53] Promising to do business differently, promising not to repeat past mistakes made by other corporations, the leaders of BP pointed to a new and prosperous era for West Papua. A global marketing campaign painted BP as a distinctive company, no longer just working with oil, a twentieth-century resource.

Amid a war among worlds, corporate visionaries attracted new followers with dazzling dreams. These speculative imaginings in West Papua were like other fictions of capitalism emerging at this time in different parts of the globe. Michael Fortun, an anthropologist who has studied biotechnology corporations in Iceland, found that corporate futures were being shaped by fantastic promises: "Just as there can be no truth without fiction, just as every operation of language is essentially promissory and thus 'unfounded' in the classical sense, there can be no science without speculation, there can be no economy without hype, there can be no 'now' without a contingent, promised, spectral, and speculated future."[54] Perhaps speculation, fantasy, and fabulation are part of all future-oriented projects.[55] But the promises made by BP were particularly spectral—ghostly, unsubstantial, unreal, difficult to pin down.

"We aim for a radical openness," claims one BP brochure printed in 2002, "a new approach from a new company: transparent, questioning, flexible, restless, and inclusive." As BP began to expand its investments in solar, wind, biofuel, and natural gas, the company structured new promises around messianic dreams—promises pinned to elusive figures of riches hidden underground, in the sun, and in the air. Executives prophesied growth in the wealth of their shareholders, as well as benefits for many different "stakeholders." With the Tangguh project, BP promised to improve the livelihoods of villagers in Bintuni Bay, bringing development funds to West Papua and tax revenue to Indonesia.[56]

BP's Tangguh base camp in Bintuni Bay, 2002. *Photograph by John Walton.*

Seen from Bintuni Bay, BP's new project lacked luster. KBR, a former Halliburton company that attracted congressional scrutiny for fraud in Iraq, was subcontracted to build two offshore drilling platforms in Bintuni Bay. More than 650 people were pushed out of their homes. Local corporate operatives made grand promises, shot through with messianic dreams of modernity, to these displaced villagers. Company agents pledged to build brand-new houses, create educational opportunities, facilitate the flow of development aid, and even offer some jobs. Villagers found themselves caught within paralytic messianic desires. They were stuck waiting for outsiders to fulfill elusive prophecies.

Public relations firms meanwhile launched a media and lobbying campaign in the United States to promote liquid natural gas (LNG), a supercooled petroleum product that would be shipped from West Papua to resource-hungry parts of the globe. According to lngfacts.org, a website representing a consortium of petroleum corporations, LNG is a cleaner fossil fuel: "The United States will need to rely on natural gas that is brought in from overseas. . . . LNG helps the nation meet its very real and pressing need for new, clean energy supplies now."[57] Promising energy security, stable prices, and a "greener energy future," industry representatives tried to recruit the imaginations of new supporters.

Claims that LNG is a "greener" and "cleaner" energy source ring hollow when they bump up against the technical specifics of BP's Tangguh project. About 12.5 percent of the gas under Bintuni Bay is carbon dioxide. The process of capturing this greenhouse gas is costly, so BP plans to release some 4.7 million tons of CO_2 directly into the earth's atmosphere every year.[58] By way of comparison, after years of hard-fought negotiations, by January 2010 global leaders had agreed to reduce global carbon emissions by only 300 million tons per year with the cap-and-trade system.[59] "Imported LNG from West Papua will carry a greenhouse gas burden that is approximately 25 percent greater than domestic natural gas," according to Bill Powers, of the Border Power Plant Working Group in San Diego.

Fictions and spectral promises proliferated when investors, rights groups, journalists, environmental organizations, policymakers, and other stakeholders attended a series of meetings in 2002 where BP executives presented their vision of the Tangguh project.[60] I was invited to one such workshop near central London in an inconspicuous office space on Wenlock Road, a dead-end street with residential units, warehouses, and a shipping facility. Similar meetings were taking place in the United States and Germany. Lunch would be served, as would cocktails and canapés at the end of the day.

David Rice, a senior executive with BP's Policy Unit, began the workshop by asking that we keep our discussions off the record. He invoked the Chatham House Rule, a protocol for meetings where information is exchanged on the condition of anonymity. Ultimately there are no sanctions for those who break the rule. It is only a sense of "morality" that binds participants to this code.[61] As participants gathered at intimate round tables, I noticed that each table had an inconspicuous omnidirectional microphone. Privately questioning BP's morality for recording our conversations, I began taking my own copious notes.

I was surprised to see a presentation by Agus Rumansara, a West Papuan figure associated with the reform movement, on the day's agenda. Rumansara was previously director of the World Wide Fund for Nature (WWF) office in Jayapura and had recently been hired by BP as a vice president. Perhaps his imagination had been captured by BP's promissory language—to be "transparent, questioning, flexible, restless, and inclusive." At any rate, at this workshop, Rumansara made spectral promises of his own.

Rumansara's presentation was about BP's "community-based approach to security."[62] In essence, he outlined plans to avoid employing Indonesian security forces to protect company facilities. BP was training its own local West Papuan security guards, a militia of sorts. One of Ruman-sara's slides stated: Indonesian "security forces' role [will be] focused on regional growth centers—not directly present at the project location itself."[63] Rumansara seemed to be imagining a future world where Indonesia's security forces would be sidelined. He seemed to be leveraging capitalism to help accomplish goals of the reform movement and human rights organizations. Rumansara was indirectly pledging to help free West Papua from terror.

After lunch, the BP executives asked us to form small discussion groups to answer a series of questions: "Is BP doing enough?" "How do we progress?" "Should we go ahead with the project?" Joining friends of mine—Lucia Withers from Amnesty International and Carolyn Marr from Down to Earth—I sat down at a table with representatives of ethical investment firms. Skepticism dominated our discussion. BP's proposed "community-based approach to security" would effectively cut the Indonesian military out of a potentially very lucrative deal. At this time, much of the military's operating budget was still coming from protection contracts.[64] Failing to reach a deal with BP would be a major blow to the military. Other companies might follow suit. In short, we argued, BP was creating an atmosphere where the Indonesian security forces had strong incentives to stir up trouble.

In response to the question "Are we doing enough?," we argued that "BP can never do enough; it is not in a position to do enough." Indonesia has a strong military on which BP has limited influence. When it came to the question "Should we go ahead?," the group was split. I joined representatives from human rights organizations in saying no, while the "socially responsible" investors said yes.[65] The investors had been captured by BP's fantastic dreams. The Tangguh project was hanging in the balance. BP's chief executives had not yet committed to spending the necessary capital. "If there were something that would be damaging to the environment and to our reputation," one executive said, "the project would be stopped."

As BP made promises that were difficult to pin down and technically off the record in London, its executives were making surprising backroom deals in Jakarta and Jayapura. BP executives were quietly paying for the operating costs of Theys Eluay's Papuan Presidium Council, funding the travel and organizing expenses of this freedom fighter.[66] At the same time, BP was signing formal contracts with Indonesian officials. A secret "production sharing contract" between BP and the Republic of Indonesia detailed the joint government and corporate expenses for developing the gas project. An oil industry analyst suggested to me, off the record, that the contract likely contained a provision guaranteeing a return on Indonesia's investment in the gas project even if West Papua becomes a sovereign nation.

Wasior, June 13, 2001

An Indonesian logging foreman named Rusdy Boeng awoke to the sound of gunfire in the middle of the night of June 13, 2001. Peering around his door, Boeng spotted six men dressed in black and carrying assault rifles. At first Boeng mistook the men in black for Indonesian police officers — crack Brimob troops — who were his next-door neighbors. The Brimob officers served as guards at the timber company base camp in the remote region of Wasior where Boeng worked as a manager. As the men in black were about to head into the jungle, Boeng shouted: "Commander! Don't go running off and leave us here without any guards." One of the men turned around and replied: "Mr. Foreman, enjoy your work. Awom has entered the arena."[67] This stranger had a muscular body and was average height. He had long flowing hair that curled over his shoulders.[68]

Foreman Boeng did not recognize the muscular stranger or any of the other men in black. They all had light Indonesian, rather than dark West Papuan, complexions. After the six mysterious men left the scene, Boeng discovered that his Brimob neighbors had been murdered, their bodies mutilated, and their six automatic rifles stolen.[69] This murder was immediately pinned on Daniel Awom, who was characterized by Antara — the Indonesian National News Agency — as a "separatist gang chief."[70] Soon after Indonesian authorities arrived by motorboat to collect the bodies, a manhunt for Awom began. He had been spotted in the region just before the attack.

On the same night as this murder, John O'Reilly, a senior vice president of BP, was visiting the remote base camp of the company in Bintuni Bay. O'Reilly, one of the executives I had met in London, was traveling with the British ambassador to Indonesia. Rumors quickly spread linking the visit of these dignitaries to the attack in Wasior. Indonesian military agents staged these attacks, human rights activists alleged, in an extortion attempt. If this was indeed the motive, then it seems to have worked. The day after the attack, Ambassador Gozney held a press conference where he asked for a "security guarantee" from the Indonesian military to ensure that similar

The logging base camp in Wasior. *Photograph by Eben Kirksey.*

incidents would not jeopardize the future of the BP project. In the same press conference, he announced that the British government would release a "crash grant" program to help enhance the security in the region.[71]

In response to the murder of their comrades, the Indonesian police lashed out and launched a campaign that was aptly named Operation Sweep and Crush. An Amnesty International report found that "over 140 people were detained, tortured or otherwise ill-treated during the course of the operation. One person died in custody as a result of torture while at least seven people are believed to have been extrajudicially executed."[72] During Operation Sweep and Crush, fifty-five houses in Wasior were burned or otherwise destroyed by security forces.[73]

Wasior is an out-of-the-way place. A coastal town in the Bird's Neck region of West Papua, Wasior is about equidistant, a daylong boat ride, from the two nearest cities, Nabire and Manokwari. Wasior boasts a small market, government and mission schools, regional police and military barracks, and several hundred tin-roofed houses. Fishing, gathering forest products like bamboo shoots, and pounding flour from sago palms provide many Wasior residents with a stable subsistence base. When logging companies began operating in Wasior in the early 1990s, some locals began collaborating with the loggers for limited wages, while others began organizing in

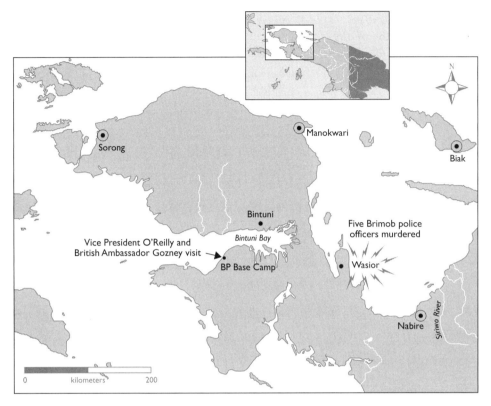

The Bird's Head. If New Guinea is shaped like a cassowary, then the mouth of the bird would be Bintuni Bay—the site of BP's Tangguh natural gas project. *Map by Damond Kyllo.*

opposition. The murdered Brimob police officers had been protecting the logging companies from the locals who opposed them.

Initial reports by human rights organizations suggested that the Brimob troops were killed as a result of a dispute between indigenous groups and the logging companies.[74] Daniel Awom, the "separatist gang chief," was reportedly helping local communities in their struggle against foreign companies. From afar I learned that Awom had ties to TPN guerrillas, but I also heard rumors linking him to Indonesian military agents. In April 1999 Indonesia's armed forces had been split in two: the police (POLRI) were given autonomy from the military (TNI).[75] The split pitted the police and the military against each other in bitter competition over scarce funds. Here, in Wasior, the security forces were reportedly at war with each other over lucrative contracts to protect logging companies.

Two years after the initial attacks, in April 2003, I visited Wasior to investigate the murky rumors surrounding Operation Sweep and Crush. I traveled and worked alongside Denny Yomaki, an old friend of mine who was secretary of Elsham, the human rights organization where I was volunteering. Denny, whose sizable belly was evidence of too much time spent pushing paperwork and attending meetings, was eager to return to the field.

It was technically forbidden for foreigners to visit Wasior at this time. After finagling a travel permit out of a high-level Indonesian official in Jakarta who had limited knowledge of West Papua's geography, we obtained a much-coveted seat on a weekly flight in a twenty-passenger Twin Otter prop plane. Denny and I were forced to work under difficult conditions. A known police informer trailed us for most of the trip. This informer, Yakobus Yoweni, made no pretense of being stealthy. When it became clear that our research in Wasior was to take place under conditions of intense surveillance, we only sought out interviews with survivors of recent assaults or family members of those killed. These people wanted to risk the chance of being seen with a foreign researcher to tell their stories. Denny and I used an elaborate protocol to protect the identity of our interviewees: we sent word to them through back channels and set up meetings in the houses of neighbors in the dark of night. We heard harrowing tales of dismembered bodies and undercover Indonesian military operations.

Daniel Awom had been killed in a firefight with Indonesian police by the time Denny and I visited in April 2003. Through a trusted intermediary, we contacted a group of local West Papuans who, according to the word on the street, had been Awom's accomplices in the 2001 murder. Huddled around a makeshift lantern—a Fanta can filled with kerosene and a wick—we chatted with four of these men, late at night, on the outskirts of town. Raucous cries of birds, cicadas, and crickets from the surrounding forest mixed with Bob Marley songs from a battery-powered boombox as we chatted in near total darkness. As Denny and I questioned the assembled men about their military ties, things suddenly became more complicated than I had bargained for. When I asked about the true identity of the muscular stranger with flowing hair, the man spotted at the crime scene just after the attack, I received a befuddling response:

"Was this man an Indonesian military intelligence agent, or was he working for Daniel Awom?" I asked.

"He was working for Daniel Awom," said one of the men. "Daniel had friends who were also members of the military here. That night, before Awom arrived on the scene, these friends had already entered the police post."

"Were they ethnic West Papuans or Indonesians?" I pressed.

Rejecting the terms of my question, a local activist replied: "No. They had to disguise themselves."

"This is supernatural stuff we are talking about," interjected Denny, amid tension-relieving laughter.

"These disguised beings entered the post first, and then Daniel came later. They disguised themselves as humans in an Indonesian form so that the cops would think that they were their friends. When Daniel Awom attacked, he was invisible. The vision of the police had been clouded."

"In other words," the activist clarified, "West Papuans also have strong command of nature [alam]."

Temporarily suspending my suspicions about Daniel Awom and the rumors linking him to Indonesian agents, I worked to unravel stories about how the revolutionary struggle worked through alam—natural and supernatural power. Ritual specialists from Wasior had reportedly convinced alam spirits to work with Awom.[76] The activists huddled around the boom box told me that Awom had links with a spectral special-ops force of the West Papuan revolutionary army: the Nature Commandos (Komando Alam). Taking on the form of Indonesian humans—friends of the Brimob police officers—the Nature Commandos reportedly entered the Brimob post before dark. They were dressed in black. The policemen were pleased to have their friends drop by unexpectedly. After dinner the visitors were invited to spend the night.[77]

Daniel Awom, who originates from the western part of Numfor Island, also employed sorcery from the traditions of his own people to facilitate the attack.[78] He used magic so that the Brimob policemen would fall fast asleep and have difficulties waking.[79] The foreman, who was at the scene of the crime, said: "In the early evening before the attack, all of the Brimob policemen went to bed at the unusually early hour of six o'clock. The policemen were 'dead asleep' when the shooting began."[80]

When the Brimob men were suddenly overcome with extreme sleepiness, their guests—the Nature Commandos in the guise of Indonesian humans—stayed awake with the one member of the platoon who was assigned to guard duty. At three o'clock in the morning, as Daniel Awom approached the post, the Nature Commandos quietly dispatched the guard.[81] Daniel Awom and "Barnabas Mawen," a man who I later interviewed, burst

through the door to kill the remaining four men. Before the Brimob policemen could stir from their beds, Awom sprayed the room with bursts from
his assault rifle. Barnabas Mawen fell on the prone victims with a knife.[82]
By the time the authorities arrived the next day, the bodies of the police
officers had been grotesquely mutilated.

The men we interviewed that night, the accomplices of Daniel Awom and
Barnabas Mawen, believed that the powers of alam let them overcome the
elite Brimob police officers. They were convinced that their erstwhile leader
had been a true freedom fighter, a revolutionary hero in the cause for independence. But these men were regarded with deep feelings of ambiguity by
different groups in Wasior. People who were loyal supporters of the Indonesian state regarded them as criminals, some fellow enthusiasts in the
merdeka movement regarded them as genuine revolutionaries, and still
other West Papuan activists saw these men as traitors who were conducting covert operations at the behest of the Indonesian military.[83]

"Theo Marey," a bearded man who had spent his youth in the city, had a
cynical and sinister interpretation of recent events. "Everyone in Wasior
knows that Daniel Awom's group of 'freedom fighters' had close ties with
the Indonesian military," he told us. "Disguised government agents killed
those police officers and then cut up their bodies for black magic rituals."
When health workers from the local clinic collected the bodies of the murdered police troops, Theo Marey had an opportunity to see them. "A few
tendons and the windpipe held the head to one of the bodies," Theo said. "It
flopped all around in unnatural positions. Another body had flesh missing
from the limbs, and the arm of another one had been shredded." Theo be-
lieves that the "friends" of the Brimob police, who lulled them into a false
sense of security before Daniel Awom's attack, were not Nature Commandos. This activist thinks that they actually were agents from an elite Indonesian military division called Kopassus.[84]

Kopassus is the notorious special forces of the Indonesian military. This is
the unit of the military that implemented Operation Illumination 2000, the
initiative to contact West Papuan guerrillas and introduce them to elected
officials. Kopassus "was established to specialize in covert domestic operations, against internal political dissenters as well as separatist movements,"
according to Damien Kingsbury, a political scientist who has published extensively on the Indonesian military. "Its methods are by definition both
political and extrajudicial." Active Kopassus agents or retired officers have
been identified as likely suspects in assassinations, bombings, and kidnap-

Mobile Brigade (Brimob) paramilitary police forces are often used in crowd control and other operations where raw power is needed (left). Kopassus soldiers, from the special forces division of the Indonesian military, specialize in covert operations. Often they conduct their operations in civilian clothes. An ice cream pushcart salesman—dressed in a white T-shirt, cheap plastic sandals, and a hat—stationed himself outside a house where I was staying. My West Papuan associates suspected that the salesman was an undercover Kopassus agent. One of my friends bought an ice cream cone to give me a pretense for taking a picture (right). Firefights have erupted between Brimob and Kopassus officers over scarce resources. *Photographs by Eben Kirksey.*

pings.[85] These suspects are rarely brought before a court of law. Kopassus agents have participated in joint training exercises with U.S. Green Berets and other branches of the U.S. military, covering topics that have included demolitions, air assault, close-quarters combat, special reconnaissance, and advanced sniper techniques.[86]

One close observer of Kopassus, a foreign military expert, has described their "deep-seated belief in animism and mysticism." The officers reportedly rely on "quasi-mystical powers" for night work and tracking.[87] A West

Papuan human rights worker later told me: "Everyone knows that Kopassus conducts exercises at the graveyard. They use magic." These supernatural powers are a hybrid combination of different indigenous sorcery practices. "Every region has its magic knowledge—power that has a connection with alam," said the human rights worker. "You can kill with ghosts. Kopassus has studied the culture of West Papua for many years now."[88]

After returning from Wasior, I discovered an anthropology manual, an instruction booklet for training soldiers, in the library of Indonesia's regional military command in Jayapura. The book outlined methods for using local cultural beliefs in psychological operations and campaigns of terror. Accounts from West Papuan activists suggest that the effectiveness of Kopassus psy ops is tied to rumors of soldiers' actual prowess in navigating supernatural realms.[89] Instead of conducting disinterested research about West Papuan cosmology, the Indonesian special forces have themselves become new hybrid specters of terror. Fusing local sorcery practices with terrifying apparitions from global culture, Kopassus agents have taken on various guises: jihad warriors, ninjas, vampires, and genies.[90]

Listening to tales about Kopassus, I found that my own imagination was being captured with terrifying dreams. Michael Taussig, an anthropologist who studies the culture of terror in Colombia, writes that paramilitaries are "soldiers who are not really soldiers but more like ghosts flitting between the visible and the invisible, between the regular army and the criminal underworld."[91] Kopassus soldiers operate similarly, flitting about in spirit worlds and in criminal realms, spreading spectral rumors as they move. Dutifully recording stories about the magical powers of Kopassus and their covert operations, I initially became lost in a murky haze where it was difficult to distinguish fact from fantasy. Finding myself amid waking nightmares, I kept meticulous notes as lurid tales captured my morbid curiosity.[92]

As Indonesia's security forces moved to implement a military solution to the "problem" of West Papua, terrifying stories spread.[93] I struggled to distinguish West Papuan separatists from Indonesian nationalists, enemies from allies. In the face of complex entanglements, I was having difficulty sorting things out.[94] A profound uncertainty is generated "when existing networks of social knowledge are eroded by rumor, terror, or social movement," in the words of Arjun Appadurai, an anthropologist who has studied violence in an era of globalization. When extreme forms of social uncertainty come into play, "violence can create a macabre form of certainty and can become a brutal technique (or folk discovery-procedure) about 'them' and, therefore, about 'us.'"[95]

Wellem Korwam (front and center) and his colleagues at the health clinic.
Photograph courtesy of the Korwam family.

Theo Marey, the person who tipped me off about Kopassus black magic in Wasior, noted that another body had been mutilated in *exactly the same* pattern as the corpses of the police officers.[96] Marey brought out a nondescript photo album that was brown with gold trim—I was expecting pictures of smiling friends posing on the beach or of a college graduation. Inside were pictures of Wellem Korwam, a thirty-two-year-old health worker. Korwam's body had been cut into seven pieces and dumped into the sea. Grotesque images of his corpse startled me with a terrifying sense of certainty amid the haze of tales about brutal violence.

Korwam was just one of many people who were executed in Wasior as part of Operation Sweep and Crush. Ghastly pictures of his body had already begun to circulate within West Papua and in human rights networks abroad, illustrating and reproducing an atmosphere of terror. The first image shows a group of some twenty people—health workers, police officers, civil servants, and civilians—struggling to deal with a large plastic bag bulging with gas and floating in the water near a palm-fringed beach. People not associated with the government were prohibited by the police from watching while the body was retrieved from the ocean. The next photograph in the series was taken indoors. A man with plastic gloves is arranging the torso in a white coffin. It is a wide-angle shot, and one can see the white, black, and pink organs inside the torso.

The subsequent picture, which is too gruesome to reproduce here, is a jumble of seven different body parts: two legs, two arms, the head and torso, and two other pieces of the body's trunk. The mouth gapes open in a distorted yawn. Whitish-green eyes stare unfocused in different directions. The nose, arms, and ears are gone. The final photo is of the burial site. Cloths worn over some of the mourners' mouths and noses helped stifle the putrefying smell.

By almost all accounts, Wellem Korwam was disappeared, murdered, and dismembered by a Brimob paramilitary police unit.[97] On the night of his disappearance, September 6, 2001, Brimob personnel accompanied him as he left work at the health clinic. Later Korwam and the Brimob troops were seen drinking and smoking near the market and a pier close to where his body was later found. No witnesses to the actual murder have emerged, but credible sources place the Brimob officers at the crime scene.[98]

Despite strong evidence linking Brimob personnel to this crime, the pattern of mutilation of the body points to an even more spine-chilling plot, according to Theo Marey. Since Korwam was dismembered in exactly the same pattern as the Brimob police officers who were previously butchered, Marey suspected that some of the spirits summoned by Kopassus soldiers were loose and on a killing spree. "These Kopassus ghosts, these Nature Commandos [Komando Alam], are running wild," he said. "People who are active in the movement, people who harbor aspirations for merdeka, aren't safe anymore."

As terrifying stories about Kopassus sorcery began to spread, West Papuan freedom fighters ramped up their efforts to fight back in supernatural realms. Viktor Kaisiepo, a West Papuan leader living in exile in the Netherlands, told me: "Papuan guerrillas have enlisted humans for their cause, but every animal, plant, and stone is also a member of the movement. Indonesian troops are just as likely to be assaulted by the rain forest and its creatures as by the human army. Forest ghouls collaborate with wild creatures as the foot soldiers of the movement." When a Brimob police officer was killed in Sanoba village, the authorities announced that he had been shot by Daniel Awom's group.[99] But a young woman, whose father is a human rights investigator, told me that a shaman turned himself into a bee and stung the Brimob officer once, killing him instantly.[100]

Local retaliation such as the incident of the cop-killing bee pales in comparison to the broader campaign of war waged against Indonesia at this time by the shamans living in Wasior. Two thousand houses were damaged

Wellem Korwam's body.
*Photographs courtesy of
LP3BH, Siegfried Zöllner,
and the Korwam family.*

in West Java, according to Channel NewsAsia, when an earthquake measuring 5.9 on the Richter scale hit on June 28, 2001.[101] While visiting Wasior, I met a young man who claimed responsibility for causing this earthquake, as well as a series of floods and volcanic eruptions in Java. He was wreaking havoc in home villages of Indonesian troops who were perpetrating human rights abuses in Wasior. The young shaman also claimed to have downed a twin-prop plane, killing ten members of the Indonesian military elite command earlier the same year, on January 8, 2001.[102] Before the crash, he wrote down the names of the regional military brass on a piece of paper. The list was placed in the forest. All the people named on the list were on board the plane that crashed. There were no survivors.[103]

Endgames

Amid warfare among multiple worlds, as well as disturbances in the natural and supernatural realms, President Gus Dur found his world fragmenting. Dreams of reform, of a reinvigorated postcolonial nationalism, were being dashed. A sense of déjà vu from the final months of the Suharto regime hung over Indonesia as earthquakes and floods destroyed cities and violence raged throughout the archipelago. Certainly some of the disorder under the Gus Dur presidency was deliberately manufactured to derail his program of reform and oust him from office.[104] Operation Illumination was just one front of a wider war against the elite of Indonesia's reform movement. Military operatives were then instigating violence in Aceh, Poso, and many other parts of the archipelago. After Gus Dur's impeachment by parliament, Megawati Sukarnoputri assumed the presidency on July 23, 2001. Megawati, a longtime champion of reform, found that her own power depended on backing from the military.

The social world of the reform movement was fragile. With the fracture between Megawati and Gus Dur, many Indonesian advocates for reform began to wonder if they might lose their world.[105] In the early days of Megawati's administration, the Indonesian military began changing its approach to West Papua's merdeka movement. Cutting back covert support to guerrillas and elite leaders, the military began to undermine the struggle. Some of the same West Papuan freedom fighters who had been outfitted and promoted by Kopassus special forces soldiers became targets for assassination.

On September 11, 2001, as the world watched the Twin Towers of the

World Trade Center collapse, the body of Wellem Onde, a TPN guerrilla, was found floating in a river near the city of Merauke.[106] The corpse had been scalped and partially skinned. Family members were only able to identify the body based on the distinctive shape of his big toe.[107] Onde had been a close associate of Kopassus. He was part of the TPN delegation that traveled to the Presidential Palace the previous year as part of Operation Illumination. The local Catholic diocese reported that Wellem Onde had likely been murdered by Kopassus because he had become increasingly difficult to control.[108]

Sightings of vampires in the suburbs of Jayapura generated widespread panic in late 2001. *Cenderawasih Pos*, a daily regional newspaper that is a branch of a conservative national chain, published a series of articles in early November 2001 about "Mrs. Dracula." A popular character from traditional Indonesian theater, "Mrs. Dracula from abroad," has inspired horror and laughter among Javanese audiences since her debut in 1969.[109] Everyone wondered with morbid curiosity what the fresh newspaper reports might mean. An owner of a food stall in the Kota Raja neighborhood was the first to see the vampire. She told reporters that a pale-faced woman with large white fangs came into the food stall one night and sat down at a table. Rumors began circulating. Six Indonesian migrants were admitted to the hospital with bite marks on their necks. As the reports spread, everyone knew not to venture out after dark. Twelve people who were foolish enough to leave home alone at night were reported killed by the vampire.[110] *Cenderawasih Pos* reports signaled that strange and sinister plans were afoot.

Amid the Dracula scare, officers from Kopassus Unit X Tribuana, the command headquarters of special forces soldiers in West Papua, hosted a reception to commemorate an important victory in Indonesia's war for independence. Kopassus agents delivered personal invitations for a reception at their headquarters to three key leaders of the West Papuan Presidium Council: Theys Eluay, Thaha Alhamid, and Willy Mandowen. Of the three, only Eluay accepted the invitation. He arrived at the Kopassus compound, along with his driver Aristoteles Masoka, in the evening just as the celebration was beginning.[111]

Theys Eluay left the party at the Kopassus complex shortly after 10:00. The commander of Kopassus Unit X was seen escorting Eluay to his car. Two Kopassus officers, named Agus Suprianto and Achmad Zulfahmi, rode in the back seat, according to *Gatra* news magazine, and Eluay sat in the front

Willem Onde's body was found floating at this spot in the river amid pieces of wood, plastic debris, and other flotsam and jetsam. *Photograph by Eben Kirksey.*

next to his driver. Later that night, these two passengers killed Theys Eluay. On the morning after the Kopassus party, the car was found in a ditch by the side of the road. Eluay's body was sprawled across the front seat. His face was black, and his tongue protruded slightly from his mouth.[112] In April 2003, seven Kopassus officers, including Suprianto and Zulfahmi, were convicted of the murder.[113] The longest sentence was three years.[114] Newspapers hailed the convicted killers as Indonesian national heroes.

The murder of Theys Eluay did not spell the death of the merdeka movement. On November 17, 2001, seven days after he was murdered, some four thousand people walked in procession with his body as it traveled forty kilometers from Jayapura to its final resting place in Sentani, a suburb bordered by hills near an expansive lake.[115] A new hero's cemetery was created for Eluay near the airport, a main point of entry for regional travelers, so that all visitors would see the grave of the martyred West Papuan leader. Several of Eluay's longtime West Papuan critics penned glorious eulogies. Many who had been suspicious of Eluay because of his continued connections to the Indonesian old guard came to understand how his collaborations had resulted in important political victories.

During a military parade in December 2001, a month after Theys Eluay's execution, President Megawati gave a speech that declared: "You can do

Willem Onde's final resting spot. He was buried in an unmarked grave in Merauke's cemetery. *Photograph by Eben Kirksey.*

your duty without worrying about being involved in human rights abuses. Do everything without doubts."[116] This speech signaled an end to her efforts to place the military under civilian control. The work of human rights, previously a social world within the broader arena of reform, was being pushed into the shadows.[117] Civil society organizations—media outlets and nongovernmental organizations—carried the goals of reform forward by exposing cases of corruption and advocating for legal action. But Megawati's speech in December 2001 signaled that the reform movement had been pushed out of the Presidential Palace.

In the new climate of terror and military impunity, few were bold enough to air aspirations for merdeka in public. Subtle and pervasive signs of Kopassus psychological operations and covert actions also began to appear. The collective West Papuan revolutionary imagination was being displaced by apparitions of deadly vampires and forest ghouls feeding on human flesh. Freedom dreams were derailed by terrifying nightmares. As reports of covert collaborations and betrayals began to circulate, stories about free-

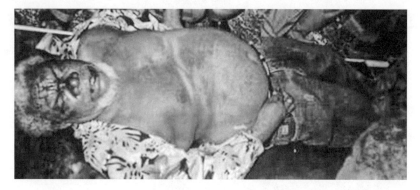

Theys Eluay was found strangled to death in his car, which had been abandoned in a roadside ditch. *Photograph courtesy of Elsham.*

dom fighters who failed to distinguish Kopassus enemy soldiers from allies, an atmosphere of suspicion and distrust began to spread. Political alliances became more difficult to forge and sustain.

The public manifestations of the figural banyan tree that Theys Eluay had helped to plant began to be absorbed into dominant Indonesian structures after his death. Eluay's organization, the West Papuan Presidium Council, persisted after his murder, although in the coming months no one was appointed to fill his position as chairman. Merdeka flourished underground. A polycentric structure began to thrive beyond the bounds of the Presidium's leaderless hierarchy. With Eluay gone, the struggle was no longer fixed on replicating the Golkar model of the nation. The movement began to slowly and quietly reconstitute itself. Like a rhizome that had been chopped up and left for dead, new hopes began to sprout from the heterogeneous fragments that remained. By the end of 2001, the movement for merdeka in West Papua entered a plateau. It was not clear what form it would take next, or what the nation might look like if it were to achieve independence. The people were searching for emergent figures that would generate the possibility of climax, of revolution.

CHAPTER FOUR

Don't Use Your Data as a Pillow

A small feast was laid out for my going-away party: salty sago pudding, fish broth, fried papaya leaves, boiled yams, and chicken. It was a modest affair, organized by Denny Yomaki, the human rights worker who traveled with me to Wasior, to mark the completion of fieldwork in May 2003. The event was scheduled to take place a few days before I returned to Oxford, where I would begin writing up my findings for a master's degree. I expected the party to be a rite of passage marking a smooth ending to my research in West Papua and a transition into a new network of obligations and duties. What actually awaited was a confrontation in Denny's living room that would question the very value of my study. Here, at my own going-away party, some of my basic research methods and guiding principles were about to meet a head-on challenge.

After Denny said a brief Christian prayer in formal Indonesian, giving thanks for our health and wishing me a safe journey, we heaped our plastic plates with food and sat on the floor of his living room to eat with spoons. Once the plates were cleared away, we moved out to the front porch to chew betel nut, a green palm-tree seed with a stringy pulp. When mixed with chalk powder and saliva, betel nut produces a sweet dark red juice that stains the mouth and produces a mild, relaxing buzz. We swapped jokes in Logat Papua, the regional slang. Propped up on my elbows and idly swatting at mosquitoes, I began chatting with Telys Waropen, a member of the National Human Rights Commission (Komnas HAM). Although we had not met before, Waropen had been invited to my party by Denny, the host. Waropen was a firebrand in his late twenties, around my own age at the time, whose government post had recently been created by Indonesia's reform movement.

Waropen originated from Wasior, where Denny and I had just been investigating the spectacular excesses of Operation Sweep and Crush. A mountain near Wasior is widely regarded as the supernatural heart of West Papua's independence movement. My ambitious research plans with Denny had also initially included plans to interview renowned shamans who lived on this mountain. Since our movements in Wasior were being closely watched, Denny and I did not risk venturing into the hills. At my going-away party, I learned that Telys Waropen had studied these shamans for his undergraduate thesis at Bird of Paradise University. As we chewed betel on Denny's front porch, I began to see Waropen as an important source who might help fill some gaps in my research.

I asked Waropen for an interview, explaining, in a well-rehearsed spiel, that I would keep his name anonymous, like the rest of my sources, to protect him from possible retribution by Indonesian security forces. Waropen recoiled. "What kind of research are you conducting," he asked, "where the identity of your sources doesn't matter? Wouldn't your data be stronger if you quoted credible sources?"[1] By the time of this party, I had conducted more than 350 Indonesian-language interviews with West Papuan politicians, survivors of violence, political prisoners, guerrilla fighters, human rights activists, and indigenous leaders. All the interviews were anonymous. As Waropen questioned the value of my research, a sinking feeling spread in my gut.

Anonymous sources are viewed with a sense of suspicion and mystery by readers of newspapers and magazines. Journalists and editors conventionally use a rigorous set of guidelines to determine when to grant someone anonymity.[2] These criteria guard against the fabrication of stories by unethical authors and the dispersal of misinformation by sources who gain the ear of reporters. Following the lead of well-known cultural anthropologists, I had approached my interviews with the idea that I might learn something even if my sources were anonymous or even deliberately lying. Most evidence about extreme violence comes in the form of stories. There are some things that are well known—about lived experiences of terror or the disappeared, for example—that cannot be spoken about in public or on the record. In short, rumor is a powerful knowledge form.

In the historical record and during anthropological interviews, it is not always possible to distinguish fact from fiction. Michael Taussig, who studied what he calls "the cultural construction of evil" in early twentieth-century century South America, suggests that we dismiss questions about the truth or falsity of spectacular reports about torture: "The meticulous historian would . . . winnow out truth from exaggeration or understatement. But the more basic implication, it seems to me, is that the narratives are in themselves evidence of the process whereby a culture of terror was created and sustained."[3] Much of my source material about violence— newspaper stories about vampires, e-mails, text messages, reports by indigenous groups, and gripping stories that were related to me in interviews—was, in this sense, helping generate widespread feelings of panic.

When Waropen confronted me about the reliability of my data, I tried to show him how insights from cultural criticism might offer fresh perspectives on the conflict in West Papua.[4] One route to merdeka, I reasoned, might be understanding how rumors produce fear. It became clear that Waropen saw a study of "the culture of terror" in Wasior as useless. West Papuan human rights workers were already playing the role of Taussig's meticulous historian. They were doing the hard work of verifying and cross-checking reports of violence to create strong forms of knowledge that might have currency in the domain of officialdom. He was already well aware that rumors help generate terror, but this insight was not helping him get traction in legal realms that required a different standard of evidence. He told me that he wanted to see members of the security forces prosecuted in Indonesian courts. Waropen saw me as a potential ally, but one who needed some serious reschooling.

I sat up as the conversation suddenly grew heated. At first I quibbled with Waropen about my anonymous sources: "Surely there are cases in human rights reporting where the identity of survivors and witnesses must be protected." After getting tired of arguing my case and justifying my research, I settled back on my elbows to listen. "Don't use your data as a pillow and go to sleep when you get back to America," Waropen insisted. "Don't just use this as a bridge to your own professional opportunities."

In part, Waropen was provoking me to become a reliable regional expert—someone who would know things with certainty and take questions of accountability seriously. Following Edward Said's critiques of Orientalist experts and Gayatri Spivak's characterization of liberal intellectuals who speak for subaltern subjects, many cultural anthropologists are understandably wary about using their research to speak to power.[5] Knowledge of the Other can be used to further colonial, imperial, or professional agendas. Regional experts often ignore demands for accountability from the people whom they study.

Perusing the latest edition of the *New York Times* reveals that most people who are fashioned as regional experts by the media—government representatives, economists, and political scientists—remain untroubled by postcolonial critiques of knowledge production. The knowledges and concerns of people who occupy structurally marginalized positions continue to be underrepresented in the public press.

Waropen asked me to rethink what counted as data in cultural anthropology. He was prompting me to be a better, more authoritative translator.[6] Along related lines, Charles Hale has recently urged anthropologists to take empiricism more seriously in activist research: "To state it bluntly, anthropologists, geographers, and lawyers who have only cultural critique to offer will often disappoint the people with whom they are aligned."[7] Waropen was challenging me to know about things that mattered and to know them well. This confrontation forced me to consider how underrepresented forms of knowledge might be translated into legible narratives that could travel abroad.

By the time I met Waropen, I had already published a number of newspaper articles about West Papua. For the *Guardian* of London, I wrote an experimental piece that explored how resistance to logging schemes and military troops was being inspired by alam—nature and supernature.[8] Was this the right kind of data to be sharing with wider audiences? Waropen was prompting me to stick to the facts, more narrowly construed. He was also demanding that I take concrete action. Our conversation led me to think about how I might begin to do more than just write words—how I might begin to bring my knowledge about West Papua to the seats of global power.[9]

After talking with Telys Waropen, I returned to the guest house where I was staying. There I placed an international call to John Rumbiak, the supervisor of Elsham, who was then traveling in New York City. John encouraged me to use my remaining few days in West Papua to pursue all remaining leads and get to the bottom of Indonesian military covert operations in Wasior. He asked me to determine the credibility of rumors linking Kopassus military agents to Daniel Awom, the guerrilla leader who murdered the Brimob police officers in Wasior on June 13, 2001. Was this killing, which coincided with the visit of BP executives and the British ambassador, an extortion attempt? With only forty-eight hours remaining in my trip, John encouraged me to interview "Barnabas Mawen"—a known associate of Daniel Awom.

After I tracked Mawen down, he admitted to murder, sparing none of the lurid details, while my tape-recorder was rolling: "Awom took up a position at the door with his gun while I slipped in the room holding my knife. I jumped on the cop closest to the door, slashing out his throat before he knew what was going on." Short, with a distinctive mane of frizzy hair, Mawen was visibly nervous. He was in hiding. "The military want to kill me because I know too much," he said. "Every morning I leave home before dawn. I spend my days fishing at a remote river and only return home after dark." Mawen was looking to me for help in escaping his entangled relations with the military—help that I was neither able nor willing to provide.[10]

Mawen explained his relationships with active-duty Indonesian soldiers, saying that he had found friends on the inside, ethnic West Papuans who supported the cause for merdeka. These military friends had enabled him to fight the Indonesian police. Petrus Kaikatui, an ethnic West Papuan who was a soldier in the Kopassus special forces, gave Mawen money, food, medical supplies, and ammunition. Kaikatui was then stationed at the district military command in Manokwari, an urban center that has administrative control over Wasior. Mawen told me that two other active-duty Indonesian military agents also supplied him with bullets: Sembra Reba, who was stationed at the local military command in Wasior, and Adrian Worengge from the district military command in Manokwari.[11]

From other sources, who insisted I protect their anonymity, I learned that Daniel Awom sent out a pair of local scouts from Wasior in mid-March 2001 on a two-week journey to conduct reconnaissance at sites near the BP base camp for a potential attack. One of these scouts told me that on this trip, he and his partner found a Brimob platoon guarding a Djayanti Group timber concession in Bintuni Bay.[12] This Brimob platoon was stationed approximately fifteen kilometers as the crow flies from the BP base camp. When the two scouts returned with favorable news that would have enabled an attack near BP's base camp, they found that Daniel Awom had already initiated an operation against the timber company in Wasior.[13]

In the weeks leading up to the murder of the Brimob police officers on June 13, 2001, Barnabas Mawen brought a shipment of ammunition to Daniel Awom. Mawen confirmed what I had heard from other sources, that members of the Indonesian military provided him with these bullets.[14] Along with the bullets, Mawen delivered a letter to Awom from the regional Indonesian military command.[15] The letter reported on the movements of

Brimob police, giving them strategic intelligence that led them to plan the attack on June 13.[16]

Even as I was able to flesh out the story about Mawen's covert collaborations with the Indonesian military, many questions remained. Mawen showed me a tattoo on his calf, a pair of dice showing a five and a three. The die with the five had a dot for each of the Brimob police officers who were killed. The other die represented the three killers: Awom, Mawen himself, and one other person. I pushed him, asking several times, about the name of this third person, but Mawen refused to reveal the name of his friend. The identity of the third person was lost in an atmosphere of intense violence. Indonesian security forces were still torturing, dismembering, and disappearing people as part of Operation Sweep and Crush, and I, for one, was not going to risk another trip to Wasior.

After I returned to graduate school in England, an opportunity arose for me to serve as an expert-in-action, even as my mind was spinning with surprising findings. In late May 2003, John Rumbiak asked me to attend a meeting at the London headquarters of BP with Dr. Byron Grote, the company's chief financial officer—the CFO, second only to the CEO. Rumbiak had secured a meeting to talk about how BP's security policy was impacting the human rights climate in West Papua. Rumbiak asked me to join the meeting so that I could present my findings about the covert operations and militia violence in Wasior. Two weeks after Telys Waropen had demanded that I do more than "use my data as a pillow," I found myself about to enter the inner sanctum of corporate power. With a gentler hand than Waropen, Rumbiak was fashioning me into a reliable witness—an expert on West Papua who would be prepared to make strong claims to knowledge. John also encouraged me to study the very institutions of power that he was trying to influence.

Before the appointment at BP's headquarters, I met up with Rumbiak, a thin man who is always quick to smile, in a coffee shop in central London. Rumbiak radiated charisma. In his words I found messianic promises. An outspoken critic of the church, Rumbiak espoused secular freedom dreams. He firmly believed in the power of international law and the ethical principles of human rights, including the right to self-determination as outlined in the United Nations charter in 1945. A native son of Biak, the original home of the Itchy Old Man, Rumbiak was on an international quest to bring rights and justice within reach of his people.

Rumbiak saw BP as an enemy. In contrast to West Papuan independence leaders who were drawing on funds from BP to support their activities, Rumbiak was not trying to garner funds for his organization. Still, he was open to diplomacy. We did not explicitly talk about our goals before going into the meeting. The previous year at the Tangguh workshop, low-level executives had said: "If there were something that would be damaging to the environment or to our reputation, the project would be stopped." I wondered if my findings about Indonesian military covert operations in Wasior might be damaging to BP's reputation, potentially embarrassing enough for the leadership to bring the project to a halt.

Not wanting to spring for a taxi, Rumbiak and I got lost on the way to the meeting with BP. Walking around on foot, we swapped stories about our recent travels, code-switching from Indonesian to English. Rumbiak was on a jet-setting schedule that would put any anthropologist to shame.[17] I came to spend time with him in Oxford, Amsterdam, Utrecht, Frankfurt, Jakarta, Washington, Santa Cruz, San Francisco, and New York, as well as different sites in West Papua. His routes also included places I was never able to visit myself—Sydney, Canberra, Dublin, Ottawa, Alberta, Wellington, Geneva, and Manila. In London we were both disoriented visitors. After asking for directions from the guards at Saint James's Palace, the official residence of the Queen, we found the BP office. We arrived twenty minutes late.

Entering through the revolving glass doors of 1 Saint James Square, a squat brick building, we were met by a smartly dressed young woman. She checked our names on a computer terminal, issued us visitors' badges, and instructed us to wait on some plush couches for our escort. When the escort arrived, we filed one by one through a turnstile where we swiped our badges. Up an elevator, down a hallway, and we sat down in a cramped room with Byron Grote, the CFO, and John O'Reilly. O'Reilly was BP's senior vice president for Indonesia, who had been visiting the gas project site when the Brimob policemen were killed.[18] Both Grote and O'Reilly had previously worked for BP in Colombia, where the company became embroiled in controversy after paramilitary death squads began assassinating environmental activists.[19] Suddenly face-to-face with some of the most powerful men in Europe, I felt adrenaline rush through my veins.

Grote opened the meeting with a request that our conversations be off the record—that we treat the discussion as strictly confidential. Rumbiak immediately countered: "I'm sorry, that just is not possible. When I meet with you, the people of West Papua want to know what we talk about."[20] Rumbiak wasted no time. He immediately presented a clear message: the BP community-based security policy was inciting violence. "Covert agents in the Indonesian military are determined to provoke violence until you relent and give them a security contract," Rumbiak said. "Your policy will cut the military out of a lucrative deal, establishing a precedent that other companies in Indonesia might follow."

"Violence is bad for business," Grote responded. "Open societies are good, and they create an environment where business thrives. Working in West Papua is a huge challenge — one that we have to take. We are convinced that the community-based security policy will still work. If we cancel this project, then another company that doesn't share our code of ethics will step in and develop this gas field." Grote's language was seductive, inviting. I privately wondered if BP could become a force to help sideline the Indonesian military in West Papua.[21]

Rumbiak asked me to present my findings from Wasior. With my heart pounding, I tried to encapsulate a series of exceedingly complex events. Looking straight at O'Reilly, a man with thick round glasses who was deceptively timid looking, I recounted my interview with Barnabas Mawen, the man with the dice tattoo: "He claims to have killed a group of Indonesian policemen, with the assistance of Indonesian military agents, the day you were visiting the base camp," I said. "The Indonesian police later used this incident as a pretext for launching Operation Sweep and Crush. Both the police and the military want to be paid to protect your project."

O'Reilly challenged my credibility. Sitting forward, he asked: "Did the militia member who murdered the police officers explicitly say that the attack was planned to coincide with our visit?" I admitted that he did not. The Indonesian military agents had sent letters to the militia with instructions to launch the attack during the week of O'Reilly's visit. But these letters did not make explicit mention of the visiting dignitaries. During a fast-paced exchange with O'Reilly, I fumbled. I failed to make the complexity of the actors and the events legible.

My stories of double agents and unlikely collaborations — Indonesian military operatives and West Papuan guerrillas working together — suddenly sounded implausible, maybe even paranoid. Rumbiak tried to intervene by providing more context: "The Indonesian police and the military are often in fierce competition over resources. Firefights among different branches of the security forces are not uncommon." O'Reilly countered: "Wasior is 160 kilometers away from our project location. There are no roads or waterways linking the two sites. A mountain range and vast tracts of forest lie in between. We don't read what is happening in Wasior as a signal." Drawing on another one of my interviews, I fired back: "Wasior is a two-week walk from your site. Members of the same militia that murdered the police officers walked this distance in March 2001 to conduct reconnaissance near your base camp."

Grote was late for his next meeting. As we hastily concluded our conversation, Rumbiak made a specific request: "Use your influence with the Indonesian government to help make sure that the perpetrators of the violence in Wasior are prosecuted." O'Reilly responded: "We are not yet confident enough about the facts of this case to approach the Indonesian authorities."

Later Rumbiak urged me to go public with my findings from Wasior. In a short Indonesian-language e-mail, he wrote: "We have to get this story published in a major paper." After our meeting at the BP headquarters, we discovered that the corporation had, in secret, already reneged on its promises not to work with the Indonesian security forces. I cold-called and e-mailed a number of newspaper editors. After being turned down by a number of papers, I connected with an editor from the *Sunday Times*, one of Britain's largest newspapers.

Jack Grimston, then the assistant foreign editor of the paper, asked if I would coauthor an article with him. He traveled to Oxford by train. After poring over my maps, interview transcripts, and field notes, he telephoned a senior editor in London. After he hung up, Grimston told me, "The paper is still very interested in the story, but cannot yet fully commit to publishing it. They want to print the name of the militia member who helped kill the police officers." Grimston took a train to London while I mulled over the implications of going ahead with the story. Would "Barnabas Mawen" be killed if we printed his name? Should he be held accountable for murder? I tried calling John Rumbiak, who was back in New York City, to ask for advice. No answer. I made my own decision and called Grimston. "We can't name the militia source," I told him. "His life might be in danger."

Over the next three days, Grimston and I worked the phones, trying to confirm the details of BP's relationships to security forces. The final article shared the back page with a story featuring a grinning picture of James Bond actor Pierce Brosnan. "Barnabas Mawen" was only mentioned in passing:

> Britain's biggest company, BP, has angered human rights groups by becoming involved with Indonesia's brutal security forces in an attempt to protect a £28 billion gas production scheme. The company is using officers from the country's feared Mobile Police Brigade (Brimob)—which has been accused of nu-

merous human rights abuses—to guard explosives. . . . Some critics believe
the army may have already staged violent incidents as a pretext for intervention. One occurred in 2001, when five police officers were killed. . . . Barnabas
Mawen, a pseudonym for one of the group which killed the policemen, told
the *Sunday Times* that Indonesian military agents had supplied him with bullets, food, and money before the attack. BP said its security policy was designed to minimize the likelihood of military involvement.[22]

Grimston and I reduced the complexity of the actors and the events that
I had learned about during my fieldwork into a few legible paragraphs. By
working with West Papuan human rights activists and a British journalist,
I had helped to translate information gleaned from structurally marginalized sources into a genre of reportage that has currency in the halls of
global power. In a sense, I had helped transform what Donna Haraway, a
feminist theorist, calls "situated knowledges" into a "view from nowhere."
Situated knowledges are faithful accounts of a real world that are simultaneously based in a no-nonsense commitment to realism and bound by
radical historical contingency. This method of knowing contrasts with a disembodied form of vision that claims to see everything from nowhere.[23] In
the article that appeared in the *Sunday Times*, "I" appeared to leave my own
point of view behind and see the world from nowhere within it.[24] "I" became
the *Sunday Times*.

My translation work was, in part, compatible with Haraway's project:
she has challenged us to "translate knowledges among very different—
and power-differentiated—communities."[25] As my partialities and situated knowing all but disappeared behind my byline in the *Sunday Times*,
I wrestled with Haraway's ideas. Rather than critique the view from nowhere as an outsider, I made an effort to rescript it from within. In writing
this text, I blended in, for a moment, to the architecture of knowledge and
power to emerge later with unexpected insights.[26]

My passing, even if just for a moment, as an unmarked author with objective authority gave the issues currency and credibility in worlds where
West Papuans are largely excluded. An emergent coalition of West Papuan groups—students, environmentalists, and human rights advocates—
wanted to see the BP project stopped. My work was being drawn into this
coalition. For some West Papuans, the publication of this short article represented a victory.

Even as the disembodied subjectivity of the unseen "I" produced the
effect of reliability and credibility, it hid painstaking research and advocacy

by scores of West Papuan human rights workers. Ultimately, in this case, I was unable to respond to Telys Waropen's demand that I name my West Papuan sources. In the hours before the story went to press, the *Sunday Times* editors cut the only sentence that quoted a West Papuan source, John Rumbiak, by name.

Even as my emergence as an expert-in-action was warmly greeted by West Papuans who opposed the BP project, I drew criticism from West Papuans who saw BP as an ally in their struggle for merdeka. Several months after my story ran in the *Sunday Times*, I took part in a public conversation about BP with a member of the Papuan Presidium Council, the independence organization that had been receiving funds from the petroleum giant.[27] The BBC World radio program had scheduled an interview with me about BP's community-based security policy. In the hours before the interview, I learned that Viktor Kaisiepo, a West Papuan independence activist who had lived much of his life in exile in the Netherlands, would be appearing on the program as well. It was to be broadcast live.

At the BBC Radio studio in Oxford, a short bike ride from my apartment, local technicians fiddled with some faulty equipment while I chatted with a producer who was coordinating the program from London. Kaisiepo was sitting in a similar radio studio in the Netherlands. As the broadcast started, I quickly summarized the evidence about covert operations by Indonesian military agents near the BP project site. I also recounted how BP had reneged on its promises to not work with Indonesian security forces. Kaisiepo did not directly engage with my claims about BP's community-based security policy but stressed the importance that the project continue: "West Papuans as a people have the right to development."[28] He lambasted the international rights groups who wanted to see the BP project stopped. Met with this challenge, sitting alone in a dim studio thousands of miles from West Papua, I found it difficult to represent the views of indigenous activists who opposed the gas project. I ended the interview inconclusively as the BBC producers quickly moved on to pressing events in another corner of the world.

Confrontations often mark moments of failure in cross-cultural mediations. When anyone attempts to translate across linguistic boundaries or gulfs of cultural difference, partial success is almost always tempered by moments of misunderstanding. Overt challenges test the allegiances of translators and culture brokers. I had come to know Viktor Kaisiepo years earlier when I was just beginning my research on aspirations for freedom in West Papua. After the BBC radio program, he sent me a friendly e-mail in the West Papuan dialect of Indonesian. He addressed me as "Napi," which means "you/friend" in the Biak language: "I'm glad to see that Napi is taking up the issue of BP and these military shenanigans. How can the international community force the Army to return to their barracks and stop all of this provocation?"[29] Here Kaisiepo suggested how we might collaborate. While he clearly wanted the BP project to continue, he also wanted to stop the military violence. He was implicitly saying, "On this, at least on this issue of military impunity, we can work together." Practical alliances, like confrontations, can produce an awareness of the relations of power that underlie the transfer of knowledge across cultural domains.[30]

Many anthropologists have become advocates for the indigenous groups they study. Charles Hale, for example, has used rigorous forms of data collection, methods of causal analysis, and new computer-based cartographic programs to aid struggles for land rights in Latin America. Positivists have long viewed politics as an influence to be purged from disinterested research. Hale has called for a rethinking of approaches to "activist" anthropology. He urges anthropologists to "deploy positivist social science methods and subject them to rigorous critique while acknowledging with acceptance the cognitive dissonance that results."[31]

Other approaches to the politics of knowledge seek to avoid cognitive dissonance, an uncomfortable feeling that comes with believing in two contradictory ideas at the same time. Many feminists see all knowledge projects as political—maintaining that researchers are never free from the values and interests of particular social locations. In short, the social and political affiliations of researchers shape the types of questions that they ask. Sandra Harding, a feminist critic who writes about the politics of knowledge, suggests that it is "far too weak a strategy to maximize the objectivity of the results of research that empiricists desire."[32] She calls for a "strong objectivity" that requires scholars to "be integrated into democracy-advancing projects for scientific and epistemological reasons as well as moral and political ones."[33]

I was now working to produce a sort of strong objectivity, the situated no-nonsense knowing demanded by Telys Waropen, that might help him and other West Papuans leverage support from policymakers. I also resisted part of Waropen's challenge. The view from nowhere, the sort of scientific realism that Donna Haraway calls "the God Trick," is poorly suited for illustrating indigenous visions that challenge Eurocentric logics.

Wedding a rigorous empiricism with a commitment to listen to unfamiliar narratives, I let West Papuan activists and visionaries pull my research in different directions, toward competing topics and alternate realisms. In trying to serve as a faithful translator, in trying to do justice to nuanced dreams of freedom in West Papua, I have done more than simply stick to the facts, narrowly construed. After working to know things that matter, and know these things well, I began crafting portraits of multiple coexistent realities in West Papua. Even as dreams were smashed amid the overt violence of ongoing military operations and the structural violence of international law, I joined West Papuans in imagining surprising futures.

CHAPTER FIVE

Innocents Murdered, Innocent Murderers

AUGUST 31, 2002

The central Jayapura office of Elsham, the human rights organization where I was volunteering, was buzzing with action when I stopped by on August 31, 2002. Three teachers—two Americans and one Indonesian—had just been shot dead near the Freeport McMoRan mine in Timika. The teachers were Freeport contract employees who worked at a local international school. John Rumbiak, Elsham's founder, was in Australia that week for a conference. The Elsham staff were scrambling to make sense of the attack. Indonesian authorities pinned the assault on Kelly Kwalik, a Tentara Pembebasan Nasional (TPN) guerrilla leader based near Timika. Before leaving for Australia, John had met with Kwalik to enlist his support in a peace initiative.

Elsham had been working with church groups and the police on a proposal to make West Papua a "Land of Peace." John had been collaborating with the police to help them gain a leg up in their struggle with the military for control of Indonesia's security forces. The Land of Peace campaign was taking place as the military was regaining power, provoking violent conflict and working to destroy the reform movement. As part of this peace process, John Rumbiak visited many guerrilla leaders, including Thadius Yogi, Melkianus Awom, Hans Yoweni, and Kelly Kwalik. He was trying to convince the veteran fighters to disarm and pursue their aspirations for merdeka through political channels. His encounters with the guerrillas were not "first contacts"; each group had already been contacted by Indonesian military agents. Aware of John's contact with militants, Indonesian authorities were alleging that he had masterminded the attack in Timika.

Working with Aloy Renwarin, a lawyer who was then assistant director of Elsham, I helped compose an English-language press release about the Timika attack: "Elsham staff members met with, and interviewed, TPN leader Kelly Kwalik last week. . . . [He has] affirmed a commitment to non-violence and peaceful dialog. We conclude from these discussions that it is not possible that yesterday's attack on the Tembagapura Road was planned by Kelly Kwalik." To avoid unwanted attention from Indonesian authorities while I was in the country, I did not include my own name in the press release. Aloy Renwarin issued it under his name. The release pointed to circumstantial evidence of Indonesian military involvement in the incident.

Why might Indonesian security forces stage an attack near Timika? One possible motive was extortion. Freeport paid a total of US$5.6 million in 2002 for "support costs for government-provided security."[1] The Sarbanes-Oxley Act of 2002 imposed new reporting requirements on U.S. companies in the wake of the Enron corporate accounting scandal. After this measure was passed into law, Freeport was forced to disclose its payments to the Indonesian military. In early 2002, Freeport conducted internal discussions about increasing the transparency of the company's relationship with the Indonesian security forces.[2] The Indonesian military may have feared that Freeport would end its security contracts. Another possible motive was to leverage funds from the U.S. government in the global war on terror. If the Indonesian military could frame a West Papuan "terrorist" group for the murder of U.S. civilians, then they would stand to reap political and financial rewards.[3]

The timing of John Rumbiak's meeting with Kelly Kwalik also left room for wild speculations. The military was alleging a conspiracy between guerrillas and leaders of nongovernmental organizations—that violence was being used in an attempt to further the cause for independence. John had publicly endorsed the right of West Papuans to self-determination, a principle codified in international law. But using violence to achieve a political goal was clearly at odds with Elsham's entire human rights campaign. Surely John would not break from his long record of working for peace. Was it at all possible that one of my closest associates in West Papua was involved in this murder?

From Australia, John called for the United States to lead an independent investigation of the murder. The Indonesian military was notorious for its history of coverups.[4] In the climate of military impunity, John saw international involvement as the only way to guarantee the transparency of the investigation. On September 2, 2002, the American embassy in Jakarta sent a secret cable to secretary of state Colin Powell about the Timika ambush.

This cable was recently declassified in response to a Freedom of Information Act request filed by the National Security Archive in Washington. It stated: "Many Papuan groups are calling for an independent investigation, led by the U.S. Calls for an independent probe are unrealistic, but we believe that Papua's Police Chief, who enjoys a good reputation with Papuan activists (and U.S.), can conduct a fair investigation."[5] In the declassified copy of this document, all specific details about the possible perpetrators of the attack were redacted.

Upon returning to West Papua, John Rumbiak partnered with the police chief to investigate the Timika ambush. The Indonesian police questioned thirty soldiers and forty-four civilians and conducted extensive forensic research. Police investigators found "a strong possibility" that Indonesian military shooters were involved.[6] Raziman Tarigan, the deputy police chief, told reporters that the thirteen guns used in the attack were the types of weapons issued to soldiers stationed in the area.[7] "Only the military and Freeport workers pass through the area," Tarigan was quoted as saying by *Koran Tempo*.[8] After making these public statements, Tarigan was transferred off the investigation.[9]

In December 2002 the Indonesian military took over the Timika investigation and promptly exonerated itself. As a result the U.S. Congress made the future of a prestigious military training program for Indonesia contingent on their cooperation with an FBI investigation into the murder. Indonesian authorities were initially hostile. At first FBI agents were only permitted short visits to Timika. Their interviews were initially conducted in the presence of Indonesian minders.[10] Despite repeated high-level requests from the U.S. government, including a personal appeal by President Bush, the FBI had continual difficulties in gaining access to witnesses and material evidence.[11] At the outset of the FBI investigation, the lines of enemy and ally, at least in the eyes of John Rumbiak, seemed to be clearly drawn. John saw the FBI investigators as partners who might help end Indonesian military impunity. He hoped to enlist these U.S. agents, no-nonsense investigators who promised to relentlessly pursue the truth, in his struggle against Indonesian security forces.

John worked closely with the FBI, helping them in the field during the early stages of their investigation. He briefed them on the details of his joint investigation with the police and assigned two Elsham staff members to work full-time with the FBI case agents. Initially the FBI seemed to scrutinize evidence offered by Elsham of Indonesian military involvement.

As the investigation proceeded, however, it became clear that the FBI had abandoned the theory that the Indonesian military was involved in the ambush. John grew increasingly skeptical of the investigation's objectivity but still continued to share information with the FBI in good faith. In late 2003, he let the FBI team copy the entire contents of his laptop when he was visiting New York City.[12]

John and other West Papuan activists began to encourage me to meet with the FBI case agents myself. I hesitated. Could I share my research with the FBI without exposing my West Papuan counterparts and sources to unwanted attention from criminal investigators? Because I was an American and an outside expert, they reasoned, I might be able to provide a credible and fresh perspective on the issue of Indonesian military involvement. In September 2004, I was in Washington to conduct research in the Smithsonian Institution archives. By this time I had finished a master's degree at Oxford and was starting the second year of my Ph.D. under James Clifford at UC Santa Cruz. Admittedly curious about the FBI, and rather apprehensive, I made an appointment to meet with the investigative team handling the Timika case.

The FBI's Washington field office is a multistory complex, northwest of the Senate office buildings, blocks away from the National Mall. It is nondescript except for the forest of communications antennae sprouting from the roof. Karen Ornstein, then the Washington coordinator of the East Timor Action Network, accompanied me during the meeting.

Entering at street level, we walked into a small reception area. An African American woman checked our identification and issued us visitor's badges. A clean-cut white man who appeared to be a few years younger than I escorted us to a waiting elevator. His own badge dangled from a neck strap printed with "U.S. EMBASSY KABUL," apparently an artifact of one of his recent assignments. A group of older white men in suits waited for us in a small office, among them Ronald C. Eowan, the primary agent on the case. As we shook hands and sat down, a knot tightened in my gut. Would these veteran investigators take my knowledge about Indonesian military operations seriously? Had I made a mistake in agreeing to this meeting in the first place?

As the discussion started, I presented the FBI team with a copy of the budget for Operation Illumination, the Indonesian military covert program to infiltrate West Papuan guerrilla groups. Eowan thanked me for the document. "We will have this translated and checked for authenticity by our experts," he said. Swallowing my anxiety, I began to summarize my findings about Operation Illumination. "Colonel Armentony, then head of Indonesian military intelligence in the Province of Papua, oversaw the implementation of this operation in 2000–2001," I told the men in suits. The operation was reportedly headquartered in Timika. "Colonel Armentony may well have masterminded this attack," I concluded. As they probed for details of Armentony's possible involvement, I admitted that I did not have any specific information linking him to the murder. My knowledge of the Timika attack was then limited to what I knew from media accounts and what I had learned through John Rumbiak.

The FBI agents began to steer the conversation away from the Indonesian military and instead toward West Papuan guerrilla fighters. They began asking me broad, seemingly innocuous, questions: "What is the organizational structure of the OPM?" "What is its relationship to the TPN?" "Can you talk about the founding of the movement?" I ended the meeting abruptly, saying that we had another appointment on the other side of town.

On the next day, I received a voicemail on my mobile phone: "Eben, this is Ron Eowan with the FBI, how are you doing. . . . I just wanted to express my appreciation for you guys coming in and talking to us. Maybe we can talk to you at a later date. Maybe we can fly out there to California. Or maybe we can arrange something along those lines. Once again, thanks for coming in, thanks for talking with us."[13] After getting advice about my legal rights and obligations from Angela Davis, a professor in my department who was hounded by the FBI in the 1970s, I decided not to return Eowan's call. He did not call back.

In June 2004, a U.S. grand jury indicted Antonius Wamang, a West Papuan farmer, for taking part in the 2002 Timika ambush. The indictment was unsealed during a press conference by U.S. attorney general John Ashcroft and FBI director Robert Mueller. Ashcroft and Mueller alleged that Wamang was a terrorist who sought independence from Indonesia.[14]

The press release accompanying the indictment made no mention of reports linking the attack to the Indonesian military. After getting a copy of the indictment, I called John Rumbiak, who was in Australia at the time. He was incensed. Over the years, he had provided FBI agents with an abundance of specific details linking the military to the attack. He felt that his goodwill, and the goodwill of his staff at Elsham, had been abused by the FBI and Bush administration officials.

Several months later, on January 19, 2005, Joseph Biden, the U.S. Senator who has since been elected Vice-President, submitted written questions about the Timika attack during the congressional hearing to confirm Condoleezza Rice for the position of U.S. secretary of state. In response, Rice wrote, "Although the investigation is not complete, the FBI has uncovered no evidence indicating TNI involvement in the Timika murders."

At the time I was back in Washington. The University of California's Washington Center had offered me a short-term teaching fellowship. John Rumbiak's colleagues had recently found new evidence of military links to the Timika ambush. Elsham had identified ties between Wamang, the indicted man, and the Indonesian military. On the heels of the testimony by Condoleezza Rice, John visited Washington to brief policymakers on these findings. I accompanied him during a busy week of meetings.

We gave presentations to the Republican and Democratic staff of the Senate Foreign Relations Committee, legislative aides for members of the Progressive Caucus in the House, the Congressional Caucus for Indonesia, and State Department officials. Nearly all these officials encouraged John to share his findings with the FBI. In the space of three days, John and I produced a five-page memo summarizing the Elsham findings about military involvement in the Timika killings. We circulated this document to John's congressional contacts and asked that they forward it to the FBI. The next day I departed for Hawaii, where I was scheduled to present a paper at the 2005 meeting of the Association for Social Anthropology of Oceania. John left Washington for a weeklong speaking tour in California and Mexico.

As I was chatting with other anthropologists in Kauai the next day, a Saturday afternoon, my cell phone rang with an unknown caller. I picked up. "Eben, this is Special Agent Paul Myers with the FBI."[15] Off guard, I struggled to put the name to a face. Later I realized that Myers had been my escort, the young man wearing the Kabul neck strap, who showed me into the meeting at the FBI Washington field office. "I need to speak with John Rumbiak in the next week," Myers said. "John is traveling in California and Mexico," I replied. "I'm not sure that he will be able meet with you right away." Myers's tone became hostile: "I want to talk with John. I don't want to have to do anything that would upset things." Special Agent Myers did not specify what he might do to "upset things." In the moment, I decided to not heed his threatening message. "John has asked that I not give out his number," I said.

Myers knew about the memo that John and I had sent to congressional offices the day before. He was not happy about the contents. "Circulating information to politicos," he charged, "puts people on the ground in danger." Precisely who was in danger was not clear. How private communications with Congress would impact people "on the ground" was equally unclear. "We will need to interview you, Eben, in addition to John," Myers added. I did not respond to this assertion, and Myers did not follow up. As long as I was not subpoenaed, I was under no obligation to speak with the FBI. Later I managed to reach John Rumbiak through his host in California. John asked me to continue to act as a go-between with the FBI. Suddenly my own entanglements with West Papuan political projects had become extremely personal and uncomfortable. Still, I agreed to John's request.

Over the next two weeks, Special Agent Myers called my cell phone repeatedly—at times very early in the morning while I was still sleeping and also late at night when I was out with friends. John eventually decided to meet with the FBI once again, against my own advice. Myers wanted to have an interrogation take place at the FBI headquarters, and he wanted John to be alone. John insisted that the meeting take place on his own terms; he wanted me and Ed McWilliams, a former State Department official, to be present. The Robert F. Kennedy Center for Justice and Human Rights, an organization with which John, McWilliams, and I were all affiliated as pro bono advocates, agreed to let us use its conference room. At the last minute, Todd Howland, a human rights lawyer and then the director of the RFK Center, agreed to join the meeting when he learned that John did not have legal representation.

At the appointed time—4:00 p.m. on Wednesday, February 23, 2005—the FBI agents arrived at RFK Center. The interrogation was to last some four hours. Paul Myers was accompanied by Brad Dierdorf, a senior investigator who had been part of the Timika investigation for several years. When I spotted Dierdorf's peculiar tie clip—a large opaque disk—some Paul Simon lyrics floated into my head: "She said the man in the gabardine suit was a spy. I said be careful, his bowtie is really a camera . . ."[16] We had planned to record the encounter, but amid a busy schedule of other meetings, we failed to find a tape recorder. I was left to scribble notes.[17] "We know the corroborative facts of this case better than anyone in the world, even the witnesses," Dierdorf began. "We are objective. We intend to confine our conversation to Mr. Rumbiak's specific knowledge of this case."

The FBI agents were trying to deploy what Donna Haraway has called "the God Trick," the view from nowhere that claims to see everything. The FBI's claims of being outside politics were pure fantasy. Recent scholarship has taught us that all knowledge projects are political. Researchers are never free from the values and interests of particular social and political locations. The subject positions of researchers shape the types of questions that are asked.[18]

Through my own political advocacy, I learned precisely how the supposed objectivity of the FBI investigation was compromised. At the time, the State Department and Pentagon were pushing to intensify military cooperation with Indonesia. Because Indonesia was the world's largest Islamic country, military strategists saw it as an important ally in the global war on terror. Evidence that the Indonesian military had murdered American schoolteachers was getting in the way of high-level political priorities.

"We have already identified some of the killers," began Dierdorf. "Now we are looking for the intellectual masterminds. We are investigating a conspiracy among the OPM and the NGO leadership." John said: "Don't go there. We aren't supporting violence, this is a peace movement." Looking directly at John, Dierdorf added: "You had a meeting with Kelly Kwalik on August 25, 2002, six days before the attack. We are investigating this." A video recording of the conversation between John and Kelly Kwalik showed them talking about the initiative to make West Papua a land of peace. Kwalik agreed to renounce violence so that merdeka could be pursued through political channels. The FBI agents alleged that Rumbiak and Kwalik held separate discussions that were not recorded. Their line of questioning indicated that they were investigating the possibility that the two men had conspired to mastermind the attack on the schoolteachers.

Two days after this troubling encounter, I took John to Union Station, where he boarded a train for New York City. The next morning, a Saturday, I called to check on him. John had just experienced a major stroke. After hearing the news, I drove up to New York. I met with the physician who had admitted him to the hospital and learned that the stroke had destroyed the language centers of John's brain. John would have aphasia—difficulties in producing and comprehending language—for the rest of his life. I learned that I was probably the last friend to speak with John before the stroke.

After John's stroke, I put other research projects on hold. I began to devote my full energies to researching the Timika case. My starting place from within the community of researchers and advocates concerned about human rights in West Papua gave me a stake in the outcome of this murder investigation. This positioned perspective was a source of insider knowledge. I worked to produce stronger claims to knowledge than research that was guided by the illusion of value neutrality. Starting with Sandra Harding's standpoint epistemology, I worked to unmask the God Trick of the FBI.[19] Standpoint theorists claim to see some things very well from their partial perspectives, rather than seeing everything from nowhere. The FBI agents were claiming the power to see but not be seen. I became determined to bring these agents out of the shadows—to shine light on their disappearing acts, their forgetting.[20]

My own political and personal commitments certainly also shaped the questions I asked during my research into this murder. When John was interrogated for the last time by Special Agents Dierdorf and Myers, he offered specific new leads that pointed toward Indonesian military involvement in the attack. John told them about a trip that Antonius Wamang, the indicted shooter, made to Jakarta. The details of this trip were still fuzzy, but Wamang reportedly had extensive contacts with military agents while he was in Indonesia's capital. From the tone and the content of the interrogation, it was clear that Dierdorf and Myers would not be pursuing these new leads. At one point, Dierdorf moved to rhetorically dismiss evidence that John was offering: "This would frankly surprise me," he said. "A lot of sourcing you've provided us is bad." I took it upon myself to follow John's leads. In March 2005 I traveled to Timika, where I began a serious empirical project that built on nearly three years of research by John's organization, Elsham.

During my own investigation, I did not pursue the allegations that John Rumbiak had masterminded the attack on the schoolteachers. I did not ask mutual friends and colleagues the hard questions that might have revealed evidence of his involvement. The FBI was already doing a rigorous job on that front. Years later, buried in courtroom documents, I discovered that the FBI later abandoned their apparent attempt to bring criminal charges against John. In April 2006, during a formal deposition to Indonesian investigators, Special Agent Eowan asked that a report about John Rumbiak's meeting with Kelly Kwalik be struck from the official record. Eowan said through an Indonesian translator: "Please erase it, because that response was not relevant to the question."[21]

Questions about Indonesian military involvement in the attack were at odds with high-level Bush administration priorities. I began to systematically ask questions that the FBI had dismissed. I learned to respect aspects of what the FBI knew about the Timika case. After all, they had access to classified details and forensic evidence deemed too sensitive for my own eyes. Still, I found that my knowledge of context—my other research on collaborations between the military and independence activists—made me able to see some things better than the case agents. Unexpected stories that would not make sense in a clear-cut world where enemies can be cordoned neatly off from allies were plausible to me. Where the FBI saw simplicity—West Papuan terrorists and innocent Americans—I found complexity.

My proclivity for taking surprising narratives seriously came to be coupled with rigorous empiricism and systematic skepticism. I partnered with Andreas Harsono, an Indonesian investigative journalist who was recently a Neiman Fellow at Harvard University. Harsono helped me translate my situated knowledge into a genre of reportage that has currency in the halls of global power.[22] Together we interviewed over fifty sources in Timika, Jayapura, Jakarta, and Washington. Through Brad Simpson of the National Security Archive, who independently submitted a Freedom of Information Act request about the case, we obtained 143 pages of declassified documents from the State Department. Many of these documents were seriously redacted, and an additional thirty-one relevant documents, identified in State Department archives, were not declassified.[23] Working closely with Harsono over the course of a year, often through multiple e-mails and phone calls every day, we pushed and challenged each other. Every sentence we wrote together was subjected to serious scrutiny. We probed our own words to ensure that they were grounded in verifiable sources and to eliminate potential legal vulnerabilities under libel law.

In time Antonius Wamang was apprehended, tried, and convicted of murder in an Indonesian courtroom. Harsono and I eventually obtained a copy of the case dossier (*Berkas Perkara*) for Wamang and six other codefendants. This dossier contained some two thousand pages of Indonesian-language documents compiled by high-level police investigators with Indonesia's Criminal Investigations Branch. During Wamang's trial, the story of his trip to Jakarta and his contacts with Indonesian military operatives was not told. Evidence from eyewitnesses and forensics experts, indicating that Indonesian military shooters may have been at the scene of the crime, was not seriously considered in court. What follows is adapted from my collaborative research and writing with Andreas Harsono, which has already been published in *Southeast Asian Research* (SEAR). It is a brief of sorts, a summary of evidence of military involvement and an inventory of questions left unanswered by the trial.

A Trip to the Big City

Antonius Wamang boarded a jet in September 2001 at Timika's airport with a mission: to get weapons and ammunition in Indonesia's capital of Jakarta.[24] Wamang hoped to secure help from Indonesian agents in Jakarta, to attack local Indonesian soldiers in Timika.[25] He had never before traveled outside West Papua. Born in the remote highland village of Beoga in 1972, Wamang was a young boy when Indonesian Brigadier General Imam Munandar launched Operation Eliminate in 1977.[26] Indonesian forces used antipersonnel daisy cutter bombs, which generate massive pressure waves that can be felt several hundred yards away, along with mortars and machine guns. Villagers armed only with bows and a few stolen rifles failed to hold their own. Nearly thirty years later, Wamang had found what he thought was an opportunity to buy arms and fight back against the Indonesian military. As he departed for Jakarta, Wamang was unknown, by all accounts a minor figure in a local group of guerrillas with vague ideas about waging war against the Indonesian military. His encounters in Jakarta opened new horizons.

When I interviewed him years later, after he had been indicted on terrorism charges by a U.S. grand jury, Wamang told me that he flew to Jakarta alone and was met at the airport by Agus Anggaibak, a Timika-based sandalwood dealer who had ties to the Indonesian military.[27] "Agus Anggaibak set up everything; he lobbied the officers and arranged the money," according to one community leader.[28] Anggaibak admits to being part of Indonesia's intelligence network and to meeting with Antonius Wamang before the attack.[29] "Everyone in Timika has met Wamang," he said.[30] Agus Anggaibak was twenty at the time of his reported trip to Jakarta with Wamang and has since been elected as a member of the regional parliamentary assembly in Timika (DPRD Mimika).

Agus Anggaibak reportedly visited Wamang's group in their jungle hideout, well before the trip to Jakarta, encouraging them to raise money to buy guns. He reportedly brought a rifle with him and showed off this weapon in Wamang's camp. Identifiers were etched into the gun: "MODEL P88–9, Col 9 MMP AK, Made in Germany."[31] Anggaibak reportedly promised to help Wamang obtain weapons like the one he was carrying, as well as other guns, from arms dealers in Jakarta.[32] But Anggaibak claims that he never had a gun. "My adjutant, who has been with me since I formed a sandalwood cooperative in high school, carries a rifle. But I have never had a weapon," he said. In Indonesia, only security forces personnel and some government officials are licensed to carry firearms. He did not explain why he had an armed personal "adjutant" in high school. Agus Anggaibak rejects the allegation that he collaborated with Wamang to stage an attack.[33]

Like all TPN groups, Wamang's men were poorly armed. The group had only three aging rifles: an SS1, an M16, and a bolt-action Mauser. Many of Wamang's comrades were newcomers to the cause. Among them were Johni Kacamol, a teenager; and Hardi Tsugumol, who had spent most of his adult life in the urban centers of Java and West Papua.[34] Tsugumol had an extensive network of "friends" who were active-duty Indonesian soldiers.[35]

Anggaibak reportedly departed for Jakarta with an advance payment from Wamang to purchase more guns. The money had been raised by several weeks of intensive gold panning and sandalwood collecting. When Wamang later flew to Jakarta, he brought sacks of sandalwood that he claims were worth more than 500 million Indonesian rupiah (US$56,000).[36] On the international market, the sandalwood would fetch even higher prices, as this rare wood is used to make incense and perfume.

According to Wamang, he and Anggaibak initially stayed in a police guest house in Jakarta. Sergeant Puji, a police officer, became Wamang's "friend." Sergeant Puji reportedly took Wamang and Anggaibak on trips around Jakarta. They toured around while Puji asked them about the West Papuan guerrillas' activities around Timika. Puji presented Wamang with a gift of six magazines of ammunition (180 bullets in total) that could be used in the M16 or SS1 rifles that Wamang's group had already secured back in Timika. Puji also gave Wamang ammunition for his bolt-action Mauser. These bullets, Wamang told us, were among those used to later launch an attack. One night in the guest house, Puji showed Wamang fifteen M16 rifles. Wamang said he paid 250 million Indonesian rupiah (US$28,000) for these guns, and Puji held them for "safekeeping."[37]

Wamang told me that he later moved to Djody Hostel at Jalan Jaksa 35, a backpacker hostel in downtown Jakarta.[38] A sandalwood middleman from Makassar, named Mochtar, introduced Anggaibak and Wamang to Indonesian army and police officers. "*Mochtar was a regular guest here,*" said Herry Blaponte, Djody Hostel front office staff. Blaponte recalled that Mochtar regularly made sandalwood business deals with his West Papuan guests. Hostel staff remembered Mochtar as having a stocky build and being a "dandy." Their memories of him are not fond, however, since he left without paying his bill. Mochtar could not be reached for comment.

Djody Hostel. *Photograph by Emy Zumaidar.*

But Blaponte and hostel security staff Mahmud Trikasno later told Indonesian chief detective Dzainal Syarief that they did not remember Wamang's stay. "I don't remember his face," said Trikasno. Four cleaning service staff also did not recognize Wamang when presented with his picture
some five years after his reported stay. The hostel has many guests, and
they said that it was entirely possible that they simply did not notice Wamang.[39]

One afternoon at Djody Hostel, according to Wamang, a stranger approached him and Anggaibak. "I hear you are looking to buy guns," Wamang quoted the stranger as saying. Eventually Anggaibak, the West Papuan sandalwood dealer who allegedly "set everything up," admitted that
they were. The stranger, Captain Hardi Heidi, said that he was an Indonesian soldier from Surabaya. Eventually Wamang paid Heidi for four guns:
two AKs and two M16s. Wamang arranged for Heidi to keep the weapons
until he was ready to depart for Timika.[40] This proved to be a naive mistake.
Heidi brought the trusting pair into a confidence scheme, a shell game of
sorts, and shuttled the rifles away beyond their reach.

Hardi Heidi introduced Anggaibak and Wamang to Sugiono, reportedly
an active-duty Kopassus officer, who pledged to help transport the weapons
to Timika.[41] Sugiono and Heidi, like Sergeant Puji, wanted to hear about the
activities of West Papuan guerrillas around Timika.

On September 21, 2001, Wamang visited with forty West Papuan delegates in Jakarta, who had just returned from the New Orleans headquarters of Freeport McMoRan. They were staying at Hotel Mega Matra. Excited to see many fellow Amungme leaders, Wamang visited the hotel a number of times. The group had just returned from negotiating a profit-sharing deal with Freeport's management.

Wamang asked many delegates for money. According to delegate Eltinus Omaleng, Wamang bragged about how he had secured a shipload of weapons that were ready to be sent to West Papua.[42] Wamang needed extra money to transport the weapons. Janes Natkime gave Wamang 1.5 million Indonesian rupiah (US$169).[43] "Five days later he came back to the hotel, saying that the ship had been rerouted to Aceh."[44]

Wamang told me that he had paid Sugiono nearly 50 million Indonesian rupiah (US$5,649) to transport the guns to Timika.[45] After a chartered boat was loaded with the weapons, Wamang claims that Sugiono and Hardi Heidi gave him the slip. The boat motored away with Wamang standing alone on the Tanjung Perak dock. Just before the boat's departure, Wamang said that he overheard a conversation between Hardi Heidi and his wife. "We should sell these in Aceh," the wife said.[46]

After calling associates in Timika for more money, Wamang traveled back alone on the passenger ship *Kelimutu*. He arrived in Timika with only the bullets that Sergeant Puji had given him.[47] Wamang's extensive contacts with Indonesian agents had given him moments of hope; his newfound friends in Jakarta, he thought at first, were genuinely committed to helping the freedom fighters of West Papua. But his mission to obtain guns had failed.

Wamang's naiveté was exploited by Agus Anggaibak, Sugiono, Mochtar, and Hardi Heidi. Each of them personally profited from Wamang's trusting gullibility. Did these Indonesian agents who "befriended" Wamang also turn Wamang's vague idea of an ambush on local military forces in Timika into something else? It is hard to imagine that in conversations with Hardi Heidi and Sugiono, Wamang never broached the subject of how he planned to use the guns. Did military intelligence agents in Jakarta hatch a plan for an ambush in Timika and then recruit Wamang for the job? Or was the ambush planned in a piecemeal, contingent fashion? Was the event "coproduced" by multiple agents with competing agendas?

The idiom of coproduction is used by Sheila Jasanoff, a theorist in the field of science and technology studies, to understand how knowledge influences the construction of the social order. Her work explores the ambivalent collaborations of different actors who work together to create ideas and infrastructures. Local contingencies figure prominently in Jasanoff's work. Rather than understand science as a centrally coordinated conspiracy that simply reinforces hegemonic and oppressive political orders, she attends to the microprocesses by which social life and cognitive understandings gain form and meaning together.[48] Appropriating the idiom of coproduction offers a new vocabulary for understanding the ambivalent and contingent collaborations that develop during covert operations and violent actions.

Many other analysts of Indonesian culture and politics use the figure of the *dalang*, the puppeteer of Javanese shadow plays, to represent the masterminds of criminal plots. The dalang puppeteer enacts shadow dramas on a projection screen by holding cut-out figures before a flickering light source. There is no evidence of a single dalang in the Timika ambush. Instead it is clear that multiple agents worked together to coproduce an act of terror. A number of actors with competing agendas came together to stage an attack.

The idiom of coproduction suggests that conspiracies are not necessarily carefully planned in advance. Chance meetings and contingent circumstances can produce unexpected outcomes. Senior Indonesian military officers, including armed forces commander General Endriartono Sutarto, discussed an unspecified operation against Freeport before the ambush, according to an article published in the *Washington Post*. Sutarto "did not detail a specific attack," according to the *Post*, nor did he "call explicitly for the killing of Americans or other foreigners." Instead general discussions about Freeport could have been understood by subordinates as a direction "to take some kind of violent action against Freeport."[49]

General Sutarto vehemently denied that he or any other top military officers discussed any operation targeting Freeport. He sued the *Washington Post* for US$1 billion and demanded an apology from the paper.[50] The paper settled out of court with Sutarto and printed a statement: further investigations "revealed no substantiation that Sutarto or other high-ranking Indonesian military officers were involved in any discussion or planning of the attack. The Post regrets publication of this report."[51]

Leaked reports on the FBI preliminary's findings later seemed to confirm the original article by the *Post*. "It's no longer a question of who did it," a senior U.S. official familiar with the investigation told the Associated Press in March 2004. "It's only a question of how high up this went within the chain of command."[52] But the U.S. embassy later issued a formal denial that the FBI found evidence of Indonesian military involvement.

During a meeting between General Sutarto and U.S. ambassador Ralph Boyce on June 16, 2003, the commander expressed concern about a new written request for an interview from the *Washington Post*. Having just settled his lawsuit with the *Post* about the Timika case, Sutarto was troubled by this new request to interview him, the Indonesian Strategic Intelligence Agency (BAIS), and chiefs of the State Intelligence Agency (BIN) regarding the ambush. According to a classified report from the meeting, "The Ambassador replied by suggesting that the upcoming *Post* article should not deter us from our main objective, which was justice in the Timika case."[53]

Antonius Wamang's visit to Jakarta presented an opportunity for mid-level Indonesian officers to further their own agendas. Naiveté on the part of Wamang, for one, was certainly an important factor that allowed enemies to come together in a contingent alliance. Wamang was apparently an "innocent," a gullible young man who was manipulated by Agus Anggaibak, his newfound Indonesian military friends in Jakarta, and other covert operatives back in Timika.

Plans for "an Action"

Back in Timika, Wamang partnered with Hardi Tsugumol, a relative newcomer to the merdeka movement. Tsugumol made it widely known he was extremely busy getting ready for "an action," according to Deminikus Bebari of the Amungme Indigenous Council (Lemassa). Tsugumol "amassed food and other supplies," wrote Bebari in a report prepared in 2002 for Indonesian police investigators.[54] The objective of this action was not initially clear.

A document circulated by Tsugumol told supporters: "Stand by at your various targets. . . . We are going to attack this big company." The company referred to in Tsugumol's document was Freeport McMoRan. Point eight of Tsugumol's document said: "Each detachment must understand human rights laws, and in keeping with this principle must be careful with West Papuan, Indonesian, and white civilians who are ordinary people and not our enemy."[55] With this proviso, seemingly Tsugumol was envisioning an action against Freeport facilities rather than against personnel.

In the lead-up to the action, Tsugumol "contacted his friends in the military to buy ammunition—300 bullets for 600,000 Indonesian rupiah [US$66], via his friends who were in the Indonesian special forces," wrote Bebari.[56] Tsugumol had an odd network of friends. When he was a boy growing up in a highland village, he wanted to be a soldier with the Indonesian military.[57] Later he lived in Java for many years, where he married an Indonesian woman.[58] After returning to Timika, Tsugumol maintained relationships with active-duty Indonesian soldiers. In contrast to Antonius Wamang, who had long been loosely affiliated with the TPN, Tsugumol cultivated contacts with guerrillas near Timika only a short time before the ambush.

Perhaps recent history led Tsugumol and Wamang to believe that it was possible to play one group of Indonesian security forces off against another. Other West Papuan activists—Thadius Yogi and Theys Eluay, for example—had staged successful events where aspirations for independence were aired with the help of Kopassus soldiers. Tsugumol may have been working to turn his special forces friends at the same time that these military agents were working to turn him. Or Tsugumol himself might have accepted an assignment to frame Wamang's band of West Papuan independence fighters in a terrorist attack. Certainly Tsugumol's plan to attack Freeport differed from Wamang's original vague ideas about waging war against the Indonesian military. Ambivalent collaborations and contingent circumstances often produce events that surprise everyone involved.

The Ambush

"I remember the night of Friday, 30 August, 2002," Steve Emma told Indonesian police investigators through an interpreter. Emma was a newly hired teacher in Tembagapura, an expatriate community in the highlands of West Papua. "I met up with friends from the school to hang out and watch a video," Emma continued. "We were all laughing a lot." The group decided to go on a picnic the next day.[59] Tembagapura is near the open-pit gold and copper mine of Freeport. Most of the pupils of the Tembagapura International School, where Emma taught, are children of expatriates who work at Freeport. The teachers were contract employees of the corporation.[60]

A winding mountain road connects Tembagapura with the coastal town of Timika. The seventy-nine-mile road has fourteen military posts manned by Indonesian security forces along with Freeport's own guards. A fleet of

Freeport vehicles—tankers, dump trucks, semitrailers—regularly ply the Timika–Tembagapura road. Freeport personnel register every car and person traveling along the road.[61] Workers have to display their employee ID cards at the checkpoints. Locals have to show special permits issued by Freeport's community liaison office. There are also special Freeport-issued visitor cards.[62]

Steve Emma and a group of ten others set out for their picnic on the morning of August 31, 2002, in a pair of white Toyota Land Cruisers. They traveled from Tembagapura down the road toward Timika. "When we reached the Mile 64 checkpoint, I felt uneasy and nervous," Emma said. "I began to think that something was wrong." The driver, Rick Spier, had to fill out a detailed form and sign it. "My feelings of unease became worse when I made eye contact with one of the soldiers at the checkpoint," continued Emma. "I nodded at him and said 'hello,' and the soldier just met me with a cold stare."[63]

The teachers stopped for their picnic at a section of old-growth cloud forest near mile 62 of the road. The group found orchids and pitcher plants. Patsy Spier, Rick's wife, said that it was rainy and foggy. "We ended up leaving the picnic early," said Patsy.[64] As the teachers traveled back toward Tembagapura, they were having a lively discussion, laughing and joking. Steve Emma said, "Suddenly there was an unexpected attack that I still can't understand. I still clearly remember my emotions and thoughts during those next 45 minutes."[65]

Rick Spier was driving the first vehicle, which carried Emma and three other passengers. Ted Burgon, the school's principal, rode next to Rick. The first four shots were distinct and methodical. "My heart skipped and my eyes opened wide when the first shot hit our windshield," said Emma. "The second shot hit Rick in the face. The third shot hit Ted, and I remember choking and almost vomiting at that instant. . . . The fourth shot hit Ted again and he toppled slowly into the middle of the jeep where Rick already lay dead."[66]

Patsy Spier was riding in the second Toyota van, driven by Ken Balk.[67] Suddenly, in the fog, Patsy Spier saw her husband's car, in front of hers, stopped by the side of the road. A third vehicle was speeding toward her on the opposite side of the road. "They ran Rick's car off of the road," Patsy Spier remembers thinking.

Ken Balk, who was in the same car, also saw this vehicle: "Another truck sped down. It was a white Toyota Land Cruiser. Seconds before we were

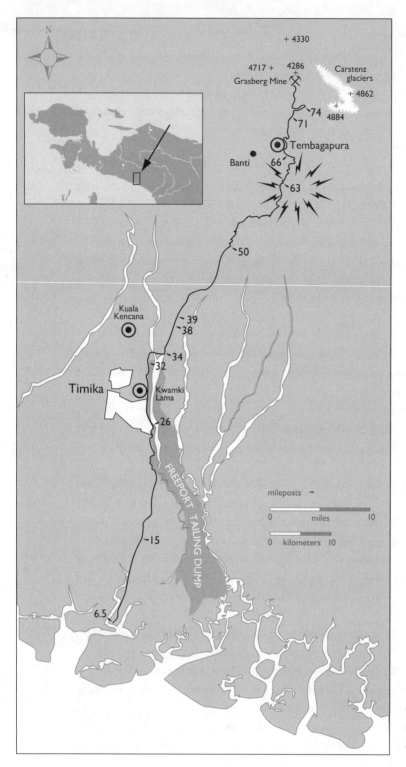

The most heavily guard[ed]
road in Indonesia.
Map by Damond Kyllo.

Timika as seen from above. The city abuts an expansive field of mining waste, called tailings, from the Freeport mine. The tailing deposition site has caused serious ecological damage to local rivers and has consequently disrupted fisheries and sago stands, important sources of food for indigenous groups. *Photograph by Eben Kirksey.*

shot, this company Toyota Land Cruiser went past us going down the mountain. They were men, officially dressed, wearing security caps. Some who I happened to see were ethnic West Papuans."[68] The Indonesian military has recruited hundreds of West Papuans as soldiers. It is possible that the men in the vehicle were West Papuan members of the military.

Patsy Spier remembers the third vehicle as a pickup truck, not a Toyota Land Cruiser. She told Indonesian investigators: "When the pickup truck went by our vehicle, I saw two grey puffs behind the truck. At that moment I also heard the sound of an explosion, and I was shot in the left side of my back."[69] She now thinks that the two "grey puffs" were bullets ricocheting off the pavement.[70]

Patsy Spier was sitting next to Bambang Riwanto, her Javanese colleague. "All of us were shot, wounded. Bambang was laying on top of me, bleeding. I was worried about my husband but the shooting just continued," said Spier.[71] Patsy's husband Rick Spier, the principal Ted Burgon, and Bambang Riwanto died in the attack.

Three other vehicles came to a stop at the ambush site amid the shooting—a yellow Mack truck and two Canadian Pacific dump trucks. These trucks were also riddled with bullets.[72] Among the eleven people who were wounded in the attack, three were Indonesian drivers. The two most seriously injured drivers, Loudwyk Worotikan and Johannes Bawan, worked for a Freeport contract company. Mastur, the third driver, sustained light injuries.

Forensics investigators found 73 holes where bullets entered and 46 holes where bullets exited the five vehicles that stopped at the ambush site.[73] A total of 208 bullets, shells, or fragments were recovered from the crime scene.[74]

Andrew Neale, a Freeport expatriate, came upon the scene from the direction of Tembagapura.[75] Seeing the chaos, Neale jammed his vehicle into reverse and drove back to a Kostrad Battalion 515 military post, less than five minutes away, at the Mile 64 checkpoint. Kostrad is the Indonesian Army's Strategic Reserve Command. According to Lexy Lintuuran, Freeport's security chief, the Kostrad company stationed at Mile 64 has more than one hundred soldiers.[76] The soldiers at Mile 64, about three hundred meters from the attack site, later claimed to not have heard any of the shooting. These soldiers say that they first learned of the attack at 12:40 p.m., when Andrew Neale arrived at their post.[77] This was the same military checkpoint where Steve Emma had an uneasy feeling earlier that day.

Neale drove back to the scene of the shooting with two of the soldiers in his car. When the Kostrad soldiers arrived at the scene, the attackers melted away. The soldiers briefly fired their guns. Then the shooting abruptly stopped.[78]

Atanasio dos Santos, a police officer stationed miles away from the ambush site at Security Post 700 in Tembagapura, said that he received a phone call at 12:15 p.m. reporting "sounds of an explosion" along the Timika–Tembagapura road. He traveled directly to the scene of the crime, but soldiers were already there when he arrived.[79] In addition to Kostrad Battalion 515 soldiers, dos Santos also saw another soldier. He told police investigators: "I saw a man armed with a rifle who was dressed in civilian clothes, a black jacket. This was around 2:00 p.m. near the ambush site at Mile 63, and I have a hunch that he was a member of Kopassus."[80] Reports of at least one Kopassus officer at the scene of the crime led police investigators to explore the possibility that the Indonesian military had staged the ambush. Given the history of Kopassus—their involvement in extrajudicial assassinations and covert operations—it was plausible that they had helped stage this act of terror.

The Shooters

Antonius Wamang admits to participating in the ambush on August 31, 2002. Wamang told me that he thought his group was attacking an Indonesian military convoy. A teenage boy named Johni Kacamol was also placed at the crime scene by an eyewitness. The Indonesian driver Mastur, saw Kacamol carrying a gun.[81] Another man, Yulianus Deikme, told investigators that he was at the crime scene but did not carry a weapon.[82] Hardi Tsugumol, the West Papuan man who reportedly obtained bullets from his friends in the special forces and helped lay plans for "an action," told investigators that he was not at the crime scene. But other witnesses place him there. Wamang claims that other gunmen, a separate group of shooters, were present at the ambush site as well.[83]

Wamang voluntarily agreed to meet with FBI agent Ronald C. Eowan on August 12, 2003. Wamang told Eowan: "I saw two white Freeport vehicles on the road as well as an Indonesian military vehicle next to the road. I also saw Indonesian soldiers shooting—like they were competing. I saw four Indonesian soldiers and one West Papuan, who was also a soldier."[84] Did Wamang fabricate the story about the second group of shooters? Perhaps he was playing up speculation about Indonesian military involvement in hopes of sending investigators down the wrong path? Still, if Wamang was solely responsible for these murders, if there were no soldiers in a vehicle on the road, why would he agree to be interviewed by the FBI in the first place? The FBI's August 2003 interview with Wamang took place three years before Special Agent Eowan apprehended him.

The FBI later discredited Wamang's report about the second group of shooters. Still, the presence of an unexplained white vehicle at the crime scene, as reported by several of the American schoolteachers, supports Wamang's claim. Ballistics evidence, victim testimony, and other crime scene witnesses also lend credibility to Wamang's initial statement.

It is not clear who fired the first four shots in the ambush, which victims remember as being distinct and methodical.[85] After Rick Spier and Ted Burgon were killed by these initial shots, there was a pause of one or two minutes. According to Steve Emma, "After one or two minutes of silence

12–14 shots destroyed the windshield."[86] According to a later autopsy report, two different types of bullets were found in Rick Spier's body.[87]

Wamang told me that he left the ambush scene shortly after the second vehicle, the Land Cruiser carrying Patsy Spier and the other teachers, arrived on the scene.[88] Wamang told police investigators that shortly after the second vehicle came to a stop, "there were shots coming from the direction of Tembagapura, from the opposite embankment, right at us. I told my companions, 'There is shooting, there is shooting.'"[89]

"We weren't there very long. We immediately retreated," Wamang told me in an Indonesian-language tape-recorded interview. I asked: "Were you there thirty minutes?" "No," Wamang replied, "thirty minutes is way too long."[90] Victim testimony about the duration of the attack is inconsistent. But many, like Steve Emma, told investigators that the shooting lasted around forty-five minutes.

Wamang told FBI Special Agent Eowan that he left the crime scene when he saw a white woman crawl out of one of the vehicles.[91] Wamang told me that he had believed up until that moment that he had been shooting at an Indonesian military convoy. No one followed as Wamang's group beat a hasty retreat on foot. As they left the scene, he says other gunmen continued shooting.[92]

Wamang told me that his group, a ragtag band of teenagers and men with limited weapons training, shot at the cars from atop an embankment. They reportedly wore black shorts, black T-shirts, and black plastic headbands. Wamang said that they were all barefoot and that they did not approach the stopped cars.[93] Victims of the attack saw some of the shooters walking along the side of the road near the vehicles. But their reports suggest that these were not Wamang's men. Ken Balk told investigators: "I saw one of the shooters clearly. He was wearing green military camouflage pants with a dark t-shirt. He wore black military boots."[94]

When I interviewed Wamang years later, he was wearing cheap plastic sandals. He told me that none of his men could afford to buy shoes. He told me that he only had three guns. "We had one M16, one SS1, and one Mauser," he said.[95] Wamang's account of his weaponry is consistent with the evidence presented by chief prosecutor Anita Asterida.[96]

At least thirteen guns were shot at the crime scene, according to a ballistics report issued by the Police Central Forensic Laboratory on December 19, 2002: five M16s, six SS1s, and two Mausers.[97] Nine weapons were identified by FBI experts as belonging to Kostrad Battalion 515, the Indonesian military detachment stationed in Timika with security checkpoints along the Timika–Tembagapura road.[98] There are no similar smoking guns linking Kopassus special forces soldiers to the crime scene. But one gun was unaccounted for by investigators. Police ballistics experts also suggested that there may have been more than thirteen weapons shot at the crime scene. Nonautomatic weapons do not necessarily leave casings behind.[99]

Were the weapons of the Kostrad Battalion 515 soldiers fired in the direction of Wamang and his men? Or were they shot into the vehicles of the teachers? The ballistics evidence presented in the Central Jakarta district court that convicted Wamang did not directly speak to these questions.[100] If Kostrad shooters were standing on the opposite embankment from Wamang, as eyewitness testimony suggests, then the question of their intended target may indeed be difficult to discern. Bullet holes on the left and right sides of the victim's vehicles indicate that hostile shooters were positioned on both sides of the road.[101] Evidence of Indonesian military attackers, or evidence that shooters had commandeered Freeport vehicles, was not pursued by the Indonesian court that convicted Wamang and his colleagues.

Atanasio dos Santos, the police officer from Tembagapura, is not the only eyewitness who saw a Kopassus soldier at the crime scene. Decky Murib, a West Papuan man who works as a military informant, told police investigators that ten soldiers picked him up at Hotel Serayu in Timika at 7:30 a.m. on the morning of the attack.[102] Murib often accompanied Indonesian officers in their operations. It is not unusual for villagers like Murib to work informally for Indonesian soldiers. Murib told me he was surprised to see Kopassus Captain Margus Arifin leading this group. "He was supposed to be in Bandung," Murib told me in a tape-recorded interview.[103] Bandung is a city in Java, thousands of miles from West Papua.

Margus Arifin had formerly been the Kopassus liaison officer at Freeport's Emergency Planning Operation (EPO) office. EPO is a Freeport division that provides logistical, transportation, and communication support for the more than three thousand Indonesian security personnel stationed in the area.[104] According to Global Witness, a London-based rights organization, "Freeport Indonesia appears to have made payments totaling U.S.$46,000 and described mostly as food costs, to Captain Margus Arifin" by March 2002.[105]

Decky Murib told police investigators that Arifin brought him in a car with license plate number 609 through the Freeport checkpoints and dropped him, with four soldiers, at Mile 62 of the Tembagapura road. Arifin reportedly continued north along the road with the remaining soldiers in the direction of the Kostrad Battalion at Mile 64.[106] Kostrad and Kopassus solders are under separate chains of command in Indonesia's military but often conduct joint operations.[107] Later Murib worked with police investigators to identify Kopassus soldiers whom he alleged were at the crime scene: Captain Margus Arifin, First Lieutenant Wawan Suwandi, Second Class Sergeant I Wayan Suradnya, and First Class Private Jufri Uswanas.[108]

Margus Arifin denied Murib's testimony, saying that he was in Bandung that day. Kopassus commander Major General Sriyanto Muntrasan explained to reporters for *Tempo* magazine that Bandung was the site of a course that Arifin was attending.

The vehicle with license plate 609 was from the vehicle fleet of the EPO, the Freeport division where Margus Arifin had been the liaison officer. "Two or three Indonesian military officers were assigned to the EPO division," Dr. Joseph Molyneux told me in a phone interview. Molyneux was Freeport's corporate chief of security at the time of the attack and was working for the FBI when I interviewed him. "They would have been able to approve the use of vehicle 609 or could have taken it on their own, since they had direct access to it."[109] According to Lexy Lintuuran, another Freeport security executive, a white Toyota Land Cruiser with the license plate 609 passed through the checkpoints on the morning of the attack. Lintuuran said that Decky Murib's statement is consistent with the Freeport record.[110]

Was this the vehicle—the white Toyota Land Cruiser, carrying men who were "officially dressed, wearing security caps"—seen by victims at the crime scene? Was this also the "Indonesian military vehicle" that Wamang described to the FBI? Decky Murib's report that vehicle 609 was at the crime scene certainly checks out with other accounts.

Another vehicle, also reportedly procured through the Indonesian officers at Freeport's EPO division, was commandeered by Wamang's group of shooters. Just before dawn on the day of the attack, Hardi Tsugumol, one of Wamang's coconspirators, and two other men were "picked up at the Pompa Dua complex in the Kwamki Lama neighborhood [a Timika suburb] by a white Toyota Land Cruiser from Freeport's Emergency Planning Operation division," according to a report written by Deminikus Bebari of the Amungme Indigenous Council (Lemassa).[111] Tsugumol said that they traveled along the Timika–Tembagapura road, past five checkpoints, that morning.[112] Checkpoints mean nothing to soldiers. "They do as they please, they don't care. The only ones we cannot control are the security vehicles," said Lexy Lintuuran, the security executive at Freeport.[113]

Did Tsugumol serve as a double agent? Did he deliberately set up Wamang and other West Papuans? Did he redirect their dreams of heroically attacking Indonesian soldiers to attacking American civilians instead? Did Tsugumol bring a group of Indonesian military shooters to the place where Wamang was waiting in ambush? We may never know the answers to these questions. Even later on his prison deathbed, Tsugumol refused to reveal the identity of the vehicle's driver, saying that he had to protect his "friend."

The Coverup

Victims of the ambush were immediately transported to SOS Tembagapura hospital and soon evacuated to larger hospitals in Australia and Indonesia. The seven expatriate survivors with the most serious injuries were flown to Townsville in northern Australia on September 1, 2002. "In their desire to keep a lid on information, the [Townsville] hospital and Freeport did not allow the patients to use the telephone for the first day and a half," according to a cable from the U.S. consulate in Sydney, which was recently declassified.[114] The victims of the attack were initially not even allowed to contact their families.

When U.S. intelligence reports linked the Timika attack to the Indonesian military, Senator Russell D. Feingold (D-Wis.) sponsored an amendment to prohibit "normalization" of the U.S.-Indonesia military relationship. Senator Wayne Allard (R-Colo.) sponsored a parallel amendment that prohibited the release of US$600,000 in military training funds. Both amendments passed in October 2003. Only "fully cooperating" with the FBI investigation would allow the Indonesian military to receive these funds.

General Susilo Bambang Yudhoyono became Indonesia's main point person for "cooperating" with U.S. diplomats and secret agents who were working to bring the Timika investigation to a swift resolution. At the time, Yudhoyono was the coordinating minister of political and security affairs. He was later elected president of Indonesia. Playing an active role in managing and influencing the direction of the investigation, demonstrating an unusual level of interest for someone of his stature, General Yudhoyono met repeatedly with U.S. diplomats, as well as low-ranking FBI field investigators, blocking their initial attempts to gain unmediated access to witnesses and material evidence.

Indonesian police suspected that the crime scene had been tampered with

Mr. X. On September 1, 2002, one day after the attack that killed the American schoolteachers, the body of Mr. X appeared near the crime scene. Indonesian military officers claimed that their troops had shot one of the Papuan guerrilla attackers. The *Washington Post* reported that Mr. X was a former military informant named Deminus Waker. Reportedly, Waker was kidnapped by security forces before the ambush, extrajudicially executed, and then dumped near the site where the teachers were ambushed. However, Indonesian officials claimed that Mr. X was Elias Kwalik, an alleged accomplice of Antonius Wamang. *Photograph courtesy of Elsham.*

from the very start. The body of "Mr. X" mysteriously appeared near the site of the attack on September 1, 2002, one day after the shooting. Several months later, on December 27, Yudhoyono wrote to the chargé d'affaires of the U.S. embassy in Jakarta: "I have dispatched a fact finding team led by one of my deputies to Timika and its surrounding[s], to find additional information and other related facts especially on broader political and security aspects of the incident." Years later Paula Makabory, who was then the Elsham field coordinator based in Timika, told journalists that this team "let the Indonesian military cover their tracks" and accused Yudhoyono of "stalling tactics." "The 'fact finders' under his command systematically intimidated witnesses and tampered with material evidence," Makabory said.[115]

The U.S. ambassador stressed in a June 2003 meeting with Yudhoyono that justice in the Timika killings was "the most important issue in the bilateral relationship."[116] But, during this period, FBI agents were given intermittent access to evidence. Yudhoyono continued to play an active role in coordinating the political aspects of the investigation. At the same time that Yudhoyono was trying to convince Washington that he was cooperating, Indonesian military agents began silencing human rights investigators who were conducting their own independent research and advocacy.

Another World Destroyed

Investigations into the attack on the schoolteachers became the site of a different battle altogether: a high-stakes conflict between the Indonesian military and West Papuan human rights advocates. Weeks after the attack, on September 26, 2002, John Rumbiak hosted a press conference where he released the preliminary results of the Elsham investigation. He presented evidence "suggesting the shooting was carried out by Indonesian military personnel or groups facilitated by the military."[117] The BBC, Radio Australia, and many West Papuan newspapers covered the report. Two days later, the Indonesian military denied the charges and announced that it was suing Elsham.

The lawsuit hung in limbo in the courts while Indonesian officials waited for a definitive signal from Washington. In 2004, less than a week after Wamang was indicted by a U.S. federal grand jury, an Indonesian district court found Elsham guilty of libel. The rights group was fined 50 million rupiah (US$5,481) and ordered to publicly apologize through national print and television media.

Paula Makabory, an Elsham field coordinator based in Timika, who met with lawmakers on Capitol Hill in June 2005, was also intimidated. I accompanied her as she presented congressional offices with specific evidence that linked the Indonesian military to Antonius Wamang. In the months after Makabory's visit to Washington, high-powered lobbyists began asking congressional aides for the names of West Papuan "separatists" who had visited Capitol Hill in the recent past. The lobbyists were employees of Richard L. Collins and Company, a firm that had been contracted by BIN, Indonesia's main intelligence agency, according to a note circulated to seventy-four congressional offices by Edmund McWilliams, a former U.S. State Department official. "There is a very strong basis for concern that any West Papuan whose names were given to BIN would face real danger," wrote McWilliams. "Several Papuan human rights advocates have recently fled West Papua because of death threats and a number of prominent Papuan human rights advocates have been detained, tortured, and murdered by security forces."[118]

After Paula Makabory returned to her home in Timika, her family was terrorized. She called me on November 15, 2005, telling me about two prowlers who tried to break into her house in broad daylight: "Yesterday my two children, Godwin and Cindy, as well as my adopted son Berto, were at home alone," she said in Indonesian. "One man tried to enter the front door without knocking. . . . At the same time there was the sound of someone clambering in back of the house. He made a racket when he stepped on a piece of tin roofing. The second man woke up my dog, which had been sleeping on the back porch. The dog began barking and chased the man away." Paula got home after the two men left, and heard the story from her children. In the coming months, she relocated to Melbourne with her children Cindy and Godwin. She has since been granted political asylum.

Paula Makabory was one node in an extended network of Elsham contacts that John Rumbiak had developed in every major urban area of West Papua. After John went into exile and then had a stroke, the regional networks faded away. Elsham was all but destroyed during its investigation of the Timika murders. As key employees sought refuge abroad and others dropped out of human rights work as a result of threats, the organization was reduced to a skeleton. Rumors spread that Elsham was a "separatist organization," and donors subsequently withdrew support.[119] From afar, international organizations like Amnesty International and Human Rights Watch continued reporting on abuses by Indonesian security forces, which showed no signs of letting up. But access to West Papua remained difficult for foreign researchers.

The social world of human rights began to evade detection, scatter along multiple lines of flight, burrow into established institutions.[120] Paranoid fears articulated by Indonesian leaders equated human rights in West Papua with separatism, distancing indigenous struggles for justice from the social world of the reform movement within the unitary state. With the marginalization of human rights research, a phantasmagoria of shadows proliferated, a shifting series of illusions, figures passing into each other and dissolving, terrifying dreams that captured the collective imagination.[121] As human rights activities went underground, U.S. secret agents also worked in the shadows. FBI agents planned an overseas operation, an increasingly common occurrence since September 11, aimed at bringing the Timika investigation to a definitive end.

A Sting

Indonesian authorities failed to capture Antonius Wamang after he was indicted by a U.S. federal grand jury. Perhaps they feared the story he might tell in court. The impasse prompted Willy Mandowen, a West Papuan politician, to begin talking with the FBI and U.S. government officials about negotiating Wamang's surrender. On December 7, 2005, Mandowen sent an e-mail to a public discussion forum for West Papuan activists: "Tomorrow at Capitol Hill, Washington, D.C., we are meeting with important representatives of the U.S. Congress who are giving full support to help us resolve our problems in West Papua in a comprehensive and humanitarian manner."[122] Congressional staffers, including Keith Luse, an aide to Senator Lugar and a professional staff member of the Senate Foreign Relations Committee, talked with Mandowen about the possibility that FBI agents might bring Wamang to stand trial in America.[123]

When Willy Mandowen came back to Timika, he told Wamang and other suspects in the killings that they would be flown to America if they handed themselves over to the FBI.[124] Special Agents Myers and Eowan invited Wamang, other suspects, and community leaders to a meeting at Hotel Amole Dua in Timika on January 11, 2006. A local church leader, Reverend Isak Onawame, delivered invitations to the meeting. Onawame joined the gathering at the hotel in an attempt to guarantee the safety of the other participants. At the meeting, the FBI agents reiterated promises to bring Wamang, his accomplices, and local leaders to America.

The FBI loaded twelve men, including Wamang and Reverend Onawame, into the back of a medium-sized truck. The agents told the men that inside the truck they would be safe from Indonesian authorities. The FBI said that this was the first stage of the journey to America. Once inside the truck, with the back door shut, the men could not see out. They did not know where the truck was headed.

The truck stopped in front of a local Indonesian police station in Kuala Kencana, a gated community built by Freeport for company employees. Indonesian troops with the elite Brimob unit were waiting in front of the station. After seeing that the twelve men were in Indonesian custody, Special Agents Myers and Eowan departed.

At first U.S. officials denied any FBI role in apprehending the men.[125] Perhaps this is because Special Agents Myers and Eowan violated Indonesian law when they detained people without a warrant.[126] Innocent people suffered through humiliating treatment and physical abuse as a result of this FBI action on foreign soil. The detainees were subjected to strip searches, deprived of sleep for over twenty-four hours, and, in one case, beaten.[127] Four of the men, who were never charged with any crime, were released the next day.[128]

Reverend Onawame, the leader who distributed invitations to the meeting at Hotel Amole Dua, was not released. He had a reputation as an outspoken advocate for merdeka and had presented briefings to U.S. policymakers on Capitol Hill. Did Indonesian authorities use his association with Wamang as a pretense to keep him in prison? Wamang has repeatedly said that Onawame was not involved in the crime. "It's fine if I am held responsible," Wamang said, "but the Reverend didn't even help us with logistics."[129] The court documents do not claim that Onawame was at the scene of the crime, but prosecutors quoted Onawame as saying: "I gave two (2) sacks of rice and one (1) plastic tent to Antonius Wamang."[130]

Two other detainees, Jairus Kibak and Esau Onawame, also told investigators that they supplied Wamang with food and camping equipment.[131] The court documents do not claim that these men were at the scene of the crime. According to a congressional aide who has been closely following the case, the FBI did not possess any other evidence implicating Reverend Isak Onawame, Jairus Kibak, and Esau Onawame in this crime other than these "confessions." All the prisoners, including the three men who confessed to giving Wamang groceries and camping gear, were soon transferred to the detention center at the Indonesian police headquarters in Jakarta, thousands of miles from West Papua. They were not given their own cells to sleep in. Instead they all shared the prison "TV room." While in jail, the men were threatened by other prisoners and the guards.[132]

Onawame has since retracted his confession about the tent. "I was in a difficult situation," Onawame told me in a phone interview from prison. "Anton Wamang had handed himself in based on my guarantee that he would be given a fair trial in America. We Amungme people cannot betray someone. If I had walked out on Anton Wamang, his relatives would have made trouble for me. I lied, I made up the story about the tent, to give Anton moral support in jail."[133]

The Trial

A simple script about terrorism in West Papua was coauthored by the FBI and Indonesian prosecutors in a Jakarta courtroom. FBI special agents, ballistics experts, and U.S. federal prosecutors were on hand to help their Indonesian counterparts. According to the official accounts that they helped compose, Wamang and his band of guerrilla fighters staged a terrorist attack in hopes of furthering the cause of independence. Facts that did not fit the script were simply left out. The courtroom accounts made no mention of the Indonesian agents whom Wamang reportedly met in Jakarta or the local special forces soldiers who reportedly supplied the group with bullets. Nor did the court seriously consider evidence of an unexplained vehicle that reportedly brought Indonesian military shooters to the scene of the crime.

During the trial, Hardi Tsugumol, the man with known ties to the Indonesian military, developed serious heart problems. After a delay of two months, he finally underwent heart surgery. Tsugumol also suffered from hepatitis and HIV/AIDS. One of the prisoners' lawyers, Riando Tambunan, repeatedly asked the court to attend to Tsugumol's health problems, but visits from doctors were infrequent.

As Tsugumol's heath deteriorated, the other men charged with the crime refused to attend the trial and went on a hunger strike until he was given proper medical attention. Attempts by the defense lawyers to piece together coherent and credible arguments were frustrated by the prisoners who were boycotting the trial proceedings. "The charges and evidence brought against them were never properly evaluated in the courtroom," said Ecoline Situmorang, one of the defense attorneys. "Without the full participation of our clients in the trial, we had difficulties in rebutting the prosecutor's allegations."[134]

Antonius Wamang and Hardi Tsugumol did not talk about their ties to the Indonesian military in the courtroom. "The threats that we were subjected to in prison made Anton Wamang afraid to tell the whole story," said Reverend Onawame in a telephone interview from prison.[135] Were Wamang and Tsugumol also trying to protect their "friends" on the inside? Were they guaranteed a light sentence and a possible early release in exchange for hiding the details of their military collaborations?

Wamang was sentenced to life in prison by the court on November 7, 2006. Two other defendants, Johni Kacamol and Yulianus Deikme, were each sentenced to seven years in jail, and the other four, Reverend Onawame, Hardi Tsugumol, Jairus Kibak, and Esau Onawame, were initially sentenced to eighteen months.[136] Tsugumol died less than a month later, on December 1, 2006.[137]

The very day that Wamang was sentenced to life in prison, Washington signaled a "new era of military co-operation" with Indonesia.[138] The Bush administration moved quickly to restore military aid programs in Indonesia. In 2006 a new Pentagon program was announced that provided US$19 million for building Indonesian military capacity. The next year, in December 2007, Congress decided to award the Indonesian military US$18.4 million in foreign military financing for the 2008 fiscal year.[139] Sidestepping evidence that the Indonesian military had killed American civilians, the U.S. government transformed enemies into allies, reinforcing relations of global hegemony, ensuring the predictable flow of natural resources and manufactured goods in the modern world system.

Entangled Stories

The rubric of coproduction explains how contingent collaborations, the connections between Wamang's group and the Indonesian military, enabled the ambush to take place. Coproduction might also help us understand the collaborations between the FBI and Indonesian officials that came to frame this attack as an act of terrorism. General Yudhoyono, the security minister who later became president, in his own words worked to coordinate the different investigations "at the political level."[140] Yet in many ways the FBI investigation proceeded independently of Indonesian authorities. The FBI had its own field agents and an independent network of informants. Each investigative team had separate microprocesses by which the case came to have form and meaning.[141] The FBI did not apparently conspire with Indonesian authorities to fabricate or destroy evidence. Instead they worked closely with Indonesian agents to construct a politically viable narrative that fit parts of the existing evidence.

FBI agents ignored evidence that did not support their simple story. Dismissing inconvenient facts, sometimes during angry outbursts in the middle of an interview, they waged discursive and epistemic violence against their subjects. Tracking the truth during high-stakes murder investigations like this one is perhaps similar to investigating claims of genocide. When genocide is taking place, the evidence is always hard to uncover. Leaders rarely state their intentions to destroy another ethnic, national, or racial group.[142] Murderers, at least ones who are trying to escape punishment for their crime, are also usually hesitant to reveal all the facts. When Bush administration officials and FBI investigators pointed to the lack of proof that Indonesian agents played a role in the murder of these teachers, they were engaging in a strategic power play.

In the aftermath of the trial that sentenced Wamang to life in prison, as I was writing up my own research for publication, I tried working the halls of Capitol Hill, presenting congressional staff members with a summary of my findings. In many of my meetings, I was joined by Karen Orenstein, the national coordinator of the East Timor Action Network (ETAN), who had accompanied me to my meeting at the FBI headquarters in September 2004. ETAN's grassroots activists had pressured the U.S. government to get behind East Timor's successful independence referendum in 1999. Indonesian soldiers who had been convicted of crimes against humanity in East Timor have since rotated to serve in West Papua, so an organic link connected our political projects. ETAN was also fighting a losing battle against the Bush administration's initiatives to give U.S. taxpayer money to the Indonesian military.

Karen knew how to work the halls of Capitol Hill, but she was not your typical Washington insider. She rode her bicycle across town to work every day, even in the winter, and often arrived at congressional meetings with her pant legs tucked into her socks—where she had stuck them for protection from her bike chain. Together we visited dozens of congressional offices, sometimes getting a polite reception, other times meeting junior staff members who sat passively with a glazed look on their face. On more than one occasion, in Republican offices, we were met with open hostility. Citing scores of interviews, thousands of pages of courtroom transcripts, and hundreds of declassified U.S. government documents, I tried to lay out the evidence pointing to an Indonesian military role in the murder of two Americans. After listening to my exhaustive presentation ad nauseam, Karen gave me a bit of critical advice. "Politics isn't about facts," said Karen, "but about stories." The FBI's simple story, backed by the power of Bush administration officials, made sense in Washington: "People of color, terrorists with guns, had attacked innocent Americans."

"Your story is too complicated," Karen continued. "Wamang was a complicated guy with connections to West Papuan guerrillas as well as the Indonesian military. His story is too complex to make intuitive sense. And your facts interrupt too many things that Washington takes for granted, the dominant and settled stories. American victims overseas is a story that Congress can easily understand. Indigenous people who are in conflict with U.S. corporations over land and resources is just not a story that most people in Washington want to hear."

Reflecting on Karen's critical advice, I searched my field notes and interview transcripts for other, more inspiring tales. The new era of U.S.-Indonesia military cooperation that emerged after the trial of Antonius Wamang seemed to show that there was little hope for West Papua on the international stage. Amid failed collaborations of the guerrilla movement, the assassination of political leaders, and the virtual destruction of Elsham, the struggle for rights, peace, and national independence seemed to be hopeless. Still, in this situation of seeming impossibility, young West Papuan activists initiated critical conversations within the movement, questioning the collaborations of independence leaders, trying to hold the older generations accountable.

III. HORIZONS

2002–2028

Bald Grandfather Willy

Merdeka is not about praying and then grabbing fistfuls of dirt to eat, starts a playful, but dead serious, critique that was posted on Komunitas Papua (The Papuan Community), a public e-mail discussion group for West Papuan activists. This e-mail subversively poked fun at Willy Mandowen, one of the so-called freedom fighters who helped the FBI capture Antonius Wamag in January 2006. "Chimbu Rose," the pseudonymous author of the critique, continues: "Land is good for planting, or building a house, or making a road, but not for eating. . . . I just want to tell Bald Grandfather Willy, to stop already, stop lying to the people. Truth will run over the liars."[1]

The truth about Willy Mandowen was already starting to come out. An Australian journalist reported that Mandowen was receiving considerable sums of money from foreign corporations operating in West Papua.[2] Some of this money helped stage the 2000 Papuan Congress, a momentous event involving the convergence of thousands of West Papuan independence activists. After the Congress, Willy Mandowen became a rich man and the moderator of the Papuan Presidium Council, the organization formerly headed by Theys Eluay. Grassroots activists such as Chimbu Rose were beginning to criticize Mandowen and other members of the Papuan Presidium Council who were personally profiting as they rallied the masses behind anticolonial nationalism.

The imagery of Willy Mandowen eating dirt—exploiting the homeland without giving anything back—accompanied a more serious allegation: that Willy was betraying the cause of freedom. The e-mail was addressed to "Willy 'Manwen' Mandowen." In the Biak language, *manwen* means ghost, a code word for Indonesian intelligence agent. On June 13, 2005, a report by SPMNews Biak directly alleged: "Willy Mandowen is channeling information to the National Intelligence Agency [BIN, or Badan Intelijen Negara]

A poster depicting Tom Beanal (left) and Willy Mandowen (right) that was
displayed at a protest outside the offices of Freeport McMoRan in Jakarta.
The caption reads: "Agents of American capitalism who struggle for the dollar."
Photograph courtesy of Elsham.

about the daily activities and long-term strategies of independence organizations."[3] Mandowen, also a subscriber to the *Komunitas Papua* e-mail discussion group, immediately denied this allegation, challenging the anonymous Internet journalist to reveal his or her identity and to come up with
"proof."

The Australian historian Peter King reports that Willy Mandowen first
"established connections with the Indonesian military through English
language teaching" when he was a professor at Bird of Paradise University.[4] After high-level negotiations with Indonesian officials in 1999, as the
groundwork was being laid for the Team of 100 national dialogue, Willy
Mandowen gave regular reports to the military.[5] Mandowen has also maintained relationships with foreign intelligence agents and criminal investigators. When he helped set up the FBI sting in January 2006, news of his
involvement was reported in the international media.[6] Some collaborations
inspire hope. Other subversions, and double-crossings, threaten to destroy
freedom dreams.

The collaborations of "Bald Grandfather" Willy were perpetuating existing inequalities rather than opening up new possibilities of freedom. Engaging with the occupiers, or the forces of global hegemony, can bring opportunities into view. But coalition building is a difficult process, especially from a subordinate position.[7] Fragile alliances can easily be infiltrated and destroyed. As illustrated by the tragic story of Theys Eluay, failing to separate enemies from allies can literally be fatal. "Without a clear vision, or purpose, collaborators drown," Chimbu Rose told me.

"Chimbu Rose" recently revealed her real name to the online *Komunitas Papua* forum: Yoneke Sabaseba. After finishing high school, she tried going to college at Gadja Mada University, one of the nation's top schools. But she quit. "I was bored with Indonesian schools that went around and around but didn't teach me how to be smart," she wrote me in an e-mail. Sabaseba started cultivating her own productive garden—growing crops of sweet potatoes, betel nut, and squash. Renting an apartment in Sentani, the suburb of Jayapura where Theys Eluay was laid to rest, she planted her vegetables high on a hill. Civil servants, lawyers, and teachers in her extended family routinely helped out with living expenses, enabling her to focus full-time on writing and activism. When we met, she did not have a paying job, but a church group was giving her free Internet access. For Sabaseba, merdeka had become a lived reality as much as it was a bundle of aspirations about a future to come.

As a farmer, an online political critic, and recently a poet, Sabaseba's lived experiences break down familiar oppositions between the indigenous urban elite and the rural peasantry.[8] Her poem "Marxism, Leninism, and Leaning Somewhat to the Left" grapples with internal tensions faced by many movements for freedom in the early twenty-first century. Punctuating lyrical verse with the sound *cuih*—the sound of hawking phlegm— she registers frustration with the contradictions inherent in revolutionary struggle. Sabaseba sent this poem to *Komunitas Papua* in August 2006:

In the middle of the Blind Night
Our friends Arnold and Sam sing sadly[9]
All about living . . . .

Full Moon stabbing at every suburb
I listen quietly

Cuih. . . . they say marxism. . . . for West Papua . . .
Cuih. . . . they say fight. . . . for West Papua . . .

Then running from West Papua towards the Colonizing Country

Cuih. . . . they say marxism. . . .
Then use them capitalist things . . .

Cuih. . . . they say leaning somewhat to the left. . . .
Then using them capitalist things . . .

Cuih . . . they say fight the Indonesian colonizers. . . .

Then. . . . still eat rice and wear them shirts made by Indonesia, That
   honorable honorable colonizer. . . .
Cuih. . . . they say use non-violent resistance. . . . .

Then Run to Java when the violence hits West Papua . . . like cats caught in
   the rain

So . . . screaming shouting like thunder and lightning . . .

Not from the Sky, only in the fugitive sky. . . . the land of the colonizer that
   is called the country of Java. . . .

Not from the Sky, only from the fugitive place . . . that is called Madang. . . .
   neighboring country . . . the unclear Place, who knows where you will be
   buried???

Cuih. . . . a glob of spit jumps from the mouth . . .

Cuih. . . . Without shame using capitalist things . . . .

Cuih . . . a glob of spit flies towards the sky . . . . . .

Cuih . . . and *cuih* . . . .

Rain comes refreshing these constructions . . . .

The poem criticizes independence leaders in exile, who have formed a "revo-lutionary council" in Madang, Papua New Guinea, safe from Indonesian military threats and far from actual revolutionary action. The lines also grapple with the difficulties of sustaining a movement for freedom under a military occupation that is supported by the forces of global capitalism. When I later met Sabaseba in Sentani, I took her out to dinner at a restau-rant run by Indonesians, since the few West Papuan-owned establishments were on the other side of town. The staple dish of our meal was rice, a crop that does not readily grow in West Papua.

Reflecting on our restaurant choice and referencing the lines of her poem about eating rice and using "capitalist things," I asked Sabaseba if her activism was constrained by material reality. "My own computer is a 'capitalist thing,' a tool that I have appropriated for the struggle," she replied. "Like the computers they sell you in the United States, the gold and copper wires in my computer are likely from the Freeport mine in Timika. But this doesn't mean I can't use it as a weapon to fight Freeport." The spit, or rain, of critics refreshes familiar constructions in Sabaseba's poem — Marxism, capitalism, West Papua, colonialism, nonviolence, nationalism. Independence activists, and Sabaseba herself, often find their imaginations forced into inherited constructs.

The script of anticolonial liberation was written by Euro-American intellectuals to further neocolonial schemes, according to Partha Chatterjee, who has written extensively about sovereignty and democracy in former colonial countries. Chatterjee suggests that the prevailing model of independent postcolonial states is copied from colonial states.[10] When new countries inherited "modular nationalism," the model of the nation described by Benedict Anderson, their possibilities for freedom were constrained. To reiterate one of Chatterjee's provocative questions: "If nationalisms in the rest of the world have to choose their imagined community from certain 'modular' forms already made available to them by Europe and the Americas, what do they have left to imagine?"[11] The imagination of West Papuan intellectuals has certainly not been limited by the models of the nation that were originally formulated abroad. West Papuan visionaries were reanimating local cosmologies and reworking alien ideas. Seeing the failings of postcolonial nationalism in a world dominated by multinational capitalism, West Papuans began to aspire for more than the partial sovereignty that comes with national independence in the early twenty-first century.

Since Otto Bauer's influential essay "The Nation" (1924), scholars have questioned the ability of small countries to thrive in the era of modern capitalism. Small nations are always forced to negotiate treaties with larger states and are almost always at a disadvantage.[12] Would an independent West Papua be in a position to protect citizens and the environment from the forces of predatory capital? If West Papuan nationalists succeed in their struggle for independence from Indonesia, will they be able to negotiate fair deals with foreign corporations and beneficial agreements with more powerful nations?

West Papuan students and young intellectuals who cut their teeth as activists under the shade of Theys Eluay's banyan tree and in the shadow of Bald Grandfather Willy had become keenly aware that the leadership had been captured by transnational capital. In the eyes of young activists like Chimbu Rose, the love of money was a fatal character flaw in these leaders. As the fickle spirit of the messianic multiple danced away from one-time independence leaders, it came to animate other figures on approaching horizons.

Even as Indonesian terror campaigns intensified, activists began to work together in the shadows, imagining new horizons of possibility in a seemingly impossible situation. Merdeka had gone back underground and online. Returning to strategies from earlier historical periods, the work of politics was again only done with discretion. Urban activists continued their organizing behind closed doors in safe, domestic spaces. Aspirations for merdeka that had been aired in public — on the streets, in church sermons, and in dialogue with Indonesian presidents — were now voiced in private. Public demands again became hidden transcripts, critiques of power articulated behind the backs of the dominant.[13] Revolutionary dreams spread in places beyond the reach of Indonesian authorities, moving from the jungle camps of guerrilla fighters, to the safe spaces of people's homes, to raucous corners of the Internet, and back again.

In 2002 an anonymous user made a surprising posting, titled *Greetings to the Republic of Indonesia!*, which mocked the hapless authorities from www.infopapua.com, an official website set up by the provincial government. On this web portal, I discovered that activists with the Organisasi Papua Merdeka (OPM), the organization that first took on the form of a rhizome in the 1960s, had become savvy to the latest digital communications technologies. Infopapua.com was established in 2000 to distribute official news about business activities, tourism, sports, and politics. It contained an early application of Web 2.0 technologies — an interactive form that allowed for public peer-to-peer discussions. The posting began: "We the West Papuan People are very proud to be called OPM. That is the truth!!! Because we are not Separatists. We are already free (merdeka)!"[14]

In claiming "we are already free," this electronic salvo announced that West Papuans were exploiting vulnerabilities within emergent cyber-infrastructures, as well as older bureaucratic institutions of domination. A radical politics of engagement, rather than oppositional resistance, or "separatism," was the principal strategy of the organization, according to this anonymous author. The posting on infopapua.com suggested that the OPM had already infiltrated nearly every sector of society. "All West Papuans are OPM," the anonymous author continued. "The Governor of Papua is OPM, the Head of the Provincial Assembly is OPM, the District Regents are OPM, the West Papuan fishermen are OPM, the West Papuan entrepreneurs are OPM, the West Papuan schoolteachers are OPM, even West Papuans who work for the government as soldiers or cops are OPM." The message painted a picture of a vast West Papuan conspiracy. Rather than forming a recognizable structure, the anonymous freedom fighters were everywhere and nowhere.[15]

I had long known that membership in the OPM is loosely defined: some West Papuans maintain that everyone with curly hair and dark skin is a member. Even some Indonesians, with lighter skin and straight black hair, are considered members or allies. Association with the OPM is contagious. Journalists, foreign aid workers, pastors, and Indonesian soldiers have all been claimed by the movement or branded by the government authorities as OPM members. Still, I was surprised when the OPM approached me.

A man with watery eyes and a long, scraggly beard came up to me one afternoon while I was chatting with some West Papuan friends in Jayapura. He was an emissary of General Melkianus Awom, a veteran OPM leader who had been evading Indonesian authorities in the forests of western Biak for some forty years. The next day, a long-distance passenger ferry was departing for Biak. The OPM scout wanted me to travel with him on this boat. He invited me to General Awom's hideout. Pausing, I weighed the implications of canceling all my appointments and suddenly leaving town or of being seen by Indonesian informants associating with the OPM. Perhaps against my better judgment, I agreed to join the elderly man on the ferry. After he left, my West Papuan friends joked that he would probably be given a higher rank by General Awom for enlisting a foreigner in the cause.

CHAPTER SIX

First Voice Honey Center

2002–2008

Before I departed for the forests of West Biak, I consulted with my West Papuan friends about the best present to bring General Melkianus Awom. Strawberry-flavored Fanta, my friends concluded, would be an appropriate tribute to bring to the elder freedom fighter. A devout Christian, Awom neither smoked tobacco nor drank liquor. But during the long decades in the jungle, he had developed a taste for this sweet soda. Along with two liters of bright red Fanta, I brought a satellite phone, a camera, a laptop computer, audio-recording equipment, a GPS tracking device, and a video-recorder to General Awom's headquarters for my own use. I was unarmed, but somehow these advanced communications and tracking technologies gave me a sense of security.

A car with dark-tinted windows had been arranged for the journey, and we sped past a series of Indonesian police and government checkpoints. We slowed down as we approached a West Papuan motorcycle courier who had been waiting for us by the side of the road. When my driver waved the pre-arranged signal, the courier jumped on his motorcycle and sped ahead of us along the road.

The head of the trail to Melkianus Awom's camp was concealed behind a village that at first glance appeared to be no different from the other villages that we had driven past in West Biak. As we pulled up to the house of the village head (*kepala desa*), we were greeted by a throng of smiling men carrying machetes, their scabbards painted in vibrant, interlocking designs. They ushered me onto the front porch of the village head's house. I was asked to write my name, passport number, and address in a register. After saying goodbye to my driver and escort from the city, I started up a trail that led me into the lush hills.

Soldiers with spears and machetes standing at attention at a checkpoint on the path to General Melkianus Awom's camp. *Photograph by Eben Kirksey.*

After walking several hours under heavy jungle cover, we eventually approached a hill. My companions told me that we were getting close. As we climbed a steep stairway made of logs, we were greeted with a series of hand-painted signs: *"Caution! Keep Out! If Afraid Don't Proceed!"* [1] The signs were kitschy. Still, my heart was beating quickly in my chest, perhaps a result of excitement, trepidation, and physical exertion. I expected the unexpected—anything could happen at any time. On the right-hand side of the trail was a small thatched hut where two uniformed guards stood at attention. They wore combat fatigues and had gold stars and stripes on red pieces of wood mounted on the shoulders of their uniforms. As we walked up, the guards saluted. When I returned their salute, they fell into step behind me.

After a few hundred meters, we reached another checkpoint. There was a gateway flanked by pieces of wood that had been carved to look like rockets and fighter jets. These mock armaments were painted in bold blues and reds. Someone had written *"I Love This Motherland"* on the side of one of the rockets. [2] Palm fronds dangled from the gateway. As I crossed the threshold, fronds brushed my face, and I again exchanged salutes with uniformed guards standing on the other side.

At the final checkpoint to General Awom's headquarters, a rectangular portal, like an airport metal detector, stood in the middle of the path. After

I walked through this wooden gate, one of the guards conducted a body search. He found my GPS tracking device in my right pocket, and after concluding that it was not a weapon, he let me pass. A humanoid statue, made out of a black, matted network of roots, stood next to the gate. A stick jutted out of the statue's mouth as if it were a cigarette.

After passing through the mock metal detector, we found ourselves at the edge of a large field. At the other end of the field, several dozen uniformed troops—armed with slingshots, bows and arrows, dart guns, machetes, and four antique bolt-action Mauser rifles—were assembled under two flagpoles that towered over the scene. As I approached the base of the flagpoles, an elderly man dressed in a purple-and-blue robe stood smiling in the door of a building that was graced with an English-language sign: FIRST VOICE HONEY, CENTER PLACE. His white beard fluttered in the breeze. I gave the man a hearty handshake, and he said one word: "Awom."

Two flags flew from the poles towering over our heads: the West Papuan Morning Star flag and the blue-and-white banner of the United Nations. The UN flag had been saved since the administration of the United Nations Temporary Executive Authority in West Papua from October 1, 1962, to May 1, 1963.[3] The flying of the Morning Star and UN flags signified that Melkianus Awom's camp was a liminal space: the people living in this community were perpetually "betwixt and between" being colonial subjects and independent West Papuan citizens.[4] I found a community in waiting. They were waiting for the UN to recognize the historical error that was made when West Papua was transferred to Indonesia instead of granted independence. They were waiting as if to expect the unexpected.

Before we began our interview, Awom invited me to photograph his troops. Each soldier shouldered thick wooden poles and marched back and forth across the field. The men wore elaborate uniforms—camouflaged, khaki, or white—emblazoned with the West Papuan state seal and with shoulder boards to indicate their rank. They were all barefoot. "*None of us wear shoes,*" Awom told me, "*because this is sacred land.*" Red wicker hats, each with a wooden button indicating membership in specific divisions, were balanced on the soldiers' heads. A group of ten women, dressed in vibrant red skirts, blue tops with shoulder boards, and wicker hats, stood at attention as they watched the men parade.

We next entered Awom's office, the building adorned with the English sign FIRST VOICE HONEY, CENTER PLACE. Later, when I asked what "First Voice Honey" means in Indonesian, one of my traveling companions told me with a puzzled look, "*Suara Rembah Madu.*" This phrase translates back

OPM soldiers marching in front of the First Voice Honey Center.
Photograph by Eben Kirksey.

into English as "Voice of Flowing Honey."[5] Awom's office was similar to many other early twenty-first-century West Papuan dwellings that I had visited—it had concrete floors, a tin roof, and cinderblock walls. Yet this building represented a major logistical accomplishment, a monument to the power of collaborative action, because it stood in the middle of the rain forest. It was four hours' walk from the nearest road. All the supplies for the structure had been carried from the road by porters. Here, imaginative visions were producing something in the world. This community was translating expansive hopes into a pragmatic program of political and economic autonomy.

Sitting in the front room of his office, I presented Awom with two liters of strawberry-flavored Fanta as I described my research. I told him that I was there to record his history. As I struggled to understand Awom and his community, he tried to understand me and my project. Only a select number of high-ranking men were permitted in the office to act as witnesses to my audience with the general. Awom spoke slowly, deliberately, into my lapel microphone as he sipped his Fanta. One of his colonels, an older man who was dressed in full uniform, took his own notes with a pen and paper. General Awom tried to recruit me as a potential collaborator, working to capture my imagination with surprising visions and dreams.

He began by contrasting his vision of merdeka with Biaks who misread myths about the Itchy Old Man, the Lord Himself who traveled abroad in disguise, in a body covered with flaky skin and oozing sores. Believers in the powers of the Itchy Old Man staged massive gatherings at various points in Biak's history, waiting for his imminent return. Freek C. Kamma, a Dutch scholar and theologian, has chronicled forty-two outbreaks of messianic movements in Biak that took place over the course of a century, from the 1850s to the Second World War.[6] General Awom explained that these groups did not know how to interpret the Itchy Old Man fables. "They were unable to differentiate between the material [*jasmani*] and the spiritual [*rohani*] dimensions of merdeka," he said.[7] Sometimes these believers had direct confrontations with the authorities, often with disastrous outcomes.

The colonel who was sitting in on our meeting looked up from his notes and started telling me about one such confrontation during the Japanese occupation of Biak in the Second World War. Believers gathered en masse amid rumors that a fleet of Allied ships was just beyond the horizon, about to usher in a new era of freedom. Before the Allies arrived, a Japanese destroyer came to investigate. A canoe full of Biak warriors, who believed that they had become invincible after being doused in holy water, charged the Japanese ship. "Lord grant me an invincible body," the colonel remembered them saying. "They advanced and fell down dead. They shouted 'Jesus, Jesus,' and continued advancing."[8] The holy water did not work, and four Biak men were killed when the Japanese opened fire.[9]

Many Biak prophets were killed by Dutch colonists or were forced to flee after getting in trouble. Still the messianic spirit lived on. In Danilyn Rutherford's words, "the prophets appealed to dreams that long outlived their own demise."[10] General Awom and his men were seeking to distance themselves from the failures of the past, making it clear that they did not believe in invincibility water, that they could distinguish the material from the spiritual. The men of the First Voice Honey Center had nonetheless inherited the spirit, the enduring dreams, that had animated so many different Biak figures throughout the ages. They had inherited the messianic multiple.

General Awom told me that God himself regularly sent angels to bring him news and show him the way. There were signs that merdeka was imminent. Awom told his personal history as salvation history—in his own biography, he found miraculous moments.[11] During the Second World War, he was still a baby, drinking milk at his mother's breast. An American bomber dropped a bomb that exploded right next to him and his mother.

"My mother was just wounded a little, even though the bomb fell very close to us. . . . There was a big hole in the earth, but we were not killed." As a teenager, Awom became a carpenter's apprentice in the city of Manokwari. When the Indonesians first arrived in the early 1960s, he watched them steal things from the people. One of his helpless neighbors lost a motorcycle. "That is when I was visited by God, flanked by two angels," he told me. "The Lord had white skin and his hair was like lightning—it was flashing with radiant light. The angels were barefoot. They had large white wings, like birds."

The angels told Awom to leave his work. He remembers their voices: "Start walking along the road of the struggle," they said. Boarding a ship in Manokwari, he traveled around the Bird's Head Peninsula to the city of Sorong. From the city, Awom walked into the forest and came upon a leper colony. "The two angels went ahead of me, announcing my arrival," he recalled. Walking all the way back to Manokwari, a journey of more than 250 miles, he was given a warm reception in small villages all along the way (see map, page 111). When he reached Manokwari, he joined West Papuans who had worked as policemen under the Dutch as they were forming a new guerrilla group, the OPM.

General Awom took part in the first OPM action. Alongside his distant relative Permenas Ferry Awom, the founder and then the undisputed leader of the OPM, Melkianus Awom was involved in the Kebar incident on July 26, 1965, where this new band of guerrillas killed a group of Indonesian soldiers and escaped into the jungle with their guns.[12] After Permenas Ferry Awom's death in November 1970,[13] Melkianus Awom was one among a multitude of charismatic figures who emerged to lead the OPM as it embodied the form of the rhizome.[14] The OPM developed numerous autonomous clusters of troops, rather than a clearly defined hierarchical command united behind a single supreme commander.[15] A competing guerrilla group, the TPN, was founded in the early 1970s. TPN soldiers like Thadius Yogi, Kelly Kwalik, and later Antonius Wamang launched new military operations independently of Awom's veteran fighters. Some of these upstarts, like Yogi, claimed the symbolic capital of the older organization, calling themselves TPN-OPM guerrillas.

Through the 1970s and 1980s, Indonesian soldiers relentlessly hunted Awom. Living in the jungle, frequently on the move, he stayed ahead of the authorities and occasionally staged surprise attacks. He told me about a special foreign operative who was hired by the Indonesians to kill him:

They brought a cowboy from America, from Texas. He wore some kind of badge and a cowboy jacket. He pursued me until we met in Manswarbo. I went there and saw him start to spin his Colt pistol, that cowboy. He raised his gun to shoot, but I shot first. It hit him in the forehead and he fell onto the ground. The Indonesian troops with him were afraid because they had placed their hopes in him, this cowboy. But I shot him dead. The Indonesians retreated back home.

He came from Texas? I asked.

Yeah, Texas. He arrived in Mardo village. He told the people to tie some thread. He shot and the strand of thread broke. . . . The people from West Biak were afraid. "Hey, he is impressive [hebat]," they said. I guess that I'm even more impressive [hebat], but yeah. That's from God. Even though he was a cowboy, I cut him down.[16]

In addition to the cowboy from Texas, Awom had met four white foreigners before my own arrival. Well aware of his community's position in the global scheme of things, Awom was seeking contact with potential allies from other worlds. Visitors from foreign lands, even those cloaked in ambiguity, were treated as honored guests. Instead of being a liability, my national identity facilitated my access to General Awom. "If you had been a West Papuan researcher, instead of a white foreigner, Awom would have immediately been suspicious of your motives for visiting his camp and recording an interview," said Daniel Randongkir, a researcher with Elsham, the human rights organization that supported my research.

Two years before my own visit, an American, who told his guides that he was a journalist, visited Awom's camp. He presented Awom's men with a video camera, sound recording equipment, and an ATM card that drew from a bank account in America. One of Awom's soldiers asked me if this person might work for the CIA. From the twinkle in this soldier's eye, it seemed that a visit from a CIA agent would actually be a mark of distinction. With the FBI investigation into the murder of schoolteachers in Timika hanging in the balance, with indications that the investigators might find Indonesian military culprits, members of Awom's community saw U.S. security forces as possible allies in the struggle for liberation from Indonesian rule.

Like other TPN and OPM leaders, Awom was not able to create a space that was beyond the reach of Indonesian operatives. The visit of the American who gave away the unrestricted ATM card was facilitated by a Biak officer named Kapitarau, who was a member of Indonesia's Kopassus Special Forces. Kapitarau had lived in Awom's camp for several months. He helped

One of General Awom's
followers wearing a hat
signaling that he is ready
to die for the cause.
Photograph by Eben Kirksey.

Awom's troops practice their marching drills and showed them the official protocol for raising their UN and Morning Star flags.

When Kapitarau sought access to the First Voice Honey Center, he said that he had been dishonorably discharged from the Indonesian military. Awom believed the story and later granted him the honorary title of colonel in the OPM. When Kapitarau later became involved in an illicit affair with a woman, Awom banished him from the camp.[17] Since this time, Kapitarau has been seen freely entering and leaving the Indonesian military head-quarters in Biak.[18] Practiced at negotiating the fluid boundary that separates enemies from allies, Awom remained open to receiving me, a potentially useful outsider, despite this recent experience of betrayal.

During my second, and final day as Awom's guest, he invited me to address his followers. After everyone assembled into orderly rows, Awom took a few steps forward, raised his right hand, and shouted *"Shalom! Shalom! Papua Merdeka!"* The greeting of *Shalom!* is common in West Papuan churches. The crowd echoed his words in a roar. Awom introduced me to his troops in the Biak language and told me in Indonesian that it was my turn to speak. Using formal Indonesian, I thanked everyone for the opportunity to come to their camp. When I told them that I was writing about the history of the merdeka movement for my doctoral dissertation, a kind of book, my words were drowned out with clapping. The clapping may simply have been the standard protocol that had developed in this community for responding to speeches, but it surprised me. This enthusiastic reception was exciting. Still, I was uneasy. The crowd assembled in front of the First Voice Honey Center was placing high expectations in me, and the book they imagined I might write, and I was not sure that I could live up to them.

With only a handful of outdated firearms, General Awom's small band of OPM soldiers was no match for the 410,000-strong Indonesian Armed Forces and their hundreds of planes, tanks, and submarines. Awom certainly knew that his men could not pose a military challenge to the established order. Seizing control of the state by force remained a distant, unrealistic hope. In the face of overwhelming odds, he was doing his best to enlist outside support for his cause, trying to capture the imagination of Indonesian soldiers and international visitors like myself. Dreams of enlisting help from powerful foreign worlds thus might be a realistic vision of possibility in a seemingly impossible situation.

Following the logic embedded in the story of the Itchy Old Man, strange foreigners are greeted as potential saviors traveling abroad in disguise. All throughout West Papua, white foreigners are regularly greeted with enthusiasm and celebration. "There is a myth that Westerners will come to save the people of West Papua," writes Benny Giay. "We must throw out this myth." In Giay's words, this is like a "virus" that paralyzes the movement. "Look at America that sees itself as the teacher of democracy and human rights in the world—still, in remote areas Freeport McMoRan cultivates intimate relations with state security forces that are destroying the West Papuan people."[19] When people are waiting for outsiders to implement "freedom dreams" serving their own interests, Giay told me that they stop working to implement their own hopes and social visions.[20]

If some readings of the Itchy Old Man tale produce paralysis, a sense of expectation that resigns the future to fate, other interpretations may certainly inspire worldly action.[21] If the story of the Itchy Old Man animates an "in-between" space where imagination bridges the gap between old and new worlds, as Rutherford has it, then it is an apt tale for understanding the lifeways of the First Voice Honey Center.[22] Spiritual and material worlds

General Awom's troops assembled under two flags, the UN banner and
West Papua's Morning Star. *Photograph by Eben Kirksey.*

came together in this liminal place under two flags, a place where people
lived betwixt and between colonial subjugation and national sovereignty, a
place where the faithful enacted visions of merdeka while anticipating transitions to come.[23]

As the issue of global food insecurity loomed large, and new locally grown
food movements cropped up all over the planet, General Awom's men actualized a vision of merdeka, a humble and realistic program of economic
autonomy.[24] Hunting, gathering, and subsistence farming were the basic
work that sustained the community at the First Voice Honey Center. Like
many Biaks living in nearby villages, the OPM soldiers worked their own
gardens of sweet potatoes, taro, and cassava. Women from the community
harvested sago trees from nearby swamps, pounding the inner pulp of the
trunks into starchy flour. Fruit trees like breadfruit, jackfruit, bananas, and
coconuts also contributed to daily meals. Wild pigs, kangaroos, and other
small marsupials like the cuscus were the favorite game of hunters.

Traditional food ways enabled Awom's community to maintain a degree
of material independence from the modern world system, even as they
secured support from further afield. Occasional bouts of wage labor, and
help from relatives and friends with salaries, also helped sustain the First
Voice Honey Center. Rice, ramen noodles, and tinned fish, as well as luxury

items like Fanta, were occasionally imported along the jungle trails.[25] Evidence of entanglements with foreign worlds notwithstanding—the UN flag flying over the compound, the contacts with Indonesian soldiers, the imported foods—Awom was largely setting the terms of his external engagements. The First Voice Honey Center was a realm of spiritual and symbolic autonomy.[26]

Rather than orient their activities around gathering funds for new weapons, like Antonius Wamang's TPN guerrilla fighters, Awom's OPM soldiers focused on living the good life. Their work regimens left plenty of time for creating a vibrant cultural scene. During my visit, dance parties with a live string band lasted until the wee hours of the morning. Instead of working to produce surplus capital, Awom's followers were working hard to actualize economic self-sufficiency and expend excess in moments of celebration.[27] Still, showing their discipline, shortly after dawn the troops assembled in straight rows for the daily flag raising ceremony.

General Awom's freedom dreams were rooted in much earlier incarnations of merdeka in island Southeast Asia. *Mardikar* areas in colonial and precolonial Java were free from any obligations to the state.[28] Peasants were forced to pay taxes in precolonial Javanese kingdoms and later under the Dutch colonial regime. Tax-free villages dating back to at least the fourteenth-century kingdom of Majapahit provided for the upkeep of religious communities, schools, grave sites, and holy places.[29] Michael Adas speculates that these villages "may have served as important antidotes to the build-up of discontent among both the peasants and the ruling social strata."[30] In this way, merdeka/mardikar was a domain of freedom that existed within the framework of the state rather than a revolutionary challenge to established order.

The First Voice Honey Center revived earlier incarnations of merdeka and became a home for West Papuan independence activists at a time when their social world was being driven underground. General Awom and his followers were "doing things together," the hallmark of any social world, while they harbored dreams about possible futures to come. Imagination and collaboration came together in this community. As they enacted a limited form of merdeka, according to their modest means, they looked abroad for help in achieving more expansive dreams.

When the time came for me to leave, Awom walked with me back through the gates and checkpoints. He held my hand in a friendly expression of affection. At the top of the steep stairway made of logs, which was marked with the series of hand-painted signs (*"Caution! If Afraid Don't Proceed!"*), we said our goodbyes. During the long walk back to the road, I reflected on my enthusiastic reception at the First Voice Honey Center. The impassioned clapping that erupted when I announced my dissertation topic to the crowd seemed wildly misplaced at the time. Before this encounter, I had met only with a single congressional aide and had published a few newspaper articles. General Awom did not give me any specific requests or make any particular demands. Clearly he wanted me to represent his aspirations to the international community. He left me to struggle with the problem of translating unfamiliar freedom dreams into idioms that might be heard in the halls of global power.

I found the messianic working within me. Being hailed as someone with the power to influence the future of West Papua led me to find possibilities of freedom in entangled worlds. Basic symbolic and material aspects of freedom that are easy to take for granted—an American passport, an affiliation at Oxford University, research grants, and fluency in English—set me apart from the people at the First Voice Honey Center. My reception by the OPM under the two flags prompted me to think critically about the privileges that I enjoy as a white American researcher. The encounter also inspired me to see how I might catalyze modest changes in the world of political elites. Like Theys Eluay, who was taught by the masses to use his connections in the Golkar banyan to further the cause, I found messianic dreams pushing me toward concrete action. Melkianus Awom taught me that anyone is potentially part of the messianic multiple.

With the Blood of Jesus You Will Become a Diplomat

"In the name of Jesus, the Lord and the bread of our life, this evening we ask for your blessing," prayed Pastor Petrus Gobai on April 5, 2003, the eve of the U.S. invasion of Iraq. As Pastor Gobai recited his dinner blessing, he expressed a hopeful ambivalence about U.S. military might. He began by voicing concern about the reckless use of raw imperial force in the Middle East: "God, you are aware of the situation between America and Iraq. Lord, this is all in your hands." At the same time that he asked God to stop the imminent U.S. military invasion, Pastor Gobai imagined how international power brokers might open up new futures in West Papua: "With the blood of Jesus you will become a diplomat to the countries that can give support for merdeka in West Papua." This request that God work to secure the independence of West Papua was also an implicit appeal for me to do the same.[31]

American military forces definitively reestablished Dutch colonial rule in West Papua at the end of the Second World War. General Douglas MacArthur landed eighty thousand men near what is now Jayapura, killing more than four thousand Japanese soldiers. Sentani—then a small village near Jayapura bordered by cool hills rising around an elongated lake—became MacArthur's headquarters. When MacArthur built a sprawling base and airfield to accommodate a thousand airplanes, this sleepy administrative outpost mushroomed almost overnight into a sizable city.[32] After the war, the Allied troops abruptly left West Papua. More than a half century later, Pastor Gobai, a Mee highlander who had recently moved to Sentani, could still see the lasting impact of the infrastructure built by the U.S. military. His house, which he purchased from an Indonesian family, had been built by General MacArthur's troops.

Like General Awom and many other West Papuans, Pastor Gobai was trying to maneuver within existing regimes of domination and engage with unlikely partners from foreign worlds. He turned expansive freedom dreams into a concrete appeal to me, a potential collaborator who might make his words accessible to you, my imagined readers in far-off lands.[33] The backdrop of the new war in Iraq, and local historical memories, led to lively discussions in Gobai's living room about how America's military could be used to free West Papua from the terror of Indonesian occupation. At first blush these freedom dreams seem fantastically unrealistic, if not downright dangerous. In a pre–September 11 world, Kurdish hopes of being suddenly saved from the regime of Saddam Hussein might have seemed similarly implausible. Kurdish dreams did come true, but they had an ambivalent outcome. After Hussein was ousted, the Kurds found themselves under a foreign military occupation and stuck in a perpetual atmosphere of violence.

West Papuans who drew me into discussions about the plausibility of U.S. military intervention, messianic dreams of sorts, were trying to understand the unpredictable whims of distant military strategists. As the U.S. campaign of shock and awe suddenly, unexpectedly, transformed the Middle East, Pastor Gobai looked abroad with guarded hope.

Pastor Gobai hosted me for dinner nearly every night over a two-month period in 2003, during my last extended period of field research. Every evening he spontaneously produced a vivid prayer before we ate. One night when I brought my tape recorder to dinner and asked him if I might record his prayer for inclusion in this book, he delivered his most spectacular performance. Along with his wife, Yosaphine, and his niece, I listened to his hopes. Pastor Gobai used prayer to ritually mark his living room, a modest space with a concrete floor and wicker furniture, as a safe bubble of freedom within the belly of what he saw as a neocolonial project. "Father, build a fence around your followers in this land with the power of your blood, with the power of your word, with the power of your spirit. Lord, we pray once again for merdeka." Pastor Gobai's faith allowed him to create an autonomous zone of freedom within a regime of inequality.[34] Amid alarming rumors, Pastor Gobai worked to keep merdeka alive.

A large barracks stood about five hundred yards from the small fenced compound where Pastor Gobai lived. As the prayer continued, Indonesian soldiers marched up the road, chanting at the top of their lungs. Pastor Gobai went on to paint the landscape of my nightmares: "Lord, you know about the woman who had been buried for three weeks in her grave," his prayer continued. "When her family tried to exhume her body, they discovered that the corpse was missing from the coffin. The culprits were motorcycle couriers working together with secret military agents, the power of Satan, and evil spirits." Recent human rights reports linked Kopassus agents to masked ninjas who were chasing independence activists through the streets.[35] This prayer asked God to deliver the land of West Papua from these evil operations. Still, it was difficult to escape the sounds of terrifying *kegouguwo* spirits, Mee demons and devils, clamoring at the window, beyond the living-room curtains that kept out the dark night.[36]

Gobai's dinner prayer temporarily resolved the terrifying uncertainties that plague people under military occupation. Noted West Papuan leaders had recently died amid rumors of poisoning. Our food—chicken, ramen noodles, boiled sweet potato leaves, and a salty sago pudding called *papeda*—had been purchased from Indonesian merchants. "Before we eat and drink the nourishment that you have prepared for our bodies, we ask that you cleanse this food. If there are any evil spirits from the market or from the stores, we reject them in the name of your blood. We order them to get out." Even as Pastor Gobai was trying to find freedom within a regime of extreme inequality, he anticipated a future where the existing global order might be radically transformed. While creating a safe space of spiritual autonomy in a compromised situation, he was also probing future horizons for signs of a coming era of peace and abundance.[37]

Pastor Gobai was watching from the sidelines as power functioned predictably in West Papua. In this time of absolute hopelessness, he was entertaining hopes that, at first, seemed entirely unrealistic.[38] This prayer was not a radical dream, in the sense of imagining sweeping changes to global power relations. Indeed, given local constraints on political activity, he was looking for stronger nations to intervene. His petition for divine salvation, and his implicit appeal to me, unquestioningly accepted global relations of hegemony.

The Genie Is Out of the Bottle

As I was departing West Papua in 2003, Pastor Gobai presented me with a net bag. Highland New Guinea net bags have long been made with a fiber from the bark of trees. Recently bag makers have imported new materials and designs. The scope of bags as metaphors has also recently been expanded.[39] The bag that Pastor Gobai gave me was a tight weave of bright yellow thread. Birds and floral designs covered one side. On the other side, a man played guitar under the Morning Star flag, a unifying symbol of West Papua's independence movement. Pastor Gobai asked that I give this bag to Kofi Annan, then the secretary general of the United Nations. Once freedom (merdeka) had been prepared for West Papua, Gobai told me, Annan should put it into the bag so that I could bring it back to the people. This going-away present, and appeals from other West Papuans, prompted me to explore openings in the architecture of global power.

Shortly after completing my fieldwork in West Papua, I was recruited as a pro bono member of the West Papua Advocacy Team at the Robert F. Kennedy Memorial Center for Human Rights in Washington. There I found the opportunity to do more than "use my data as a pillow." For three months in 2005, I lived in Washington and helped conduct a focused campaign of advocacy. Securing an appointment with a particular key official, I came to learn, could be a significant achievement. I had over one hundred meetings with congressional offices in the House of Representatives and over thirty meetings in the Senate. I also met with Bush administration officials at the Department of State, the National Security Council, and the Department of Justice. We presented U.S. policymakers with reports about political prisoners, a study of genocide, and materials about the Indonesian takeover in the 1960s.

Working with other activists, I learned the importance of incremental and partial victories. Meetings often involved specific "asks," or requests for action. Sometimes these encounters resulted in bringing a new ally into a fragile, contingent coalition that backed a particular initiative. In presentations to policymakers, I simplified the ideal of merdeka: it turned into familiar stories about justice, human rights, and national awakening. The complexity of the situation—the issues that were left off the advocacy agenda and unquestioned assumptions underlying the familiar rights discourses—remained in my peripheral vision.

My advocacy work in Washington produced limited results. In early 2005, George W. Bush had just begun his second term as president. Congress was controlled by Republicans, and the global war on terror was the guiding foreign policy focus. Few policymakers in key positions of power were readily inspired by freedom dreams from West Papua.

To enlist the support of the congressman from my home district, I helped coordinate a petition that was signed by fellow graduate students, professors, union leaders, schoolteachers, community activists, and the mayor. Our congressman was Sam Farr, a member of the Progressive Caucus, an influential block of Democrats in the House of Representatives who were united around issues of social justice, environmental protection, and ending U.S. involvement in the Iraq war. The petition began: "We write as citizens of Santa Cruz and Monterey Counties who appreciate the many courageous stands you have taken against violations of human rights and the natural environment, both at home and abroad. We are confident that given reliable information about another towering injustice, you will do the right thing once again." The letter discussed a number of issues: importing liquid natural gas from West Papua to California, the coverup of Indonesian military involvement in the murder of Americans in Timika, and historical political grievances. We asked Representative Farr to help "search for a peaceful and democratic solution to the sufferings of the inhabitants of this occupied territory."

At the same time that West Papuans were reaching abroad for help in their cause, Indonesian authorities were attempting to limit their encounters with foreign nationals. Aid workers, foreign journalists, human rights researchers, anthropologists, and biologists had recently been blocked from visiting West Papua. In the summer of 2005, I collaborated with Representative Farr's staff to write a letter to President Yudhoyono of Indonesia. Once the draft was finalized, Farr signed it. Working with professional human rights activists from the Robert F. Kennedy Memorial Center for Human Rights and the East Timor Action Network (ETAN), I helped collect signatures from thirty-four other members of Congress. The letter called for a lifting of restrictions on travel in West Papua: "In all areas of West Papua outside of major urban centers, foreigners are required to carry *surat jalan* travel permits. . . . We call on you to abolish the travel permit system and allow for the freedom of movement throughout Indonesia. Visa policies are in place that restrict access of international journalists, researchers, and NGO workers to West Papua. We urge you to abolish these visa restrictions." The president of Indonesia never wrote back. Although our letter did not achieve any clear change in Indonesian policies, many of my fellow campaigners regarded it as a small victory. The letter was a successful effort at educating members of Congress and their staff about developments in West Papua.[40] After this letter, the issue of international access to West Papua has been included in the language of congressional legislation. State Department officials now regard access to West Papua as an ongoing concern and are required by law to write an annual report about the issue for Congress. By beginning to pry at the bureaucratic gates that were keeping members of the international community out of West Papua, I hoped that this initiative would help set the stage for future encounters among entangled worlds. I hoped that it would open the door to future collaborations, to visits by other people whose imagination might get captured by the messianic spirit.

In January 2006, I presented Pastor Gobai's net bag as a gift to Representative Farr. I wanted to thank him for supporting recent initiatives on West Papua. As I gave Farr the present, I recounted the nuanced cultural history of net bags and Pastor Gobai's specific request for freedom. Farr is the only member of Congress with a UN flag outside his door. I asked Farr if he might pass Pastor Gobai's request for freedom up the chain to Secretary General Kofi Annan. Farr did not take up the issue of independence, although his office continued to support human rights concerns.

On the other side of the Atlantic, in London, a decades-long campaign by Carmel Budiardjo about human rights in Indonesia had produced a political climate that was receptive to West Papuan demands for independence. Budiardjo, who was born in England in 1925, spent three years of her life under detention in Indonesian prisons. At the time of her arrest in 1968, Budiardjo had spent sixteen years in Indonesia, teaching English, working for the government, and lecturing at universities. She was detained without trial, on suspicion of being a communist, and held in squalid condi-

Presenting Pastor Gobai's net bag to Representative Sam Farr.
Photograph by Pam Sexton.

tions where she witnessed torture, sexual violence, and other excesses by prison guards. "I see myself as someone who became a human rights activist because of my own bitter experiences at the hands of a harshly repressive regime," she wrote in a memoir.[41] Shortly after Budiardjo was released from prison in 1971, she founded Tapol, the Indonesian Human Rights Campaign. Tapol means "political prisoner" in Indonesian. After working to free many of her fellow prisoners, Budiardjo turned to broader human rights concerns—like the issue of self-determination in West Papua.

In January 2007, a year after I gave Pastor Gobai's net bag to Representative Farr, Budiardjo helped bring the issue of West Papua before the British House of Lords in an open debate. The British Parliament is inhabited by nobility and notables of all sorts—the Earl Marshal, the Lord Great Chamberlain, the Lords of Appeal in Ordinary, and the Gentleman Usher of the Black Rod. Here the grievances of the titled men of the First Voice Honey Center were eloquently voiced in an alien tongue. "Lord Harries of Pentregarth rose to ask Her Majesty's Government what representations they are making to further the independence of West Papua," reads the official account of the debate from the Lords Hansard. "West Papua may seem far away and its problems small compared with the very grave situation in the Middle East," said Lord Harries. "To its people those problems are immediate and painful, and the principles at stake are fundamental to civilized life in the modern world."[42]

Richard Harries, a life peer, provided his colleagues with historical context about West Papua's annexation: "The so-called Act of Free Choice consisted of 1,022 people being forced at gunpoint to vote for integration with Suharto's Indonesia." This was the sham referendum that Agus told me about years before when he waylaid me outside the library. Before this debate in the House of Lords, the British government had acknowledged that the Act of Free Choice involved "handpicked representatives and that they were largely coerced into declaring for inclusion in Indonesia." Citing this admission, Lord Harries looked toward the future. "The question now is: what can be done to rectify this historical wrong and what is the next step? In particular, what steps are the Government taking? The 1969 Act of Free Choice was both cynical and wrong." Lord Harries concluded by asking the British government to push for a new independence referendum according to principles of international law: "We have every criterion for the right to self-determination. The principle is declared in Article 1.2 of the United Nations charter and further enshrined in the two human rights covenants of 1966."

Lord Judd, a Life Baron, rose to speak: "My Lords, I congratulate the noble Lord, Lord Harries of Pentregarth, on introducing this important debate tonight. There were many reasons for wanting to intervene. Perhaps the whole issue of human rights, to which the noble Lord referred, would be sufficient in itself." Judd recounted his travels to East Timor just before this country achieved independence from Indonesia: "I see in the situation too many sinister and ominous parallels." In this context, he expressed his concern about lending support to any and every breakaway nationalist movement: "Obviously, it is not convincing to contemplate a world in which every ethnic group has a national identity of its own. That would make neither political nor economic sense." Ultimately, Lord Judd concluded, sentiments for nationalism would not disappear in West Papua. In closing, he said simply: "The genie is out of the bottle."[43]

Despite the principled arguments of Lord Judd and Lord Harries, the conclusion of the debate in the House of Lords ended with a definitive statement from Her Majesty's Government: "I have listened carefully to the debate," said Baroness Royall of Blaisdon, "but must start with a clear statement that the UK does not support independence for West Papua."[44] The governments of Australia and the Netherlands had recently issued similar statements in support of the status quo in Indonesia. Stories about the promise of nationalist revolutions, once part of a widely embraced logic of postcolonial liberation, are bouncing off the architecture of power in the early twenty-first century. Seeing violent turmoil in many new breakaway states, particularly the unrest in East Timor after independence from Indonesia, many decision makers have lost faith in the promise of new nationalist struggles.

Given the opposition of powerful governments to independence for West Papua, the cause seemed hopeless. Still, it is not always easy to see probable futures within the broader field of historical possibility. An inventory of over sixty important "mini-nationalist movements," compiled in 1982, did not even mention East Timor or West Papua.[45] In the early 1980s, it may have seemed completely unrealistic that East Timor would gain independence, that the Berlin Wall would fall, and that apartheid would end in South Africa. In the face of seeming impossibility, I learned nonetheless to look for signs of hope. West Papuans had taught me to anticipate many different future events, horizons of change, and potential saviors.

New Figures of Hope

While I was working to build a grassroots advocacy campaign in support of Congressman Farr's letter about access, a startling development emerged within the House of Representatives itself. In February 2005, congressman Eni Faleomavaega, a delegate with the Democratic Party representing American Samoa, issued a statement to the press: "Today newly appointed U.S. Secretary of State, the Honorable Condoleezza Rice, testified before the House International Relations Committee. During the hearing, Faleomavaega asked Rice to support West Papua's right to self-determination." At the time, Faleomavaega was the ranking Democratic member of the Subcommittee on Asia, the Pacific, and the Global Environment.

Over the years, a handful of West Papuan leaders—John Rumbiak, Octovianus Mote, and several others—had met with Faleomavaega when they passed through Washington. I had been aware of Faleomavaega's interest in West Papua since 2000, when he voiced opposition to a proposed dam project. But this was a radical new direction. The press release quoted a recent State of the Union address by President Bush. Faleomavaega drew parallels between Bush's language and the freedom dreams of the West Papuan people: "We now have a President who has publicly stated that 'we are all part of a great venture—to extend the promise of freedom in our country, to renew the values that sustain our liberty, and to spread the peace that freedom brings.'"

"In my opinion," Faleomavaega wrote, "the President's mantra must and should include West Papua."[46] Was this the contingent opening in the architecture of power that the West Papuans had been waiting for? Had the people of West Papua found a new champion of their cause? Was this an answer to Pastor Gobai's prayers? The press release was silent about Rice's response. Curious, and plainly excited, I tried to contact Congressman Faleomavaega's staff. After a series of unsuccessful e-mails and phone calls, I simply went to Capitol Hill and stuck my head in the door of his office one afternoon. A receptionist, a young man from Samoa, greeted me in the vestibule. When I told him about my advocacy on West Papua, he directed me to Lisa Williams, Faleomavaega's chief of staff, who welcomed me with a light southern accent. Clearly overworked, juggling innumerable tasks at once, Williams paused and chatted with me for a few minutes. She helped me set up a meeting with the congressman in the following week.

In preparing for my meeting with Faleomavaega, I readied materials about the 1969 Act of Free Choice. At that point, a number of politicians and influential intellectuals had joined a petition to the United Nations asking for a formal review of this controversial plebiscite. These leaders included Archbishop Desmond Tutu, a majority of Irish Parliamentarians, Lord Harries, Lord Judd, and several other members of the House of Lords. Diplomats from Nauru and Vanuatu, small island countries in the Pacific, spoke out in the year 2000 at the UN General Assembly in favor of formally reviewing the Act of Free Choice.[47] Few other member nations of the General Assembly, and no members of the powerful Security Council, had yet lent support to calls for a new independence referendum in West Papua. Could Congressman Faleomavaega help leverage pressure on the UN?

Arriving early for my appointment with the congressman, I studied the decorations on his walls: a picture of him in Samoan customary dress showing his fully tattooed thighs and hips, a plaque from Chicken of the Sea, a company that sells canned tuna fish, a picture of "The Rock"—a Hollywood actor who I later learned was Faleomavaega's cousin. Faleomavaega, a mustached man with a broad smile, suddenly came in, and I rose to shake his hand. After exchanging pleasantries and telling him about my research,

I asked him about the hearing with Secretary Rice. Chuckling a little, he said, "Well, I seem to have caught her a bit off-guard. It wasn't immediately clear from her response that she had heard of West Papua before." We chatted for the better part of an hour. He suggested that Secretary Rice might take an interest in the issue, since she, like West Papuans, was black. Faleomavaega's parents had been missionaries in Papua New Guinea, and their stories had sparked his initial interest in the region. When he heard other politicians from Pacific nations raise the issue of independence at a recent meeting, Faleomavaega decided to take action himself.

The lengthy list of signatories to the UN petition about the Act of Free Choice—at that point 174 parliamentarians and representatives of eighty nongovernmental organizations—surprised Faleomavaega when I showed him. After recounting the Biak protest in 1998, where unarmed people waiting under a water tower for Kofi Annan were mowed down with machine gun fire, I moved to further contextualize the UN petition. "Annan, a citizen of Ghana, was already working for the UN in 1969, the year that the General Assembly discussed the Act of Free Choice," I told the congressman.[48] In November 1969, Ghana led a group of African nations that opposed the exercise for being undemocratic. African diplomats called for a new referendum. In the end the UN General Assembly voted to simply "take note" of reports about the Act of Free Choice and move on to other business.[49] "Given Annan's historical connections to the issue," I concluded, "many West Papuans are hoping for UN action before he leaves office." With a wink, congressman Faleomavaega pledged to support the effort.

Over the coming weeks, I encountered Faleomavaega and his staff several times—at a hearing and when I ducked my head in the office on the way to other meetings. Rumors were circulating on Capitol Hill that he was working on a new initiative relating to the Act of Free Choice. When I asked his chief of staff, Lisa Williams, about the initiative directly, she did not want to discuss the details.

In March 2005, I was back in West Papua investigating the Timika shooting. One afternoon, out of the blue, Congressman Faleomavaega called me on my Indonesian cell phone. I had shared this number with his office and with a number of other congressional contacts, but his call still startled me. "Thirty-seven members of the Congressional Black Caucus have just written to Kofi Annan and Secretary Rice asking for a review of the Act of Free Choice," Faleomavaega told me. He asked for my help in spreading news of this development in West Papua.

Apprehensive about my ability to translate and transmit this news—not wanting to stir up false hopes—I sent out a brief note on a public e-mail list for West Papuan activists. Attaching an electronic copy of the letters and suggesting that people thank the congressman for his efforts, I passed along the general e-mail address and fax number for Faleomavaega's office. The West Papuan pioneers who met with Faleomavaega over the years had cracked open the door to his office, and my e-mail pushed it open a little wider. Through this contingent crack in the architecture of power, a flood began to rush in. Stepping back from my contacts with Faleomavaega, I watched from afar as a multitude of West Papuans sought him out as an ally. In the coming months, Faleomavaega was clearly overwhelmed with the response from West Papua. Thousands of messages poured in, often in Indonesian or broken English. At this moment, merdeka was largely under-ground, embodying a polycentric structure. Faleomavaega searched in vain for West Papuan leaders who represented the merdeka movement, who could advise his office about how best to aid the struggle.

Years passed, and Kofi Annan left the UN, while West Papuans antici-pated Faleomavaega's next move. In July 2007, he traveled to Indonesia along with Republicans David Drier and James Moran, as well as Democrat Donald Payne. The group made it no further than Jakarta, after being in-formed that the security situation in West Papua was not "conducive." After a thirty-minute meeting with Indonesian president Yudhoyono, Faleoma-vaega told reporters: "I am relieved to see there has been a complete change in the commitment and priorities that the government of Indonesia has taken towards the need of the people of West Papua."[50] Privately, when I called on him again in his office, Faleomavaega told me that senior West Papuan leaders—elected government officials, renowned figures in civil so-ciety, and independence leaders in exile—had urged him to stop supporting independence. Faleomavaega told me that he was not prepared to go out on a limb with continued calls for freedom if West Papua's leadership was not clearly unified and behind him.

Reclaiming the Messianic Promise

West Papuans were struggling for sovereignty at a historical moment when emerging nationalist movements were not fashionable with influential intellectuals and power brokers in the global North. Jacques Derrida is one among many prominent intellectuals who have dismissed nationalism as an "archaic phantasm." "Nationalisms of the native soil not only sow hatred, not only commit crimes," writes Derrida, "they have no future, they promise nothing even if, like stupidity or the unconscious, they hold fast to life." He contends that the root problem of sovereignty and territorially bounded nation-states, what he regards as the "old concepts of politics," is that these phenomena are grounded in what he calls "ontopology." The idea of ontopology links the "ontological value of present-being [*on*]" with a stable locality, "the *topos* of territory, native soil, city, body in general."[51]

"Derrida's dismissal of nationalism is too hasty," cautions Pheng Cheah, a literary critic who writes about globalization. Despite the failed promises of postcolonial nationalism — in light of widespread misery and suffering in an era of uneven globalization — Cheah contends that the nation is still a form that can enable ethical and political transformations. Popular nationalist movements have arisen in the postcolonial South to resist the forces of economic transnationalism. Instead of dismissing these movements as "essentially and irredeemably ontopologocentric," Cheah argues, "one can see them as spectral promises."[52] Nationalism can thus allow for the promise of the messianic. Rather than Derrida's messianicity without messianism, where hope is detached from any particular present-being (*on*) or place (*topos*), nationalism contains definitive objects of desire.

The nation is just one figure that was animated by the spirit of merdeka, a messianic consciousness containing multiple objects of desire. Rather than being oriented toward utopia — an imagined state of perfection, literally no-place (Greek *ou* + *topos*) — in West Papua hopes were grounded in the topos of territory, the bodies of historical actors, and other grounding figures. With many policymakers sharing Derrida's basic sentiments about nationalism, merdeka became stuck in a plateau as it began traveling to Congress and the House of Lords. Still, indigenous visionaries managed to keep hope alive in an era of seeming impossibility, reworking emerging ideas of freedom that were gaining currency abroad.

With George W. Bush still in office, many West Papuans proved to be attentive listeners to the language of American power. Like Congressman Faleomavaega, who played with Bush's own words "to spread the peace that freedom brings" in West Papua, indigenous activists were talking about their dreams in terms that might somehow capture the imagination of White House staff. Certainly the messianic spirit was at play in the Bush White House. "I think a light has gone off for people who've spent time up close to Bush," said Bruce Bartlett, a domestic policy adviser to Ronald

Reagan and a treasury official for the first President Bush. "He's always talking about this sort of weird, Messianic idea of what he thinks God has told him to do."[53] After meeting Bush at the White House in 2002, Jim Wallis, a theologian and civil rights activist, described the president as "a messianic American Calvinist. He doesn't want to hear from anyone who doubts him." Many of Bush's evangelical followers believed that he had been anointed by God.[54] George W. Bush was playing to widespread elements of the U.S. political imagination. According to Kathleen Stewart and Susan Harding, anthropologists who study the cultures of the contemporary United States, "American nationalism rests both on the millennial claim that American-style democracy and technological progress will save the world and on an apocalyptic paranoia that imagines external enemies, 'thems' who are out to get 'us.'"[55]

Bush himself publicly said: "I trust God speaks through me." Specifically he said that God told him to go to war in Iraq.[56] By invading Iraq, Bush was implementing the messianic visions of the Project for a New American Century—"a neoconservative organization supporting greater American militarization, challenging hostile governments, advancing democratic and economic freedom."[57] This organization, founded by disgruntled Republicans in response to the "incoherent" foreign policy of the Clinton administration, imagined a new international order where increased defense spending would lead to a future of peace and prosperity for the American people. The Project for a New American Century was explicitly secular, though many of its leading figures (like Dan Quayle, Donald Rumsfeld, Paul Wolfowitz, and Dick Cheney) depended on a base of evangelical Christians for political support. The Project for a New American Century certainly achieved elements of its vision: defense spending more than doubled from $259 billion in 1997, when the group was launched, to $651 billion in fiscal year 2009.[58] But these changes in fiscal policy failed to bring about the promised peace and prosperity for the American people. During Bush's final months in office—as the economy fell into disarray and specters of terrorism continued to flicker across the national stage—the messianic spirit left the president, at least in the eyes of all but the most faithful.

Ultimately, even with help from senior Democratic members of Congress, freedom dreams from West Papua failed to gain purchase in the world of U.S. foreign policy at this historical juncture. In advocating for small, molecular transformations in the final years of Bush's presidency, and with a Republican-controlled Congress, I learned that more dramatic transformations could come only with wildly contagious visions of hope. A grassroots coalition in the United States launched a project that grounded imagination in the politics of collaboration. Collective freedom dreams coalesced around a single event—the election of the first African American president of the United States. The Obama campaign in 2008 worked to embody the messianic spirit, rallying the masses behind hope, quoting Martin Luther King Jr.'s famous plea about "the fierce urgency of now." Obama promised to close the gap between the imagined and possible future real, in the words of John Hartigan, a cultural anthropologist who writes about race.[59]

My friends in West Papua got caught up in the revolutionary excitement surrounding Obama's election campaign. When Obama was a boy, growing up in Java, his stepfather, Lolo, served a tour of duty as an Indonesian soldier in West Papua. Lolo returned with scars from leech bites and troubling stories of killing "weaker men."[60] West Papuans, descendants of these "weak men," hoped that memories of these troubling tales, and a shared sense of black consciousness, might lead Obama to chart a radical new future for their homeland if he were elected president.[61]

After the 2008 presidential election, it quickly became clear, to me at least, that there would be radical continuities between Bush administration and Obama administration policies toward Indonesia. People with direct links to human rights abuses in Indonesia were appointed to Obama's cabinet, millions in U.S. taxpayer dollars continued to flow as aid for the Indonesian military, and the U.S. embassy supported business as usual at the Freeport mine and the BP natural gas project.[62] In the coming months, many erstwhile Obama supporters in the United States became disillusioned as the president intensified combat operations in Afghanistan, struggled to implement a healthcare reform package, and failed to close Guantanamo Bay. Real changes from the Bush administration had occurred, but many of the dreams that had been fixed on Obama's election went unrealized. Still, the people of West Papua clung to the elusive promise of hope.

Congressman Faleomavaega, West Papua's champion from American Samoa, had assumed an influential position after the Democratic Party took control of the House of Representatives in 2006. He was appointed chairman of the Foreign Relations Subcommittee on Asia, the Pacific, and the Global Environment. Faleomavaega had become the key player shaping U.S. policies toward West Papua. In his new position, he had the power to hold congressional hearings. As chairman, he also had more clout among fellow members of Congress. Galvanizing support behind particular initiatives would be easier for him now. Doors were open to Faleomavaega—at the White House or the United Nations—that were closed to someone like me, an ordinary U.S. citizen, or junior members of Congress who did not chair important committees.

Still, Faleomavaega was constrained. In the wake of the Bush administration, the power of the executive branch eclipsed that of the legislative and the judiciary. At this moment in history, U.S. foreign policy was being enacted by bureaucrats in the administration—at the State Department, the National Security Council, the Pentagon, and the CIA—who had more de facto power than directly elected representatives like Faleomavaega. Tenacious lobbyists representing foreign governments like Indonesia, as well as multinational corporations like BP and Freeport, were also quietly working behind the scenes.

Like me, Faleomavaega had clearly felt the messianic spirit of merdeka moving within him. Like me, he had also experienced his share of frustrations with the movement. The people of West Papua had placed expansive hopes in him, desires that were not entirely realistic. Many people who claimed to represent merdeka, some with hidden agendas, were competing for his attention. Faleomavaega's statement of July 2007, his announcement lauding the Indonesian government for their "complete change" in policies toward West Papua, was a public signal of his disappointment with the discord among leaders. The struggle, which lacked a clear leader following the assassination of Theys Eluay, was failing to interface with this sympathetic figure, an influential ally who had the capacity to articulate their collective desires within the labyrinthine structure of U.S. power. After John Rumbiak's stroke, without a clear leader to rally behind, my own enthusiasm as an advocate for the cause, as a pro bono volunteer, had also begun to wane.

When tens of thousands of people took to the streets of West Papua in June and July 2010, demanding dialogue and an official vote on the issue of independence, the messianic spirit began to stir in me again. Reaching out to Faleomavaega, I learned that he shared my enthusiasm for the news from the streets. Faleomavaega asked me to draft up a letter to President Obama, giving background on the issue and encouraging him "make West Papua one of the highest priorities of the administration." After consulting with friends back in West Papua, the key architects of the recent protests, I put a formal request in the letter to President Obama, asking him to meet with the Team of 100, during an upcoming trip he had scheduled to Indonesian in November 2010. More than a decade earlier, the Team of 100 had the historic national dialogue with Indonesian president B. J. Habibie on February 26, 1999. Now they desired an international dialogue.

After finalizing the draft of this letter, working with the staff in Faleoma-vaega's office, I watched from the sidelines as he worked to enlist the support of fifty other congressional representatives — members of the Congressional Black Caucus, men and women who fought for civil rights in America in the 1960s, and members of the Hispanic Caucus, as well as the last remaining member of the Kennedy family in Congress, Patrick Kennedy from Rhode Island. After the letter was sent, I began to look toward the White House with cautious optimism. Previously I had been critical of the president for rallying the people behind empty hopes, for cultivating something akin to messianicity without messianism with Obama's own figure as the only content. With Democratic members of Congress who carried serious moral authority backing this initiative, the vacuous idea of hope, in my own political imagination, came to settle on a possible event approaching on the horizon. If a meeting took place between Obama and the Team of 100, perhaps the president would be inspired to take their freedom dreams to heart.

Meanwhile in West Papua, the messianic spirit was dancing about like liquid mercury, moving in different directions, coalescing around multiple future events, figures of hope, animating messianic formations beyond strictly human realms.[63] A new cohort of young West Papuan activists reinvigorated the movement for merdeka, imagining sweeping changes, pushing beyond the visions of older generations of freedom fighters. Rather than emulate the struggle of bygone heroes like Theys Eluay and Bald Grandfather Willy, who leveraged covert support from multinational corporations and military agents in their nationalist struggle, the emerging generation was more careful in its coalition building. Students and activists in rural areas again took to the streets, rallying behind the cry of merdeka, wrapping their freedom dreams around the architecture of the modern world system.

The Tube

2006–2028

One morning an e-mail with a single Indonesian-language word in the subject line arrived in my mailbox: *Merdeka!!!* The message came from an address I didn't recognize, akeharvest@yahoo.com, and announced startling news: "Praise be to God! Today at mile 73 the gold pipe of the thief has broken open."[1] Unsolicited e-mails from West Papua had become routine surprises for me. This note was different. Ake Harvest reported that the flow of wealth out of his land was being disrupted and rechanneled.

The "thief" referred to Freeport McMoRan Copper and Gold Inc., whose slurry pipe burst open on March 9, 2006, at about 5:00 a.m. "Gold is flowing out. . . . Everyone is going out with buckets to collect the gold," Ake Harvest announced. Later, the corporate communications representative at Freeport told a local newspaper that the pipe had simply worn out. Word on the streets, I learned after placing calls to friends, was that the pipe, a blue tube about eight inches in diameter, had deliberately been cut open about one hundred yards from an Indonesian military post.[2]

At seventy miles long, Freeport's slurry pipe was a relatively small piece of the world's supply chain for gold and copper. Still, this short pipe had become a literal and figural embodiment of global economic injustice. The breaking open of Freeport's pipeline was not a singular event. It offers an opportunity to reflect on the inequalities built into the architecture of the modern world system over the longue durée of history.[3]

West Papua's literal pipelines were extensions of figural pipes that crisscrossed other parts of the world at earlier moments of history. A "transatlantic tube" connected the Caribbean to the modern world system in the sixteenth century, according to Antonio Benítez-Rojo, a noted Latin American novelist and cultural theorist. Diverse valuables—gold, silver, sugar, coffee—traveled through this figural tube from the Caribbean to Seville. This "sucking iron mouth" was a bricolage, a coupling of diverse machines, an assembled network of organisms and objects. Cobbling together the mine, the plantation, the mule train, the *flota* (fleet) system, and the warehouse, early modern architects assembled a magical and powerful system. Benítez-Rojo describes how the transatlantic tube was installed simultaneously in a variety of locales in the Caribbean. Since then, this architecture of resource extraction has replicated itself until it reached all the seas and lands of the earth.[4]

During a different historical moment and geographic location—maritime Southeast Asia at the beginning of the twenty-first century—the flow of goods is channeled by a multiplicity of figural tubes. The mechanical components of the early modern pipeline have been replicated, modified, and supplemented. Some systems, within the larger vacuuming bricolage, are still recognizable replicates of the originals—the mine, the plantation, and the warehouse. Railroads, highways, and trucks have replaced mule trains. Spanish galleons have been replaced by supertankers.

The Pacific Fleet of the U.S. Navy, according to a recent government press release, "has command and control of more than 45 percent of the earth's surface."[5] Its frigates, destroyers, and battleships watch over the predicable flow of goods. In the archipelago of contemporary Indonesia, natural products and manufactured goods—like rice, coffee, cocoa, footwear, timber products, textiles, precious metals, palm oil, copra, and petroleum—are sucked from rural to urban areas. Joining commodities from other parts of the global South, these goods are piped to nodes in the multicentered matrix of Northern power. Aside from exceptional moments—natural disasters, public protests, looting sprees, acute military conflicts—the tube continues to function predictably, vacuuming, storing, transporting, depositing. Asymmetries are exacerbated. Resentments grow.

The broken Freeport pipe signaled to local West Papuan communities that global disparities in wealth would, at least temporarily, be reversed. With this incident, West Papuan indigenous communities living in the shadow of the Freeport mine found hopeful possibilities trickling from a small crack in the infrastructure of resource extraction. Thousands of West Papuans and Indonesians flocked to the growing pool of slurry. They filled up buckets, water bottles, and motorcycle helmets with the precious muck. Some Indonesian police and soldiers also joined in the free-for-all and began carting away the muddy mess in trucks.[6]

Hopes of selling buckets of gold at the local market were quickly dashed. The liquid concentrate oozing onto the ground was about 30 percent copper and contained gold in concentrations of about thirty parts per million. Elaborate chemical processes were necessary to extract the precious metals. As Freeport maintenance crews fixed the pipeline on March 11, 2006, and the pool dried up, the crowds withdrew. Even if the indigenous communities around the mine were not able to suddenly resolve long-standing economic injustices, even if the people could not suddenly enjoy direct access to the wealth of their land, the incident catalyzed a moment of political possibility. West Papuan activists began to articulate visions about reconfiguring the architecture of resource extraction.[7]

Elements of Decky Pigome's dreams from the 1980s, his plans for creating Freeport Sweet Potato Distribution Inc., a community-run gold mine and humanitarian aid organization, suddenly resurfaced and gained widespread popular support. Pigome's dreams of transforming the theft of natural resources into a gift, his hopes of achieving national independence as a first step toward reconfiguring global interdependencies, began to gain renewed currency.[8] Highlanders began to imagine a future when resources and revenue would no longer steadily stream from their land to corporate coffers, a time when they would give away the wealth from their land as gifts to the world, gaining political allies and economic debtors who could be called on in times of need.

Calls for the closing of Freeport emerged from many different corners. Indigenous groups who wanted substantial shares of the revenue from their land, West Papuan students and intellectuals who were critics of capitalism, Indonesian politicians who were fighting U.S. imperialism, and Indonesian environmental activists who wanted stricter regulations on pollution all suddenly found cause for a temporary coalition. Local Indonesian soldiers, who were rumored to have cut open the pipeline in the first place, showed their support tacitly by allowing the protests to take place. Diverse worlds temporarily put aside their own conflicts, their incompatible visions, and united in opposition against a common enemy. Through surprising collaborations, a seemingly impossible objective, shutting down Freeport's tube, was coming in reach. Multiple entangled worlds were finding freedom together, engaging with each other in a strategic alliance despite conflicting visions for the future.[9]

Protests spread from the Freeport mining site in Timika to cities throughout West Papua and other islands in the Indonesian archipelago. West Pap-

West Papuans gathered in protest, demanding the closure of the Freeport mine, at an iconic fountain on Jalan Thamrin, the main thoroughfare of Indonesia's capital, Jakarta. *Photograph courtesy of Elsham.*

uan students—decked out in penis sheaths, fluorescent plastic skirts, and face paint—marched the streets of Java carrying signs that read: *Shut Freeport Down Right Now*, *Freeport: Stop Sucking Up the Wealth of West Papua*, and simply, in English, "Freeport Fuck Off." Another sign poked fun at two West Papuan "freedom fighters," Tom Beanal and Willy Mandowen (Bald Grandfather Willy), who both had close ties to Freeport. Grinning images of these two leaders appeared amid stacks of hard currency and a message: *Agents of American Capitalism Fighting for the Dollar*. Indonesian human rights and environmental activists joined some of the protests against Freeport in Java, while other actions exclusively involved West Papuans.[10]

In Jakarta the movement to shut down Freeport began to link up with other political initiatives. Indonesian politicians demonstrated outside the Jakarta Convention Center on March 15, 2006, while dignitaries from the United States and other countries were speaking inside. The Indonesian activists were trying to block a new trade agreement that would give Exxon-Mobil rights to develop a field of oil and natural gas offshore of Java.[11] Investors began to wonder, "Is it time to steer clear of Indonesia?", when in the next week fifty unidentified people razed the exploration camp of Newmont, the world's largest gold-mining company, which was developing a new mine on Sumbawa Island.[12]

Multiple worlds came together to oppose Freeport and other foreign companies, uniting behind a clear goal: bringing the flow of capital under control. Activists wanted to shut resource extraction projects down until equitable deals could be reached. "Capital flows away from locations that cannot or will not produce inviting climates," writes Jeffrey Winters, a political economist who is an Indonesian specialist. . Winters suggests that the reverse flow of funds "punishes the community with declining investment rates."[13] The opposite dynamic was happening with these protests. Local communities were punishing the people who were profiting from the tube by interrupting their access to desired resources.

A showdown between West Papuan students and Indonesian police took place on March 16, 2006, the day after the protests at the Jakarta Convention Center. The students set up a series of blockades in front of Bird of Paradise University, stopping all traffic between Jayapura and the suburb of Sentani. When protesters and security forces faced off on this road, an unknown group began throwing rocks. The police responded by releasing tear gas. Obeth Epa, a police officer based at the Abepura station, suddenly shot his pistol twice, hitting a woman in the chest. The crowd exploded. Three Indonesian policemen and a military intelligence agent were beaten to death in a gruesome scene that was captured by journalists and replayed for the Indonesian public. Eight students sustained serious gunshot wounds. Following the incident, security forces launched a sweeping operation, arbitrarily detaining dozens of people from the streets and ransacking student dormitories. Several detainees were tortured. Charges were later brought against a total of twenty-four suspects.[14]

The violence in front of Bird of Paradise University took the wind out of the sails of the movement to shut down Freeport. The temporary alliances between West Papuan and Indonesian activists, and between indigenous people and security forces, unraveled as the dead were counted and courtroom battles began. After the events in 2006, Freeport increased its annual payments to Indonesia's security forces from an average of $5.2 million a year to a total of $8 million in 2008.[15] Bloodshed again disrupted Freeport's operations and put employees on edge when between July 2009 and January 2010, over a dozen sniper attacks occurred near the mine. Spawning feelings of déjà vu by recalling the investigation into the killings in 2002

Protesters and police forces clashed at Bird of Paradise University in Jayapura. *Photograph courtesy of Elsham.*

near the Freeport mine, the police initially indicated that military agents were the likely culprits.[16]

Still, the tube functioned predictably—vacuuming, transporting, and redistributing the wealth of West Papua. Amid the sniper attacks in 2009, gold prices soared to record highs, and Freeport McMoRan was added to the S&P 100 Index. Another sort of tube, a multimedia pipeline, channeled messianic dreams about Freeport Gold and Copper to the inboxes and mailboxes of investors. A travel ban was still in force for journalists and researchers, in effect prohibiting a serious investigation of the recent attacks. Media pundits, stockbrokers, and investors were free to wildly speculate in the vacuum of credible information from the Freeport mine site in Timika. Digital interruptions like the e-mail from akeharvest@yahoo.com appeared as minor blips of static in the information highway, a transnational infrastructure of digital pipes and tubes.[17]

The tube proliferated and spread in West Papua even as Freeport struggled to keep its employees at work under the constant threat of new attacks. The monstrous vampire assemblage continued assimilating new people and working components, probing seemingly remote corners of New Guinea, seeking to feed, seeking novelties to redistribute around the globe. The enormous Tangguh gas field in West Papua, with 18.3 trillion cubic feet of proven and probable reserves and an additional 5.4 trillion cubic feet of possible reserves, had been discovered years earlier by the multinational vacuum cleaner. This gas field had the prospects of meeting the energy needs of major countries for years to come. In the United States, for example, consumers were using only an average of 22.5 million cubic feet of natural gas each year between 2000 and 2008.[18]

BP inspired other companies and national governments to construct a retrofit "machine of machines" for transporting liquid natural gas (LNG) from West Papua to energy-hungry regions around the world. Supercooling the gas to a liquid state, loading it on oceangoing tankers, BP coupled and conjoined devices, carefully calibrating flows and evaluating potential interruptions. Reconfigured naval machines, military machines, territorial machines, geopolitical machines, bureaucratic machines, and commercial machines—assemblages with genealogical origins that Benítez-Rojo has traced back five centuries—began to bring the Tangguh LNG (liquid natural gas) into their regimes of calculation and control.[19] BP quietly put the finishing touches on its new transporting contraption in 2009 and began channeling natural gas from West Papua into pipelines that were spreading throughout the western United States, China, South Korea, and Japan.

When Sempra Energy, a San Diego–based company, proposed a terminal near Ensenada, Mexico, to receive the LNG from West Papua, a strong coalition emerged across the U.S.-Mexico border in opposition. Multiple social worlds united to fight the LNG terminal: local fishermen, coastal resort owners, environmental activists, a transborder surfing organization, and Mexican indigenous groups. Sempra Energy proceeded nevertheless. When I visited Ensenada just after Sempra began construction in 2004, I found that the form of the tube mirrored what I had come to know on the other side of the Pacific Rim in West Papua. Sempra logos graced local police cars. The U.S. Navy and Coast Guard were quietly plying the shoreline, watching over the construction site, maintaining the predicable flow of some goods while policing the movement of people. A new pipe—forty-five miles long and thirty inches in diameter—was laid, going from Ensenada, across the border at Otay Mesa, and plugging into the tubular architecture of natural gas distribution in the United States.[20]

New initiatives to import LNG were undermining dreams of energy independence. "We are embroiled in wars in the Middle East due to a large

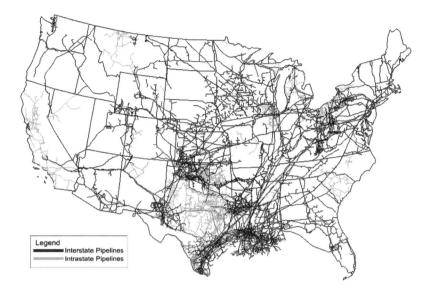

Major natural gas transportation corridors of the United States as of 2008. Once the LNG receiving terminal near Ensenada, Mexico, begins to receive gas from West Papua, new arteries will appear along the North Baja Pipeline, which enters the United States near Mexicali and Otay Mesa. The facility near Ensenada will be able to process one billion cubic feet of gas per day. *Image courtesy of Ann Whitfield of the U.S. Energy Information Administration.*

degree to the perceived need to secure the region to keep oil imports flowing to the U.S.," said Bill Powers of the Border Power Plant Working Group. "Voluntarily shifting from relatively abundant U.S. and Canadian natural gas to imported LNG from West Papua invites the same type of entanglement." Desires for regional autonomy, desires to apply principles of justice to the distribution of natural resources, were undercut as the tube burrowed and spread.

In Tijuana I met with Carla García Zendejas, a young lawyer who had grown up on the U.S.-Mexico border. Harold Green, a black activist from Los Angeles who founded the Pan-African Coalition for the Liberation of West Papua, joined us. Over a rich meal of chicken covered with *mole*, Carla told us: "We are bearing all the safety risks and environmental costs of this LNG terminal. This is like an energy *maquiladora*—a factory on the border that ships everything north to the United States."[21] Security concerns led communities in the United States to block LNG terminals in their own backyards. James Fay, a professor emeritus of mechanical engineering at the Massachusetts Institute of Technology, has modeled explosions of LNG tankers and warns that the thermal radiation could set fire to thousands of homes and cause significant casualties within a one-mile radius.[22]

According to a twenty-year contract, between Sempra and BP, the gas from West Papua should flow to the United States through 2028. Cargoes of LNG were scheduled to start arriving from West Papua in 2008, shortly after Sempra finished building its $875 million terminal in Mexico. But by the close of 2009, regular shipments of gas were not yet arriving. Shifting political and economic forces had routed precious energy resources elsewhere. The LNG previously earmarked for Sempra had found a buyer in South Korea willing to pay a higher price.[23] Politicians in Indonesia also began agitating to reroute the flow of gas to meet their own domestic energy needs. Sempra spokesman Art Larson told me that the company was receiving "diversion fees" every time the energy cargoes were routed elsewhere. "The amount of these fees are proprietary," Larson continued, "but the diversion has no impact on Sempra financially."[24] The Sempra terminal was standing unused—a ghostly monument to changing power dynamics in the modern world system. It seemed that the people of the Americas might be waiting for cargo that would never come.[25] By May 2010, the gas began flowing to the United States in fits and starts. Sempra's terminal in Ensenada began receiving about three cargoes a month from the Tangguh plant in West Papua.[26]

Vast networks of tubes were feeding off of consumers too, in Mexico, southern California, and other parts of the globe, as resources trickled through. As millions of people around the world used natural gas—cooking, heating their homes, and fueling water heaters—millions of meters quietly ticked away, measuring off cubic feet or imperial meters. As pipelines did the invisible work of transporting and redistributing, corporate profits soared, and asymmetries were exacerbated.[27] Resentments were growing. In lean economic times, with volatile energy prices, ratepayers started to grumble about utility bills, and drivers grew outraged at the price of gasoline at the pump. Spikes in the price of food, clothing, shoes, and precious metals like gold signaled that the tube was becoming unpredictable.

Anna Tsing, a cultural theorist, has invited us to play the game of global futures. "Unexpected connections can make new things come into being," she writes. "New technologies, new economies, new identities and political visions: futures of all sorts are forged in the contingencies of strange connections."²⁸ In collaboration with Elizabeth Pollman, a legal scholar who writes about corporate rights, Tsing has designed an actual game with a deck of cards that contain figural imaginings. Each player receives a mission in the Game of Global Futures: "Create a revolution," for example, or "Corrupt a nation's government," or "Revitalize an ancient philosophy." During each turn, players are dealt future-making cards—iconic images from global culture, indigenous societies, and world history.

"In this game," write Tsing and Pollman, "you imagine a global future that might develop from the possibilities of what we call a 'coalescence'—the historical force that arises from a transformative coming together of disparate groups, institutions, or things. You tell the story of this coalescence, and if your fellow players accept the story, it makes history: it becomes a part of the world of the game."²⁹ Playing this game is an opportunity to explore the interplay of imagination and collaboration. Playing this game led me to explore possibilities of freedom in entangled worlds.

I invite you to become players, to become *bricoleurs*, to make do with "whatever is at hand."³⁰ Feel free to grab a pair of scissors and cut out the pictures in my book. Consider creating new future-making cards and playing the Game of Global Futures, West Papuan style.³¹ And think about a new mission: "Take over the tube." A grassroots coalescence around the tube might involve disrupting and transforming the bureaucratic machines, the commercial machines, the geopolitical machines, and the military machines that govern the global architecture of resource distribution. Maybe start on a modest scale—perhaps tinker with your utility meter, figure out how to get natural gas for free, and then donate the money you save to a deserving cause. If you aren't a tinkerer, or don't imagine yourself risking a larceny charge, perhaps you might start playing the Game of Global Futures by seeking a position on a state public utilities commission. After your initial move, scale up and take over the whole monstrous assemblage. The details are up to you. Once you have figured out how to take over the tube, consider taking on a new mission.

One mission in Tsing and Pollman's Game of Global Futures, "Corrupt a nation's government," seems like an easy accomplishment in the current historical moment. During the mid-twentieth century, emergent nationalist movements were oriented toward seizing control of the state from colonial powers. But many anticolonial independence struggles failed to find freedom, even after achieving sovereignty on paper. Leaders of newly independent countries found that they were caught in sticky entanglements, transnational webs of obligation being spun by corporations and more powerful nations. Small nations were pitted against each other in a war among mighty worlds as capitalism battled communism. As capital seemed to win this war, nations around the globe began opening their arms to multinational corporations, lifting barriers to trade, inviting these flighty guests to dig in and stay awhile.[32]

Despite histories of corruption and co-optation, it is still possible to reinvigorate established political structures with a new spirit. Popular nationalist movements have the potential to serve as a vehicle of ethical and political transformation in an era when predatory agents of capital are running wild.[33] Bringing the tube under democratic control would not necessarily demand new utopian institutional forms. Imagine joining with your friends to encircle and penetrate existing architectures of power—town councils, corporate boardrooms, national parliamentary assemblies—like a multitude of banyan tree saplings slowly growing up and around the canopy trees of a forest.

As the tube began hiccupping in a global financial crisis—as the price of energy spiraled out of control and associated commercial machines began to fail—dramatic actions by national governments tried to preserve its predictable functioning. With the global elite struggling to contain the coughing and convulsing vacuum cleaner, a multitude of hopeful activists watched from the sidelines, biding their time, waiting for strategic moments to make interventions of their own. New multinational coalescences began forming. As pragmatic strategies of collaboration met up with imagination, the future became ripe with open-ended possibility.

Acknowledgments

Over the past twelve years, countless people in West Papua, Indonesia, Europe, and the United States have enabled my research and writing. I owe thanks to a few of these people in particular:

To my Papuan mentors—Benny Giay, Octovianus Mote, and John Rumbiak—whose courage opened my eyes to new possibilities. To Maria Vesperi, a sage guide who had a hand in this project from start to finish. To my intellectual elders—James Clifford, Anna Tsing, Donna Haraway, Donald Brenneis, Mike O'Hanlon, and Peter Carey—who collectively gave me healthy doses of both rigor and imagination. To Susan Leigh Star, Geoff Bowker, Louise Lennihan, Jesse Prinz, and Joan Richardson for giving me the time and space to work on West Papua when my day job was science studies. To my writing buddies—Rebecca Schein, Scout Calvert, John Marlovits, David Machledt, Astrid Schrader, Conal Guan-Yow Ho, Yen-ling Tsai, Sloan Mahone, Joshua Bell, John Manton, Steinur Bell, Berna Zengin, and Anita Chan—who taught me to think with care. To Benedict Anderson and Terence Ranger, whose critical insights pushed me to explore new horizons. To Claudia Vandermade, Will Kirksey, and Gina Clark, whose generous readings helped me imagine how my work might travel across disciplinary boundaries and beyond the ivory tower.

To fellow scholars, activists, and authors—Danilyn Rutherford, Brigham Golden, Rupert Stasch, Carolyn Marr, Carmel Budiardjo, Paul Barber, Adrian Arbib, George Monbiot, Nick Angelopoulos, Jay Griffiths, Kiki van Bilsen, J. A. D. Roemajauw, Pieter Drooglever, Henkie Rumbewas, Sophie Richardson, Edmund McWilliams, Katherine Wilson, Lucia Withers, Signe Poulsen, John Saltford, Siegfried Zöllner, Susan Harding, Sarah Bracke, William Girard, Maria Puig de la Bellacasa, Daniel Randongkir, Anis Rumere, Angela Davis, Gopal Balakrishnan, Gordon Bishop, Mary Kaplan, Sarah Haughton,

Melissa Andrews, Hengke Rumbiak, Markus Iyai, Brad Simpson, Alberth Rumbekwan, Kelelawar, Theo Sitokdana, Ronald Tapilatu, Neles Tebay, Andreas Harsono, Miriam Young, Charles Farhadian, Abigail Abrash, John Miller, Karen Orenstein, Pam Sexton, Max White, Carl Ross, Jesse Greist, Daniela Marini, Chimbu Rose, and Denny Yomaki—who have been sources of inspiration, ideas, and information. A multitude of institutions and individuals who are not public figures enabled my research in West Papua. Naming them here would subject them to unwanted scrutiny from government agents. So, above all, I owe thanks to those I have not named.

My research in West Papua was costly. Suzanne Janney, who is now special assistant to the president of New College, worked with me to secure funding for my undergraduate and graduate research in West Papua: with her help I was awarded a British Marshall Scholarship and was nominated to the USA Today All Academic Team. In 2000 a WWF-U.S. Conservation Grant supported my field research in West Papua. A number of travel grants have also supported my research: from the New College Anthropology Fund, the Sir John Hicks Fund, Wolfson College, U.S. Indonesia Society, the Oxford Faculty of Modern History, the Oxford Committee for Graduate Studies, and the History of Consciousness Program at UC Santa Cruz. Paul Taylor at the Smithsonian Institution's National Museum of Natural History facilitated my access to archives in Washington when I was a research collaborator in his Asian Cultural History Program. Freek Colombijn, Wouter Feldberg, and Wim Stokhof hosted me as a research guest at the International Institute of Asian Studies (IIAS) in Leiden, where I was supported by a Scatcherd European Scholarship. Essential Information funded my trip to Timika in 2005. During my final years of dissertation writing and rewriting, a Chancellor's Fellowship and an Institute of Humanities Research Finishing Grant paid my bills at UC Santa Cruz, where Sheila Peuse and Anne Tuttle worked wonders behind the scenes.

A grassroots funding program, Kickstarter, enabled me to include pictures of Papuan leaders in this book. Thirteen donors supported this initiative. In particular I would like to thank Dorion Bennet, Remko Caprio, and Akihisa Matsuno for their generosity.

A National Science Foundation Postdoctoral Fellowship in the Science and Society Program enabled me to embark on a new ethnographic research project in Panama and Costa Rica even as I was still tinkering with my West Papua manuscript. While in Monte Verde, Costa Rica, I had the pleasure of sharing my work with a group of talented and insightful undergraduates—

Matt Cohen-Price, Sweta Adhikari, Helena Touhey, and Sarah Lince—who were enrolled in the Global-Local Challenges to Sustainability course with Jim Weil and Lynn M. Morgan. In Panama, Damond Kyllo lent me his design skills as we pored over maps together and recrafted West Papua's cartographic imaginary.

Kiki van Bilsen, Shanta Barley, Terry McClain, and Emy Zumaidar generously donated photographs to the cause. The generous use policy of the U.S. government enabled me to include some remarkable imagery. In particular, thanks are due to Robert Simmon of the NASA Earth Observatory and Ann Whitfield of the U.S. Energy Information Administration.

"Don't Use Your Data as a Pillow," an earlier version of chapter 4, originally appeared in *Anthropology off the Shelf* (Wiley-Blackwell, 2011), a collection of essays edited by Alisse Waterston and Maria D. Vesperi, where leading anthropologists consider the craft of writing and the deeply rooted passions that fuel their desire to write books. Chapter 5 was originally published online by Joyo News and Pantau in a series of online reports called "Murder at Mile 63." A revised collection of these reports was published as "Criminal Collaborations? Antonius Wamang and the Indonesian Military in Timika," *Southeast Asia Research* 16, no. 2 (2008): 165–97. I had the honor of researching and writing these earlier drafts of chapter 5 in collaboration with Andreas Harsono, one of the most rigorous, uncompromising, and distinguished journalists working in Indonesia today. Andreas is publishing an Indonesian-language translation of "Murder at Mile 63" in a forthcoming book and posts original reporting about West Papua in English and Indonesian on his blog, http://andreasharsono.blogspot.com.

Coffee shops in California, Florida, and Costa Rica provided me with writing space and kept me caffeinated—Café Pergolesi, the Octagon, and Lulu Carpenters in Santa Cruz; Libreria Chunches, Paseo de Stella, and Dulce Marzo in Monte Verde; and Café Bohemia in Saint Petersburg. Other institutions that gave me critical support include Santa Clara University, the University of Pittsburgh, the Smithsonian Institution, and the CUNY Graduate Center. On the heels of finishing my Ph.D. in January 2008, New College of Florida hosted me as an alumni fellow for the spring semester. Maria Vesperi, Jay Sokolovsky, Jono Miller, and Julie Morris provided shelter and good conversation during a critical period of sustained work on the manuscript. The Cruz family of Monte Verde—Eladio, Anais, Arturo, Ana Rita, José Andreas—provided me with camaraderie and good food as I tinkered with the manuscript while learning about the natural cultural history of the cloud forest. During my final push to finish the book in the woods of western Maryland, Benny Giay proved to be a stalwart writing companion, a source of startling insights. The steady eye and careful hand of William G. Henry turned my manuscript into a proper book. Sincere thanks are due to the staff of Duke University Press—especially Ken Wissoker, Leigh Barnwell, Bonnie Perkel, Neal McTighe, Cherie Westmoreland, Katie Courtland, and Tim Elfenbein—for shepherding this book through to publication.

Notes

Preface

1. This book would have been very different if the work of Danilyn Rutherford had not come first. Readers will find conversations with Rutherford's work spread throughout this book. Here I am indebted to her for a description of Biak magic, as well as the comparison between flying tourists and flying fish (*Raiding the Land of the Foreigners*, 80–90).

2. A number of older anthropological texts, as well as more recent travelogues, describe West Papuans as "Stone Age" people (e.g., Koch, *War and Peace in Jalémó*; Gibbons, *Where the Earth Ends*).

3. "If Biaks lured fish with foreigners," writes Rutherford, "they lured foreigners with a dance . . . bringing them off the airplane and, with luck, out of the airport, to take in Biak's cultural riches." These performers seem to be following Indonesian authorities who were bent on promoting tourism, but Rutherford hints: "there was more to their complicity than met the eye." My own book picks up where Rutherford left off. She concluded her period of major fieldwork in 1994, just as I was first traveling to Indonesia. Departing from the playful trickery of these airport encounters, this book explores political possibilities emerging with unexpected encounters and collaborations (Rutherford, *Raiding the Land of the Foreigners*, 100, 107).

4. The debate about whether the killings, massacres, disappearances, and structural elimination of indigenous peoples amount to genocide is fruitless and potentially diversionary, according to the historian Tracey Banivanua-Mar. She uses the case of West Papua to focus on the kinds of discursive and epistemic violence—tropes about cannibalism and violent savages—that provide the enabling backbone and camouflage for genocidal practices. "The word *genocide*," observes the West Papuan pastor and anthropologist Benny Giay, "is usually defined by institutions and powerful states that are perpetrators of violence. West Papuans have the right to define this word for ourselves. We have experienced a genocide during the last 40 years of Indonesian rule" (Banivanua-Mar, "A Thousand Miles of Cannibal Lands"; Benny Giay, interview, January 15th, 2010, McHenry, Md.).

The question of genocide in West Papua has nonetheless recently been hotly debated by Stuart Upton (who argues against using the word "genocide") and Jim

Elmslie (who makes a case that genocide is taking place). Both of these authors agree on some basic points: that West Papua has experienced a large-scale demographic transformation, that the economy is dominated by Indonesian settlers, and that West Papuans suffer disadvantages in education, employment, and health. They also both agree that significant human rights abuses have been perpetrated by the Indonesian security forces. "A demographic catastrophe is happening in West Papua," writes Jim Elmslie, "and this is the basis for the genocide claim." "Stuart Upton, in contrast, calls genocide an "emotive term" and suggests that the decrease of the numbers of West Papuans (in relative terms) can be explained as "part of the normal pattern of inter-island migration" (Chauvel, "Genocide and Demographic Transformation in Papua"; Elmslie, "Not Just Another Disaster"; Upton, "A Disaster, but Not Genocide").

In the United Nations convention of 1948, "genocide means any of the following acts committed with intent to destroy, in whole or in part, a national, ethnical, racial or religious group, as such: (a) Killing members of the group; (b) Causing serious bodily or mental harm to members of the group; (c) Deliberately inflicting on the group conditions of life calculated to bring about its physical destruction in whole or in part; (d) Imposing measures intended to prevent births within the group." The Allard K. Lowenstein International Human Rights Law Clinic of Yale University has published a preliminary investigation about the application of the UN genocide convention to the case of West Papua. The study documented the above listed acts of genocide by the Indonesian government in West Papua, but concluded that more research is needed to document the "intent to destroy" West Papuans as a national, ethnic, or racial group. This research is difficult to conduct because of ongoing problems faced by human rights researchers, journalists, and diplomats who seek access to West Papua (Brundige et al., "Indonesian Human Rights Abuses in West Papua").

Documenting the intent of one group to destroy another group is extremely challenging. Leaders who are conducting campaigns of genocide are usually reluctant to state their intentions for fear of international intervention. Even still, in 2007 Col. Burhanuddin Siagian, an Indonesian military commander who faces two indictments in East Timor for crimes against humanity, stated: "If I encounter elements that use government facilities, but still are betraying the nation, I will destroy them." At the time, Col. Siagian was the regional commander (DANREM) of the Indonesian military stationed in Jayapura, the capital of West Papua. "It is a fact of history," he went on to say, "Papua is part of the Republic of Indonesia." The Indonesian original reads: "Jika saya temukan ada oknum-oknum orang yang sudah menikmati fasilitas negara, tapi masih saja menghianati bangsa, maka terus terang saya akan tumpas . . . sesuai fakta sejarah, Papua sudah masuk menjadi NKRI" ("Danrem: Penghianat negara harus ditumpas," *Cenderawasih Pos*).

5. The exact number of West Papuans who have been killed as a direct result of military and police actions is unknown. In the words of the human rights investigators Carmel Budiardjo and Soei Liong Liem: "Accounts of military operations show that at certain times, thousands of people were killed by bombing and strafing and that thousands have died as the result of neglect, famine and maltreatment. Esti-

mates of the death toll range from 100,000 to 150,000. We would prefer not to support any particular figure, only to state the conviction that the loss of life suffered by the West Papuan people at the hands of their Indonesian colonizers has been on such a scale as to threaten their very survival as a people" (Budiardjo and Liem, *West Papua*, vii).

6. In 2008 a study by the *Medical Journal of Australia* reported: "Treatable diseases, particularly pneumonia and diarrhea, are common causes of mortality in children. Data from across West Papua suggest that malaria, upper respiratory tract infections and dysentery are the major causes of childhood morbidity. Maternal mortality is three times higher than for the remainder of Indonesia." Government "family planning" (*keluarga berencana*) programs aggressively promoted birth control at earlier historical periods in West Papua, despite an extremely sparse population relative to other areas of the country (Rees et al., "Health and Human Security in West Papua").

7. The territory has various names, each with charged political connotations. On October 19, 1961, the Papuan National Committee issued a manifesto renaming their nation West Papua from the previous name, Netherlands New Guinea. After a UN-brokered deal ceded sovereignty of the territory to Indonesia in 1963, the official name of the new province became West Irian, and later Irian Jaya. On January 1, 2000, Indonesian president Gus Dur issued a presidential decree to rename the territory Papua. Further complexity was introduced in 2003 with a controversial move that split the territory into the province of Papua and the province of West Papua. To avoid undue confusion to readers, I use the name West Papua to refer to the entire territory for all recent historical periods. In everyday speech, most people who trace their roots to the indigenous groups of this place refer to themselves as ethnic Papuans, in addition to members of one or more of the 263 tribes (*suku*). In this book I depart from my previous writing to call these people "West Papuans." Making this switch, after much deliberation, is intended to distinguish them from "Papuans" who live in the neighboring country of Papua New Guinea. The name *West* Papuan also highlights the power of arbitrary cartographic boundaries in shaping nations and collective identities.

8. Many human rights researchers have not turned away. During the thirty-two-year Suharto regime, human rights research was extremely difficult and dangerous work. As a result, most studies of violence from the 1970s and 1980s—notably *Indonesia's Secret War* by Robin Osborne (1985) and *West Papua: The Obliteration of a People* by Carmel Budiardjo and Liem Soei Liong (1983)—were conducted from a distance, relying on sporadic reports from the ground. In the late 1990s and the early years of the twenty-first century, Amnesty International and Human Rights Watch were able to gain intermittent access to West Papua, resulting in a series of reports about specific massacres, sweeping operations, and political prisoners (e.g., Human Rights Watch, *Indonesia*; Withers and Poulsen, *Grave Human Rights Violations in Wasior*; Human Rights Watch, *What Did I Do Wrong?*). After the expulsion of Amnesty International researchers from West Papua in 2003, international organizations came to rely on indigenous counterparts for their information.

9. Dominant historical narratives about West Papua "all fail adequately to address the views, or provide a space for the voices, of the indigenous communities," in the words of the Australian anthropologist Chris Ballard. Quoting Ezra Pound— "And even I can remember a day when the historians left blanks in their writing"— Ballard pointed to the absence of these voices as blanks in the writing of West Papua's history. Since Ballard published a review of the historical literature in 1999, some of these blanks have been filled in by anthropologists and indigenous West Papuan intellectuals. Readers who have a serious interest in West Papua should consult the collaborative bibliographic project of the University of Papua, Cenderawasih University, and the Australian National University, http://www.papuaweb.org. My book, which covers a decade in West Papua's history, engages many of the sources on Papua Web and adds more indigenous voices to the conversation. Inevitably I have privileged some voices, and some events, over others—leaving more blanks to fill in (Ballard, "Blanks in the Writing," 151). For a basic technical description of the languages of West Papua, see Gordon, *Ethnologue*.

10. Day, *Identifying with Freedom*, 2.

11. These expansive subtexts are modeled after *Negara*, by Clifford Geertz (1980). I thank an anonymous reviewer of this manuscript for making this suggestion.

12. This book draws on primary historical documents from a number of different archival collections. I studied colonial reports and correspondence, Christian missionary records, materials generated during ethnographic expeditions, newspaper clippings, and reports from human rights organizations. This research took place in collections that are housed at the Smithsonian National Museum of Natural History, the U.S. Library of Congress, the Netherlands General State Archives in the Hague (Algemeen Rijksarchief, or ARA), the Royal Netherlands Institute of Southeast Asian and Caribbean Studies at Leiden (KITLV), Elsham in Jayapura (the Institute for Human Right Studies and Advocacy), the Kodam VIII Trikora History Center in Jayapura, TAPOL (the Indonesian Human Rights Campaign in London), the Public Record Office (PRO) at Kew, the British Library in London, and the Center for the Study of Christianity in the Non-Western World at the University of Edinburgh.

13. Marcus, "Ethnography in/of the World System," 96–117.

14. At the conclusion of my undergraduate fieldwork in West Papua in 1998, my ability to speak Indonesian was formally rated as "advanced high" fluency by the American Council on the Teaching of Foreign Languages. As a graduate student, I learned Papuan slang, or Logat Papua, which is all but unintelligible to speakers of standard Indonesian. Most of my interviews were a mix of standard Indonesian and Logat Papua. My sources also incorporated fragments of five Papuan languages and one other European language into our interviews: Wandamen, Lani, Yali, Mee, Biak, and Dutch. I speak both Mee and Dutch at an elementary level and relied on Wandamen, Lani, Yali, and Biak translators. I tape-recorded 146 of my interviews. A total of 405,000 words were transcribed from a selection of the recorded interviews. The multiple sites in West Papua where I conducted these interviews include Jayapura, Wamena, Biak, Angguruk, Manokwari, Wondama, Merauke, Demta, Nabire, and Paniai. I have also interviewed members of the West Papuan diaspora and inter-

national solidarity network in the United Kingdom, the United States, the Netherlands, Germany, and eastern Indonesia.

15. Cf. Siegel, *Solo in the New Order*, 115–16; LiPuma, *Encompassing Others*, 4.

16. Cf. Haraway, *When Species Meet*, 4.

17. Jameson, "Marx's Purloined Letter," 62.

18. My project is allied with the work of John and Jean Comaroff, who have written about civil society and the political imagination in Africa. A "future-oriented memory," in their words, contrives "a past to conceptualize the continuous present . . . to transgress conventional limits, hybridize and compromise identities, to put into flux and movement what was considered stable, normative" (Comaroff and Comaroff, introduction to *Civil Society and the Political Imagination in Africa*, 5).

Introduction

1. In *Imaginative Horizons*, Vincent Crapanzano suggests that we can take pleasure in the unreality of imaginary hinterlands—the possibilities and the play they facilitate (100–102).

2. Ibid., 114.

3. Ester Nawipa, tape-recorded interview, Sentani, August 2, 2002.

4. Among the Huli, living in the highlands of twenty-first-century Papua New Guinea, women who have sex out of wedlock (either at knifepoint or otherwise) often find it impossible to say whether they had "consented." These women do not "own" their sexuality—their reproductive capacity is often thought of as a family and clan resource. In rape cases among the Huli, the most pressing issues are usually sociopolitical and economic. If a marriage ensues, with the appropriate bride price, or if the rapist provides adequate compensation, then the woman's immediate family feels vindicated. The feelings of the individual woman, and any abuse she may have suffered, are regarded as secondary to the economic considerations (Wardlow, *Wayward Women*, 114).

5. Pospisil, *Kapauku Papuan Economy*, 63, 324; Giay, *Zakheus Pakage and His Communities*, 32.

6. Marilyn Strathern has studied the intersection of kinship, personhood, and the arithmetic of ownership in the highlands of New Guinea. "It matters how people count the number and *kinds* of parents they have and even the number of offspring." In Melanesia the "right" to reproduce is sustained not by a legal apparatus but by the person in the appropriate and necessary ontological state to exercise the right. Ester found herself trapped in this violent confrontation between indigenous Melanesian notions of property and the reckless lust of the young Indonesian soldiers (Strathern, *Kinship, Law, and the Unexpected*, 82; 154).

7. Leslie Butt and Jenny Munro have studied conflicts among indigenous sexual mores and the norms of Indonesian civilian settlers. In the article "Rebel Girls," they explore the predicament of young West Papuan women who have babies out of wedlock, under the omnipresent "settler gaze" of Indonesian officials.

8. Departing from Marx's theory of use value, Donna Haraway argues: "To be in a relation of use to each other is not the definition of unfreedom and violation. Such relations are almost never symmetrical ('equal' or calculable)." Ester and I entered into a mutually agreeable use of her tragic biographical story amid the asymmetrical relations of power that often define ethnographic encounters. She and I discussed frankly the possible risks that her name's appearing in print might pose for her and her family. Ultimately I decided to respect her decision to use her encounter with me as an opportunity to become a public figure (Haraway, *When Species Meet*, 74).

9. Deciding who is a friend and who is an enemy was a central existential problem for Carl Schmitt. In the words of Gopal Balakrishnan, a scholar of Schmitt, the distinction between friend and enemy "cannot be determined by moral or even utilitarian criteria. . . . The enemy is the other, the stranger, with whom there is the real possibility of a violent struggle to the death." Schmitt was interested in "the potentially groundless, high-stakes decision as to whether a particular group of men are to be considered friends or enemies." Departing from Schmitt, I track the clever engagements of indigenous peoples and their movement among hostile social worlds (Balakrishnan, *The Enemy*, 108; cf. Derrida, "For a Justice to Come," 21).

10. Tapol, "Dead Bodies Found in West Papua," August 27, 2002.

11. Tsing, "Becoming a Tribal Elder," 162.

12. Tsing, *Friction*, 13.

13. D. Moore, *Suffering for Territory*, 4.

14. Nicolas Thomas brought the notion of entanglement to anthropology with his work on "entangled objects"—things with different careers, roles in transactions, and uses of material artifacts at different phases of their lives. He resuscitated multifaceted histories from entangled objects, describing a long history of interconnections between indigenous economies and global capitalism. Transactions involving material objects are forms of "entanglement that most of us cannot step outside." Patricia Spyer, an anthropologist who works just south of West Papua on the Aru Islands, recently brought entanglement out of the narrow domain of material culture to understand "centuries-long engagements within extended networks of commerce and communication and, on the other, by modernity's characteristic repressions and displacements." Entanglement, for Spyer, is a way to think about "the longer durée." My own use of entanglement points to emergent possibilities as much as past connections. I am in dialogue with Karen Barad, who has traced the notion of entanglement to mid-twentieth-century particle physics. Two entangled electrons can communicate with each other faster than the speed of light. "To be entangled," writes Barad, "is not simply to be intertwined with another, as in the joining of separate entities, but to lack an independent, self-contained existence. . . . Individuals emerge through and as part of their entangled intra-relating" (Thomas, *Entangled Objects*, 5; Spyer, *The Memory of Trade*; Barad, *Meeting the Universe Halfway*, ix).

15. Only the participants in a given conflict are well placed to judge what is at stake, according to Carl Schmitt. From an outside perspective, from the perspective of a nonpartisan, the differences separating bitter enemies seem arbitrary and

inconsequential. As I was recruited as an ally by West Papuan activists, I gained an increasingly nuanced understanding of their conflicts and collaborations with different powerful institutions (Balakrishnan, *The Enemy*, 108).

16. Here I am building on James Clifford's notion of "indigenous articulations," links between local traditions and foreign cultural elements. Clifford explores how antagonism among cultural groups is contained by contingent, nonguaranteed alliances and links. His work on the subject can be traced to Antonio Gramsci's ideas about hegemony, or the ability of one class to articulate the interests of other social groups to its own (Clifford, "Indigenous Articulations"; see also Hall, "Signification, Representation, Ideology"; Laclau, *Politics and Ideology in Marxist Theory*, 10).

17. With her current familial duties, Ester by no means has freedom in any absolute sense. Cynics might say that she has traded the raw exploitation of sexual slavery for a more widely accepted form of patriarchal domination. Still others might be critical of her dream to explore possibilities of freedom in theology. The Christian Church has an ambivalent legacy in West Papua. Early missionaries regarded indigenous West Papuan belief systems with distain. In more recent historical periods, large church organizations have worked in close coordination with the Indonesian government. Still, West Papuan human rights activists have also used the church as a vehicle for liberatory politics and human rights. Walter Post Theological School, where Ester's husband earned a master's degree, offers a curriculum informed by liberation theology. In 2003, when I interviewed Ester, I was teaching a postcolonial theory course to the Walter Post students. Periodically the Indonesian government has attempted to shut down Walter Post. Still, the theological school remains a site where indigenous intellectuals, like Ester, come to reflect on their lived experiences under the Indonesian military occupation.

18. Note that I was not asked if I would help the Yali people. The Yali became "West Papuans" during the last fifty years of contact with Europeans, Indonesians, and West Papuan groups from the lowlands.

19. Anna Tsing was told a similarly startling history of the world when she entered "the Realm of the Diamond Queen," a shared conceptual space that she created with Uma Adang, her primary interlocutor. Uma Adang would take "the words out of foreigners' mouths and juxtapose them wildly. The effect was disconcerting; a wall of broken mirrors fastened at odd angles, overlapping and askew" (Tsing, *In the Realm of the Diamond Queen*, 273).

20. The Yali had their first experiences of intense Indonesian military violence in 1968 when two white missionaries went missing on their land. Sensationalist accounts in the media, which turned out to be false, reported that the Yali had cannibalized the missionaries. One of the missionaries who went missing, a self-described "spiritual commando," was determined to burn all Yali religious artifacts, objects that he regarded as "fetishes." It is likely that the Yali killed the missionaries, but there is no evidence that the corpses were eaten. An Indonesian patrol marched into the village near where the pair had disappeared, set up a machine gun tripod, and, without warning, showered the village with heavy fire. Five Yali villagers were killed in this encounter. In the late 1970s, Indonesian airstrikes, bomb-

ing campaigns, and ground assaults took place on Yali lands. A widespread "sweeping" campaign by Indonesian security forces resulted in a number of deaths in the nearby highland town of Wamena in October 2000. At the time of my own visit to Yali villages in April 2003, a gun heist in Wamena sparked a fresh Indonesian military operation (Richardson, *Lords of the Earth*, 330–33; Budiardjo and Liem, *West Papua*; Rumbiak, "Testimony 17 tahanan tragedi Wamena").

21. Zöllner, *The Religion of the Yali*, 174.

22. Soccer was certainly a visible part of early colonialism in the highlands of New Guinea. A popular memoir by a Dutch colonial official reports on a soccer match that took place in the late 1930s, at the highland outpost of Enarotali, on the heels of initial adventures by whites in the region. Poking fun at indigenous forms of clothing, the official wrote: "West Papuans feel that they are completely dressed with the penis gourd, it completely satisfies their feelings of decency. . . . When de Bruyn [a Dutch police captain] organized a soccer match, the joking aim of the game became hitting the penis sheaths of the other players. With a direct hit one gourd exploded into pieces and the owner suddenly stood 'naked.' He then ran into the bushes and squatted there until someone brought him more 'pants'!" This story of broken penis sheaths is hardly utopic. When whites and blacks first played soccer together in the highlands of New Guinea, their games took place against a backdrop of racism and material inequality (Rhys, *Jungle Pimpernel*).

23. Yali actors, who inked binding contracts with thumbprints, received a one-time cash payment for participating in a Discovery Channel television documentary called "The Yali of Moon Mountain."

24. While navigating a similar contact zone—the Putumayo region of Colombia, where terror, colonialism, and gold are all in play—Michael Taussig reflects on his own experience in being "a white" (Taussig, *Shamanism, Colonialism, and the Wild Man*).

25. Ira Bashkow, a cultural anthropologist, found complex and ambivalent images of white men among the Orokaiva in Papua New Guinea. The Orokaiva are critical of the greediness that drove whites to colonize foreign lands. But at the same time, they remember that the whites vanquished disease-causing spirits with the power of Christianity (*The Meaning of Whitemen*, 93).

26. I borrow this phrase from Edward LiPuma, *Encompassing Others*, 4.

27. Battaglia, *On the Bones of the Serpent*, 9.

28. Jameson, "Science-Fiction as a Spatial Genre," 51.

29. The Freeport gold-mining operations have been subject to nuanced analysis by anthropologists who have studied the culture of terror, millennial expectations that get wrapped into political projects, and corporate philanthropy (Ballard, "The Signature of Terror"; Golden, "Gold, Violence, and the Rise of a Political Millenarianism"; Jacobs, "Kamoro Arts Festival"; Jacobs, "United Colours of Papua").

30. "Freeport," *Dow Jones Newswire*, March 15, 2006.

31. F. Wilson, *The Conquest of Copper Mountain*, 199.

32. In the pidgin English spoken across the border in the independent country of Papua New Guinea, the word *kago* is translated as "baggage, cargo, supplies." Logat

Papua does not have an equivalent word. During encounters with agents of capitalism and modernity, the figure of cargo in Papua New Guinea became "a reduction of Western notions like profit, wage-labor, and production," according to Roy Wagner (Murphy, *The Book of Pidgin English*; Wagner, *The Invention of Culture*, 31).

Lamont Lindstrom has traced the genealogy of the phrase "cargo cult" back to 1945, when it first appeared in print in the context of slowly dying colonial ambitions. Since its birth in borderline racist rhetoric, the cargo cult idea has come to influence colonial policy throughout Melanesia and beyond. In the words of Doug Dalton, "The term 'cargo cult' was used by colonial authorities to de-legitimize and criminalize the behavior of their subjects." Some observers—among them Indonesian intelligence agents—have called the independence movement in West Papua a "cargo cult" (Lindstrom, *Cargo Cult*, 15–26; Dalton, "Cargo Cults and Discursive Madness").

Rather than deliberately developing conceptual tools to facilitate the implementation of colonialism, anthropologists who contributed to the literature on cargo cults in the mid-twentieth century were attempting to respond to indigenous discontent with foreign rule. Jean Guiart saw cargo cults as the "forerunners of Melanesian nationalism." His overview in 1951 of the Melanesian cargo cult literature found that in some locations "one can easily notice the wish for independence in religious as well as secular affairs." Yet Guiart saw the cargo cult movements as being a long way from progressing to "modern political methods." Peter Worsley also portrayed cargo cults as "proto-national formations" that would progressively be replaced by "more advanced, secular political movements" in rural regions (Burridge, *New Heaven, New Earth*, 128; Guiart, "Forerunners of Melanesian Nationalism," 89–90; Worsley, *The Trumpet Shall Sound*, 255).

Numerous elements of my book owe a debt to classic anthropological studies of cargo cults in Melanesia and Oceania. Still, I argue that branding West Papuan nationalists as "cargo cultists" reinscribes European colonial discourses—delegitimizing and criminalizing the behavior of indigenous political agents. The complex diplomatic negotiations I chronicle in this book suggest that the West Papuan people are indeed savvy about "modern political methods."

33. Joel Robbins, who studied millenarian Christian thought among the Urapmin of Papua New Guinea, found that indigenous Papuan notions of time had been inflected with the apocalyptic dreams of Pentecostal Christian missionaries. The Urapmin were "everyday millenarians" who mixed a strong belief in the imminent end of the world with a steady commitment to carrying out the tasks of everyday life. Kiwak's parable of the hole contained elements of messianic thinking—feelings of expectation that were divorced from a particular messiah or from a specific period of time, for example the millennium (Robbins, "Secrecy and the Sense of an Ending," 526).

34. This "Good News" reached many parts of West Papua's highlands in the mid-twentieth century. Newly converted West Papuan Christians faced off against "pagans" in a series of violent encounters. Some expatriate missionaries encouraged fetish-burning ceremonies, where important indigenous ritual objects were

destroyed by fire. These public demonstrations of conversion were initiated by West Papuan evangelists who foretold the coming of the Christian millennium (Obeth Komba, tape-recorded interview, Utrecht, the Netherlands, May 27, 2003. See also Hitt, *Cannibal Valley*, 16; Hayward, *The Dani of Irian Jaya*, 135).

35. Many other West Papuans share such dreams about the Second Coming. The Imyan, an indigenous group in the Bird's Head Peninsula, "use local forms of Christianity to interpret past, present, and future events. Imyan read world news and reports about regional events through the Book of Revelation, which promises an end to oppression and a thousand-year kingdom of Jesus Christ. Silas Kiwak maintained a steady commitment to carrying out the tasks of everyday life, like the Urapmin across the border in Papua New Guinea. He attentively listened to his single-sideband radio, waiting for news of an event that would transform the existing political and social order (Timmer, "Erring Decentralization," 30; Robbins, "Secrecy and the Sense of an Ending," 526).

36. Derrida, "Marx and Sons," 253. Paul de Man is also regarded as a founder of deconstruction.

37. Derrida, *Specters of Marx*, 74.

38. Haraway, *When Species Meet*, 4.

39. Chimerical visions are imaginary. They are things with "no ground or truth," according to the same dictionary, the *Dictionarium Britannicum*. Donna Haraway has argued that we are all chimeras—products of technological, linguistic, cultural, political, and biological fusions. "By the late twentieth century, our time, a mythic time," writes Haraway, "we are all chimeras, theorized and fabricated hybrids of machine and organism; in short, we are cyborgs." The chimera—a fabled fire-breathing monster of Greek mythology with a lion's head, a goat's body, and a serpent's tail—has also served as a way for biologists to think about how tissues of genetically different individuals coexist as a result of grafting or an analogous process in nature. Haraway, a member of my doctoral dissertation committee, has deeply influenced how I think about figures—how they bring hopes into focus on imaginative horizons, how they engender possibilities of freedom (Bailey, *Dictionarium Britannicum*; Haraway, *Simians, Cyborgs, and Women*, 150; Haraway, "Speculative Fabulations for Technoculture's Generations," 304n3).

40. "Figures collect the people through their invitation to inhabit the corporeal story told in their lineaments," continues Haraway. "Figures are not representations or didactic illustrations," she argues, "but rather material-semiotic nodes or knots in which diverse bodies and meanings coshape one another" ("Speculative Fabulations for Technoculture's Generations," 4).

Charles Sanders Peirce, an American philosopher, defines a "representation" as "an object which stands for another so that an experience of the former affords us a knowledge of the latter." This definition of representation plays up the materiality—historicity, flesh and bloodiness, and entangledness—of all signs. Departing from Peirce, Webb Keane, an anthropologist who also works in Indonesia, argues that representations are things and acts in the world: "They are enunciated in speech events," says Keane "enacted in rites, embodied in clothing, and portrayed in physical media; they circulate as goods and live in the form of human delegates" (Peirce, *Writings of Charles S. Peirce*, 257; Keane *Signs of Recognition*, 8).

Peircians thus might quibble with Haraway's assertion ("figures are not representations") claiming a materiality of all signs. In this book, I treat figures as a particular kind of representation with more palpable substance when compared with other species of sign. The materiality of speech acts is arbitrary with respect to denoted objects. Like metaphors, figures are not literal and self-identical—they diffract our visions. Figures exist in the borderlands between metaphorical allegory and sacramental actuality. Substances and symbols come together in figures to coshape and coconstitute institutions, bodies, and worlds. By pinning their hopes on specific figures, the people of West Papua brought substantive objects within the reach of desire (see also Haraway, *Modest_Witness*, 11; G. Bateson, *Steps to an Ecology of Mind*, 33–37).

41. Figural interpretation connects two things (e.g., events or persons) that are separated in time. In the words of Eric Auerbach, the two poles of a figure are linked, so that "the first signifies not only itself but also the second, while the second involves or fulfills the first. . . . They are both contained in the flowing stream which is historical life, and only the comprehension, the *intellectus spiritualis*, of their interdependence is a spiritual act." Auerbach's work, a rich study of mimesis in traditions of Western Christian realism, illustrates how salvation history *is* history. As such, it is a particularly apt guide to describing merdeka in West Papua (Auerbach, *Mimesis*, 73).

A new mode of representation, figural realism, emerged out of Auerbach's work. "The heart of figural realism," writes Haraway, "is the Christian practice of reading the story of Christ into Jewish scripture. Although in Christian figuration both figure and fulfillment are materially real, history is fully contained in the eternal plan of Divine Providence, which alone can supply the key to historical meaning." Christ competes with other extraordinary figures in West Papua—holes that contained the magic of modernity, pipelines that transported the wealth of global capitalism, and multiple messiahs—that contain hope and depict otherwise elusive aspects of reality (White, *Figural Realism*; Haraway, *Modest_Witness*, 9–11).

42. Crapanzano, *Imaginative Horizons*, 114.

43. Benny Giay, "Eben Kirksey's Thesis in West Papuan History," note to author, Washington, November 23, 2007.

44. "PT Freeport pays US$899m in Taxes, Royalties," *Jakarta Post*, August 30, 2010.

45. Tedjasukmana, "Why Jakarta Needs to Pay More Attention to Papua," August 16, 2010.

46. Vincent Crapanzano has discussed the distinction between hope and desire at length. In dialogue with the psychiatrist Eugène Minkowski, Crapanzano suggests that desire enables us to settle on something. Desire builds, he proposes, when there is an oscillation of revelation and concealment. Hope, for Crapanzano, invokes an ever-further horizon, a mysterious beyond (Crapanzano, *Imaginative Horizons*, 103–4, 146).

47. Social worlds involve collective action. They are classically defined as people "doing things together" (Becker, *Doing Things Together*, 21; Clarke and Star, "Social Worlds/Arenas/Discourse Framework," 113).

48. Strauss, "A Social World Perspective," 119.

49. Clarke, *Disciplining Reproduction*, 15.

50. Donna Haraway has written about what she calls "SF worlding"—the worlds of science fiction or speculative fabulation. Worlding generates new horizons of possibility by wedding imaginative dreams with insights that come from being worldly, from being attentive to emergent opportunities. Anna Tsing's related notion of "worldmaking" is illustrated with the figure of a flowing creek cutting through a hillside. As the water rushes down, it carves rock and moves gravel. Tsing invites us to imagine the landscape that channels these flows as being composed of a multitude of agents: ethnic groups, corporations, refugees, nongovernmental organizations, social movements, and social scientists, among others. Separately, Tsing has invited scholars to imagine their own worldmaking projects and has invented a playful exercise called the "Game of Global Futures." This game involves imaging strange coalescences, assemblages of unlikely allies and agents (Haraway, "Speculative Fabulations for Technoculture's Generations"; Tsing, "The Global Situation"; Tsing, *Friction*; also see my epilogue in this book).

51. Adele Clarke and Susan Leigh Star have written about the moment when worlds fracture and become "large and crisscrossed with conflicts, different sorts of careers, viewpoints, funding sources" (Clarke and Star, "Social Worlds/Arenas/Discourse Framework," 113).

52. Latour, *War of the Worlds*, 3.

53. Wallerstein, *The Capitalist World Economy*, 18.

54. Wallerstein, *The Decline of American Power*, 237; *World-Systems Analysis*, 18–19.

55. Identifying a single global hegemon, a unified conspiratorial force, fails to account for the countervailing powers of heterogeneous alterworlds (cf. García Canclini, *Hybrid Cultures*).

56. Anzaldúa, *Borderlands*.

57. Speculative fictions and fabulations are key imaginative elements of worldmaking. Figures grab hold of the imagination, compelling worldly action—often in complex, countervailing, directions (Haraway, "Speculative Fabulations for Technoculture's Generations").

58. The political imaginary, according to Susan Buck-Morss, keeps the enemy within the position of the "other." In occupying this position, Buck-Morss argues (in opposition to Carl Schmitt) that the enemy loses its absolute character. As long as the enemy stays in its place—so long as the enemy behaves like the enemy—it is not a threat in the absolute sense. The truly dangerous enemy operates on the metalevel, threatening the imaginary system itself. This absolute enemy operates in the great political divide between imaginary systems. The friend-enemy distinction is not usually clear for people who inhabit imagined political borderlands or are entangled with multiple worlds at war (Buck-Morss, *Dreamworld and Catastrophe*, 33–34).

Indonesian freedom fighters, struggling for liberation from Dutch colonial rule in the mid-twentieth century, found that if they were discovered by the authorities, they might suddenly end up on the Dutch side. "One could be punished, even killed, by the Dutch," writes James Siegel, a historian and anthropologist. "But one might also be subtly wooed to their side. Perhaps without being aware of it, one could find that one changed sides." These dynamics were replayed during the Indonesian occupation of West Papua. Amid competing visions—freedom dreams from West Papuan revolutionaries, and promises of security from the Indonesian state—people struggled to figure out which side they were on. West Papuans reexperienced the anxieties inherent to recognition described by Siegel—people worried that they might suddenly become a traitor (Siegel, *Fetish, Recognition, Revolution*, 185).

59. Clinton Fernandes misrepresents an earlier iteration of this point that I made in my master's thesis. He quoted me as saying that merdeka is "interdependence rather than independence; *merdeka* in this sense means self-sufficiency in terms of food production and access to clean water. Kirksey's insights are valuable because they show that what West Papuans desire are new systems of governance based on indigenous modes of authority that ought to be achievable without separating from Indonesia." Certainly some articulations of merdeka relate to desires to maintain economic autonomy from the modern world system (see chapter 6 in the present volume). But the dominant meaning of merdeka in West Papua references the desire for national sovereignty. Postnational visions of freedom include desires for new interdependencies, not just an autochthonous form of national independence. In short, West Papuans desire national independence and also hope to actualize a new model of nationalism that does not replicate the well-rehearsed scripts of postcolonial suffering that have been played out in many different corners of the globe (Fernandes, *Reluctant Indonesians*, 11).

60. Van Eekelen et al., *Shock and Awe*, 1.

61. Some of these meanings have already been explored in a short book on the subject, *Identifying with Freedom*, edited by Tony Day, with contributions from leading scholars of Indonesia. This pamphlet explores the idea of merdeka during a new age of Indonesian democracy amid American military agendas and the emergence of China as a dominant economic power in Southeast Asia. Among other valances of this powerful, polysemic word, the authors explore how it plays out in discourses on gay and lesbian rights, as well as among the *preman*—thugs who regard themselves as "free men."

62. Echols and Shadily, *Kamus Indonesia-Inggris*, 371.

63. Words are in constant motion, according to Webb Keane. "In some circumstances," he writes, "people's ideas about words, things, and people include assumptions *about* history—for example, that history can be understood as a narrative of moral liberation." In the mid-twentieth century, merdeka was embedded within global narratives about progress and liberation. It also came to include messianic assumptions about historical process—the sense that anything could happen at any time (Keane, *Christian Moderns*, 5).

64. Reid, *Slavery, Bondage, and Dependency in Southeast Asia*, 21; Monier-Williams,

A Sanskrit-English Dictionary, 494; Nick Allen, "Maharddhika," e-mail sent on October 24, 2003, from nick.allen@anthropology.oxford.ac.uk.

65. Freed slaves, who were called the *maharddhika* or *mardijkers*, brought the root of this powerful word from India at some point before the fifteenth century. The 1623 Dutch/Malay *Vocabularium* by Sebastiaan Danckaerts defines *mardijker* as "freeman, non-slave, or *mardeka*" (Taylor, *The Social World of Batavia*, 47–49; de Haan, "De Laatste Der Mardijkers").

66. In the first half of the twentieth century—amid colonial decline, revolution, and war—the rise of Indonesian nationalism competed with many different political alternatives. By 1950 "political leaders reached a compromise to institutionalize the Indonesian nation in the form of a unitary state and modern, liberal democratic political institutions" (Bertrand, *Nationalism and Ethnic Conflict in Indonesia*, 28).

67. Anderson, *Imagined Communities*, 4.

68. Print capitalism, Anderson argued, made the vernacular languages of early modern Europe homogeneous. In Anderson's early work, he essentially agreed with Ernest Gellner in assuming that nations have key traits: homogeneity, literacy, and anonymity. In Gellner's words, nations are "based on a culture striving to be a high (literate) culture; they are large enough to sustain the hope of supporting the educational system which can keep a literate culture going; they are poorly endowed with rigid internal sub-groupings; their populations are anonymous, fluid, and mobile. West Papuan nationalists scored surprising political victories at the dawn of the twenty-first century although they did not have the characteristics deemed essential by Anderson and Gellner (Anderson, *Imagined Communities*, 37–46; Gellner, *Nations and Nationalism*, 138).

69. Members of these imagined communities do not necessarily *do things together*, aside from reading the daily newspaper or watching national events unfold on television (Anderson, *Imagined Communities*, 25).

70. One of Anderson's longtime critics, Partha Chatterjee, asks: "If nationalisms in the rest of the world have to choose their imagined community from certain 'modular' forms already made available to them by Europe and the Americas, what do they have left to imagine?" West Papua's visionaries have reanimated political forms that they inherited from abroad, and have developed their own surprising freedom dreams (Chatterjee, *The Nation and Its Fragments*, 5).

71. Cited in Siegel, *A New Criminal Type in Jakarta*, vii.

72. In 1999 East Timor had a historic independence referendum. In the days after the Timorese people cast their votes, choosing an independent future by a clear margin, the Indonesian military conducted a scorched-earth campaign, killing civilians and destroying basic infrastructure. One survivor of this violence "recalled seeing heads, severed from their bodies, rolling on the ground. Many hundreds of people were there with her, witnessing the horror. They were screaming and attempting to flee those who were attacking, stabbing, hacking, and beheading her compatriots. But the heads on the ground created a different sort of scene. It was 'as if they were playing soccer,' she recounted." In Aceh, Indonesian military campaigns intensified after the fall of Suharto. A devastating tsunami on December 26, 2004, which

left some 170,000 dead or missing in Aceh, prompted the international community to intervene. The Helsinki Peace Process concluded in August 2005, resulting in a cease-fire between Acehnese guerrillas and the Indonesian military. Aceh now enjoys a high degree of genuine autonomy (Nevins, *A Not-So-Distant Horror*, 4; Kingsbury, *Peace in Aceh*).

73. Kelley, *Freedom Dreams*, ix.

74. Maria Puig de la Bellacasa, a scholar and an activist with the Next Generation Network, helped me understand the distinction between the European alter-globalization projects and the antiglobalization rallies in the United States.

75. In other corners of the globe, indigenous groups were also beginning to reemerge after long periods of suffering under settler colonialism (see, e.g., Clifford, "Indigenous Articulations"; Cattelino, *High Stakes*, 163).

76. The Department of Anthropology at UC Santa Cruz has launched a new initiative to study "emerging worlds." This represents a departure from norms that prevailed in twentieth-century anthropology to study "vanishing worlds"—cultures that were purportedly disappearing as a result of modernization and progress. World-making networks, geographies, innovations, and assemblages are carrying us into the future. In the words of Anna Tsing, one of the key theorists behind the Santa Cruz emerging-worlds initiative, "Cosmopolitans, like diasporas, promote projects of world-making, but . . . the projects they endorse enlarge the hegemonies of northern centers even as they incorporate peripheries. In contrast, the world-making projects of southern diasporas and poor migrants form an oppositional accompaniment to northern hegemonies, limiting their attempts at universalization and criticizing their center-periphery perspective. They limit, rather than spread, Northern hegemonies" (Tsing, "The Global Situation," 86).

77. Merdeka is what James Clifford would call a "translation term," which privileges a number of different "original" meanings. The Imyan, who live in the Bird's Head region of West Papua, for example, equate merdeka (freedom) with *berkat* (blessings, profit). Among the Biak, merdeka is equated by many indigenous intellectuals with the ideal of *koreri*, a utopia of material plenty where everyone "eats in one place." The Dani highlanders' notion of *nabelan kabelan*, where the ideal of eternal life is measured practically in modern times through food security, healthcare, and general prosperity, informs indigenous perceptions of Christian salvation and national liberation. Translation terms are imperfect equivalences. Rather than gloss over different meanings of merdeka, this book follows expansive indigenous freedom dreams as they exploded along multiple lines of flight (Clifford, *Routes*, 11–2; Timmer, "The Return of the Kingdom," 300; Rutherford, *Raiding the Land of the Foreigners*; Farhadian, *Christianity, Islam, and Nationalism in Indonesia*, 17).

78. In *The Spectre of Comparison*, Benedict Anderson considered the role of new communications technologies in popularizing nationalism. He writes: "Radio brought even illiterate populations within the purview of the mass media, and its reception was never effectively limited to nation-state audiences. . . . Subsequently, the telephone and telex, film, television, cassettes, video recorders, and the personal computer accelerated and enormously magnified nearly everything that radio had

initiated." In contrast to the standardized national languages generated by earlier forms of print capitalism, the technologies of nation making in West Papua (the Internet, the single-sideband radio, and the cell phone) actively generated new sorts of linguistic heterogeneity on top of existing indigenous diversity. Logat Papua, long an oral linguistic form with no major written works or even a published dictionary, was only one of the 271 distinct indigenous languages animating West Papua's independence movement. The struggle for merdeka began to achieve surprising political results without a standardized language, widespread literacy, and other sorts of cultural homogeneity that Anderson deemed important in his early work (Anderson, *The Spectre of Comparison*, 66–67).

79. In the National Archives of Fiji, the anthropologist Hirokazu Miyazaki encountered Fijian lawyers, consultants, and clan heads who were pursuing historical documents that had bearing on a controversial land dispute. These people who frequented the archives hoped that they might find documents showing that they were entitled to receive compensation for loss of their ancestral lands. Like West Papuans who clung to promises of international treaties, these Fijian researchers were struggling to gain traction in a world where political power in the present mediated the sorts of truth that might be told about history (Miyazaki, *The Method of Hope*).

80. Jameson, "Marx's Purloined Letter," 62.

81. These quotes are drawn from a forthcoming book, *Spectral Sovereignties: Colonialism, Nationalism, and the Idea of an Audience in West Papua*, where Danilyn Rutherford explores how culture-jamming with Obama's words and imagery on YouTube allowed "West Papuans and their supporters to enjoy a glimpse of freedom, and . . . imagine attracting the world's gaze."

82. Here I am revoicing the title of *Histories of the Future*, a collection of essays by Daniel Rosenberg and Susan Harding.

Interlude: The King Has Left the Palace

1. Hill, "The Indonesian Economy," 93–103; Vidal, "Poison Fog Blanket Threatens World Climate," September 27, 1997; "Drought Disaster and Snowfall in West Papua," *Kompas*, October 23, 1997; Walters, "Malaria Compounds Irian Jayans' Misery," December 6–7, 1997; Bird, "Indonesia in 1997," 172–75; Lioe, "Indonesia on the Boil," February 26, 1998.

2. "From a millenarian perspective, things are always getting worse," writes Donna Haraway. "Oddly, belief in advancing disaster is actually part of a trust in salvation, whether deliverance is expected by sacred or profane revelations, through revolution, dramatic scientific breakthroughs, or religious rapture" (Haraway, *Modest_Witness*, 41).

3. Anderson, *Language and Power*, 33.

4. Tesoro, *The Invisible Place*, 21.

5. Tales have long tried to shape history in Indonesia. Maier, "In Search of Memories," 99–121.

6. Edmund McWilliams, interview, Washington, April 11, 2007.

7. Said, *Orientalism*, 26.

8. Robinson, "The Post-coup Massacre in Bali," 118; Colmey and Liebhold, "The Family Firm"; J. Pemberton, *On the Subject of Java*, 3, 315; Sidel, "Macet Total," 164.

9. Many specialists on Indonesia will likely disagree with me on this point. The student activists who were at the political vanguard of the Indonesian Reformasi movement looked on indigenous prophecy, and messianic hopes grounded in religion, as unhelpful superstition. These secular revolutionaries had faith that was not tied to religion. Still, they believed in profound transformations to come. My intention is to stretch meaning of the word "messianic"—to blur the boundaries between secular and religious desires. This book works to reclaim the political possibilities contained in messianic desires (cf. Aspinall, "Guerrillas in Power," 213; Benjamin, *Illuminations*; Haraway, *Modest_Witness*; Derrida, "Marx and Sons"; Jameson, "Marx's Purloined Letter").

10. The phrase "homogeneous, empty, time," which I use to refer to the Suharto era, has also been purloined from Benjamin. Benedict Anderson also uses the phrase: "The idea of a sociological organism moving calendrically through homogeneous, empty time is a precise analogue of the idea of the nation, which also is conceived as a solid community moving steadily down (or up) history" (Benjamin, *Illuminations*, 261; Anderson, *Imagined Communities*, 26).

11. Jameson, "Marx's Purloined Letter," 62; Benjamin, *Illuminations*, 263–64.

12. Derrida, "Marx and Sons," 253; italics mine.

13. Derrida, "For a Justice to Come," 24–25.

14. Derrida also regards messianicity "as *promise* and not as onto-theological or teleo-eschatological program or design" (Derrida, *Specters of Marx*, 28, 74, 167).

15. The messianic spirit was animating a secular political formation, rather than a religious ideology. Kenelm Burridge, a student of indigenous history and politics in New Guinea, writes: "Faith is faith whether thought of as religious or secular" (Burridge, *New Heaven, New Earth*, 7; See also Derrida, *Specters of Marx*, 167).

16. Derrida is clear to distinguish messianicity from messianism. Since the spirit of messianicity is not fixated on a particular outcome, in this case the resignation of Suharto, it cannot fail. By the same token, since messianicity never settles on anything in particular, I argue that it can never succeed. If one expects the unfigurable, one will never know when it arrives (cf. Derrida, "Marx and Sons," 253).

17. Aspinall, *Opposing Suharto*, 223.

18. Social worlds often involve such "implicated actors" who are "silenced or only discursively present—constructed by others for their own purposes" (Clarke and Star, "Social Worlds/Arenas/Discourse Framework," 119).

19. Octovianus Mote, telephone interview, September 2009.

20. The *Far Eastern Economic Review* (FEER) conducted an interview in February 1998 with Gingrich about congressional support for an IMF bailout of Indonesia's failing economic institutions: "FEER: In Indonesia, it's complicated because of the political factors, the uncertainty of succession, like President Suharto stepping down. Gingrich: Maybe that should be the goal. FEER: But that cannot be an IMF de-

mand. Gingrich: In that case we cannot give them money." Such decrees from Washington produced economic turmoil and suffering for the people of Indonesia. They also created the conditions for a social revolution (Chanda, "Strings Attached").

21. Forrester, "A Jakarta Diary, May 1998," 24–25.

22. McCarthy, "Indonesia Burning," 44.

23. Tsing, *Friction*, 227.

24. Yen-ling Tsai, who earned her Ph.D. in anthropology at uc Santa Cruz, has written about Chinese communities in the city of Medan. She is writing about the fortifications erected by Chinese shop owners during the looting that took place during the mass mobilization of the "reform" era.

25. Aspinall, *Opposing Suharto*, 232; U.S. Embassy, "Travel Advisory," June 3, 1998; Sidel, "Macet Total," 164.

26. Forrester, "A Jakarta Diary, May 1998," 5.

27. Jameson, "Marx's Purloined Letter," 62.

28. Certainly many Indonesians had long imagined the possibility of Suharto's resignation. Despite quiet grumbling, and occasional open expressions of dissent, "public demonstrations of opposition [were] relatively unusual" during the Suharto regime. Dreams of deposing Suharto, even those harbored by influential power brokers, seemed impossible during the halcyon days of his regime. As the students occupied parliament on May 18, 1998, no one knew if this extraordinary moment would bring the impossible within realms of possibility (Sidel, "Macet Total," 175; J. Pemberton, "Notes on the 1982 General Election," 3).

29. Derrida's writings about the messianic are concerned with the undecidable and indeterminable nature of specific figures—particular events, people, and objects—and the transformations that they foretell. Benjamin's "Critique of Violence" is also a useful reference point here. He argues that only God can determine whether a given event constitutes mythological violence (which is lawmaking, threatening, and bloody) or divine violence (which is law destroying and lethal without spilling blood). Messianic hopes operate according to a similar logic. Ultimately only the messiah himself or herself can decide about making an appearance or imbuing an event with revolutionary force. The moments leading up to Suharto's renouncing of power contained a certain undecidability—people wondered if the impossible event would happen or if the power of the president would persist despite the revolutionary momentum (Derrida, "For a Justice to Come," 207–11; "Marx and Sons," 253; Benjamin, *Illuminations*, 282–85).

30. Sidel, "Macet Total," 188–89.

31. "What I call messianicity without messianism," Derrida says, "is a call, a promise of an independent future for what is to come, and which comes like every messiah in the shape of peace and justice, a promise independent of religion, that is to say universal. . . . And I believe we must seek today, very cautiously, to give force and form to this messianicity, without giving in to the old concepts of politics (sovereignism, territorialised nation-state), without giving in to the Churches or to the religious powers, theologico-political or theocratic of all orders" (Derrida, "For a Justice to Come").

32. "Messianicity without messianism," writes Derrida, "remains, for its part, undeconstructible, like justice." In dialogue with this passage from Derrida, Owen Ware writes: "Derrida's notion of messianicity is thus in no way a secularization of Judeo-Christian messianism (Marxism, Hegelianism, or Kantianism, on the other hand, are perfect examples of secular eschatology), because the very nature of the messianic is undetermined—it has no content. The indeterminateness of messianicity likewise prevents it from ever being a 'return' to religion, in any orthodox sense" (Derrida, "Marx and Sons," 253; Ware, "Dialectic of the Past," 110).

33. In this section, I am indebted to Danilyn Rutherford for helping me clarify my interpretation of Derrida's nuanced writings about messianicity. Here, with the questions about the postrevolutionary moment, I am directly borrowing from comments that Rutherford made on a draft of this manuscript pointing to correspondences between Derrida's work and my own argument.

34. Derrida writes of "critical moments (pre-revolutionary or post-revolutionary), moments of hope or disappointment, in short, dead ends during which a simulacrum of messianism serves as an alibi" (Derrida, "Marx and Sons," 253).

Chapter 1. The Messianic Multiple

1. Rutherford, *Raiding the Land of the Foreigners*, 154–55.

2. Ibid., 24; 160; Kamma, *Koreri*, 31–36.

3. There are three authoritative sources for the Itchy Old Man myth, according to Rutherford: a dynamic corpus of Biak songs called *wor*, a 328-page book written by a Dutch colonial official, and the Bible, which according to Biak legend was missing its first page, where the secrets of the Itchy Old Man were revealed. I conducted interviews on this subject with Biaks and have also consulted obscure primary sources (Rutherford, *Raiding the Land of the Foreigners*, 150–51; Ircham, *Mansren Koreri*; Thimme, "Manarmakeri," 21–49).

4. Here *merdeka* stands in as a translation term for the indigenous Biak notion of koreri. "One can describe *koreri* as utopia, an imagined state of pleasure and perfection," writes Danilyn Rutherford. The fabled time of koreri is prophesied to bring food in abundance, to sustain perpetual youth, and to transform slaves into masters (Rutherford, *Raiding the Land of the Foreigners*, 25; Kamma, *Koreri*, 18–19).

5. Susan Harding, who coined the phrase "revoicing" to understand the discursive practices of evangelical Christians in North America, has deeply influenced my thinking about related issues in West Papua. Revoicing involves occupying, colonizing, and deeply disturbing the worlds of cultural others. The tale of the Itchy Old Man is an indigenous revoicing—a diffracted repetition of global stories, culture jamming that parodies world religion (Harding, "Get Religion," 345–46).

6. Rutherford, *Raiding the Land of the Foreigners*, 27.

7. Jesus is the son of the Itchy Old Man, the disguised Lord Himself, in the version of the tale I have reproduced here. Identities are blurred in other versions. Early missionaries working in Biak were accused of ripping out the first page of the Bible

where it was written that Jesus was really the Itchy Old Man (Kamma, *Koreri*, 161; Rutherford, "The White Edge of the Margin").

8. Rutherford, *Raiding the Land of the Foreigners*, 26–27.

9. The messianic multiple is at play in the borderlands where hope meets desire. Departing from Vincent Crapanzano, who maintains a distinction between hope and desire, I suggest that the slippage between these two sentiments generates revolutionary possibilities. When generalized feelings of collective hope become articulated to multiple specific objects of desire—coming events, material concessions, or historical figures—mass movements begin to gain political traction (Crapanzano, *Imaginative Horizons*, 103–4, 146).

10. Words are "like drops of liquid mercury splashing about, moving in any direction," writes the Chinese poet Gu Cheng. Like liquid mercury, merdeka is difficult to contain. It runs through figural holes and travels abroad in unlikely disguises. All manner of heterogeneous and seemingly contradictory elements are contained in the fluidity of merdeka—hopes for national independence, capitalist wealth, socialist equality, Christian salvation, and indigenous sovereignty. These imperfect equivalencies allowed a massively popular grassroots movement to coalesce in West Papua after the fall of Suharto. Thanks to Katie Peterson and Li Dong for bringing Gu Cheng's work to my attention during our time together at Deep Springs College (Weinberger, "Diary").

11. The multitude, a swarm of creative agents, is distinct from my notion of the messianic multiple—a revolutionary logic that can work in the imagination of an individual visionary. When the spirit of the messianic multiple catches hold of a crowd, possibilities multiply beyond control (Hardt and Negri, *Multitude*, 56–57).

12. De Bruijn, "Anthropological Research," 137.

13. The indigenous people of New Guinea are complicit in constructing images of "paradise." Constructing West Papua as paradise—either as an idyllic Pacific haven or as an anthropological "living laboratory"—has given some indigenous communities the opportunity to encounter powerful foreigners. These encounters become occasions for surprising interruptions of idealized images, the site of collaboration and mutual exploitation (O'Hanlon, *Paradise*; Clifford, *Routes*).

14. "During the 1990s, apocalypticism, and, somewhat less flamboyantly, its millennialist twin, have become a constant and unavoidable presence in everyday life" (Stewart and Harding, "Bad Endings," 289–90).

15. Haraway, *Modest_Witness*, 41.

16. Clifford, "Saving Indigenous Time," presented at "Saving Time: An Interdisciplinary Conference on Memory and Memorialization," Cowell College, UC Santa Cruz, November 18, 2005.

17. Cf. Tsing, "Indigenous Voice," 39.

18. Komer to Rostow, February 17, 1961, White House. Quoted in G. Pemberton, *All the Way*, 86.

19. Subandrio, J. H. van Rouen, and C. W. A. Schurmann, "The New York Agreement," August 15, 1962 (original document in UN archives in New York).

20. In written testimony for a U.S. congressional hearing about West Papua,

Pieter Drooglever suggested that the New York Agreement ruled out the possibility of a referendum on the issue of independence: "There were certainly no clear plans for a plebiscite on the basis of universal suffrage and individual vote—which would have been hardly practicable in the isolated but densely populated highland areas. Instead the documents stipulated that an Indonesian-style *Musyawarah*, or 'traditional consultation,' would be an essential part of the Act of Free Choice. This 'consultation' allowed for manipulation from above. Thus, the foundations for the inadequate Act of Free Choice were already laid down in the agreement itself." The English-language translation of Drooglever's monograph on this subject reached me in 2010 as I was preparing my own book manuscript for copyediting. While I did not have the opportunity to fully engage with the nuanced historical material that Drooglever discovered in the archives, my knowledge of the New York Agreement text (informed by lively debates in the early twenty-first century among West Papuan intellectuals) leads me to suspect that a *musyawarah*, or "traditional consultation," was not the only practical option available to the parties charged with implementing the treaty. The original text of the New York Agreement suggests that all West Papuans should have been eligible to participate. Indonesia was responsible for ensuring "the eligibility of all adults, male and female, not foreign nationals to participate in the act of self-determination to be carried out in accordance with international practice" (Drooglever, *An Act of Free Choice*; *Crimes against Humanity: When Will Indonesia's Military Be Held Accountable for Deliberate and Systematic Abuses in West Papua?:Hearing Before the Subcommittee on Asia, the Pacific and the Global Environment*, 111th Cong., September 22, 2010).

21. Drooglever, *An Act of Free Choice*, 758.

22. Saltford, *United Nations and the Indonesian Takeover*, 180.

23. Rutherford, "Waiting for the End," 56; Danilyn Rutherford, personal communication, Santa Cruz, Calif., August 13, 2009.

24. This text and the ones that follow are excerpts from my field notes that have been condensed and rewritten.

25. The student who had been shot in the head later died in the hospital. Associated Press, "One Student Killed in Clash with Security Personnel," July 3, 1998.

26. Danilyn Rutherford points us to this quote from George Orwell's essay "Shooting an Elephant," about a crowd in Burma who became "all happy and excited over this bit of fun." In Rutherford's forthcoming collection of essays about West Papua, she uses Orwell's encounter with elephants and crowds in Burma as an opportunity to explore ideas about sovereignty.

27. "Rumors offer a clue to knowledge not yet generally established by suggesting where powerful centers may shift," according to Anna Tsing. "Like changing market prices, rumors cannot be ignored where quick evasions are necessary for survival" (Tsing, *In the Realm of the Diamond Queen*, 91).

28. Rutherford, "Waiting for the End," 56.

29. Anonymous tape-recorded interview, Biak, September 3, 2002.

30. Deutsche Presse-Agentur, "U.N. Envoy Due in Indonesia on East Timor Conflict," July 4, 1998.

31. Rutherford, *Raiding the Land of the Foreigners*, 25.

32. This army is described in Judges 4. Years later I interviewed several members of the Deborah and Barak prayer group, on the condition of strict anonymity. In the Biak language the word *barak* also refers to supernatural power that pilgrims sought from the Sultan of Tidore during the period of indirect colonial rule (Rutherford, *Raiding the Land of the Foreigners*, 17).

33. Anonymous tape-recorded interview in Indonesian, Biak, September 3, 2002; Benny Giay, "Eben Kirksey's Thesis in West Papuan History," note to author, Washington, November 23, 2007; Timmer, "The Return of the Kingdom," 30.

34. Anonymous tape-recorded interview in Indonesian, Biak, September 3, 2002; Rutherford, *Raiding the Land of the Foreigners*, xvii–xviii.

35. Elsham, "Nama tanpa pusara, pusara tanpa nama," 11.

36. Jameson, "Marx's Purloined Letter," 62.

37. Elsham, "Nama tanpa pusara, pusara tanpa nama," 10–11.

38. Ibid., 13–14.

39. Reviewing Derrida's work, Fredric Jameson writes: "We ought to be able to distinguish an apocalyptic politics from a messianic one, and which might lead us on into some new way of sorting out the Left from the Right, the new International in Marx's spirit from that in the world of business and state power. The messianic is spectral, it is the spectrality of the future, the other dimension, that answers to the haunting spectrality of the past which is historicity itself. The apocalyptic, however, announces the end of spectrality" (Jameson, "Marx's Purloined Letter," 63–64).

40. Derrida, *Specters of Marx*, 28.

41. The people of Biak, in Danilyn Rutherford's words, "fetishized the foreign." Rutherford's ideas about the fetish exceed the associations of popular parlance— mystical qualities attached to inanimate objects, the sexual attraction to objects or body parts not conventionally regarded as erotic, or even the commodity fetishism described by Karl Marx. The fetish analytic, as elaborated by Marx and Freud, looks for misplaced concreteness. In Rutherford's argument, "the foreign" is not a specific fetish object but something more expansive and elusive. She suggests that the Biak people "turned what is foreign into a source of agency and an object of desire" (Marx, *Capital*, 1:165; Haraway, *Modest_Witness*, 146–48; Rutherford, *Raiding the Land of the Foreigners*, 4; Rutherford, "Waiting for the End," 56).

42. Human Rights Watch, *Indonesia*.

43. Rutherford, *Laughing at Leviathan*.

44. Peter Worsley, who studied messianic movements in New Guinea in the aftermath of the Second World War, distinguished "movements which anticipate that the millennium will occur solely as a result of supernatural intervention, and those which envisage that the action of human beings will be necessary" (Worsley, *The Trumpet Shall Sound*, 12).

45. Divine violence is an element of all revolutions, according to Benjamin, but it is never possible to pinpoint the order-destroying moment. "Divine violence," he concludes, "which is the sign and seal but never the means of sacred execution, may be called sovereign violence." For Rutherford, this Biak protest contained the

potential of divine violence—the potential of destroying the order of Indonesian law. When the crowd rallied behind Filep Karma's demands for independence, many people undoubtedly wondered if God would mark the event with a divine seal (Benjamin, "Critique of Violence," 285; Rutherford, *Laughing at Leviathan*).

46. Susan Harding, "Imagining the Last Days," 14–44.

47. Elsham, "Nama tanpa pusara, pusara tanpa nama," 19–20.

48. Anonymous tape-recorded interview in Indonesian, Biak, September 3, 2002.

49. Ibid.

50. Anonymous tape-recorded interview in Indonesian, Bosnik, Biak, September 5, 2002.

51. First Infantry Lieutenant Hermanus Yeninar reportedly burst into tears when he told a close family member the number of people killed in the initial assault (Elsham, "Nama tanpa pusara, pusara tanpa nama," 31, 34).

52. Ibid., 22.

53. I did not attempt to systematically verify this number, but from my interviews with other eyewitnesses, it is within the realm of possibility. The source is a faxed appeal to Dr. Kofi Annan from the Komite Solidaritas Rakyat Irian Kosorairi, which cites eyewitness accounts, as well as reports from the largest protestant Church in West Papua (GKI), of dead bodies appearing on the beaches of Biak. This faxed appeal was posted on the West Papua Newsgroup (Polet, "Human Rights Violations in West Papua," e-mail message, August 12, 1998).

54. Anonymous tape-recorded interview, Biak, September 3, 2002.

55. Elsham, "Nama tanpa pusara, pusara tanpa nama," 56–58.

56. "Bodies Found Near Biak 'May Be Shooting Victims,'" *Jakarta Post*, July 30, 1998.

57. Elsham, "Nama tanpa pusara, pusara tanpa nama," 60.

58. Polet, "Human Rights Violations in West Papua," August 12, 1998.

59. Anonymous tape-recorded interview, Bosnik, Biak, September 5, 2002.

60. "Bodies Found Near Biak 'May Be Shooting Victims,'" *Jakarta Post*, July 30, 1998.

61. Elsham's report was published in July 1999, several months after preliminary reports by journalists, Human Rights Watch, and Survival International. Rutherford has compiled an extensive list of reports about the event that emerged on the Internet and in the press (Human Rights Watch, *Indonesia*; Rutherford, "Waiting for the End," 39–40).

62. My line of argument here is made in counterpoint to Rutherford's interpretation of the same event. She writes that the Biak protesters "envisioned international acknowledgement of the West Papuan nation as leading to an eschatological transformation". Eschatology, according to the *Oxford English Dictionary*, is "the department of theological science concerned with 'the four last things: death, judgment, heaven, and hell.'" Rutherford suggests that Biaks were waiting for an "eschatological moment [that] was—and remains—a focus of longing and hope." There is little evidence that the people who gathered in the harbor longed for death, judgment, and hell. The collective imagination of the crowd settled on clear figures

of hope. Certainly protesters were "waiting for the end" of Indonesian rule, and anxiety about a possible crackdown by Indonesian security forces was also at play in the crowd. The charismatic leaders who rallied the crowd did not seek redemption through death but looked for political and theological transformations through peace. Like the Indonesian students who had willed Suharto out of office, these West Papuan protesters were waiting for a seemingly impossible event. They were waiting to be granted independence (Rutherford, *Raiding the Land of the Foreigners*, 25; Rutherford, "Waiting for the End," 54).

63. Demonstrators destroyed the Sorong government offices and mosques, as well as shops, restaurants, hotels, and drugstores owned by Indonesians. In response, Indonesian troops opened fire on the crowd, killing a pregnant woman and a man (Alua, *Dialog nasional Papua*, 8).

64. Deleuze and Guattari, *On the Line*, 17–18.

65. Ibid., 10.

66. Islam, *Sejarah TNI Jilid V (1984–2000)*, 126.

67. Ismail, Rapanoi, Said, and Hutasuhut, *Praja ghupta vira*, 245–46; Melkianus Awom, tape-recorded interview, Biak, September 1, 2002.

68. Deleuze and Guattari, *A Thousand Plateaus*, 8–9.

69. When I interviewed Melkianus Awom, a distant relative of Permenas Ferry Awom, he confirmed that Filep Karma was not involved with his group of guerrilla soldiers.

70. Derrida, "Marx and Sons," 253.

71. In a normative, even programmatic, passage in *Specters of Marx*, Derrida insists on embracing "emancipatory desire," which he regards as "the condition of a re-politicization" (74–75).

72. Cf. Clifford, "Indigenous Articulations," 481.

Chapter 2. From the Rhizome to the Banyan

1. Barrett, "Ficus in Florida," 118–83.

2. The Imyan people, who live in the Bird's Head region of West Papua, remember giving President Sukarno powerful things when he visited West Papua: a *beringin* (banyan) tree and a mythical Garuda eagle. The Garuda and the banyan tree both figure in the seal of the Indonesian republic to symbolize the Pancasila state ideology (Timmer, "The Return of the Kingdom," 53).

3. Reeve, *Golkar of Indonesia*, 280.

4. J. Pemberton, "Notes on the 1982 General Election in Solo," 2.

5. J. Pemberton, *On the Subject of Java*, 160.

6. Soeseno, "Berkah di antara dua beringin" and "Beringin dan tradisi" (1999), http://www.indomedia.com/intisari/1999/november/beringin.htm (accessed November 2, 2007).

7. Mahmud, *Beringin berkabut*, 2001.

8. "Berlindung di bawah beringin," *Jawa Pos*, August 8, 2004.

9. Anderson, "Indonesia's Struggle."

10. Deleuze and Guattari, *A Thousand Plateaus*, 21; Foucault, "Nietzsche, Genealogy, History," 144–46.

11. In "Erring Decentralization and Elite Politics in Papua," Jaap Timmer has already explored how the twinned strategies of collaboration and resistance were at play in this period. The Papuan Spring was a time when symbolic concessions were granted by Indonesian officials even as different West Papuan leaders jockeyed for power. This period has also been the subject of extensive studies by political scientists: Chauvel, *Constructing Papuan Nationalism* and "The Papuan Spring"; McGibbon, "Pitfalls of Papua"; King, *West Papua and Indonesia since Suharto*; and Fernandes, *Reluctant Indonesians*.

12. Deleuze and Guattari, *On the Line*, 17.

13. Bourdieu's work on the universe of possible discourse (*Outline of a Theory of Practice*, 191) and James Scott's writing about hidden transcripts (*Domination and the Arts of Resistance*, 1–14) have influenced my understanding of the performative dynamics of language.

14. In this section, I draw extensively on the work of Agus Alua, a theology professor and close ally of Theys Eluay, who published a series of official histories about the movement. Alua recorded speech-in-action at momentous political occasions. My quotes from Eluay are translated from Alua's original Indonesian-language quotes. Alua, *Dialog nasional Papua dan Indonesia 26 Februari 1999*, 15.

15. Giay, *Peristiwa penculikan dan pembunuhan Theys H. Eluay 10 Nopember 2001*, 72.

16. Ibid., 17.

17. Octovianus Mote, telephone interview, New Haven, Conn., August 19, 2010.

18. Giay, *Peristiwa penculikan*, 74.

19. Ibid., 125.

20. Acts 9:3–19.

21. Writing about indigenous political movements in New Guinea, Kenelm Burridge notes: "Some participants may see the activities as a vehicle of spiritual salvation; and others may seem more concerned for their own immediate material advantage" (*New Heaven, New Earth*, 1). For Theys Eluay, the spiritual was entangled with the material. His conversion from being an Indonesian politician to a West Papuan freedom fighter certainly let Eluay pursue personal material rewards. Ultimately it is impossible to know if his spiritual salvation was genuinely heartfelt or staged for purely cynical reasons.

22. Deleuze and Guattari, *A Thousand Plateaus*, 7.

23. All figs in the English folk category of banyan, or the corresponding Indonesian folk category of beringin, are stranglers. An article published on indomedia.com, the online portal associated with *Kompas* newspaper, identifies the beringin trees planted at Javanese palaces as *Ficus benjamina*. The article contrasts *F. benjamina* with several other *Ficus* species that are planted in Indonesia and known by different folk names. *F. benjamina* has the habit of a strangler and can form large groves when the aerial roots grow into tree trunks. Corner, "The Climbing Species of Ficus"; Soeseno, "Berkah di antara dua beringin" and "Beringin dan tradisi."

24. Thomson, Herre, Hamrick, and Stone, "Genetic Mosaics in Strangler Fig Trees," 1214–16.

25. Putz, Romano, and Holbrook, "Comparative Phenology of Epiphytic and Tree-Phase Strangler Figs," 183–89.

26. Deleuze and Guattari, *A Thousand Plateaus*, 7.

27. "All of tree logic is a logic of tracing and reproduction," write Deleuze and Guattari. "The tree articulates and hierarchizes tracings. The rhizome is altogether different, a *map and not a tracing*." Following their distinction between the map (an experimentation in contact with the real) and the tracing (a reproduction of something that comes ready-made), I suggest the banyan, an arboreal rhizome, is a hybrid figure: an inherited structure that might be reanimated by contact with the messianic spirit (Deleuze and Guattari, *Thousand Plateaus*, 12).

28. "When Suharto resigned as the country's president," writes Kenneth George, he became "its preeminent political ghost, an unseen figure whose corrupt and deathly touch had unnerved and silenced the country since the civilian massacres of 1965 and 1966" ("Violence, Culture, and the Indonesian Public Sphere," 26).

29. D. Moore, *Suffering for Territory*, 4.

30. Boy Eluay, recorded interview in Indonesian, Sentani, West Papua, May 6, 2003.

31. Giay, *Peristiwa penculikan*, 118–19.

32. Balakrishnan, *The Enemy*, 108.

33. The meeting between Theys Eluay and former president Suharto was facilitated by Yorris Raweyai, a Chinese Indonesian businessman who specializes in debt collection. Born in West Papua, Yorris spent most of his adult life in Jakarta, the center of power in Indonesia. In Jakarta, Yorris became a prominent leader in an Indonesian nationalist paramilitary gang called Pemuda Pancasila (Youth for National Ideology). Under Suharto (in office 1966–98), Yorris and his gang flourished. The Pemuda Pancasila were useful to the president in securing business deals and squelching political dissent. In 1996, for example, Yorris and about 1,200 of his followers ransacked the headquarters of Megawati Sukarnoputri, a political critic who later became the president of Indonesia ("Yorris Arrested in Connection to July 27 Case"). According to the National Commission on Human Rights (Komnas HAM), at least 5 people died, 149 were injured, and 23 went missing during the violence. The Pemuda Pancasila remain active today. The day after the meeting with Suharto, on August 12, 1998, a new "indigenous" leader emerged. The West Papuan warrior dance at the International Tourism Hotel was part of an elaborate installation ceremony that made Yorris Raweyai the Jakarta representative of West Papua's Indigenous Peoples Council (Lembaga Masyarakat Adat). (Ryter, "Youth, Gangs, and the State in Indonesia"; Anonymous tape-recorded interview in Indonesian, Jayapura, May 7, 2003.)

34. Rutherford, "Why Papua Wants Freedom," 361–89.

35. Here I am reworking the words of Theys Eluay in an idiom used by American converts to Christianity (see Walker, "Sauling Around").

36. News of cash donations to Eluay's personal coffers was later widely reported.

He had multiple wives. In a confidential interview with someone close to Eluay, I was shown pictures of women with whom he reportedly slept while traveling abroad. (See, e.g., Keagop and Ramandey, *Menelusuri jejak kasus pemimpin bangsa Papua Theys Hiyo Eluay*, 146; Recorded interview in Indonesian, Sentani, West Papua, April 24, 2003.)

37. Alua, *Dialog nasional*, 15.

38. Ibid.

39. Giay, *Peristiwa penculikan*, 118.

40. Ipenburg, "The Life and Death of Theys Eluay," 2002.

41. Deleuze and Guattari, *On the Line*, 13.

42. Ibid., 21.

43. Tsing and Pollman, "Global Futures," 107.

44. Foucault, "Nietzsche, Genealogy, History," 140.

45. Ibid., 144.

46. Boy Eluay, recorded interview in Indonesian, Sentani, West Papua, May 6, 2003.

47. Lijphart, *The Trauma of Decolonization*, 15.

48. Eurasians, a people with mixed Dutch and Indonesian descent, fled the Dutch East Indies by the thousands during the early years of Indonesian independence. They faced racial discrimination in the Netherlands and few other countries willing to accept them as "colored" immigrants. Many historians agree that the motive behind the Dutch program to keep West Papua as a colony was to find a new homeland for the Eurasians. By the 1950s, the Dutch began to govern West Papua with a colonial policy that was "explicitly based on the principle of self-determination" (Lijphart, *The Trauma of Decolonization*, 89–90; Drooglever, *An Act of Free Choice*, xiv, 337).

49. Tsing, *Friction*, 82.

50. Chauvel argues that at the time of Theys Eluay's youth, independence aspirations were largely confined to West Papua's elite (*Constructing Papuan Nationalism*, 3).

51. Anonymous, recorded interview in Indonesian, Sentani, West Papua, April 9, 2003.

52. "*Mau merdeka, kok minta obat dan rokok*," *Tifa Irian*, third week of January, 6.

53. Thomson, Dent-Acosta, Escobar-Paramo, and Nason, "Within-Crown Flowering Synchrony in Strangler Figs," 291–97.

54. Hall is a critic in the British tradition of cultural studies. See also Clifford, "Indigenous Articulations," 481.

55. Simpson and Weiner, "Articulation," *OED Online*, http://dictionary.oed.com.

56. Laclau, *Politics and Ideology in Marxist Theory*, 10.

57. Hall and Grossberg, "On Postmodernism and Articulation," 53.

58. Hall, "Signification, Representation, Ideology," 113.

59. Deleuze and Guattari, *A Thousand Plateaus*, 7.

60. Alua, *Dialog nasional*, 32.

61. Ibid., 41–42.

62. Cf. Bourdieu, *Outline of a Theory of Practice*, 191–92.

63. Octovianus Mote, telephone interview, New Haven, Conn., August 19, 2010.

64. Here I am adopting the language of Scott, *Domination and the Arts of Resistance*, xiii.

65. Alua, *Dialog nasional*, 38–39.

66. Ibid., 55.

67. Ibid.

68. Van den Broek and Hernawan, *Memoria passionis di Papua 2000*, 8–12.

69. Ibid., 10–11.

70. Octovianus Mote, telephone interview, October 2007.

71. In this referendum a clear majority of the East Timorese chose independence. Once the result was announced, East Timor went "from guarded euphoria to ground zero," in the words of Joseph Nevins. The Indonesian military and paramilitary militias went on a rampage, murdering civilians and destroying basic infrastructure. Soldiers went from house to house, building to building, burning them down. The violent aftermath of the referendum sent a chilling message to the people of West Paupa who were beginning to harbor renewed hopes for a similar plebiscite (Nevins, *A Not-So-Distant Horror*, 102).

72. Golden, "Gold, Violence, and the Rise of a Political Millenarianism."

73. Reeve, *Golkar of Indonesia*, 117.

74. Alua, *Kongres Papua 2000*, 65–68.

75. In the words of Rodd McGibbon, a senior Australian intelligence official, Theys Eluay's group "essentially adopted a strategy of non-violent political activism, in contrast to the OPM's limited armed struggle which was no longer effective in an open democratic environment. As the OPM's tactics became increasingly anachronistic, the leadership of Papua's independence cause passed to this emerging group." At this moment in history, in June 2000, the tactics of the OPM, a rhizomorphic anti-organization, might well be seen as "anachronistic," out of step with historical forces that were enabling public political dialogue. But in the coming months, as the influence of Indonesia's reform movement began to wane, guerrilla tactics once again became the order of the day (McGibbon, "Pitfalls of Papua," 33).

76. Benny Giay, recorded interview in Indonesian, Washington, November 29, 2007.

77. Brigham Golden, a doctoral candidate at Columbia University who was close to the Congress organizers, originally told me about the BP and Freeport donations. Later Benny Giay joined me in interviewing Taha Al Hamid, one of the Congress organizers, who confirmed this in an Indonesian language tape-recorded interview at his home (Golden, personal communication, New Orleans, November 20, 2002; Al Hamid, Entrop, Jayapura, April 14, 2003).

78. See my discussion in the interlude about Freeport Sweet Potato Distribution Company regarding these power relations with respect to Jessica Cattelino's study of philanthropic giving by the Seminole Tribe of Florida and work by Karen Jacobs about art exhibits sponsored by Freeport McMoRan (Jacobs, "Kamoro Arts Festival"; Jacobs "United Colors of Papua"; Cattelino, *High Stakes*).

79. Van den Broek and Hernawan, *Memoria passionis di Papua*, 92–95.

80. In the months after the Congress of June 2000, these small protests took place even as Eluay continued to rally the masses during public events. Eluay was again jailed on November 29, 2000, and later faced a prolonged legal battle for charges of "rebellion." The movement again arrived at a plateau in 2001 with a pitched intensity of activity that held little promise of climax (Van den Broek and Hernawan, *Memoria passionis di Papua: Kondisi hak asasi manusia dan gerakan aspirasi merdeka—gambaran 1999*, 124).

81. Benny Giay, interview in Indonesian, Washington, December 1, 2007.

82. Giay, *Peristiwa penculikan*, 118–19.

83. Keagop and Ramandey, *Menelusuri jejak kasus pemimpin bangsa Papua Theys Hiyo Eluay*, 146.

84. Chatterjee, "Whose Imagined Community?," 214.

85. Pheng Cheah writes that prominent scholars of nationalism (i.e., Benedict Anderson and his critic Partha Chatterjee) "share a basic distrust of the state as an instrument of dead capital and its corollary, a basic belief in the spontaneous transfigurative power of the people" ("Spectral Nationality," 229, 232).

86. "Compromise," in English texts from 1448, meant "promise or mutual promise." In later centuries it came to mean "A joint promise or agreement made by contending parties" (Oxford English Dictionary, http://www.oed.com).

87. Anonymous, recorded interview in Indonesian, Sentani, May 1, 2003.

88. G. Bateson, *Steps to an Ecology of Mind*, 112.

89. Ibid., 113.

90. Ibid., 114–15.

91. The phrase "peripheral visions" comes from a book title by Mary Catherine Bateson, the daughter of Gregory Bateson and Margaret Mead. Much of Gregory Bateson's work on Bali was done in collaboration with Mead.

92. Bateson's essay on Bali does not mention the Indonesian revolution even though it was published in 1949, four years into the anticolonial war. When the essay was reprinted in 1972, it made no reference to the approximately eighty thousand people who were killed in Bali, mostly by fellow Balinese, during Suharto's rise to power. By this time the atmosphere of policed calm under the Golkar banyan had replaced the Dutch colonial regime (Robinson, *The Dark Side of Paradise*, 1–7).

93. After suffering defeats in 1846 and 1848, the Dutch attacked a key Balinese stronghold in 1849 with some fifteen thousand troops. Only after a sustained campaign against the Balinese, whom some officers described as their "most formidable military opponents" in the Indies, could the Dutch claim victory (Robinson, *The Dark Side of Paradise*, 23).

94. In the mid- to late 1930s, little revolutionary activity took place in the public spaces of Bali, in contrast to earlier decades in the twentieth century, which saw open protests and outright military conflicts. At this moment, nationalist organizing was happening quietly in places like the independent Taman Siswa schools (Robinson, *The Dark Side of Paradise*, 69, 109).

95. I am indebted to Rebecca Schien for helping me refine my language here.

Interlude: Freeport Sweet Potato Distribution Inc.

1. These new policies are detailed hereafter in the context of the special autonomy legislation.

2. At least US$1.2 million of these funds were routed back to Freeport coffers through a plan that enlisted West Papuans as shareholders in the company. Freeport McMoRan, *Underlying Values*, 8–10.

3. Cattelino, *High Stakes*, 174.

4. Karen Jacobs has written a nuanced analysis of Freeport McMoRan's sponsorship of Asmat and Komoro art auctions. Jacobs explores how Freeport philanthropic projects seek to paper over the environmental and social ruptures caused by the mine (Jacobs, "Kamoro Arts Festival"; Jacobs, "United Colors of Papua").

5. Cattelino, *High Stakes*, 193.

6. The sweet potato (*Ipomoea batatas*) was domesticated in South America. Pre-Columbian trade networks brought this tuber to Polynesia by 1000 AD or even earlier. The archaeologist James Watson has challenged portrayals of West Papuans as "the most isolated peoples on earth" by suggesting that an "Ipomoean revolution" transformed highland New Guinea societies some two hundred years before European explorers arrived. According to some proponents of this hypothesis, highland New Guinea societies were still in the midst of changes brought by the sweet potato when the first European explorers arrived in the mid-twentieth century (Watson, "From Hunting to Horticulture," 295; Hather, "Archaeobotany of Subsistence in the Pacific," 75; Scaglion and Soto, "A Prehistoric Sweet Potato," 259).

7. Cf. Clifford, "Indigenous Articulations," 468.

8. Cattelino, *High Stakes*, 188.

9. Marcel Mauss has famously described how three obligations—to give presents, to receive them, and to reciprocate—structure binding social relationships and informal contracts (Mauss, *The Gift*, 7, 13).

10. Competitive exchanges, called *moka*, are the traditional channel for obtaining status of big man (*wuə nyim*) among the groups around Mount Hagen in the highlands of Papua New Guinea. During moka exchanges, rival groups compete with each other to give away the most lavish gifts. Spectacular exchanges on this scale are not a feature of Mee society, but the political and economic tactics of the tonowi are analogous to those used by the wuə nyim. For the big man, writes Andrew Strathern, "it is not the fact of wealth but its deployment which is important" (*The Rope of Moka*, 187).

11. Pospisil, *Kapauku Papuan Economy*, 323–24; *Kapauku Papuans and Their Law*, 79–85.

12. Pospisil, *Kapauku Papuan Economy*, 214–15.

13. All of Pospisil's publications refer to the Mee as the "Kapauku." In the words of one West Papuan intellectual, "The word Kapauku means Mountain People or Backwards Mountain People. This name is not well received by this ethnic group because Kapauku connotes someone who is ignorant." Some interlocutors told me that the name Kapauku means "cannibal." The Mee were known as the "Ekari" during much

of the 1970s and 1980s. An exhaustive discussion of these ethnonyms can be found in my undergraduate thesis (Kudiai, "Religi suku Ekagi," 2; Kirksey, "Saya Makan Sembarang").

14. Pospisil, *Kapauku Papuan Economy*, 214–15.

15. Benny Giay's doctoral dissertation describes a charismatic Mee leader, Zakheus Pakage, who led a popular movement against the tonowi (rich men) shortly after Christian missionaries established their first schools in the region. Pakage was persecuted by Dutch authorities, but villages centered around his communitarian ideals have persisted through the decades (Giay, *Zakheus Pakage and His Communities*, 115).

16. Stuart Kirsch has built on the work of Roy Wagner to show how West Papuans use the strategies of "reverse anthropology" to understand modernity. In Kirsch's words, "The focus on reverse anthropology . . . [privileges] indigenous understandings and interpretations." Indigenous West Papuans have analyzed how the colonial political economy impacts their own exchange practices. Citizens of Papua New Guinea have taken legal action to gain monetary compensation from the Ok Tedi copper and gold mine (Wagner, *The Invention of Culture*; Kirsch, *Reverse Anthropology*, 5, 104; Kirsch, "Indigenous Movements," 2007).

17. Kelley, *Freedom Dreams*, ix.

18. This account of the Durban Conference draws on the reporting of Naomi Klein. Her article about the Obama administration's boycott of Durban II—the 2009 United Nations Durban Review Conference—argues that Obama should structure a new stimulus package around a coherent idea, rather than abstract macroeconomic principles. Stimulus money that was directed toward righting historical wrongs, through reparations to African Americans who are descendants of slaves, would mark a groundbreaking historical transition (Klein, "Minority Death Match," 57).

19. Marr, "Court Orders Freeport to Clean Up Its Act," November 2001.

20. Hernawan, "Human Rights Conditions in Papua," February 26–28, 2002.

21. International Crisis Group, *Indonesia*, 18. Exchange rates calculated for January 1, 2001, at http://www.oanda.com/convert/classic.

22. Quoted in International Crisis Group, *Indonesia*, 18.

23. In 2001 Indonesia's legislature passed this comprehensive special autonomy package for West Papua, radically changing the formula for distributing funds. After a delay of several years, the special autonomy funds began to flow. In the 2008 fiscal year, the government disbursed 3.6 trillion rupiah ($390 million) under the new program. Amid charges of corruption and financial mismanagement, the governor announced that he would disburse 100 million rupiah ($10,800) of the autonomy funds to each village (InfoPapua, "Rp 3,59 triliun uang dibagi-bagi," InfoPapua.com, February 21, 2008, http://www.infopapua.com). The original text of the special autonomy legislation is available at http://www.papuaweb.org. See also Octovianus Mote's critical analysis of special autonomy at http://www.etan.org/issues/wpapua/1207spaut.htm.

24. The Indonesian government failed to win the hearts and minds of the East Timorese with a similar autonomy package. In a referendum, the people of East

Timor choose national independence instead of broad autonomy within Indonesia. "For East Timorese today," writes Doug Kammen "'pro-autonomy' and 'pro-independence' parallel the master-slave metaphor. Pro-autonomy does not simply connote a political preference, but also an inferior relationship to a foreign master. . . . Pro-independence, of course, means freedom from colonial 'slavery' and becoming 'masters' of one's own future" (Kammen, "Master-Slave," 83).

25. Sem Karoba, "[wpcore] M. Wenda on PDP Failure and Autonomy," e-mail from skaroba@yahoo.com to wpcore@yahoogroups.com on August 23, 2001, 05:21 GMT.

26. Haraway, "Speculative Fabulations for Technoculture's Generations," 100–107.

Chapter 3. Entangled Worlds at War

1. Das, *Life and Words*, 2, 123–33.

2. Writing of collaborations during Indonesia's anticolonial struggle for independence, James Siegel makes a similar point—describing how Indonesian revolutionaries who were discovered by the Dutch would be offered opportunities within the colonial administration (Siegel, *Fetish, Recognition, Revolution*, 185).

3. Mydans, "Indonesia Chooses an Islamic Cleric as New President," October 21, 1999.

4. Mietzner, "Between Pesantren and Palace," 183.

5. Barton, *Abdurrahman Wahid*, 13.

6. For a discussion of syncretic Islam in Java, see the classic study by Clifford Geertz, *The Religion of Java*.

7. Barton, *Abdurrahman Wahid*, 120.

8. In Aceh, Gus Dur had tried a similar conciliatory gesture in December 2000. In the words of Damien Kingsbury, who was involved in brokering a peace accord between Acehnese independence fighters and the Indonesian government: "While as President, Gus Dur had made the resolution of the Aceh problem one of his highest priorities, he seemed unable to bridge the divide between the demands for independence by GAM and wider 'nationalist' pressure for the maintenance of the unity of the state, in particular from the army. Gus Dur even visited the provincial capital, Banda Aceh, in December 2000, although GAM leaders refused to meet with him" (Kingsbury, *Peace in Aceh*, 11).

9. "Di penghujung tahun Irian Jaya berubah menjadi Papua," *Kompas*, January 1, 2000.

10. Haraway, *Modest_Witness*, 44.

11. For the Urapmin of Papua New Guinea, the subject of "rapture" (*repse*) is a recurrent focus of dreams, visions, and general discussion (Robbins, *Becoming Sinners*).

12. "Di penghujung tahun Irian Jaya berubah menjadi Papua," *Kompas*, January 1, 2000.

13. Dr. Benny Giay, my Mee mentor, sat at the same dinner table as President Gus Dur, along with other West Papuan civil society leaders. The president was flanked by senior Indonesian military officers. "Gus Dur began with an apology," said Dr. Giay. "He apologized for the many years of suffering experienced by the

Papuan people under Indonesian rule. 'The behavior of the Indonesian military has been despicable,' the president declared to the dinner guests. These words were like a slap in the face for the officers sitting next to him." Benny Giay, interview in Indonesian, McHenry, Md., February 4, 2010.

14. The politics of naming are exceedingly complex here. In this meeting, Tom Beanal asked that the president rename the province West Papua, while Theys Eluay asked that it be named Papua. For a more detailed discussion of these competing names, see also the notes in my preface.

15. According to Partha Chatterjee, postcolonial nationalist movements have largely failed to live up to their promises because of elite leaders who cynically pursue their private interests in collaboration with agents of imperialism. Still, hope seemed alive in Gus Dur's reinvigorated program of merdeka within Indonesia's nationalist framework (Chatterjee, "Whose Imagined Community?" 214; cf. Anderson, "Indonesian Nationalism Today and in the Future").

16. "Papuans Allowed to Fly 'Morning Star' Freedom Flag," *Agence France Presse*, June 8, 2000.

17. "Highlights of Indonesian Wahid's State of Nation Speech," *Dow Jones Newswire*, August 7, 2000.

18. Barton, *Abdurrahman Wahid*, 300–301.

19. Bourchier, "Conservative Political Ideology in Indonesia," 199.

20. Drexler, *Aceh, Indonesia*, 36.

21. Benny Giay, interview in Indonesian, McHenry, Md., January 5, 2010.

22. A linear nonrepeating account of chronological time structured Yogi's narrative. Indigenous peoples, "peoples without history," often tell historical narratives that are at odds with the dominant understanding of temporality prevailing in the industrial world. J. Clifford, "Saving Indigenous Time," presented at "Saving Time: An Interdisciplinary Conference on Memory and Memorialization," Cowell College, UC Santa Cruz, November 18, 2005.

23. Obeth Komba, tape-recorded interview in Indonesian, Utrecht, the Netherlands, May 25, 2003.

24. Sularto, "Mereka yang terpaksa mengungsi," *Kompas*, November 28, 1977; Budiardjo and Liem, *West Papua*, 119–20; Osborne, *Indonesia's Secret War*, 145.

25. Budiardjo and Liem, *West Papua*, 119–24.

26. Thadius Yogi, tape-recorded interview in Indonesian, Enarotali, April 8, 2001; Budiardjo and Liem, *West Papua*, 119, 121.

27. Anonymous, tape-recorded interview in Indonesian, Enarotali, April 8, 2001.

28. Echols and Shadily, *Kamus Indonesia-Inggris*, 11.

29. Much of the specificity of Mee cosmology is lost in conversations about alam with West Papuans from other groups. *Alam* is what James Clifford calls a "translation term," an approximation privileging certain original meanings. Alam has become a revolutionary model of ontological and cosmological order throughout West Papua (Clifford, *Routes*, 11, 39).

30. See, e.g., LiPuma, *Encompassing Others*; Stephen, *A'aisa's Gifts*; Kirsch, *Reverse Anthropology*; Stasch, *Society of Others*; Zöllner, *The Religion of the Yali*.

31. Anonymous, tape-recorded interview in Indonesian, Enarotali, April 9, 2001.

32. The category of snake (*yina*) in Mee taxonomy includes worms, grubs, larvae, and caterpillars, as well as snakes of the reptilian variety. These "snakes" are capable of shape-shifting: larvae turn into bugs, grubs become beetles, and caterpillars change into butterflies. The origin story of Yogi clan is centered on a primordial metamorphosis: A lonely man lived at Nagiitouda. He really had nothing to do, for he lived there all by himself. One day a snake appeared on one of the leaves of a water lily in a corner of the pool opposite the man. The snake gave birth to a monster on the leaves of namu and poku tree ferns. This monster child had an exceptionally big skull. The man took the child into his house and tenderly cared for it. He cared for it so well that at last it became human. In fact, it became four humans: two males and two females. They were the first members of the Yogi clan. Metamorphic transitions are not regarded by the Mee as permanent or stable. Upon death, humans become unseen spirits or, in the case of some shamans, animals (Steltenpool, *Ekagi-Dutch-English-Indonesian Dictionary*; Hylkema and Wolke, "Ekagi Texts"; Kirksey, "Saya Makan Sembarang," 105–6).

33. Anonymous interview in Indonesian, Sentani, April 6, 2003.

34. In other parts of Indonesia, among the Anakalangese of Nusa Tenggara, people speak of a historical epoch, the "free age" (*masa merdeka*) when Christianity and the state replaced an age animated by spirits. Cultural change in West Papua's highlands did not take place along a before-after axis with a "traditional" baseline preceding the arrival of "outside" influences. In Yogi's world, Mee spirits, the language of global Christianity, and state agents meet in a heady mix. Future horizons, Yogi's own masa merdeka, are populated by lively spirits and a new order defined by universal rights and international law (Keane, *Christian Moderns*, 161–62; O'Hanlon, *Paradise*; Clifford, *Routes*).

35. Kusni Kasdut, an Indonesian criminal who was famous up through his execution in 1980, "was reported to have supernatural power that he exercised particularly in escaping from prison," writes James Siegel. These magic powers contributed to newspaper accounts about Kusni Kasdut's criminal behaviors "because he held on to a fetishistic power after the period when his fetishism was legitimate." Yogi's magic, and the social world formed by his followers, was a direct affront to the power of Indonesian sovereigns—the supernatural and material order that should prevail in the nation. Like Kusni Kasdut, Yogi later went on to become a media sensation, regularly appearing on Indonesian television news shows. Yogi was regarded both as a traditional bandit (*jago*) and as a revolutionary (cf. Siegel, *A New Criminal Type in Jakarta*, 48–49; cf. Anderson, *Language and Power*, 41).

36. This dance, called *waita tai*, was traditionally performed among the Mee to express displeasure or to shame an opponent. Megawati has not publicly commented about this encounter. Based on reports of her reaction, as well as popular stereotypes about West Papuans that prevail in the Indonesian national imaginary, I suspect that she perceived the dancers as naked (*telanjang*), wild (*liar*), and backward (*terbelakang*).

37. Thadius Yogi, tape-recorded interview in Indonesian, Enarotali, April 8, 2001.

38. Anonymous interview in Indonesian, Sentani, April 6, 2003.

39. Anonymous, tape-recorded interview in Indonesian, Enarotali, April 9, 2001; anonymous interview in Indonesian, Sentani, April 6, 2003.

40. Theo van den Broek, interview in Indonesian, Jayapura, March 30, 2001.

41. Personal observation, Paniai, April 12, 2001.

42. Other OPM and TPN guerrilla leaders named in the budget include Hans Yoweni, Kelly Kwalik, Mathias Wenda, Hans Bomai, Wellem Onde, and Bernadus Mawen.

43. These details about the logistics of Operation Illumination 2000 come from the classified Indonesian military letter that was photocopied and given to me by a West Papuan human rights activist: KODAM XVII Trikora, R/129/IV/2000, A. Inkiriwang, Rahasia: Sinar 2000 Tahap-2, April 27, 2000. Original document on file with author. Exchange rates calculated for April 27, 2000, http://www.oanda.com/convert/classic.

44. Many Indonesian military officers, as well as their hired thugs, understand these personal freedoms as an embodiment of merdeka. Loren Ryter's work among the *preman*, Indonesia's gangsters, illustrates this point most clearly. One of Ryter's informants told him: "Preman means a free person, exactly free-man. I am one of these. A preman is a person who is free, not tied by any knot, free to determine his own life and death, so long as he fulfills the requirements and the laws of this country" (quoted in Day, *Identifying with Freedom*, 8; see also Ryter, "Youth, Gangs, and the State in Indonesia").

45. Human Rights Watch, *Too High a Price*.

46. Ingo, "Here Come the Kostrad Boys—Again!"

47. Barton, *Abdurrahman Wahid*, 313.

48. "Indonesian Vice-President Meets Free Papua Delegation," BBC *Monitoring*, May 30, 2000.

49. In 1996, only four years earlier, thugs linked to the Suharto regime had attacked Megawati's PDI-P party headquarters. Yorris Raweyai, a gangster who was born in West Papua, coordinated this assault on Megawati's followers. In April 2000, Yorris was arrested for his involvement in this incident. The next month, Yorris was given a public role in West Papua's independence movement: he was appointed to the thirty-two-member Presidium Council at the 2000 Papuan Congress. Given Megawati's very real personal grievances with this key figure in West Papua's merdeka movement, it is hardly surprising that Megawati began to develop a hard-line stance ("Yoris Arrested in Connection to July 27 Case," *Jakarta Post*).

50. Barton, *Abdurrahman Wahid*, 339–40.

51. Hyams, "Petrol in Papua," 53.

52. Data from 2000–2008 available at http://tonto.eia.doe.gov/dnav/ng/hist/n9140us2A.htm.

53. Vidal, "Shattered Illusions," March 19, 2008.

54. Fortun, "Mediated Speculations," 146.

55. New horizons of possibility emerge when imaginative dreams are wed with insights that emerge from being worldly, from being attentive to concrete opportunities (Haraway, "Speculative Fabulations for Technoculture's Generations").

56. "Beneath Bintuni Bay lies a valuable source of clean energy: a world-class reserve of high quality natural gas," wrote BP executives in a company report. "With the participation of a wide range of partners—and with innovative, pro-active planning—this resource can become a catalyst for sustainable development and a brighter future" (BP Indonesia, "Tabura: The Tangguh LNG Project Newsletter," first edition, fourth quarter 2001, Jakarta).

57. The Center for Liquefied Natural Gas (CLNG) is a trade association of LNG producers, shippers, terminal operators and developers, energy trade associations, and natural gas consumers. CLNG, "LNG Future" (2008), http://lngfacts.org/LNG-Future/default.asp (accessed January 14, 2010).

58. The environmental organization Down to Earth has reviewed the environmental assessment documents for the Tangguh project, as summarized and updated in 2005 by the Asian Development Bank, and has concluded: "The project will still produce 4.67 million tonnes of carbon dioxide per year to produce 7.6 MT LNG per year. The CO_2 produced by burning the LNG will produce a further 20.9 MTPA. While this represents a reduction in CO_2 emissions from coal (calculated as producing 40.88 MTPA for the same amount of energy) it is still hard to see how 25.57 million tonnes of CO_2 can be described as environmentally benign." "ADB to Fund BP's Tangguh Gas Project," *Down to Earth* 68 (February 2006).

59. By January 2010 only 300 million carbon credits—each representing one ton of carbon dioxide—had been generated in the global cap-and-trade system. Schapiro, "Conning the Climate," 32.

60. In late February 2002, I received an unsolicited invitation from BP to this workshop. At the time I was a Marshall Scholar at the University of Oxford. Before accepting this invitation, I sent an e-mail to my West Papuan counterparts, asking them if I should attend. One rights worker wrote: "Attendance should not be seen as support for the project." The other invitees included representatives from the British Foreign and Commonwealth Office, a number of international environmental and human rights organizations, and investment firms. The nongovernmental organizations included Amnesty International, World Wide Fund for Nature (WWF-UK), Flora and Fauna International, TAPOL (the Indonesian Human Rights Campaign), Down to Earth, Conservation International, Save the Children, and Survival International.

61. Chatham House, "Chatham House Rule" (2002), http://www.chathamhouse.org.uk (accessed January 15, 2008).

62. Beyond Petroleum, "BP.com: Location Reports—Indonesia," http://www.bp.com (accessed March 29, 2002).

63. Rumansara, PowerPoint presentation, Tangguh Workshop (London), March 26, 2002.

64. Human Rights Watch, *Too High a Price*.

65. The investors present at the Tangguh Workshop represented Henderson Global Investors, International Business Leaders Forum, Morley Fund Management, Standard Life Investments, Friends Ivory and Sime, Dresdner RCM Global Investors, and Co-operative Insurance Society.

66. Richards, "Way beyond Petroleum," 14–16.

67. This quote is taken from the case dossier (*berkas berkara*) for a court trial about the incident that was prepared by the police. PolRes Manokwari, *Berkas perkara Ronald Ramandey dan Amalina Kiri*, 3.

68. Yan Christian Warinussy and Denny Yomaki, tape-recorded interview in Indonesian, Manokwari, April 20, 2003.

69. PolRes Manokwari, *Berkas perkara Ronald Ramandey dan Amalina Kiri*, 3.

70. In contrast to Melkianus Awom, one of the founders of the OPM, Daniel Awom only recently became involved with the guerrilla movement. Melkianus Awom shares a family name with Daniel, but the two are not closely related. Melkianus Awom, tape-recorded interview, Biak, September 5, 2002.

71. "Dubes Inggris Minta Jaminan Keamanan," *Papua Post*, July 16, 2001.

72. Withers and Poulsen, *Grave Human Rights Violations in Wasior, Papua*.

73. *Kejahatan kemanusiaan*, attachment 6.

74. Withers and Poulsen, *Grave Human Rights Violations in Wasior, Papua* 9; "The Logging of West Papua," *Down to Earth* 55 (November 2002).

75. King, *West Papua and Indonesia since Suharto*, 98.

76. Anonymous interview in Indonesian, Abepura, Jayapura, April 2, 2003.

77. Anonymous, tape-recorded interview in Indonesian, Wondiboi, Wondama, April 24, 2003.

78. In Logat Papua the word *adat* (custom) is frequently used to denote sorcery (Kirksey, "Saya Makan Sembarang").

79. Barnabas Mawen (pseud.), tape-recorded interview in Indonesian, Jayapura, August 8, 2002.

80. Anonymous, tape-recorded interview in Indonesian, Padang Bulan, Jayapura, August 22, 2002.

81. Anonymous, tape-recorded interview in Indonesian, Wondiboi, Wondama, April 24, 2003.

82. PolRes Manokwari, *Berkas perkara Ronald Ramandey dan Amalina Kiri*, 3; Barnabas Mawen (pseud.), tape-recorded interview in Indonesian, Jayapura, May 1, 2003.

83. The would-be West Papuan freedom fighters in Wasior were caught at the intersection of multiple norms and standards. Their magic placed them in opposition to modern rationality and visions of national order (cf. Siegel, *A New Criminal Type in Jakarta*, 45).

84. Anonymous, tape-recorded interview in Indonesian, Wasior, April 2003.

85. Kingsbury, *Power Politics*, 29, 94.

86. Such joint exercises reportedly stopped when the Clinton administration initiated a ban on military assistance to Indonesia in 1999 after the scorched-earth campaign in the wake of East Timor's vote for independence. After September 11, the Bush administration stepped up technical training programs for Indonesian intelligence services. Shortly after Hillary Clinton became secretary of state, she began to promote engagement with the Indonesian military. Defense Secretary Gates announced in July 2010 that U.S. forces would resume joint training exercises with Kopassus agents (Nairn, "U.S. Intelligence Is Tapping Indonesian Phones").

87. Quoted in Kingsbury, *Power Politics*, 105.

88. Anonymous, tape-recorded interview in Indonesian, Nabire, August 14, 2002.

89. Much like General Thadius Yogi, and the Indonesian criminals described by James Siegel, these Kopassus soldiers were reportedly using "a fetishistic power after the period when his fetishism was legitimate." Also like Yogi, Kopassus agents occupied an ambivalent role in Indonesian society. They are variously understood as traditional bandits (*jago*) and Indonesian freedom fighters (*pejuang*) (Siegel, *A New Criminal Type in Jakarta*, 48–49).

90. Aditjondro, "Ninjas, Manggalas, Monuments, and Mossad Manuals," 158–88.

91. Taussig, *Law in a Lawless Land*, ix.

92. Like Valentine Daniel, I found that I could not write about torture without letting the prurience of violence leak in. Daniel asks: "How else could the average reader, living in an antiseptic even if not an uncaring world, have an inkling of the foul scent that he or she has been spared?" (Daniel, *Charred Lullabies*, 5).

93. Kenneth George has written a critique of a journalist who displayed "fascination with the grotesque and the primitive, and in its occasional credulity" while depicting violence in Indonesia. This reporter helped spread lurid stories about the Dayak people, who were reportedly "casting themselves as headhunting cannibals who devour the brains, blood, and hearts of their Madurese victims." George calls for an accounting of politics, history, and the state's role in spreading violent rumors. Responding to George's call, I have situated graphic stories, tales of magic, and horrifying pictures within accounts of political maneuvers by diverse actors and countervailing economic forces (George, "Violence, Culture, and the Indonesian Public Sphere," 41; see also Kirsch, "Rumor and Other Narratives," 53–79; Butt, "'Lipstick Girls' and 'Fallen Women,'" 412–41).

94. Here I am playing with the language of Bowker and Star, *Sorting Things Out*.

95. Appadurai, "Dead Certainty," 225.

96. Among the Korowai, on the south coast of West Papua, all deaths are believed to be caused by witches who surreptitiously eat the insides of their victims' bodies. Suspected witches are ambushed and reportedly cannibalized. Indonesian soldiers joined a mimetic cycle of violence to try to stop the killing of witches. Novel forms of Indonesian torture directed at the alleged witch killers—rolling people around in barrels; making them stand overnight in a leech-infested pond; forcing them to eat tobacco, chili peppers, animal feces, and unripe papaya—have in turn been copied by the Korowai and used against alleged witches (Stasch, "Giving Up Homicide," 43; cf. Arens, *The Man-Eating Myth*; Sahlins, "Artificially Maintained Controversies"; Obeyesekere, *Cannibal Talk*).

97. I managed to secure interviews about Wellem Korwam's murder with key sources in Nabire, Manokwari, and Wasior. The sources included family members, church workers, village leaders, and fishermen. While keeping all my sources anonymous to protect them from potential retribution, I have rigorously cross-checked all their accounts.

98. Revealing details of this evidence would put my sources in danger.

99. *Kejahatan kemanusiaan*, attachment 5.

100. Anonymous interview in Indonesian, Padang Bulan, Jayapura, July 23, 2002.

101. "Quake Rocks Indonesia, 2000 Houses Damaged," *Channel NewsAsia*, June 29, 2001.

102. "Mily Rules Out Sabotage in Disappearance of Navy Aircraft," *Antara*, January 9, 2001.

103. Anonymous interview in Indonesian, Kota Raja, Jayapura, May 9, 2003.

104. Barton, *Abdurrahman Wahid*, 300–301.

105. Das, *Life and Words*, 123–33.

106. This killing took place several hours before the World Trade Center was hit by airplanes. The two events are not connected.

107. Anonymous tape-recorded interview in Indonesian, Merauke, August 24, 2002.

108. Merauke Catholic Diocese, *Mengapa pembunuhan terhadap Willem Onde dan John Tumin Kandam belum diinvestigasi?*

109. Siegel, *Solo in the New Order*, 91.

110. Giay, *Peristiwa penculikan*, 23. Elsham, "Penculikan dan pembunuhan terhadap Theys Hiyo Eluay terencana dan bermotif politik," unpublished report, 2002.

111. Giay, *Peristiwa penculikan*, 24; Keagop and Ramandey, *Menelusuri jejak kasus*, 7.

112. Giay, *Peristiwa penculikan*, 24–27.

113. The convicted soldiers (abbreviated Indonesian ranks and name as reported in media) were Letkol Inf Hartomo, Kapten Inf Rionaro, Sertu Asrial, Praka A Zulfahmi, Mayor Inf Doni Hutabarat, Lettu Agus Supriyanto, and Sertu Laurensius Li (Keagop and Ramandey, *Menelusuri jejak kasus pemimpin bangsa Papua Theys Hiyo Eluay*, 278–79).

114. Powell, "Kopassus Assassins Get Light Jail Terms," 8; Sugiharto, "Berkasnya dibacakan, terdakwa kasus Theys semaput," detik.com, May 14, 2004.

115. Giay, *Peristiwa penculikan*, 41–42.

116. Quoted in Hernawan, "Human Rights Conditions in Papua," February 26–28, 2002.

117. Clarke and Star, "Social Worlds/Arenas/Discourse Framework," 113.

Chapter 4. Don't Use Your Data as a Pillow

1. Telys Waropen, interview in Indonesian, Kota Raja, Jayapura, May 9, 2003.

2. Andreas Harsono, an investigative reporter who collaborated with me to research and write chapter 5, first informed me about these guidelines. The guidelines are (1) promises of anonymity must be authorized by the editor; (2) anonymous sources should be used only for a just cause; (3) anonymous sources should be used only as a last resort; (4) sources should be as fully identified as possible with reasons for anonymity explained in the story; (5) proportionality: editors should balance the potential harms and benefits in any use of anonymous sources; (6) anonymous sources can only be used with just intentions by the reporter, the media, and the source; (7) just means: use of anonymous sources requires independent verification by a second source (Boeyink, "Anonymous Sources in News Stories," 233–46).

3. Taussig, "Culture of Terror—Space of Death," 482.

4. Leslie Butt has taken this approach to understand rumors about HIV being deliberately introduced to West Papua to kill the independence movement: "The question is not 'Is it true?' but, rather, 'How are the political conditions constitutive of the truth claims so formulated?'" (Butt, "'Lipstick Girls' and 'Fallen Women,'" 414).

5. Said, *Orientalism*; Spivak, "Can the Subaltern Speak?," 271–313.

6. "What Taussig referred to as 'the problem of writing effectively against terror' is the risk we run of representing terror as a rational economy of behavior, and thus extending its reach," writes Chris Ballard, an Australian anthropologist. Ballard points to indigenous West Papuans who "escape the circle of mirrors, the totality of representation. . . . Their success in this evasion can perhaps be characterized as a form of resistance." Telys Waropen's struggle, as an indigenous agent operating within the state, illustrates the possibilities that emerge with strategies of political engagement rather than resistance. He was working to escape from the hall of mirrors by translating terrifying rumors about violence into forms of knowledge that arguably have the potential to upset prevailing relations of power (Ballard, "The Signature of Terror," 23).

7. Hale, "Activist Research versus Cultural Critique," 96–120.

8. Kirksey, "Spirited Fight."

9. Maria Vesperi, my undergraduate advisor at New College of Florida, has been a steady guide in helping me navigate these problems over the years. My language for representing these difficult translation problems comes from an abstract that she and Vincent Crapanzano wrote for a presidential session at the American Anthropological Association conference in 2007 called "Just Words." I had the honor of contributing a paper to this session.

10. "Barnabas Mawen," (pseud.) tape-recorded interview in Indonesian, Jayapura, August 8, 2002.

11. Direct family ties between Daniel Awom's group and members of the Indonesian military facilitated the flow of goods and tactical advice. Sembra Reba is related (through his wife) to Ottis Koridama, who was one of Daniel Awom's men. Anonymous, phone interview in Indonesian, May 2003.

12. Anonymous, tape-recorded interview in Indonesian, Wondiboi, Wasior, April 23, 2003.

13. *Kejahatan kemanusiaan*, 3.

14. "Barnabas Mawen," (pseud.) tape-recorded interview in Indonesian, Jayapura, May 1, 2003.

15. Written correspondence between Awom's men and Indonesian military agents was also reported in a separate interview with Awom's affiliates in Wasior. "Barnabas Mawen," (pseud.) tape-recorded interview in Indonesian, Jayapura, May 1, 2003.

16. "Barnabas Mawen," (pseud.) tape-recorded interview in Indonesian, Jayapura, August 8, 2002, and April 29, 2003; Anonymous interviews in Indonesian, Manokwari, April 27, 2003; Wasior, April 29, 2003; Nabire, May 2, 2003; and Jayapura, May 9, 2003.

17. Like many other anthropologists who work in the era of globalization, I used the methods of multisited ethnography to "follow the people" and "follow the conflict" (Marcus, "Ethnography in/of the World System").

18. "Dubes Inggris minta jaminan keamanan," *Papua Post*, July 16, 2001.

19. Gillard, "Colombia Murder Claim Hits BP," April 21, 2002.

20. English conversation reconstructed from notes, London, May 23, 2003.

21. Jeffrey Winters has already captured the power dynamics at play in such meetings. "The power of capital controllers is deep, structural, and daunting, but it is also contingent—incessantly contested and remade in daily conflicts." A subtext, containing veiled threats, was running beneath the inviting language of Byron Grote. The specter of a new company, without BP's "code of ethics," threatened to derail any peace-building initiatives (Winters, *Power in Motion*, x–xi).

22. Kirksey and Grimston, "Indonesian Troops for BP Gas Project," July 20, 2003.

23. Haraway, "Situated Knowledges," 581.

24. Nagel, *The View from Nowhere*.

25. Haraway, "Situated Knowledges," 580.

26. Later, when I began my Ph.D. research at UC Santa Cruz, Donna Haraway became a member of my dissertation committee.

27. Brigham Golden, personal communication, New Orleans, November 20, 2002; Taha Al Hamid and Benny Giay, tape-recorded interview, Entrop, Jayapura, April 14, 2003.

28. Kaisiepo, BBC *East Asia Today*, September 17, 2003.

29. Kaisiepo, "Hei Napi," September 17, 2003.

30. James Clifford sees failure as being inevitable in projects of cross-cultural mediation. Here I have borrowed heavily from his language for understanding the contingent alliances that emerge amid conflicts ("Indigenous Articulations," 182).

31. Hale, "Activist Research versus Cultural Critique," 113.

32. Sandra Harding, "Rethinking Standpoint Epistemology," 241.

33. Sandra Harding, *The Feminist Standpoint Theory Reader*, 136.

Chapter 5. Innocents Murdered, Innocent Murderers

1. Quoted in Global Witness, *Paying for Protection*, 4.

2. Reverend David Lowry, then the vice president for social and community relations at Freeport McMoRan, told researchers with Global Witness that "[the discussion] was a good number of months prior to 31 August [2002]" (Global Witness, *Paying for Protection*).

3. Writing in the pre–September 11 era, Michael Taussig describes a pervasive and perpetual state of emergency "in an age as defined by Pentagon theorists as one of 'low intensity warfare.'" Taussig argued that the armed forces "have as much to gain from disorder as from order—and probably a good deal more" (Taussig, *The Nervous System*, 17).

4. Perhaps the most notorious of these coverups relates to the Balibo massacre.

During the Indonesian invasion of East Timor in 1975, five Australian journalists were executed by Indonesian forces (Lawless, "The Indonesian Takeover of East Timor", 959).

5. Cable from U.S. embassy, Jakarta, to the Secretary of State (priority 0033), "The Perpetrators of the August 31 Attack on a Pt Freeport Convoy in Papua Remain Unclear," September 2, 2002. All State Department documents referenced in this chapter are on file at the National Security Archive, George Washington University, Washington, archive 20060105FBI002.

6. Quoted in Priest, "Nightmare and a Mystery."

7. Dudon Satiaputra, "Rahasia: Laporan Hasil Sementara Pemeriksaan TKP Penembakan Kary. PT. Freeport," Jakarta, December 19, 2002. Copy of the document on file with author. "Police Say Indonesian Army behind Papua Ambush," *Agence France Presse*, December 26, 2002.

8. Hyland, "Police Blame Army for Papua Ambush," December 27, 2002; "Police Say Indonesian Army behind Papua Ambush," *Agence France Presse*, December 26, 2002.

9. Elegant, "Murder at the Mine," February 10, 2003.

10. Priest, "Nightmare and a Mystery."

11. M. Moore, "Find Freeport Killers, Bush Tells Megawati," December 21, 2002.

12. John Rumbiak, interview in English, Washington, February 24, 2005.

13. Ronald C. Eowan, voicemail, September 22, 2004, 9:57 a.m.

14. Ashcroft et al., "Papuan Separatist Charged with the Murders of Two Americans, Attempted Murders of Others during 2002 Ambush in Indonesia" (2004), http://www.usdoj.gov/opa/pr/2004/June/04_crm_439.htm (accessed September 8, 2010).

15. Paul Myers, phone call from Washington to Kauai, Hawaii, February 5, 2005, 2:35 p.m.

16. Simon, "America," *Bookends* (Columbia Records, 1968).

17. These notes filled twenty-seven pages of an 8.5 x 11 inch notebook. Paraphrased dialogue from these notes appears in quotes.

18. Sandra Harding, "Rethinking Standpoint Epistemology," 128, 241; Haraway, "Situated Knowledges," 176.

19. Sandra Harding, *The Feminist Standpoint Theory Reader*, 136, 128; Haraway, "Situated Knowledges," 176.

20. Here my language is inspired by Haraway, *Simians, Cyborgs, and Women*, 188.

21. This section relies heavily on the *berkas perkara*, the case dossier assembled by police prosecutors (Badan Reserse Kriminal Polri) in the trial of Antonius Wamang and his codefendants. The English-speaking witnesses were interviewed by police investigators with an Indonesian translator present. I have back-translated quotes from these interviews into English. Undoubtedly this has introduced minor errors. When possible I have cross-checked the quotes from these interviews with other sources. These documents, and all other documents cited in this chapter, are on file with the author. Zainal Syarief, Indonesian-language interview with Ronald C. Eowan, April 20, 2006, in Berkas Perkara No. Pol.: BP/05/III/2006/KAMTRANNAS.

22. The following sections of this chapter have been adapted from Kirksey and

Harsono, "Criminal Collaborations," 197–230. In the following notes, "AH" desig-
nates source material collected by my coauthor Andreas Harsono.

23. Margaret P. Grafeld to Mary Curry, archive 20060103D0031, June 4, 2007,
National Security Archive, Washington.

24. Antonius Wamang, tape-recorded interview in Indonesian, Kwamki Lama, Timika, March 25, 2005; interview by AH in Indonesian, Indonesian police headquarters detention center in Jakarta, October 8–9, 2006.

25. Similar collaborations have taken place between Indonesian soldiers and
GAM guerrillas in Aceh. In East Timor resistance figures have been turned by Indo-
nesian intelligence agents. Eurico Guterres, a notorious Indonesian militia leader,
was reportedly "an activist in the pro-independence clandestine movement Santo
Antonio," fighting for East Timor's independence in his youth. Guterres "was always
more a street fighter who followed the money than a political player" (Kilvert,
"Whisky Friends"; Aspinall, "Guerrillas in Power"; Van Klinken and Bourchier, "Key
Suspects," 91, 95).

26. Sularto, "Mereka yang Terpaksa Mengungsi"; Budiardjo and Liem, *West Papua*,
119–24; Osborne, *Indonesia's Secret War*, 145.

27. Antonius Wamang, tape-recorded interview, Timika, March 25, 2005; John
Rumbiak, interview, Washington, February 24, 2005.

28. Janes Natkime, interview by AH in Indonesian, Jakarta, November 6, 2006.
Natkime knows both Wamang and Anggaibak and heads the Warsi Foundation in
Timika.

29. Anggaibak told me that he once traveled to Jakarta with someone named
Anton, Antonius Wamang's preferred nickname. Midway through our conversation,
however, he seemed to catch himself, claiming that this person was a member of BIN
(Badan Intellegen Negara), one of Indonesia's intelligence agencies, not Anton Wamang. Agus Anggaibak, telephone interview in Indonesian, June 2008.

30. Agus Anggaibak, telephone interview in Indonesian, June 2008. Indonesian
original: *"Anton, orang Timika semua orang ketemu."*

31. An activist attended the meeting and copied the specifications of the gun
down in his notebook. I saw this notebook in Timika on March 24, 2005.

32. Antonius Wamang, tape-recorded interview in Indonesian, Timika, March 25,
2005; John Rumbiak, interview in English, Washington, February 24, 2005.

33. Agus Anggaibak, telephone interview in Indonesian, June 2008.

34. In the police documents, Johni Kacamol's name is spelled "Joni Kasamol." But
Kacamol himself spells his name "Johni Kacamol." Johni Kacamol, interview by AH
in Indonesian, Jakarta, October 8, 2006.

35. It is extremely difficult to discern where Tsugumol's political commitments
lay, or those of his "friends" on the inside. The Indonesian military has a long history
of co-opting guerrilla fighters. Many militia members who worked as Indonesian
operatives in East Timor were previously independence activists. "Following their
surrender," writes Douglas Kammen, "they were forced to participate in paramilitary organizations or become informants." The term "militia member" thus does
not necessarily mean that the individual in question shares the political goals of

Indonesian authorities. A remarkable novel, *The Redundancy of Courage*, by Timothy Mo (2002), charts the complex moral turmoil of a fictional Chinese hotel owner, Adolph Ng, who struggles for survival in the aftermath of Indonesia's invasion of East Timor. Ng joins the freedom fighters and is then pressed into service of the Indonesian military once he is caught. From his entangled position in the intimate spaces of military compounds, Ng engages in further covert actions in support of independence (Van Klinken and Bourchier, "Key Suspects," 91–95; Kammen, "Master-Slave," 82).

36. Antonius Wamang, tape-recorded interview in Indonesian, Timika, March 25, 2005; Deminikus Bebari, interview by AH in Indonesian, Jakarta, October 13, 2006. Exchange rate calculated for September 1, 2001, using data from http://www.xe.com/ict.

37. Antonius Wamang, tape-recorded interview in Indonesian, Timika, March 25, 2005. Exchange rate calculated for September 1, 2001, using data from http://www.xe.com/ict.

38. Antonius Wamang, tape-recorded interview in Indonesian, Timika, March 25, 2005.

39. Herry Blaponte and Mahmud Trikasno, interview by AH in Indonesian, Jakarta, November 6, 2006. Police chief commissioner Zainal Syarief, who headed the Indonesian police investigation, declined to comment. AH showed Wamang's photo to five other hotel employees. None remembered his face. They said they have many guests. The hotel management does not keep its guest record.

40. Antonius Wamang, tape-recorded interview in Indonesian, Timika, March 25, 2005.

41. John Rumbiak, interview in Indonesian, Washington, February 24, 2005; Antonius Wamang, tape-recorded interview in Indonesian, Timika, March 25, 2005.

42. Eltinus Omaleng, interview by AH in Indonesian, Jakarta, November 6, 2006.

43. Exchange rate calculated for September 1, 2001, using data from http://www.xe.com/ict.

44. Like West Papua, Aceh is an Indonesian province with an active nationalist movement, which declared independence in December 1976. Aceh guerrilla fighters regularly attack Indonesian military positions. Some of the most daring attacks took place in 2001. Free Aceh guerrillas signed a peace agreement with Jakarta in August 2005 after a tsunami wiped out much of the population.

45. Exchange rate calculated for September 1, 2001, using data from http://www.xe.com/ict.

46. Antonius Wamang, tape-recorded interview in Indonesian, Timika, March 25, 2005; Antonius Wamang, interview by AH in Indonesian, October 8–9, 2006.

47. Antonius Wamang, tape-recorded interview in Indonesian, Timika, March 25, 2005.

48. Jasanoff, *States of Knowledge* and *Designs on Nature*; see also Reardon, *Race to the Finish*, 6–9.

49. Nakashima and Sipress, "Indonesia Military Allegedly Talked of Targeting Mine," A18.

50. Lubis, "Lawyer for Washington Post says Indonesian Military Failed to Follow Procedure," November 22, 2002.

51. Nakashima and Sipress, "Indonesia Military Allegedly Talked of Targeting Mine," A18.

52. Lekic, "Indonesian Army Ordered Deadly Ambush," March 3, 2004.

53. Cable from U.S. Embassy, Jakarta, to Secretary of State, Washington, June 17, 2003.

54. Deminikus Bebari, "Kesaksiaan saudara Hardi Tsugumol tentang pelaku penembakan di mill 63," Lemassa internal report.

55. "Perintah Oprasi," Tentara Pembebasan Nasional (TPN), Makodap III, Nemangkawi, Papua Barat, June 27, 2002. Document obtained from Paula Makabory.

56. Bebari, "Kesaksiaan saudara Hardi Tsugumol tentang pelaku penembakan di mill 63," Lemassa internal report. AH checked this information with Bebari in Jakarta, November 13, 2006.

57. Hardi Tsugumol, interview in Indonesian, Timika, March 22, 2005.

58. Many West Papuans who are staunch supporters of independence—pastors, intellectuals, and civil servants—have also married Indonesian women, attracting criticism from die-hard activists in rural areas.

59. Stephen Francis Emma, interview with Fajaruddin and Ahmad, May 8, 2006, in *Berkas Perkara* No. Pol.: BP/05/III/2006/KAMTRANNAS.

60. These security forces include Kostrad (Army Reserves) Battalion 515, Army Battalion 752, units from the marines and the army's cavalry, the air force's elite unit Paskhas, police paramilitary Mobile Brigade troops (Brimob), and Kopassus Special Forces.

61. PT Freeport Indonesia Corporate Communications Department, Pedoman Kunjungan, Jakarta, August 2005. This manual prints a map of the mining area with the military posts, or "Milpos."

62. Lexy Lintuuran, interview by AH in Indonesian, Jakarta, November 6, 2006.

63. Stephen Francis Emma, interview with Fajaruddin and Ahmad, May 8, 2006, in *Berkas Perkara* No. Pol.: BP/05/III/2006/KAMTRANNAS.

64. Patsy Spier, interview by AH in English, Jakarta, October 13, 2006.

65. Stephen Francis Emma, interview with Fajaruddin and Ahmad, May 8, 2006, in *Berkas Perkara* No. Pol.: BP/05/III/2006/KAMTRANNAS.

66. Ibid.

67. Patsy Spier, interview by AH in English, Jakarta, October 13, 2006.

68. Kenneth M. Balk, interview with Zainal Syarief and Jeldi Ramadhan, May 9, 2006, in *Berkas Perkara* No. Pol.: BP/05/III/2006/KAMTRANNAS.

69. *Berkas Perkara* No. Pol.: BP/05/III/2006/KAMTRANNAS, Spier interview, p. 3.

70. Patsy Spier, interview in English, Washington, November 30, 2007.

71. Patsy Spier, interview by AH in English, Jakarta, October 13, 2006.

72. Dudon Satiaputra, "Rahasia: laporan hasil sementara pemeriksaan TKP penembakan kary. PT. Freeport," Jakarta, December 19, 2002.

73. Chomsi Syafrian S., interview with Fajarudin and Ahmad, January 23, 2006, in *Berkas Perkara* No. Pol.: BP/05/III/2006/KAMTRANNAS.

74. Dudon Satiaputra, "Rahasia: laporan hasil sementara pemeriksaan TKP penembakan kary. PT. Freeport." Chomsi Syafrian, a ballistics expert with the Indonesian police, reiterated the data contained in the original ballistics report on September 29, 2006, in the Central Jakarta district court. The lab analyzed 30 bullets of 5.56 caliber, 77 bullet fragments, 94 bullet casings of 5.56 caliber, 7 bullet casings of 7.62 caliber. Of the six magazines given to Wamang by Sergeant Puji, he claims that only 1½ magazines (about 45 bullets of 5.56 caliber) were used by his men that day.

75. Priest, "Nightmare and a Mystery."

76. Lexy Lintuuran, interview by AH in Indonesian, Jakarta, November 6, 2006.

77. *Berkas Perkara* No. Pol.: BP/05/III/2006/KAMTRANNAS, p. 17.

78. Priest, "Nightmare and a Mystery."

79. *Berkas Perkara* No. Pol.: BP/05/III/2006/KAMTRANNAS, p. 13.

80. Chomsi Syafrian interview with Fajarudin and Ahmad, January 23, 2006, in *Berkas Perkara* No. Pol.: BP/05/III/2006/KAMTRANNAS.

81. Puzzlingly, the courtroom documents referred to Johni Kacamol, the teenager placed at the scene of the crime by an eyewitness, as "Agus Anggaibak." The real Agus Anggaibak, who reportedly inspired Wamang's attack and helped him get bullets in Jakarta, now regards himself as an up-and-coming young leader in the government regional assembly in Timika.

82. "Wamang Divonis Seumur Hidup," *Pikiran Rakyat*, November 8, 2006.

83. Antonius Wamang, tape-recorded interview in Indonesian, Timika, March 25, 2005. Antonius Wamang, interview by AH in Indonesian, October 8–9, 2006, Jakarta.

84. Ronald C. Eowan, interview with Zainal Syarief and Fajaruddin (Cherrilyne Goodenough Pakpahan translator), April 20, 2006, in *Berkas Perkara* No. Pol.: BP/05/III/2006/KAMTRANNAS.

85. Wamang told me that he does not know who started shooting first. In a summary of the evidence, prepared by Zainal Syarief, a senior police investigator, a man named "Emi Aim," an apparent pseudonym, fired the first five shots from a Mauser rifle. Emi Aim was allegedly part of Wamang's group and was reported dead in the court documents. Antonius Wamang, tape-recorded interview, Timika, March 25, 2005; *Berkas Perkara* No. Pol.: BP/05/III/2006/KAMTRANNAS, p. 24.

86. Stephen Francis Emma, interview with Fajaruddin and Ahmad, May 8, 2006, in *Berkas Perkara* No. Pol.: BP/05/III/2006/KAMTRANNAS.

87. *Berkas Perkara* No. Pol.: BP/05/III/2006/KAMTRANNAS, p. 34.

88. Antonius Wamang, tape-recorded interview, Timika, March 25, 2005.

89. *Berkas Perkara* No. Pol.: BP/05/III/2006/KAMTRANNAS, p. 24.

90. Antonius Wamang, tape-recorded interview in Indonesian, Timika, March 25, 2005. Confirmed by AH on October 9, 2006 with Wamang.

91. Ronald C. Eowan, interview with Zainal Syarief and Fajaruddin, April 20, 2006, *Berkas Perkara* No. Pol.: BP/05/III/2006/KAMTRANNAS.

92. Antonius Wamang, tape-recorded interview in Indonesian, Timika, March 25, 2005.

93. Ibid. Surat Dakwaan, Kejaksaan Negeri Jakarta Pusat, June 2006, in *Berkas Perkara* No. Pol.: BP/05/III/2006/KAMTRANNAS.

94. Kenneth M. Balk, interview with Zainal Syarief and Jeldi Ramadhan, May 9, 2006, in *Berkas Perkara* No. Pol.: BP/05/III/2006/KAMTRANNAS.

95. Antonius Wamang, tape-recorded interview in Indonesian, Timika, March 25, 2005.

96. Surat Dakwaan, Kejaksaan Negeri Jakarta Pusat, June 2006, in *Berkas Perkara* No. Pol.: BP/05/III/2006/KAMTRANNAS.

97. Dudon Satiaputra, "Rahasia: laporan hasil sementara pemeriksaan TKP penembakan kary. PT. Freeport," Jakarta, December 19, 2002.

98. *Berkas Perkara* No. Pol.: BP/05/III/2006/KAMTRANNAS, p. 33.

99. Chomsi Syafrian, an Indonesian police ballistics expert who testified at the trial, noted: "Bullet casings fly out of guns with magazines when they are used for automatic or semi-automatic shooting. Thus, casings from these guns are often found at crime scenes. Guns that have cylinders where bullets are inserted do not eject bullet casings." Chomsi Syafrian, interview with Ahmad A., January 23, 2006, in *Berkas Perkara* No. Pol.: BP/05/III/2006/KAMTRANNAS.

100. *Berkas Perkara* No. Pol.: BP/05/III/2006/KAMTRANNAS, p. 33.

101. *Berkas Perkara* No. Pol.: BP/05/III/2006/KAMTRANNAS, Lampiran 3b.

102. "Saran tindak lanjut BAP saksi Sdr Decky Murib (TBO Kopassus)," Timika, September 28, 2002. This is a police document from the archives of Elsham.

103. Decky Murib, tape-recorded interview in Indonesian, March 26, 2005.

104. Lexy Lintuuran and Saul Tahapary, respectively PT Freeport Indonesia's senior manager of corporate security and security consultant, interview by AH in Indonesian, Jakarta, November 6, 2006.

105. Global Witness, *Paying for Protection*, 28.

106. "Kesaksian Deky Murib di Polda Papua tentang penembakan di mile 62–63 Tembagapura," Polda, Jayapura, September 18, 2002. "Saran tindak lanjut BAP saksi Sdr Decky Murib (TBO Kopassus)," *Timika*, September 28, 2002.

107. For details of one such joint operation, see Alfian Hamazah, "Kejarlah daku kau kusekolahkan," *Pantau*, January 2003.

108. "Saran tindak lanjut BAP saksi Sdr Decky Murib (TBO Kopassus)," *Timika*, September 28, 2002.

109. Joseph Molyneux, phone interview in English, October 2007.

110. Lexy Lintuuran, interview by AH in Indonesian, Jakarta, November 6, 2006.

111. Demi Bebari, "Kesaksiaan saudara Hardi Tsugumol tentang pelaku penembakan di mill 63," Lemassa internal report.

112. The Kwamki Lama neighborhood is located near Timika. One has to pass five checkpoints manned by Freeport's security and the Indonesian military to reach Mile 63. The five checkpoints include Mile 28, Mile 32, Mile 34, Mile 50 (one of the strictest), and Mile 58. Wamang told me inconsistent stories about how he arrived on the scene. At times he indicated that he had traveled up and down the road by car in the days leading up to the attack; at other times he said that he arrived on foot.

113. Lexy Lintuuran, interview by AH in Indonesian, Jakarta, November 6, 2006.

114. Cable from American Consul, Sydney, to Secretary of State, Washington, September 2, 2002.

115. Declassified State Department documents related to Indonesian President Yudhoyono's role in overseeing the FBI investigation were released on the internet in July 2009 by ETAN, the East Timor and Indonesia Action Network. Cable from American Embassy, Jakarta, to FBI Headquarters, Washington, December 27, 2002. The original documents are available at http://www.etan.org/news/2009/06Timika .htm.

116. Cable from American Embassy, Jakarta, to Secretary of State, Washington, June 16, 2003, available at http://www.etan.org/news/2009/06Timika.htm.

117. Elsham, "What Happened at Freeport," public report, September 26, 2002.

118. Edmund McWilliams, "Warning about Indonesian Intelligence Agency Activities in Congress," December 16, 2005; Harsono and Heller, "Jakarta's Intelligence Service," September 7, 2006.

119. Veena Das has written about how rumors can destroy social worlds. In part, the force of rumors derives from their lack of signature, the impossibility of tracing them to an individual agent (Das, *Life and Words*, 132–33). The rumors about Elsham being a separatist organization emerged during the Timika investigation as allegations spread about John Rumbiak helping mastermind the attack. Tales about Elsham's contacts with guerrillas, meetings with people like General Thadius Yogi to talk about disarmament, fueled further allegations.

120. Cf. Deleuze and Guattari, *On The Line*, 17.

121. The phrase "phantasmagoria of shadows" comes from Lacan. Here I am in dialogue with the writing of Veena Das about rumor, as well as with the common dictionary definition of "phantasmagoria" (Lacan, *The Psychoses*, 79; Das, *Life and Words*, 132).

122. Willy Mandowen, "Kami Tidak Berpesta Atas Keringat Orang!," e-mail message sent December 7, 2005.

123. Octovianus Mote, telephone interview in Indonesian, January 2006.

124. Rulianto and Levi, "Timika's 'Flight Club' Grounded," January 17–23, 2006.

125. After reading an account that I circulated on Joyo Indonesia News Service, "The Arrests of January 2006—A Preliminary Account," reporters from the *New York Times*, *Washington Post*, and *Wall Street Journal* interviewed me about the FBI's role in Wamang's capture (Nakashima, "FBI Said Involved in Arrest of 8 Indonesians"; Bonner, "FBI Said Involved in Arrest of 8 Indonesians"; Pura and Hiebert, "Arrest Helps U.S.-Indonesian Ties").

126. Johnson Panjaitan, telephone interview in English, March 2006.

127. On the day after the detention, I spoke with one of the detainees, an elderly man named Jairus Kibak, via the mobile phone of an Elsham rights worker who was visiting him in prison. Kibak told me that an Indonesian interrogator had punched his head.

128. Nakashima, "FBI Said Involved in Arrest of 8 Indonesians," January 14, 2006.

129. Antonius Wamang, interview by AH in Indonesian, Jakarta, October 9, 2006.

130. *Berkas Perkara* No. Pol.: BP/05/III/2006/KAMTRANNAS, p. 87.

131. Esau Onawame told Indonesian police investigators that he supplied Wamang with food, cigarettes, batteries, a flashlight, and a light bulb. Jairus Kibak told the same investigators that he provided Wamang with rice, sugar, coffee, and condensed milk. *Berkas Perkara* No. Pol.: BP/05/III/2006/KAMTRANNAS.

132. Demi Bebari, "Re: Mogok makan dan teror," e-mail message sent to author September 20, 2006.

133. Isak Onawame, telephone interview in Indonesian, June 2008.

134. Ecoline Situmorang, interview in Indonesian, Jakarta, May 19, 2008.

135. Isak Onawame, telephone interview in Indonesian, June 2008.

136. "Wamang divonis seumur hidup," *Pikiran Rakyat*, November 8, 2006.

137. After the convictions, lawyers for the group filed an appeal at the Jakarta High Court. In January 2007 the court upheld the life imprisonment of Wamang. Surprisingly, the court increased the sentences of the other defendants: Kacamol and Deikme were sentenced to eight years in jail (increasing their sentence from seven years), and the other four were sentenced to five years (increasing their sentence from eighteen months). The West Papuan villagers appealed to the Supreme Court. This appeal was rejected. The Supreme Court found no procedural fault in the High Court trial ("Ma tetap hukum terpidana Freeport penjara seumur hidup," *Antara*, September 26, 2007).

138. Radio Australia, "U.S.: Washington Signals New Era of Military Co-operation," November 11, 2006.

139. The majority of these funds, U.S. $15.7 million, were automatically awarded to the Indonesian military in FY2008. The remaining U.S. $2.7 million was awarded once the U.S. Department of State completed a report about the assassination of the human rights activist Munir, access to West Papua, and general reforms in Indonesia. Miller, "ETAN Statement on Military Assistance to Indonesia in the FY2008 Consolidated Appropriations bill (HR 2764)," http://www.etan.org/news/2007/12app .htm.

140. For more information on the role that President Yudhoyono played in steering the investigation, see Kirksey, "Indonesia's Bleak Record," July 7, 2009.

141. Cf. Jasanoff, *States of Knowledge*.

142. Banivanua-Mar, "A Thousand Miles of Cannibal Lands," 583.

Interlude: Bald Grandfather Willy

1. Rose, "Buat Tebo Willy 'Manowen' Mandowen," July 23, 2005.

2. Richards, "Way beyond Petroleum," 14–16.

3. Suara Papua, "KOMUNITAS PAPUA Willy Mandowen Agen BIN," June 13, 2005.

4. King, *West Papua and Indonesia since Suharto*, 40.

5. This is according to two of Willy Mandowen's close associates at the time: Benny Giay and Denny Yomaki. Both Giay and Yomaki had a falling out with Mandowen over the issue of his military ties. Mandowen denies making reports to the military headquarters during the Team of 100 negotiations. Benny Giay, interview

in Indonesian, Washington, November 28, 2007. Denny Yomaki, interview in Indonesian, Jayapura, West Papua, June 2, 2008. Willy Mandowen, telephone interview in English, April 2005.

6. Nakashima, "FBI Said Involved in Arrest of 8 Indonesians," January 13, 2006.

7. Gramsci has detailed the challenges faced by organic intellectuals who attempt to wage a "war of position" within the institutions of hegemony (*Selections from the Prison Notebooks*).

8. This distinction is critiqued in Cheah, "Spectral Nationality," 229, 232.

9. This line refers to Arnold Ap and Sam Kapisa, two West Papuans who used music as a medium to carry a political message. Ap, an anthropologist at Cenderawasih University, was jailed in 1984. He was shot dead by Indonesian soldiers during a staged "escape" attempt.

10. Nationalism might be seen as a copy of a copy of a copy of a copy, rather than a repeating module with definitive characteristics. The original module is missing. See Harootunian, "Ghostly Comparisons," 140.

11. Chatterjee, *The Nation and Its Fragments*, 5, 14.

12. Bauer, "The Nation," 39–77.

13. Scott, *Domination and the Arts of Resistance*, xii.

14. Anonymous, "Selamat Buat Pemerintah Indonesia!!," posted April 30, 2002, at 02:42, http://www.infopapua.com.

15. By 2007 infopapua.com had been completely taken over by West Papuan activists; they used it to report on the visit of UN Special Envoy Hina Jilani, a new Indonesian intelligence operation aimed at West Papuan activists living abroad, and an audit of provincial government funds that was hidden from public view. When the webmaster announced that the domain name was up for sale, no buyers emerged, and the site was shut down.

Chapter 6. First Voice Honey Center

1. The Indonesian originals read: "Awas! Dilarang masuk! Kalau takut jangan maju!"

2. The Indonesian original reads: "Aku cinta tanah air ini."

3. For a detailed account of the period of UN administration in West Papua, see Saltford, *The United Nations and the Indonesian Takeover of West Papua*.

4. Turner, "Betwixt and Between," 4–20.

5. During translation, a negotiation takes place between the source text and the target language. Following the dictum of "keep it strange," a translator can give increased weight to the form and the content of source text instead of seamlessly rendering a passage into the target language. For the speakers of Biak and Indonesian at Awom's camp, this "English" sign is also strange (Eco, *Experiences in Translation*).

6. Kamma, *Koreri*, 102–56.

7. Melkianus Awom, tape-recorded interview in Indonesian, Pusat Perwomi, Biak, September 5, 2002.

8. Ibid.

9. See also Kamma, *Koreri*, 173, 178–79.

10. Rutherford, *Raiding the Land of the Foreigners*, 190.

11. Bleeding the distinction between historical time and messianic time, General Awom was deploying the interpretive tactics of figural realism (cf. Auerbach, *Mimesis*, 73; Haraway, *Modest_Witness*, 9–10).

12. Ismail, Rapanoi, Said, and Hutasuhut, *Praja ghupta vira*, 125–26.

13. Many West Papuan guerrillas, such as Kelly Kwalik, trace their roots to the TPN. When Seth Rumkorem founded the TPN on July 1, 1971, it was initially a rival guerrilla group to the OPM. Now some observers view the TPN as the "military arm" of the OPM.

14. Ismail, Rapanoi, Said, and Hutasuhut, *Praja ghupta vira*, 245–46.

15. The OPM might be understood as a hybrid fusion of the "polycentric network" and the "full-matrix" that has been described by Michael Hardt and Antonio Negri. The polycentric network is characterized by "numerous, relatively autonomous centered clusters . . . in which each hub commands its peripheral nodes and communicates with other hubs," whereas the full-matrix has "no center and all nodes can communicate directly with all others" (Hardt and Negri, *Multitude*, 56–57).

16. Melkianus Awom, tape-recorded interview in Indonesian, Pusat Perwomi, West Biak, September 4, 2002.

17. Anonymous interview in Indonesian, Biak, September 6, 2002.

18. Anonymous interview in Indonesian, Biak, April 17, 2003.

19. Giay, *Misi gereja dan budaya kekerasan di Tanah Papua*, 199.

20. Benny Giay, interview in Indonesian, McHenry, Md., January 22, 2010. See also Giay, *Zakheus Pakage and His Communities*, 205.

21. Crapanzano, *Imaginative Horizons*, 114.

22. Rutherford, *Raiding the Land of the Foreigners*, 26–27.

23. Turner, "Betwixt and Between," 235.

24. Hunter-gatherers are "original affluent societies," according to Marshall Sahlins. Despite comparative poverty in terms of accumulated material goods, hunter-gatherers have an abundance of leisure time. In the early twenty-first century, key West Papuan intellectuals were advocating for revitalizing local subsistence strategies, though their discourses were about work rather than leisure: "One route to merdeka for the Papuan people is for us to get busy working in our sweet potato gardens and to raise lots of pigs," said Socratez Sofyan Yoman, a Baptist pastor. Like many other West Papuan communities in rural areas, the First Voice Honey Center was already enacting Yoman's vision (Sahlins, *Stone Age Economics*; Socratez Sofyan Yoman, interview in Indonesian, Abepura, Jayapura, May 30, 2008).

25. I reconstructed this list of foods from personal observations, with help from Danilyn Rutherford, and by consulting French, *Food Plants of Papua New Guinea*.

26. Chatterjee, *The Nation and Its Fragments*, 6.

27. Surplus value, according to Marx's theory of labor and value, represents the measurable portion of the worker's productive capacity that does not return to him or her as a wage. The writing of Georges Bataille explores another sort of surplus,

an immeasurable excess, which does not return to the production process but is ex-
pended "unproductively." In *The Accursed Share*, Bataille suggests that a process of
expenditure, "the lavish loss of an object given up," lies at the base of all precapitalist societies. Celebrating events of excessive consumption—from the potlatch, to
Roman games, and the construction of medieval cathedrals—Bataille proposes that
we reject capital's ethic of accumulation and utility. The First Voice Honey Center
does rely on precapitalist subsistence strategies—indigenous food ways and cultiva-
tion practices that have roots reaching back past Biak's long history of colonial encounters. This community is also postcapitalist in some respects. Many of the people
who congregated at the First Voice Honey Center had tasted life in urban areas on
the periphery of capitalistic systems of production and had developed strategies for
exiting modernity (Brenkman, "Introduction to Bataille," 61–62; cf. García Canclini,
Hybrid Cultures).

28. Peter Carey, personal communication, Oxford, April 19, 2002.

29. These villages were known as *desa perdikan*. In contemporary Javanese, the
word *mardika* (free, freedom, liberty, or independence) is a synonym of *pardika* or
pĕrdika (free, unencumbered by taxes) (Horne, *Javanese-English Dictionary*, 361–62;
430; see also Carey, "Civilization on Loan," 726; Geertz, "The Javanese Kijaji," 231).

30. Adas, "From Avoidance to Confrontation," 239.

31. Donald Brenneis has suggested that understanding the political dimensions
of discourse involves the interpretation of texts and the unraveling of carefully
veiled intentions (Brenneis, "Straight Talk and Sweet Talk," 70).

32. Muller, *New Guinea*, 44–45.

33. Pastor Gobai's previous encounters with Americans—largely missionaries
from conservative Protestant backgrounds—colored his perception of my potential
readers. Gobai was revoicing the political aspirations of West Papua in terms that
might appeal to the Religious Right of America. Pastor Gobai was appropriating the
revoicing strategies of American Christians, rethinking and respeaking their political discourses in a surprising new idiom (cf. Susan Harding, "Get Religion," 350).

34. Petrus Gobai, tape-recorded interview in Indonesian, Sentani, April 5, 2003.

35. George Aditjondro has described Kopassus ninja operations at length in "Ninjas, Manggalas, Monuments."

36. Geradus Adii, another Mee pastor, has written a book containing evidence
about "a centralized government of Satan on earth," titled *Free of Dark Forces in
the Land of Papua*. Adii offers an extensive taxonomy of devilish spirits, listing
fifty-three demons that terrorize Papuans. This taxonomy appears next to a list of
twenty-six names for Satan from the Bible. Adii describes a "World Satanic Conference" where the devil and evil spirits meet and decide on their agenda. In discussing
this book with me, Pastor Gobai said that Osama bin Laden had been involved in
this conference and that the Indonesian government is also in on the plans.

37. Partha Chatterjee suggests that spiritual autonomy is a driving force behind
emerging nationalist movements: "By my reading, anticolonial nationalism creates
its own domain of sovereignty within colonial society well before it begins its political battle with the imperial power. It does this by dividing the world of social

institutions and practices into two domains—the material and the spiritual. . . . The greater one's success in imitating Western skills in the material domain, therefore, the greater the need to preserve the distinctness of one's spiritual culture. This formula is, I think, a fundamental feature of anticolonial nationalisms in Asia and Africa" (*The Nation and Its Fragments*, 6).

38. Cf. Jameson, "Marx's Purloined Letter," 62.

39. O'Hanlon, *Paradise*.

40. Obtaining signatures on the letter involved a coordinated campaign of phone calls, e-mails, and meetings with congressional aides. Here I worked with other members of the RFK West Papua Advocacy Team and the East Timor Action Network. Reaching congressional offices through activists in their local districts or through trusted human rights advocates who already had relationships with the congressional offices proved the best way to get a signature. Ann Vaughan in Congressman Farr's office played a key role in coordinating this effort.

41. Budiardjo, *Surviving Indonesia's Gulag*, ix.

42. Lords Hansard, "West Papua," January 8, 2007, available at http://www.publications.parliament.uk.

43. Jacques Bertrand has made a similarly elegant point: "Papuan nationalism was a reality that would not disappear" (*Nationalism and Ethnic Conflict in Indonesia*, 159). Lords Hansard, "West Papua," March 30, 2007.

44. Lords Hansard, "West Papua," March 30, 2007.

45. Snyder, *Global Mini-nationalisms*, 253.

46. Faleomavaega, "Faleomavaega Asks U.S. Secretary of State to Support West Papua New Guinea's Right to Self-Determination," press release, February 17, 2005, http://www.house.gov/list/press/as00_faleomavaega/papuanewguinea.html (accessed January 15, 2008).

47. Orenstein, "ETAN Calls for U.N. Review of Papua Act of 'Free Choice,'" press release, November 13, 2002, http://www.etan.org/news/2002a/11wpap.htm (accessed January 15, 2008).

48. Nobel Foundation, "Kofi Annan Biography" (2002), http://nobelprize.org/nobel_prizes/peace/laureates/2001/annan-bio.html (accessed January 15, 2008).

49. For more information about Ghana's role in opposing the Act of Free Choice, see Saltford, "United Nations Involvement with the Act of Self-Determination in West Irian," 90.

50. Ali, "U.S. Congressman Says Progress in Indonesia's Papua," July 5, 2007.

51. Derrida, *Specters of Marx*, 82–83; Derrida, "For a Justice to Come," 24; Cheah, *Spectral Nationality*, 392.

52. Cheah, *Spectral Nationality*, 392–93.

53. Suskind, "Faith, Certainty, and the Presidency of George W. Bush."

54. Jones, "The Liberal Antichrist," 102.

55. Stewart and Harding, "Bad Endings," 293.

56. Newport, preface to *Expecting the End*, x.

57. "Project for a New American Century," http://rankdirectory.org/site/www.newamericancentury.org (accessed September 9, 2010).

58. These figures come from GPO Access, the official portal for information about the budget of the U.S. government. I consulted the following two pages: http://www.gpoaccess.gov/usbudget/fy97/pdf/guide.pdf, http://www.gpoaccess.gov/usbudget/fy09/pdf/budget/defense.pdf (accessed July 14, 2011).

59. John Hartigan, "Millennials for Obama," in "The Promise of the Messianic," American Ethnological Society Session at the 108th Annual Meeting of the American Anthropological Association, Philadelphia, December 5, 2009.

60. Obama, *Dreams from My Father*, 39–45.

61. Danilyn Rutherford offers a more in-depth treatment of how Obama was claimed by West Papuan independence activists. She also writes of the troubled times that the president and his mother lived through, arriving in 1967 on the heels of the Indonesian massacres of 1965. "At this time," writes Rutherford, "neither Obama nor his mother had a clear understanding of the tumultuous events that had just transpired in Indonesia. One cannot help but imagine the specters that would have haunted his Jakarta neighbourhood a few short months after Suharto's rise to power. Villagers suffered in the killings, but they also participated in the killings: communities like Obama's neighbourhood were literally filled with ghosts" (Rutherford, *Laughing at Leviathan*).

62. Obama appointed Admiral Dennis Blair as director of national intelligence in November 2008, making it clear that his policies toward Indonesia would not be a major shift from those of the Bush administration. Blair was infamous in human rights circles for disobeying orders from the Clinton administration to stop spectacular human rights violations by the Indonesian military in East Timor when he was commander in chief of the U.S. Pacific Command in 1999. Blair was dismissed by Obama in May 2010 as the result of an unrelated scandal. See Nairn, "U.S. Complicity in Timor," September 27, 1999.

63. Weinberger, "Diary," 2005.

Epilogue

1. Ake Harvest, "Merdeka!!!," March 9, 2006.

2. "Pipa Freeport Bocor," *Cenderawasih Pos*, March 11, 2006. Mandowen, "Re: Komunitas Papua Willy Mandowen moderator Pt. Freeport Indonesia," March 9, 2006.

3. Cf. Wallerstein, *The Decline of American Power*, 237.

4. Benítez-Rojo, *The Repeating Island*, 3–9.

5. Stewart, "CPF Opens New Command Center," NAVY.mil Story Number: NNS060615-09 June 18, 2006, http://www.navy.mil/.

6. "Pipa Freeport bocor," *Cenderawasih Pos*, March 11, 2006.

7. "Tumpahan konsentrat emas Freeport sudah kering," Liputan6.com, March 11, 2006.

8. National independence in the early twenty-first century translates into new interdependencies, according to the sociologist Mohammed Bamyeh. "Scotland, when and if it secedes from Britain, will not become independent, but will immedi-

ately apply to join the European Union," writes Bamyeh. "No one wants to be independent today and the rhetoric of independence only serves as a symbolic assertion of sovereignty in a world in which sovereignty is impossible" (Bamyeh, "Postnationalism").

9. Clarke and Star, "Social Worlds/Arenas/Discourse Framework," 113.

10. This is according to postings on the Komunitas Papua electronic discussion group.

11. Amri, "Rice Pidato di JCC, Anggota DPR-DPD demo tolak Exxon," detikNews, March 15, 2006, http://us.detiknews.com/.

12. Nones, "Is It Time to Steer Clear of Indonesia?," March 20, 2006.

13. Winters, *Power in Motion*, ix.

14. Hotland and Somba, "SBY Orders End to Papua Violence," March 17, 2006; Leo L. Ladjar, Andreas Ayomi, and Hermann Saud, "Executive Summary of the Preliminary Report of the Abepura Case 16 March 2006," The Ecumenical Council of Churches in Papua, Jayapura, September 29, 2006.

15. In 2008 Freeport paid $8 million in support costs to security forces, according to filings with the U.S. Securities and Exchange Commission. Of this amount, $1.6 million went to "allowances" for military and police officers. The payments to the military technically violated a 2007 ministerial decree handing over all security for "vital national projects" to the police (Belford, "U.S. Mining Giant Still Paying"; see also Global Witness, *Paying for Protection*, 4).

16. Major General Ekodanto, the provincial chief of police, was quick to admit that the weapons used in the attack were standard issue for security forces: "It's clear they (the attackers) were using weapons belonging to the police or the military." Shortly after making this statement, Ekodanto retired from his post, and new teams of police from Jakarta launched a manhunt to find the snipers. The shooting continued even after security forces rounded up some twenty-four West Papuan men and boys. In December 2009, when police shot and killed Kelly Kwalik, a TPN guerilla commander, they declared that he was responsible for the sniper attacks; but the sniper attacks continued in January 2010 ("Gunmen Pre-planned Fatal Shooting in Papua: Police," *Agence France-Presse*, July 11, 2009; "Police Still Studying Evidence on Timika Shooting Incident," *Antara*, January 26, 2010).

17. This minor noise, static, and interference is related to the idea of the parasite as articulated by Michele Serres, a French posthumanist thinker who "speaks in figures to those who speak in figures." In French, *parasite* is polysemic, signifying the common English association of a biological or social freeloader as well as the static dots that appear on television screens. Ake Harvest was working to interrupt the meal of the vampire, creating static in the information highway—figural speculations that might result in literal actualities (Serres, *The Parasite*, 7).

18. "U.S. Natural Gas Total Consumption (Million Cubic Feet)," Independent Statistics and Analysis, U.S. Energy Information Administration, http://tonto.eia.doe.gov/dnav/ng/hist/n9140us2A.htm (accessed May 31, 2011).

19. Benítez-Rojo, "The Repeating Island," 435.

20. Sempra was put on trial for manipulating markets in the 2000–2001 Cali-

fornia energy crisis. The company eventually paid out $7.2 million to settle allegations that it had manipulated energy supplies to charge higher prices. Sempra owns and controls key components of the energy infrastructure in southern California, Mexico, and beyond (Rose, "Sempra Energy Settles").

21. Carla García Zendejas, interview, Tijuana, Mexico, December 28, 2004.

22. Institute for the Analysis of Global Security (IAGS), "Study: LNG—Not in My Backyard" (2004), http://www.iags.org/n0121041.htm (accessed February 10, 2010).

23. See also Elias, "Reality Might Well Intrude on Positive Poll Findings on LNG," 2009.

24. Larson was coy with me on the phone, declining to comment about current processing activities, about how long the diversions might continue, or about possible replacement LNG cargoes from other sources. Art Larson, telephone interview, January 2009.

25. The phrase "cargo cult" was first used in Melanesia to refer to villagers who were waiting for ships to appear with fabulous goods and material wealth. With the flows of capital and resources hidden behind a smoke screen of public relations, perhaps Melanesian notions of "cargo" might be imported as an explanatory device—a way of understanding the magic of modernity (see the note on this subject in the introduction).

26. Fineren, "Sempra Says to Keep Mexico LNG Terminal Open," *Reuters*, June 21, 2010.

27. "No work is inherently either visible or invisible," argue Susan Leigh Star and Anselm Strauss, who have conducted a nuanced analysis of these issues in networks of computer-supported cooperative work. "On the one hand, visibility can mean legitimacy, rescue from obscurity or other aspects of exploitation. On the other, visibility can create reification of work, opportunities for surveillance, or come to increase group communication and process burdens." By making the tube hypervisible, I hope to provoke conversations about bringing it more firmly under democratic control (Star and Strauss, "Layers of Silence, Arenas of Voice," 10).

28. Tsing and Pollman, "Global Futures," 107.

29. Ibid., 108–9.

30. "The 'bricoleur,'" in the words of Claude Lévi-Strauss, "is adept at performing a large number of diverse tasks; but, unlike the engineer, he does not subordinate each of them to the availability of raw materials and tools conceived and procured for the purpose of the project. His universe of instruments is closed and the rules of his game are always to make do with 'whatever is at hand,' that is to say with a set of tools and materials which is always finite and is also heterogeneous because what it contains bears no relation to the current project, or indeed to any particular project, but is the contingent result of all the occasions there have been to renew or enrich the stock or to maintain it with the remains of previous constructions or destructions" (Lévi-Strauss, *The Savage Mind*, 17).

31. The Game of Global Futures appears in the book *Histories of the Future*, edited by Daniel Rosenberg and Susan Harding.

32. Michel Serres has written at length about the distinction between hosts and

guests: "It might be dangerous not to decide who is the host and who is the guest, who gives and who receives, who is the parasite and who is the *table d'hôte*, who has the gift and who has the loss, and where hostility begins within hospitality." Nation-states that have long hosted capital might start bringing the hostility back into hospitality (Serres, *The Parasite*, 15–16).

33. Cheah, "Spectral Nationality," 250–51.

Bibliography

Adas, Michael. "From Avoidance to Confrontation: Peasant Protest in Precolonial and Colonial Southeast Asia." *Comparative Studies in Society and History* 23, no. 2 (1981): 217–47.

Adii, Geradus. *Bebas dari kuasa kegelapan di Tanah Papua*. Jayapura: Gereja Kemah Injil Indonesia, 2002.

Aditjondro, George. "Ninjas, Manggalas, Monuments, and Mossad Manuals: An Anthropology of State Terror." In *Death Squad: The Anthropology of State Terror*, ed. Jeffrey Sluka, 158–88. Philadelphia: University of Pennsylvania Press, 2000.

Ali, Muklis. "U.S. Congressman Says Progress in Indonesia's Papua." *Reuters*, July 5, 2007.

Alua, Agus. *Kongres Papua 2000: 29 Mei-4 Juni*. Jayapura: Biro Penelitian STFT Fajar Timur, 2002.

———. *Dialog nasional Papua dan Indonesia 26 Februari 1999*. Jayapura: Biro Penelitian STFT Fajar Timur, 2001.

Anderson, Benedict. "Indonesia's Struggle: Conquering a Legacy of Avarice and Vice." *The Age*, May 12, 2001.

———. "Indonesian Nationalism Today and in the Future." *Indonesia* 67 (April 1999): 1–12.

———. *The Spectre of Comparisons: Nationalism, Southeast Asia, and the World*. New York: Verso, 1998.

———. *Imagined Communities: Reflections on the Origin and Spread of Nationalism*. Rev. ed. London: Verso, 1991.

———. *Language and Power: Exploring Political Cultures in Indonesia*. Ithaca: Cornell University Press, 1990.

Anzaldúa, Gloria. *Borderlands: The New Mestiza / La Frontera*. San Francisco: Spinsters/Aunt Lute, 1987.

Appadurai, Arjun. "Dead Certainty: Ethnic Violence in the Era of Globalization." *Public Culture* 10, no. 2 (1998): 225–47.

Arens, William. *The Man-Eating Myth: Anthropology and Anthropophagy*. New York: Oxford University Press, 1979.

Aspinall, Edward. "Guerillas in Power." *Inside Indonesia* 90 (2007). Available at http://www.insideindonesia.org.

———. *Opposing Suharto: Compromise, Resistance, and Regime Change in Indonesia*. Stanford: Stanford University Press, 2005.

———. "The Indonesian Student Uprising of 1998." In *Reformasi: Crisis and Change in Indonesia*, ed. Arief Budiman, Barbara Hatley, and Damien Kingsbury, 212–38. Clayton: Monash Asia Institute, 1999.

Auerbach, Erich. *Mimesis: The Representation of Reality in Western Literature*. Princeton: Princeton University Press, 1953.

Bailey, Nathan. *Dictionarium Britannicum*. New York: Georg Olms, 1730.

Balakrishnan, Gopal. *The Enemy: An Intellectual Portrait of Carl Schmitt*. New York: Verso, 2000.

Ballard, Chris. "The Signature of Terror: Violence, Memory, and Landscape at Freeport." In *Inscribed Landscapes: Marking and Making Place*, ed. Bruno David and Meredith Wilson, 13–26. Honolulu: University of Hawaii Press, 2002.

———. "Blanks in the Writing: Possible Histories for West New Guinea." *Journal of Pacific History* 34, no. 2 (1999): 149–55.

Bamyeh, Mohammed A. "Postnationalism." *Bulletin of the Royal Institute for Inter-Faith Studies* (BRIIFS) 3, no. 2 (2001). Available at http://www.riifs.org.

Banivanua-Mar, Tracey. "'A Thousand Miles of Cannibal Lands': Imagining Away Genocide in the Recolonization of West Papua." *Journal of Genocide Research* 10, no. 4 (2008): 583–602.

Barad, Karen Michelle. *Meeting the Universe Halfway: Quantum Physics and the Entanglement of Matter and Meaning*. Durham: Duke University Press, 2007.

Barrett, Mary F. "Ficus in Florida. III. Asiatic Species." *American Midland Naturalist* 45, no. 1 (1951): 118–83.

Barton, Greg. *Abdurrahman Wahid: Muslim Democrat, Indonesian President*. Honolulu: University of Hawaii Press, 2002.

Bashkow, Ira. *The Meaning of Whitemen: Race and Modernity in the Orokaiva Cultural World*. Chicago: University of Chicago Press, 2006.

Bataille, Georges. *The Accursed Share: An Essay on General Economy*. Vols. 2 and 3. New York: Zone Books, 1991.

Bateson, Gregory. *Steps to an Ecology of Mind: Collected Essays in Anthropology, Psychiatry, Evolution, and Epistemology*. San Francisco: Chandler, 1972.

Bateson, Mary Catherine. *Peripheral Visions: Learning along the Way*. New York: Harper Collins, 1994.

Battaglia, Debbora. *On the Bones of the Serpent: Person, Memory, and Mortality in Sabarl Island Society*. Chicago: University of Chicago Press, 1990.

Bauer, Otto. "The Nation." In *Mapping the Nation*, ed. Gopal Balakrishnan, 39–77. New York: Verso, 1996.

Becker, Howard. *Doing Things Together: Selected Papers*. Evanston: Northwestern University Press, 1986.

Belford, Aubrey. "U.S. Mining Giant Still Paying Indonesian Military." *Agence France-Presse*, March 23, 2009.

Benítez-Rojo, Antonio. *The Repeating Island: The Caribbean and the Postmodern Perspective*. Trans. James E. Maraniss. Durham: Duke University Press, 1996.

———. "The Repeating Island." *New England Review and Bread Loaf Quarterly* 7, no. 4 (1985): 430–52.

Benjamin, Walter. "Critique of Violence." In *On Violence: A Reader*, ed. Bruce B. Lawrence and Aisha Karim, 268–85. Durham: Duke University Press, 2007.

———. *Illuminations*. New York: Schocken Books, 1968.

Bertrand, Jacques. *Nationalism and Ethnic Conflict in Indonesia*. Cambridge: Cambridge University Press, 2004.

Bird, Judith. "Indonesia in 1997: The Tinderbox Year." *Asian Survey* 38, no. 2 (1998): 168–76.

Boeyink, David E. "Anonymous Sources in News Stories: Justifying Exceptions and Limiting Abuses." *Journal of Mass Media Ethics* 5, no. 4 (1990): 233–46.

Bonner, Raymond. "FBI Said Involved in Arrest of 8 Indonesians." *New York Times*, January 14, 2006.

Bourchier, David. "Conservative Political Ideology in Indonesia: A Fourth Wave?" In *Indonesia Today: Challenges of History*, ed. Grayson Lloyd and Shannon Smith, 112–25. New York: Rowman and Littlefield, 2001.

Bourdieu, Pierre. *Outline of a Theory of Practice*. New York: Cambridge University Press, 1977.

Bowker, Geoffrey C., and Susan Leigh Star. *Sorting Things Out: Classification and Its Consequences*. Cambridge: MIT Press, 1999.

Brenkman, John. "Introduction to Bataille." *New German Critique* 16 (1979): 59–63.

Brenneis, Donald Lawrence. "Straight Talk and Sweet Talk: Political Discourse in an Occasionally Egalitarian Community." In *Dangerous Words: Language and Politics in the Pacific*, ed. Donald Lawrence Brenneis and Fred R. Myers, 69–84. New York: New York University Press, 1984.

Brundige, Elizabeth, Winter King, Priyneha Vahali, Stephen Vladeck, and Xiang Yuan. "Indonesian Human Rights Abuses in West Papua: Application of the Law of Genocide to the History of Indonesian Control." New Haven: International Human Rights Clinic, Yale Law School, 2003.

Buck-Morss, Susan. *Dreamworld and Catastrophe: The Passing of Mass Utopia in East and West*. Cambridge: MIT Press, 2000.

Budiardjo, Carmel. *Surviving Indonesia's Gulag: A Western Woman Tells Her Story*. New York: Cassell, 1996.

Budiardjo, Carmel, and Soei Liong Liem. *West Papua: The Obliteration of a People*. Thornton Heath: Tapol, 1988.

Burridge, Kenelm. *New Heaven, New Earth: A Study of Millenarian Activities*. New York: Blackwell, 1969.

Butt, Leslie. "'Lipstick Girls' and 'Fallen Women': AIDS and Conspiratorial Thinking in Papua, Indonesia." *Cultural Anthropology* 20, no. 3 (2005): 412–41.

Butt, Leslie, and Jenny Munro. "Rebel Girls? Unplanned Pregnancy and Colonialism in Highlands Papua, Indonesia." *Culture, Health, and Sexuality* 9, no. 6 (2007): 585–98.

Carey, Peter. "Civilization on Loan: The Making of an Upstart Polity: Mataram and Its Successors, 1600–1830." *Modern Asian Studies* 31, no. 3 (1997): 711–34.

Cattelino, Jessica R. *High Stakes: Florida Seminole Gaming and Sovereignty*. Durham: Duke University Press, 2008.

Chanda, Nayan. "Strings Attached." *Far Eastern Economic Review*, February 26, 1998.

Chatterjee, Partha. "Whose Imagined Community?" In *Mapping the Nation*, ed. Gopal Balakrishnan, 214–25. New York: Verso, 1996.

———. *The Nation and Its Fragments: Colonial and Postcolonial Histories*. Princeton: Princeton University Press, 1993.

Chauvel, Richard. "Genocide and Demographic Transformation in Papua." *Inside Indonesia* 97 (2009). Available at http://www.insideindonesia.org.

———. *Constructing Papuan Nationalism: History, Ethnicity, and Adaptation*. Washington: East-West Center, 2005.

———. "The Papuan Spring: The Passing of a Season." *H & A Asies: Revue Pluridisciplinaire de Sciences Humaines Strasbourg* 1 (2002).

Cheah, Pheng. *Spectral Nationality: Passages on Freedom from Kant to Postcolonial Literatures of Liberation*. New York: Columbia University Press, 2003.

———. "Spectral Nationality: The Living on (*Sur-Vie*) of the Postcolonial Nation in Neocolonial Globalization." *Boundary 2* 26, no. 3 (1999): 225–52.

Clarke, Adele. *Disciplining Reproduction: Modernity, American Life Sciences, and the Problems of Sex*. Berkeley: University of California Press, 1998.

Clarke, Adele, and Susan Leigh Star. "The Social Worlds/Arenas/Discourse Framework as a Theory-Methods Package." In *The New Handbook of Science and Technology Studies*, ed. Michael Lynch, Olga Amsterdamska, and Ed Hackett. Cambridge: MIT Press, 2008.

Clifford, James. "Indigenous Articulations." *Contemporary Pacific* 13, no. 2 (2001): 468–90.

———. *Routes: Travel and Translation in the Late Twentieth Century*. Cambridge: Harvard University Press, 1997.

Cohn, Norman. *The Pursuit of the Millennium: Revolutionary Messianism in Medieval and Reformation Europe and Its Bearing on Modern Totalitarian Movements*. New York: Harper Torchbooks, 1961.

Colmey, John, and David Liebhold. "The Family Firm." *Time*, May 24, 1999.

Comaroff, John, and Jean Comaroff. Introduction to *Civil Society and the Political Imagination in Africa: Critical Perspectives*, 1–43. Chicago: University of Chicago Press, 1999.

Corner, E. J. H. "The Climbing Species of Ficus: Derivation and Evolution." *Philosophical Transactions of the Royal Society of London* B 273, no. 925 (1976): 359–86.

Crapanzano, Vincent. *Imaginative Horizons: An Essay in Literary-Philosophical Anthropology*. Chicago: University of Chicago Press, 2004.

Dalton, Doug. "Cargo Cults and Discursive Madness." *Oceania* 70 (2000): 345–61.

Daniel, E. Valentine. *Charred Lullabies: Chapters in an Anthropography of Violence*. Princeton: Princeton University Press, 1996.

"Danrem: Penghianat negara harus ditumpas," *Cenderawasih Pos*, May 12, 2007.

Das, Veena. *Life and Words: Violence and the Descent into the Ordinary*. Berkeley: University of California Press, 2007.

Day, Tony, ed. *Identifying with Freedom*. New York: Berghahn Books, 2007.

De Bruijn, J. V. "Anthropological Research in Netherlands New Guinea since 1950." *Oceania* 29 (1958): 123–63.

De Haan, F. "De Laatste Der Mardijkers." *Bijdragen tot de Taal-, Land- en Volkenkunde* 73 (1917): 219–29.

Deleuze, Gilles, and Félix Guattari. *A Thousand Plateaus: Capitalism and Schizophrenia*. London: Athlone Press, 1988.

———. *On the Line*. New York: Semiotext(e), 1983.

Derrida, Jacques. "For a Justice to Come." Proceedings of the Brussels Tribunal, April 14–17, 2004, Brussels, Belgium. Available at http://www.brusselstribunal.org.

———. "Marx and Sons." In *Ghostly Demarcations: A Symposium on Jacques Derrida's Specters of Marx*, ed. Michael Sprinker, 213–69. New York: Verso, 1999.

———. *Specters of Marx: The State of the Debt, the Work of Mourning, and the New International*. New York: Routledge, 1994.

———. *Glas*. Lincoln: University of Nebraska Press, 1986.

Drexler, Elizabeth F. *Aceh, Indonesia: Securing the Insecure State*. Philadelphia: University of Pennsylvania Press, 2008.

Drooglever, Pieter J. *An Act of Free Choice: Decolonisation and the Right to Self-Determination in West Papua*. Oxford: Oneworld, 2010.

Echols, John, and Hassan Shadily. *Kamus Indonesia-Inggris (An Indonesian-English Dictionary)*. Jakarta: PT Gramedia, 1990.

Eco, Umberto. *Experiences in Translation*. Toronto: University of Toronto Press, 2001.

Elegant, Simon. "Murder at the Mine." *Time*, February 10, 2003.

Elias, Tom. "Reality Might Well Intrude on Positive Poll Findings on LNG." *Santa Monica Mirror*, November 6, 2008.

Elmslie, Jim. "Not Just Another Disaster: Papuan Claims of Genocide Deserve to Be Taken Seriously." *Inside Indonesia* 97 (2009). Available at http://www.insideindonesia.org.

Elsham. "Nama tanpa pusara, pusara tanpa nama." Jayapura: Elsham, July 1999.

Fanon, Frantz. *The Wretched of the Earth*. New York: Grove, 1965.

Farhadian, Charles E. *Christianity, Islam, and Nationalism in Indonesia*. New York: Routledge, 2005.

Fernandes, Clinton. *Reluctant Indonesians: Australia, Indonesia, and the Future of West Papua*. Melbourne: Scribe Short Books, 2006.

Fineren, Daniel. "Sempra Says to Keep Mexico LNG Terminal Open," *Reuters*, June 21, 2010.

Forrester, Geoffrey. "A Jakarta Diary, May 1998." In *The Fall of Suharto*, ed. Geoffrey Forrester, 24–69. Bathurst: Crawford House, 1998.

Fortun, Michael. "Mediated Speculations in the Genomics Futures Markets." *New Genetics and Society* 20, no. 2 (2001): 139–56.

Foucault, Michel. "Nietzsche, Genealogy, History." In *Language, Counter-memory, Practice: Selected Essays and Interviews*, ed. Donald F. Bouchard, 139–64. Ithaca: Cornell University Press, 1977.

"Freeport: Grasberg Illegal Protests Over, No Impact on Ops." *Dow Jones Newswire*, March 15, 2006.

Freeport McMoRan. *Underlying Values: 2006 Working toward Sustainable Development Report*. New Orleans: Freeport McMoRan Copper and Gold, 2007.

French, Bruce R. *Food Plants of Papua New Guinea*. Sheffield, Tasmania: Australia Pacific Science Foundation, 1986.

García Canclini, Néstor. *Hybrid Cultures: Strategies for Entering and Leaving Modernity*. Minneapolis: University of Minnesota Press, 2005.

Geertz, Clifford. *Negara: The Theatre State in Nineteenth-Century Bali*. Princeton: Princeton University Press, 1980.

———. "The Javanese Kijaji: The Changing Role of a Culture Broker." *Comparative Studies in Society and History* 2, no. 2 (1960): 228–49.

———. *The Religion of Java*. Glencoe, Ill.: Free Press, 1960.

Gellner, Ernest. *Nations and Nationalism: New Perspectives on the Past*. Ithaca: Cornell University Press, 1983.

George, Kenneth M. "Violence, Culture, and the Indonesian Public Sphere: Reworking the Geertzian Legacy." In *Violence*, ed. Neil L. Whitehead, 25–54. Santa Fe: School of American Research, 2002.

Giay, Benny. *Misi gereja dan budaya kekerasan di Tanah Papua*. Jayapura, Indonesia: Deiyai, 2006.

———. *Peristiwa penculikan dan pembunuhan Theys H. Eluay 10 Nopember 2001*. Jayapura, Indonesia: Deiyai, 2003.

———. *Zakheus Pakage and His Communities: Indigenous Religious Discourse, Sociopolitical Resistance, and Ethnohistory of the Me of Irian Jaya*. Amsterdam: VU University Press, 1995.

Gibbons, Alice. *Where the Earth Ends: Stone Age People Tell Their Story*. Longwood, Fla.: Xulon Press, 2009.

Gillard, Michael. "Colombia Murder Claim Hits BP." *Sunday Times*, April 21, 2002.

Global Witness. *Paying for Protection: The Freeport Mine and the Indonesian Security Forces*. Global Witness, July 2005.

Golden, Brigham. "Gold, Violence, and the Rise of a Political Millenarianism: Freeport's Mine and Papua *Merdeka*." Paper presented at the Annual Meeting of the American Anthropological Association, Chicago, 2003.

Gordon, Raymond G. *Ethnologue: Languages of the World*. 15th ed. Dallas: SIL International, 2005.

Gramsci, Antonio. *Selections from the Prison Notebooks of Antonio Gramsci*. Trans. Quintin Hoare and Geoffrey Nowell-Smith. London: Lawrence and Wishart, 1971.

Guiart, Jean. "Forerunners of Melanesian Nationalism." *Oceania* 22, no. 2 (1951): 81–90.

Hale, Charles. "Activist Research versus Cultural Critique: Indigenous Land Rights and the Contradictions of Politically Engaged Anthropology." *Cultural Anthropology* 21, no. 1 (2006): 96–120.

Hall, Stuart. "Signification, Representation, Ideology: Althusser and the Poststructuralist Debates." *Critical Studies in Mass Communication* 2, no. 2 (1985): 91–114.

Hall, Stuart, and Lawrence Grossberg. "On Postmodernism and Articulation: An Interview with Stuart Hall." *Journal of Communication Inquiry* 10, no. 2 (1986): 45–60.

Haraway, Donna. *When Species Meet*. Minneapolis: University of Minnesota Press, 2007.

———. "Speculative Fabulations for Technoculture's Generations: Taking Care of Unexpected Country." In *(Tiernas)Criaturas/(Tender)Creatures*, ed. Patricia Piccinini, 100–107. Vitoria: Egileak, 2007.

———. *Modest_Witness@Second_Millennium.FemaleMan©_Meets_OncomouseTM: Feminism and Technoscience*. New York: Routledge, 1997.

———. *Simians, Cyborgs, and Women: The Reinvention of Nature*. London: Free Association Books, 1991.

———. "Situated Knowledges: The Science Question in Feminism and the Privilege of Partial Perspective." *Feminist Studies* 14, no. 3 (1988): 575–600.

Harding, Sandra, ed. *The Feminist Standpoint Theory Reader: Intellectual and Political Controversies*. New York: Routledge, 2004.

———. "Rethinking Standpoint Epistemology: What Is 'Strong Objectivity'?" In *Feminism and Science*, ed. Evelyn Fox Keller and Helen E. Longino, 235–48. New York: Oxford University Press, 1996.

Harding, Susan Friend. "Get Religion." In *The Insecure American: How We Got Here and What We Should Do about It*, ed. Hugh Gusterson and Catherine Bestman, 345–61. Berkeley: University of California Press, 2010.

———. "Imagining the Last Days: The Politics of Apocalyptic Language." *Bulletin of the American Academy of Arts and Sciences* 48, no. 3 (1994): 14–44.

Hardt, Michael, and Antonio Negri. *Multitude: War and Democracy in the Age of Empire*. New York: Penguin, 2004.

Harootunian, Harry D. "Ghostly Comparisons: Anderson's Telescope." *Diacritics* 29, no. 4 (1999): 135–49.

Harsono, Andreas, and Nathaniel Heller. "Jakarta's Intelligence Service Hires Washington Lobbyists." International Consortium of Investigative Journalists, September 7, 2006. Available at http://projects.publicintegrity.org.

Hather, Jon G. "The Archaeobotany of Subsistence in the Pacific." *World Archaeology* 24, no. 1 (1992): 70–81.

Hayward, Douglas. *The Dani of Irian Jaya: Before and after Conversion*. Sentani: Regions Press, 1980.

Hernawan, J. Budi. "Human Rights Conditions in Papua." UNHCR Regional Seminar on Emergency Management and Contingency Planning, Bali, Indonesia, 2002.

"Highlights of Indonesian Wahid's State of Nation Speech." *Dow Jones Newswire*, August 7, 2000.

Hill, Hal. "The Indonesian Economy: The Strange and Sudden Death of a Tiger." In *The Fall of Soeharto*, ed. Geoffrey Forrester and R. J. May, 93–103. Bathurst: Crawford House, 1998.

Hitt, Russell T. *Cannibal Valley*. Grand Rapids: Zondervan, 1962.

Horne, Elinor McCullough Clark. *Javanese-English Dictionary*. Yale Linguistic Series. New Haven: Yale University Press, 1974.

Hotland, Tony, and Nethy Dharma Somba. "SBY Orders End to Papua Violence." *Jakarta Post*, March 17, 2006.

Human Rights Watch. *What Did I Do Wrong?: Papuans in Merauke Face Abuses by Indonesian Special Forces*. New York: Human Rights Watch, June 2009, http://www.hrw.org.

———. *Too High a Price*. New York: Human Rights Watch, June 2006.

———. *Indonesia: Human Rights and Pro-Independence Actions in Irian Jaya*. New York: Human Rights Watch, December 1998.

Hyams, Keith. "Petrol in Papua." *Ecologist*, June 2001, 52–57.

Hyland, Tom. "Police Blame Army for Papua Ambush." *The Age*, December 27, 2002.

Hylkema, S., and W. Wolke. "Ekagi Texts: Myths." Leiden: unpublished manuscript, 1988.

Ingo, W. "Here Come the Kostrad Boys—Again!" *Watch Indonesia! Critical Contributions to Current Affairs* 2 (November 11, 2000).

International Crisis Group. *Indonesia: Keeping the Military under Control*. Report no. 33. Jakarta, 2001.

Ipenburg, At. "The Life and Death of Theys Eluay." *Inside Indonesia* 70 (2002). Available at http://www.insideindonesia.org.

Ircham, M. C. *Mansren Koreri: Mengenal beberapa suku dan ceritera rakyat Irian Jaya*. Bandung, Indonesia: Penerbit Binacipta, 1980.

Islam, H. M. Sjaiful. *Sejarah TNI Jilid V (1984–2000)*. Jakarta: Pusat Sejarah dan Tradisi TNI, 2000.

Ismail, A., Supardi Rapanoi, Sjamsuar Said, and H. Hutasuhut. *Praja ghupta vira: Irian Barat dari masa ke masa*. Jakarta: Sedjarah Militer Kodam XVII, 1971.

Jacobs, Karen. "United Colours of Papua." In *Identity Theft: Cultural Colonisation and Contemporary Art*, ed. Jonathan Harris. Liverpool: Chicago University Press, 2008.

———. "Kamoro Arts Festival." In *Kamoro Art: Tradition and Innovation in a New Guinea Culture*, ed. Dirk Smidt, 66–71. Amsterdam: KIT Publishers, 2003.

Jameson, Fredric. "Marx's Purloined Letter." In *Ghostly Demarcations: A Symposium on Jacques Derrida's "Specters of Marx*," ed. Michael Sprinker, 26–67. New York: Verso, 1999.

———. "Science-Fiction as a Spatial Genre: Generic Discontinuities and the Problem of Figuration in Vonda McIntyre's *The Exile Waiting*." *Science Fiction Studies* 14, no. 2 (1987): 44–59.

Jasanoff, Sheila. *Designs on Nature: Science and Democracy in Europe and the United States*. Princeton: Princeton University Press, 2005.

———. *States of Knowledge: The Co-production of Science and Social Order*. New York: Routledge, 2004.

Jones, Darryl. "The Liberal Antichrist—Left Behind in America." In *Expecting the End: Millennialism in Social and Historical Context*, ed. Kenneth G. C. Newport and Crawford Gribben, 113–30. Waco: Baylor University Press, 2006.

Kamma, Freerk. *Koreri: Messianic Movements in the Biak-Numfor Culture Area*. The Hague: Nijhoff, 1972.

Kammen, Douglas. "Master-Slave, Traitor-Nationalist, Opportunist-Oppressed: Political Metaphors in East Timor." *Indonesia* 76 (2003): 69–85.

Katyasungkana, Nursyahbani. "Exchanging Power or Changing Power? The Problem of Creating Democratic Institutions." In *Indonesia in Transition: Social Aspects of Reformasi and Crisis*, ed. Chris Manning and Peter van Diermen, 259–68. London: Zed Books, 2000.

Keagop, Paskalis Worot, and Frits Bernard Ramandey. *Menelusuri jejak kasus pemimpin bangsa Papua Theys Hiyo Eluay*. Jayapura: Lembaga Studi Pers dan Otsus Papua, 2007.

Keane, Webb. *Christian Moderns: Freedom and Fetish in the Mission Encounter*. Berkeley: University of California Press, 2007.

———. *Signs of Recognition: Powers and Hazards of Representation in an Indonesian Society*. Berkeley: University of California Press, 1997.

Kejahatan kemanusiaan: Dibalik operasi penyisiran dan penumpasan Di Wasior, Manokwari. Indonesian-language report. Jayapura: Tim Advokasi Untuk Wasior, March 2002.

Kelley, Robin D. G. *Freedom Dreams: The Black Radical Imagination*. Boston: Beacon, 2002.

Kilvert, Andrew. "Whisky Friends." *Inside Indonesia* 60 (1999). Available at http://www.insideindonesia.org.

King, Peter. *West Papua and Indonesia since Suharto: Independence, Autonomy, or Chaos?* Sydney: University of New South Wales Press, 2004.

Kingsbury, Damien. *Peace in Aceh: A Personal Account of the Helsinki Peace Process*. Jakarta: Equinox Publishing Indonesia, 2006.

———. *Power Politics and the Indonesian Military*. New York: Routledge Curzon, 2003.

Kirksey, Eben. "Don't Use Your Data as a Pillow." In *Anthropology Off the Shelf: Anthropologists on Writing*, ed. Maria D. Vesperi and Alisse Waterston, 146–59. Malden, Mass.: Wiley-Blackwell, 2009.

———. "Indonesia's Bleak Record." *Saint Petersburg Times*, July 7, 2009.

———. "Spirited Fight." *Guardian*, May 29, 2002, Society, 9.

———. "Saya Makan Sembarang (I Eat Anything): The Changing World of the Oge Bage Mee." B.A. thesis, Department of Anthropology, New College of Florida, 2000.

Kirksey, Eben, and Jack Grimston. "Indonesian Troops for BP Gas Project." *Sunday Times*, July 20, 2003.

Kirksey, Eben, and Andreas Harsono. "Criminal Collaborations? Antonius Wamang and the Indonesian Military in Timika." *South East Asia Research* 16, no. 2 (2008): 165–97.

Kirsch, Stuart. "Indigenous Movements and the Risks of Counterglobalization: Tracking the Campaign against Papua New Guinea's Ok Tedi Mine." *American Ethnologist* 34, no. 2 (2007): 303–21.

——. *Reverse Anthropology: Indigenous Analysis of Social and Environmental Relations in New Guinea*. Stanford: Stanford University Press, 2006.

——. "Rumor and Other Narratives of Political Violence in West Papua." *Critique of Anthropology* 22, no. 1 (2002): 53–79.

Klein, Naomi. "Minority Death Match: Jews, Blacks, and the 'Post-racial' Presidency." *Harper's Magazine*, September 2009, 53–67.

Koch, Klaus-Friedrich. *War and Peace in Jalémó: The Management of Conflict in Highland New Guinea*. Cambridge: Harvard University Press, 1974.

Kudiai, V. P. F. "Religi suku Ekagi." Undergraduate thesis, Department of Anthropology, Universitas Cenderawasih, 1980.

Lacan, Jacques. *The Psychoses*. Trans. Russell Grigg. New York: W.W. Norton, 1993.

Laclau, Ernesto. *Politics and Ideology in Marxist Theory*. London: Verso, 1982.

Latour, Bruno. *War of the Worlds: What about Peace?* Chicago: Prickly Paradigm Press, 2002.

——. *We Have Never Been Modern*. Trans. Catherine Porter. Cambridge: Harvard University Press, 1993.

Lawless, Robert. "The Indonesian Takeover of East Timor." *Asian Survey* 16, no. 10 (1976): 948–64.

Leith, Denise. *The Politics of Power: Freeport in Suharto's Indonesia*. Honolulu: University of Hawaii Press, 2003.

Lekic, Slobodan. "Indonesian Army Ordered Deadly Ambush." *Associated Press*, March 3, 2004.

Lévi-Strauss, Claude. *The Savage Mind*. Chicago: University of Chicago Press, 1966.

Lijphart, Arend. *The Trauma of Decolonization: The Dutch and West New Guinea*. New Haven: Yale University Press, 1966.

Lindstrom, Lamont. *Cargo Cult: Strange Stories of Desire from Melanesia and Beyond*. Honolulu: University of Hawaii Press, 1993.

Lioe, Fanny. "Indonesia on the Boil." *Far Eastern Economic Review*, February 26, 1998.

LiPuma, Edward. *Encompassing Others: The Magic of Modernity in Melanesia*. Ann Arbor: University of Michigan Press, 2000.

Lubis, Todung Mulya. "Lawyer for Washington Post Says Indonesian Military Failed to Follow Procedure Regarding Media Complaints." *Radio New Zealand*, November 22, 2002.

Mahmud, A. *Beringin berkabut*. Jakarta: Seri Bacaan Sastra Anak Nusantara, 2001.

Maier, Hendrik M. J. "In Search of Memories: How Malay Tales Try to Shape History." In *Beginning to Remember: The Past in the Indonesian Present*, ed. Mary S. Zurbuchen, 99–121. Seattle: University of Washington Press, 2005.

Marcus, George E. "Ethnography in/of the World System: The Emergence of Multi-sited Ethnography." *Annual Review of Anthropology* 24 (1995): 96–117.

Marr, Carolyn. "Court Orders Freeport to Clean Up Its Act." *Down to Earth Newsletter* 51 (2001). Available at http://dte.gn.apc.org.

Marx, Karl. *Capital*. Vol. 1. London: Penguin Classics, 1976.

Mauss, Marcel. *The Gift: The Form and Reason for Exchange in Archaic Societies*. New York: W. W. Norton, 1990.

McCarthy, Terry. "Indonesia Burning." *Time*, May 25, 1998.

McGibbon, Rodd. "Pitfalls of Papua: Understanding the Conflict and Its Place in Australia-Indonesia Relations." *Lowy Institute Paper 13* (2006). Available at http://www.lowyinstitute.org.

Merauke Catholic Diocese. *Mengapa pembunuhan terhadap Willem Onde dan John Tumin Kandam belum diinvestigasi?* Peace and Justice Office report, 2002.

Mietzner, Marcus. "Between Pesantren and Palace: Nahdlatul Ulama and Its Role in the Transition." In *The Fall of Suharto*, ed. Geoffrey Forrester and R. J. May, 179–99. Bathurst: Crawford House, 1998.

Miyazaki, Hirokazu. *The Method of Hope: Anthropology, Philosophy, and Fijian Knowledge*. Stanford: Stanford University Press, 2004.

Mo, Timothy. *The Redundancy of Courage*. London: Paddleless Press, 2002.

Monier-Williams, Monier. *A Sanskrit-English Dictionary: Etymologically and Philologically Arranged*. Oxford: Clarendon, 1960.

Moore, Donald S. *Suffering for Territory: Race, Place, and Power in Zimbabwe*. Durham: Duke University Press, 2005.

Moore, Matthew. "Find Freeport Killers, Bush Tells Megawati." *Sydney Morning Herald*, December 21, 2002.

Muller, Kal. *New Guinea: Journey into the Stone Age*. Lincolnwood: Passport Books, 1993.

Murphy, John Joseph. *The Book of Pidgin English*. New York: AMS Press, 1980.

Mydans, Seth. "Indonesia Chooses an Islamic Cleric as New President." *New York Times*, October 21, 1999.

Nagel, Thomas. *The View from Nowhere*. Oxford: Oxford University Press, 1986.

Nairn, Allan. "U.S. Intelligence Is Tapping Indonesian Phones." *CounterPunch*, December 12, 2007.

———. "U.S. Complicity in Timor." *The Nation*, September 27, 1999.

Nakashima, Ellen. "FBI Said Involved in Arrest of 8 Indonesians." *Washington Post*, January 13, 2006.

Nakashima, Ellen, and Alan Sipress. "Indonesia Military Allegedly Talked of Targeting Mine." *Washington Post*, November 3, 2002.

Nevins, Joseph. *A Not-So-Distant Horror: Mass Violence in East Timor*. Ithaca: Cornell University Press, 2005.

Newport, Kenneth G. C. Preface to *Expecting the End: Millennialism in Social and Historical Context*, ed. Kenneth G. C. Newport and Crawford Gribben. Waco: Baylor University Press, 2006.

Nones, Jon A. "Is It Time to Steer Clear of Indonesia?" *Resource Investor*, March 20, 2006.

Obama, Barack. *Dreams from My Father: A Story of Race and Inheritance*. New York: Random House, 2004.

Obeyesekere, Gananath. *Cannibal Talk: The Man-Eating Myth and Human Sacrifice in the South Seas*. Berkeley: University of California Press, 2005.

"Office of Rights Group Probing Papua Shootings Attacked." *Jakarta Post*, October 28, 2002.

O'Hanlon, Michael. *Paradise: Portraying the New Guinea Highlands*. London: British Museum Press, 1993.

"One Student Killed in Clash with Security Personnel." *Associated Press Worldstream*, July 3, 1998.

Orwell, George. *Facing Unpleasant Facts: Narrative Essays*. Orlando: Harcourt, 2008.

Osborne, Robin. *Indonesia's Secret War: The Guerilla Struggle in Irian Jaya*. London: Allen and Unwin, 1985.

Peirce, Charles S. *Writings of Charles S. Peirce: A Chronological Edition*. Bloomington: Indiana University Press, 1982.

Pemberton, Gregory. *All the Way: Australia's Road to Vietnam*. London: Allen and Unwin, 1987.

Pemberton, John. "Notes on the 1982 General Election in Solo." *Indonesia* 41 (1986): 1–22.

———. *On the Subject of Java*. Ithaca: Cornell University Press, 1994.

"Police Say Indonesian Army behind Papua Ambush." *Agence France Presse*, December 26, 2002.

PolRes Manokwari. *Berkas perkara Ronald Ramandey dan Amalina Kiri: Tindak pidana kejahatan terhadap keamanan negara*. Manokwari Regional Police (PolRes) court dossier. January 24, 2003.

Pospisil, Leopold J. *Kapauku Papuans and Their Law*. New Haven: Human Relations Area Files Press, 1964.

———. *Kapauku Papuan Economy*. New Haven: Yale University Publications in Anthropology, 1963.

Powell, Sian. "Kopassus Assassins Get Light Jail Terms." *Australian*, April 22, 2003.

Priest, Dana. "Nightmare and a Mystery." *Washington Post*, June 22, 2003.

Pura, Raphael, and Murray Hiebert. "Arrest Helps U.S.-Indonesian Ties: Bilateral Efforts Lead to 12 Suspects Held in Teacher's Slayings." *Wall Street Journal*, January 13, 2006.

Putz, F. E., G. B. Romano, and N. M. Holbrook. "Comparative Phenology of Epiphytic and Tree-Phase Strangler Figs in a Venezuelan Palm Savanna." *Biotropica* 27, no. 2 (1995): 183–89.

"Quake Rocks Indonesia, 2000 Houses Damaged." *Channel NewsAsia*, June 29, 2001.

Radio Australia. "U.S.: Washington Signals New Era of Military Co-operation." *Radio Australia*, November 11, 2006.

Rafael, Vicente L. "The Cell Phone and the Crowd: Messianic Politics in the Contemporary Philippines." *Public Culture* 15, no. 3 (2003): 399–425.

Reardon, Jenny. *Race to the Finish: Identity and Governance in an Age of Genomics*. Princeton: Princeton University Press, 2005.

Rees, Susan J., Remco van de Pas, Derrick Silove, and Moses Kareth. "Health and Human Security in West Papua." *Medical Journal of Australia* 189, nos. 11–12 (2008): 641–43.

Reeve, David. *Golkar of Indonesia: An Alternative to the Party System*. New York: Oxford University Press, 1985.

Reid, Anthony. "Introduction: Slavery and Bondage in Southeast Asian History." In *Slavery, Bondage, and Dependency in Southeast Asia*, ed. Anthony Reid, 1–43. New York: St. Martin's, 1983.

Rhys, Lloyd, *Jungle Pimpernel: The Story of a District Officer in Central Netherlands New Guinea.* London: Hodder and Stoughton, 1947.

Richards, Chris. "Way beyond Petroleum." *New Internationalist* 344 (2002): 14–16.

Richardson, Don. *Lords of the Earth.* Glendale: G/L Regal Books, 1977.

Robbins, Joel. *Becoming Sinners: Christianity and Moral Torment in a Papua New Guinea Society.* Berkeley: University of California Press, 2004.

———. "Secrecy and the Sense of an Ending: Narrative, Time, and Everyday Millenarianism in Papua New Guinea and in Christian Fundamentalism." *Comparative Studies in Society and History* 43, no. 3 (2001): 525–51.

Robinson, Geoffrey. "The Post-coup Massacre in Bali." In *Making Indonesia: Essays on Modern Indonesia in Honor of George Mct. Kahin,* ed. Ruth McVey, 118–43. Ithaca: Cornell Southeast Asia Studies Program, 1996.

———. *The Dark Side of Paradise: Political Violence in Bali, Asia, East by South.* Ithaca: Cornell University Press, 1995.

Rose, Craig D. "Sempra Energy Settles Power Market-Manipulation Allegations for $7.2 Million." *San Diego Union-Tribune,* July 29, 2004.

Rosenberg, Daniel, and Susan Friend Harding, eds. *Histories of the Future.* Durham: Duke University Press, 2005.

Rulianto, Agung, and Cunding Levi. "Timika's 'Flight Club' Grounded." *Tempo,* January 17–23, 2006.

Rumbiak, John. "Testimony 17 tahanan tragedi Wamena." ELS-HAM report. October 27.

Rutherford, Danilyn. *Laughing at Leviathan: Sovereignty and Audience in West Papua.* Chicago: University of Chicago Press, 2012.

———. "Why Papua Wants Freedom: The Third Person in Contemporary Nationalism." *Public Culture* 20, no. 2 (2008): 361–89.

———. *Raiding the Land of the Foreigners: The Limits of the Nation on an Indonesian Frontier.* Princeton: Princeton University Press, 2003.

———. "The White Edge of the Margin: Textuality and Authority in Biak, Irian Jaya, Indonesia." *American Ethnologist* 27, no. 2 (2000): 312–39.

———. "Waiting for the End: Violence, Order, and a Flag Raising." *Indonesia* 67 (April 1999): 39–59.

Ryter, Loren Stuart. "Youth, Gangs, and the State in Indonesia." Ph.D. diss., University of Washington, 2002.

Sahlins, Marshall. "Artificially Maintained Controversies: Global Warming and Fijian Cannibalism." *Anthropology Today* 19, no. 3 (2003): 3–5.

———. *Stone Age Economics.* Chicago: Aldine-Atherton, 1972.

Said, Edward W. *Orientalism.* New York: Vintage Books, 1979.

Saltford, John. *The United Nations and the Indonesian Takeover of West Papua, 1962–1969.* London: Routledge Curzon, 2003.

———. "United Nations Involvement with the Act of Self-Determination in West Irian (Indonesian West New Guinea) 1968 to 1969." *Indonesia* 69 (2000): 71–92.

Scaglion, Richard, and Kimberly A. Soto. "A Prehistoric Sweet Potato?" In *Migration and Transformations: Regional Perspectives on New Guinea,* ed. Andrew Strathern and Gabriele Sturzenhofecker, 257–94. Pittsburgh: University of Pittsburgh Press, 1994.

Schapiro, Mark. "Conning the Climate: Inside the Carbon-Trading Shell Game." *Harper's*, February 2010, 31–39.

Scott, James C. *Domination and the Arts of Resistance: Hidden Transcripts*. London: Yale University Press, 1990.

Serres, Michael. *The Parasite*. Minneapolis: University of Minnesota Press, 2007.

"Shooting of Papuan Human Rights Activist's Family May Be Related to Timika Incident." *Tempo Interactive*, December 28, 2003.

Sidel, John T. "Macet Total: Logics of Circulation and Accumulation in the Demise of Indonesia's New Order." *Indonesia* 66 (1998): 159–94.

Siegel, James T. *A New Criminal Type in Jakarta: Counter-revolution Today*. Durham: Duke University Press, 1998.

———. *Fetish, Recognition, Revolution*. Princeton: Princeton University Press, 1997.

———. *Solo in the New Order: Language and Hierarchy in an Indonesian City*. Princeton: Princeton University Press, 1986.

Simon, Paul. "America." In *Bookends*. Columbia CK 09529, compact disc. Originally released in 1968.

Simpson, Bradley. *Economists with Guns: Authoritarian Development and U.S.-Indonesian Relations, 1960–1968*. Stanford: Stanford University Press, 2008.

Snyder, Louis Leo. *Global Mini-nationalisms: Autonomy or Independence*. Westport: Greenwood Press, 1982.

Somba, Nethy Dharma. "Wife of Human Rights Activist Shot at Papua-PNG Border." *Jakarta Post*, December 29, 2002.

Spivak, Gayatri Chakravorty. "Can the Subaltern Speak?" In *Marxism and the Interpretation of Culture*, ed. Cary Nelson and Lawrence Grossberg, 271–313. Chicago: University of Illinois Press, 1988.

Spyer, Patricia. *The Memory of Trade: Modernity's Entanglements on an Eastern Indonesian Island*. Durham: Duke University Press, 2000.

Star, Susan Leigh, and James R. Griesemer. "Institutional Ecology, 'Translation,' and Boundary Objects: Amateurs and Professionals in Berkeley's Museum of Vertebrate Zoology, 1907–1939." *Social Studies of Science* 19 (1989): 387–420.

Star, Susan Leigh, and Anselm Strauss. "Layers of Silence, Arenas of Voice: The Ecology of Visible and Invisible Work." *Computer Supported Cooperative Work* 8 (1999): 9–30.

Stasch, Rupert. *Society of Others: Kinship and Mourning in a West Papuan Place*. Berkeley: University of California Press, 2009.

———. "Giving Up Homicide: Korowai Experience of Witches and Police (West Papua)." *Oceania* 72 (2001): 33–52.

Steltenpool, J. *Ekagi-Dutch-English-Indonesian Dictionary*. The Hague: Martinus Nijhoff, 1969.

Stephen, Michele. *A'aisa's Gifts: A Study of Magic and Self*. Berkeley: University of California Press, 1995.

Stewart, Kathleen, and Susan Friend Harding. "Bad Endings: American Apocalypses." *Annual Review of Anthropology* 28 (1999): 285–310.

Strathern, Andrew. *The Rope of Moka: Big Men and Ceremonial Exchange in Mount Hagen, New Guinea*. Cambridge: Cambridge University Press, 1971.

Strathern, Marilyn. *Kinship, Law, and the Unexpected: Relatives Are Always a Surprise*. New York: Cambridge University Press, 2005.

Strauss, Anselm. "A Social World Perspective." *Studies in Symbolic Interaction* 1 (1978): 119–28.

Suskind, Ron. "Faith, Certainty, and the Presidency of George W. Bush." *New York Times Magazine*, October 17, 2004.

Taussig, Michael. *Law in a Lawless Land: Diary of a Limpieza in Colombia*. New York: New Press, 2003.

———. *The Nervous System*. New York: Routledge, 1992.

———. *Shamanism, Colonialism, and the Wild Man: A Study in Terror and Healing*. Chicago: University of Chicago Press, 1986.

———. "Culture of Terror—Space of Death: Roger Casement's Putumayo Report and the Explanation of Torture." *Comparative Studies in Society and History* 26, no. 3 (1984): 467–97.

Taylor, Jean Gelman. *The Social World of Batavia*. Madison: University of Wisconsin Press, 1983.

Tedjasukmana, Jason. "Why Jakarta Needs to Pay More Attention to Papua." *Time*, August 16, 2010.

Tesoro, Manuel Jose. *The Invisible Place: The True Story of a Journalist's Murder in Java*. Jakarta: Equinox, 2004.

Thimme, Hans Martin. "Manarmakeri: Theological Evaluation of an Old Biak Myth." *Point* (1977): 21–49.

Thomas, Nicholas. *Entangled Objects: Exchange, Material Culture, and Colonialism in the Pacific*. London: Harvard University Press, 1991.

Thomson, James D., Sara Dent-Acosta, Patricia Escobar-Paramo, and John D. Nason. "Within-Crown Flowering Synchrony in Strangler Figs, and Its Relationship to Allofusion." *Biotropica* 29, no. 3 (1997): 291–97.

Thomson, James D., E. Allan Herre, J. L. Hamrick, and J. L. Stone. "Genetic Mosaics in Strangler Fig Trees: Implications for Tropical Conservation." *Science* 254 (1991): 1214–16.

Timmer, Jaap. "Erring Decentralization and Elite Politics in Papua." In *Renegotiating Boundaries: Local Politics in Post-Suharto Indonesia*, ed. Henk Schulte Nordholt and Gerry van Klinken, 459–82. Leiden: KITLV Press, 2007.

———. "The Return of the Kingdom: Agama and the Millennium among the Imyan of Irian Jaya, Indonesia." *Ethnohistory* 47, no. 1 (2000): 29–65.

Tsing, Anna Lowenhaupt. "The Global Situation." In *The Anthropology of Globalization: A Reader*, ed. Jonathan Xavier Inda and Renato Rosaldo. New York: Wiley-Blackwell, 2007.

———. "Indigenous Voice." In *Indigenous Experience Today*, ed. Marisol de la Cadena and Orin Starn. New York: Berg, 2007.

———. *Friction: An Ethnography of Global Connection*. Princeton: Princeton University Press, 2005.

———. "Becoming a Tribal Elder, and Other Green Development Fantasies." In

Transforming the Indonesian Uplands: Marginality, Power, and Production, ed. Tania Murray Li, 159–202. London: Harwood Academic Publishers, 1999.

———. *In the Realm of the Diamond Queen: Marginality in an Out-of-the-Way Place*. Princeton: Princeton University Press, 1993.

Tsing, Anna Lowenhaupt, and Elizabeth Pollman. "Global Futures: The Game." In *Histories of the Future*, ed. Daniel Rosenberg and Susan Friend Harding, 107–22. Durham: Duke University Press, 2005.

Turner, Victor W. "Betwixt and Between: The Liminal Period in Rites de Passage." In *Symposium on New Approaches to the Study of Religion*, ed. American Ethnological Society, 4–20. Seattle: University of Washington Press, 1964.

"U.N. Envoy Due in Indonesia on East Timor Conflict." *Deutsche Presse-Agentur*, July 4, 1998.

Upton, Stuart. "A Disaster, but Not Genocide." *Inside Indonesia* 97 (2009). Available at http://www.insideindonesia.org.

Van den Broek, Theo, and Budi Hernawan. *Memoria passionis di Papua: Kondisi hak asasi manusia dan gerakan aspirasi merdeka—gambaran 1999*. Jakarta: SKP Keuskupan Jayapura, 2001.

———. *Memoria passionis di Papua: Kondisi sosial politik dan hak asasi manusia— gambaran 2000*. Jakarta: SKP Keuskupan Jayapura, 2001.

Van Eekelen, Bregje, Jennifer Gonzalez, Bettina Stotzer, and Anna Lowenhaupt Tsing, eds. *Shock and Awe: War on Words*. Santa Cruz: New Pacific, 2004.

Van Klinken, Gerry, and David Bourchier. "The Key Suspects." In *Masters of Terror: Indonesia's Military and Violence in East Timor in 1999*, ed. Richard Tanter, Desmond Ball, and Gerry van Klinken, 67–82. Oxford: Rowman and Littlefield, 2005.

Vidal, John. "Shattered Illusions." *Guardian*, March 19, 2008.

———. "Poison Fog Blanket Threatens World Climate." *Guardian*, September 27, 1997.

Wagner, Roy. *The Invention of Culture*. Chicago: University of Chicago Press, 1981.

Walker, Madeline Ruth. "Sauling Around: The Trouble with Conversion in African American and Mexican American Autobiography, 1965–2002." Ph.D. diss., University of Victoria, 2008.

Wallerstein, Immanuel Maurice. *World-Systems Analysis: An Introduction*. Durham: Duke University Press, 2004.

———. *The Decline of American Power: The U.S. in a Chaotic World*. New York: New Press, 2003.

———. *The Capitalist World Economy*. New York: Cambridge University Press, 1980.

Walters, Patrick. "Malaria Compounds Irian Jayans' Misery." *Weekend Australian*, December 6–7, 1997.

Wardlow, Hollow. *Wayward Women: Sexuality and Agency in a New Guinea Society*. Berkeley: University of California Press, 2006.

Ware, Owen. "Dialectic of the Past / Disjuncture of the Future: Derrida and Benjamin on the Concept of Messianism." *Journal of Cultural and Religious Theory* 5, no. 2 (2004): 99–114.

Watson, James. "From Hunting to Horticulture in the New Guinea Highlands." *Ethnology* 4, no. 3 (1965): 295–309.

Weinberger, E. "Diary: Next Stop, Forbidden City." *London Review of Books* 27, no. 12 (June 23, 2005): 42–43.

White, Hayden V. *Figural Realism: Studies in the Mimesis Effect*. Baltimore: Johns Hopkins University Press, 1999.

Wilson, Forbes. *The Conquest of Copper Mountain*. New York: Atheneum, 1981.

Wilson, Rob, and Christopher Leigh Connery. *The Worlding Project: Doing Cultural Studies in the Era of Globalization*. Santa Cruz: New Pacific, 2007.

Winters, Jeffrey A. *Power in Motion: Capital Mobility and the Indonesian State*. Ithaca: Cornell University Press, 1996.

Withers, Lucia, and Signe Poulsen. *Grave Human Rights Violations in Wasior, Papua*. Amnesty International report. London. AI-index: ASA 21/032/2002. Available at http://www.amnesty.org.

Worsley, Peter. *The Trumpet Shall Sound: A Study of "Cargo" Cults in Melanesia*. London: MacGibbon and Kee, 1957.

"Yoris Arrested in Connection to July 27 Case." *Jakarta Post*, April 19, 2000.

Zöllner, Siegfried. *The Religion of the Yali in the Highlands of Irian Jaya*. Point Series No. 13. Goroka, Papua New Guinea: Melanesian Institute, 1988.

Index

Page references in italics indicate maps and figures; those followed by "n" indicate endnotes.

EBEN KIRKSEY IS A MELLON FELLOW AT

THE CITY UNIVERSITY OF NEW YORK GRADUATE CENTER.

THIS IS HIS FIRST BOOK.

Library of Congress Cataloging-in-Publication Data

Kirksey, Eben, 1976–
Freedom in entangled worlds :
West Papua and the architecture of global power / Eben Kirksey.
p. cm.
Includes bibliographical references and index.
ISBN 978-0-8223-5122-1 (cloth : alk. paper)
ISBN 978-0-8223-5134-4 (pbk. : alk. paper)
1. Papua (Indonesia) — History — Autonomy and independence movements.
2. Papua (Indonesia) — Politics and government — 1963–
3. Indonesia — Politics and government — 1998–
I. Title.
DU744.5.K565 2012
995.1′04 — dc23
2011048244